100 QUESTIONS YOU SHOULD ASK ABOUT YOUR PERSONAL FINANCES

100 QUESTIONS YOU SHOULD ASK ABOUT YOUR PERSONAL FINANCES

And the Answers You Need to Help You Save, Invest, and Grow Your Money

Ilyce R. Glink

TIMES BUSINESS

RANDOM HOUSE

Copyright © 1999 by Ilyce R. Glink

All rights reserved under International and Pan-American Copyright Conventions. Published in the United States by Times Books, a division of Random House, Inc., New York, and simultaneously in Canada by Random House of Canada Limited, Toronto.

Library of Congress Cataloging-in-Publication Data

Glink, Ilyce R.
   100 questions you should ask about your personal finances : and
the answers you need to help you save, invest, and grow your money /
Ilyce R. Glink.
      p.   cm.
   Includes index.
   ISBN 0-8129-2741-9 (alk. paper)
   1. Finance, Personal. 2. Investments. I. Title.
HG179.G552 1999
332.024—dc21   98-41101

Random House website address: www.atrandom.com

Published in the United States of America

9 8 7 6 5 4 3 2

First Edition

In memory of my grandfather, Paul,
who taught me you don't always have to buy low and sell high to
make money in the stock market; and for his brother, Meyer, who
remembered to his dying day the value of a nickel in 1910: you could
buy a half pound of bologna and a loaf of bread, or two red hots while
watching the Chicago Cubs at the West Side Grounds.

And for Sam, Alex, and Michael, who give me things money can't buy.

Contents

ix

xi

xiii

Preface

How many times have you thought about cleaning out your family closet, only to find something else, anything else, to do instead? Even as you go about your daily grind, you know the closet needs to be cleaned, and it weighs on you. It's a jumbled mess of shoes, boots, mittens, winter coats, old clothes, sports equipment, luggage, next year's birthday presents, last year's broken holiday gifts, old Halloween costumes, your spouse's prewedding china, spare card-table chairs, your high school papers from twenty years ago (just in case your kids need them some day), sleeping bags, and unpacked boxes of stuff Aunt Jeanne left you in her will. Just thinking about organizing that closet, and then organizing and giving away all the clothes that don't fit you anymore and the stuff you don't want, is enough to give anyone a case of the willies. Even opening that closet door is cause for consternation. It reminds you of that Groucho Marx movie, where dozens of people pile into a room. And when the last person finally opens the door, a sea of humanity flows out.

As hard as it is to tackle that closet (eventually, that day—or weekend—does come), some folks find organizing their personal finances even more frightening. There's nothing more daunting than sitting down at your kitchen or dining room table (or a desk, if you're lucky enough to have one at home), facing a huge pile of receipts, bills, and statements. The mound may be so high, and so discouraging, that you need a broom to sweep everything off the table and back into the shoebox, bootbox, or brown cardboard box that once contained paper for the office copying machine.

Part of the problem is that the amount of time we dedicate to organizing, fixing, and managing our finances is minute, compared to the importance we place on our money. We do this with a lot of important things; we always find a way to push them to the bottom of the list. Why? It's our psychological resistance: the more important the task in front of us, the less time we assign to completing it. If you're a writer, you might call it writer's block. It's why time management experts often advise their clients to tackle their most difficult or least favorite project first. Throwing yourself into your least favorite project while you still have all your mental energy and clarity is one way to give yourself a psychological boost—and finish an unappealing job.

I like to call our intuitive resistance to actively managing our finances a "Money Block." For most of us, managing our finances is something akin to, say, doing our annual tax return or choosing whether we want to be buried or cremated. We know all too well that we'll never be able to avoid death and taxes, so why deal with either until we have to? That's why so many people think about filing their tax return on April 14th (some folks start the frantic search for documents, information, and tax forms on April 15th, around 4:00 P.M.), and leave their heirs to decide what to do with their remains.

If you think you'll "grow into the job" of managing your personal finances, or that you'll deal with them "one day, maybe when I'm retired, when I have the time," here's my first piece of advice: *Stop kidding yourself.* Unless you've got an in with the personal finance fairy (a very distant relative of the tooth fairy), the only way to get your financial life in order is to tackle it head-on.

I wrote *100 Questions You Should Ask About Your Personal Finances*, as a place to start. The goal of this book is to help you think about, organize, and manage your personal finances in a way that makes sense—a way that is fun, exciting, and satisfying enough to keep you coming back, week in and week out, throughout your life. You don't have to be a great stock picker or mutual fund manager to be good at managing your money. Nor do you have to hire someone to do it for you, though you might want some professional assistance down the line.

All you really need to know are what questions to ask, and how to apply the answers to your own life and finances. I wrote *100 Questions You Should Ask About Your Personal Finances* to help you think through the big issues you'll face on the way to organizing, repairing, growing, and managing your financial life. Like anything else, managing your money is a process you learn step-by-step. Once you learn the language (and the jargon) and how the system works, you'll begin to feel at ease with the plethora of information available. You'll find yourself regularly dipping into and out of your finances, perhaps even trading online (for as little as $5 per trade, as we went to press, no matter how many shares of a company you buy or sell). You'll find ways to organically trim your budget and add to your savings. You'll learn to cut out the middlemen and get exactly what you need when you need it. And you'll learn to plan for the future you want, without waiting until it's handed to you on a platter of procrastination.

I decided to write this book after readers of my previous books, *100 Questions Every First-Time Home Buyer Should Ask*, *100 Questions Every Home Seller Should Ask*, and *10 Steps to Home Ownership* came to me for advice on fixing up their personal finances before they bought their next home. They wanted to know how to organize, budget, and plan for the future. They wanted a full and fancy life with all the trimmings today, *and* a platinum retirement. They wanted to fix their credit *and* spend more than they actually had. And they wanted to find the next Intel or Microsoft in which to invest all of their savings. In researching and writing this book, it became clear to me that managing personal finance can be complicated and emotionally trying. But it can also be extremely satisfying. In the past decade of writing about real estate and personal finance, I've come to realize that the two are inextricably intertwined. To make the most of your real estate opportunities, you have to be in control of your financial life. And once you're in control of your finances, you can sit back and enjoy living in your home.

If you have a bad case of Money Block, you won't remember to ask every question. And those unanswered questions are usually the ones that come back to haunt you. *100 Questions You Should Ask About Your Personal Finances* is designed to help you find your bearing. I've tried to organize this book so that it will mirror your own experiences, and I've phrased questions in a way I thought you'd ask them yourself. There are two ways to read this book: (1) start with the introduction and work your way through Question 100, or (2) pick it up, thumb through, and find a specific question that addresses an urgent need. I recommend that you do both.

One final thought. You *can* get through life without ever tackling that closet. You don't even have to open the door, though it may mean you'll do without some of the things that would have made your life happier, more fulfilled, and more secure. But think about this: Someone will eventually have to open that door. Someone will have to clean out that closet, take stock of the contents, organize them, give them away, sell them, manage them.

Shouldn't it be you?

ILYCE R. GLINK
October, 1998

P.S. If you have a question that isn't answered in this book, or if you'd like to share your personal finance horror stories or experiences, feel free to write to me at the following address: Ilyce R. Glink, Real Estate Matters Syndicate, P.O. Box 366, Glencoe, Illinois 60022. My Internet address is IlyceGlink@aol.com and my website address is www.thinkglink.com.

100 QUESTIONS YOU SHOULD ASK ABOUT YOUR PERSONAL FINANCES

Introduction

Gearing up to work on your personal finances may require a fundamental shift in your perspective: from paying off your past to preparing for your future. Not everyone can make the leap. For some folks, the idea of taking responsibility for their financial life is too much to handle. They'd rather pass off the responsibility and, I suppose, hope for the best.

This seems to me to be a particularly haphazard way to live. It might turn out all right, especially if you've married well and your spouse earns a great living, is trustworthy, and won't run off with the family nest egg. Or if you've inherited a sizable trust fund that's managed well and continues to grow. Or if you win a $178 million powerball lottery, and get an annual payment of $8.9 million (before taxes) for twenty years. (Even I would have a hard time spending the after-tax take of about $4 million a year.)

Then again, you could be like one woman who, after twenty-five years of work, marriage, and raising kids suddenly found out her husband had kept, separate from their family's finances, all the money his parents had given them through the years. And, he'd spent her cash (she contributes one-third of the household income) while forcing her to live on a monthly stipend of $600 for everything other than groceries. The final shocker? Her name isn't on anything except the house. She wants to know what she should do.

My advice: Find a therapist and a get good divorce lawyer.

Twenty-five years of financial illiteracy is just about twenty-five years too much. And there's no excuse for it. Each partner in the relationship should know: the amount of your annual household income; what it costs to live; what you have, separately and together; where it's kept; and where the keys are to the place where the papers, stock certificates, and wills are kept. At least once a year, and preferably every six months, the two of you should sit down and go over everything you have. Assess what works and what doesn't. And make changes as you go along. If you have cash, property, or children, you should have a valid will (and possibly trusts set up) so that things happen the way you want them to. Don't leave things to chance—or the courts.

One friend of mine and his wife split the duties and trade off every other year or so. One year he does the taxes, the next year she does them. Same thing with paying household bills, buying insurance, and other financial matters. It works out well for them. Except she hasn't bought homeowner's insurance in three years. If your spouse or partner is irresponsible about paying the bills, don't let him or her wreck your credit. Step in and do it together. Money management isn't about genetics or sex. It's about Common $ense and learning. Most of all, it's about doing rather than procrastinating.

A Change of Attitude

Perspective is everything when it comes to money. A lot of people fear it. They think a truckful of cash is the answer to their prayers, but if they actually got all of the money they say they want, they wouldn't know what to do with it. A few years ago, one survey said that about 80 percent of Americans consider households with an annual income of $100,000 to be rich. In a few years, the level of "rich" might be $150,000. To families already bringing in $100,000 or more a year, rich is more like $200,000 per year. And so on.

When is any amount enough money? When you realize that money can't buy you the important things in life: love, happiness, friendship, security. If you have enough money, you can guarantee that you won't go to bed hungry. But you can't guarantee that you won't be lonely.

Bob's Story

Bob was 12 when his parents bought their first car, a 1936 Chevrolet. He loved riding in the car and, being within spitting distance of being old enough to drive, he spent a fair amount of time imagining how he'd tool around in it with his friends.

But his mother was pregnant. And in those days, you had to come up with cash to pay the doctor who delivered your baby, as well as the accompanying hospital bill. As Bob remembers it, if you didn't pay, the baby couldn't come home.

Those were tough years. When the time came, Bob's dad realized he didn't have enough money to pay the hospital bill. So he sold the car to the dealer down the street for $300. Bob's dad asked the dealer to let him use the car to bring his wife and the baby home from the hospital. And so he got the money, drove over to the hospital, and paid the bill. He brought Bob's mom and baby brother home, got them safely upstairs, and then slowly drove the car back to the dealer's lot. He walked home.

Bob says he'll always remember that car, and the amount of money the dealer paid for it. His family didn't own another car until Bob earned enough money, at age 18, to buy one.

You may need to make some drastic changes to achieve your financial goals. Then again, you may be a lot further along than you'd imagined. One thing is certain: The sooner you start, the better off you'll be.

So, let's get started.

Organization

HOW SHOULD I ORGANIZE MY PERSONAL FINANCES?

Organizing your personal finances is just like cleaning out that dreaded family closet. You have to clear out all of the stuff you don't need, can't use, and won't want in the future. Then you have to create some sort of childproof/dogproof/neighborproof space in which you can store what you *will* need. Believe me, the paperwork—and the space you'll need for it—is a lot less than you think. A shoebox isn't the perfect size, but you *can* manage your personal finances with (1) a plastic storage facility with hanging files and (2) a bound ledger. Total cost? Less than $20.

Tracking Your Personal Finances

Keeping track of your personal finances is the only way you'll become intimately familiar with them. To create the financial future you want, you have to get a handle on where you are today. Here are several ways you can keep track of your personal finances.

Option 1: Paper and Pencil

How well does this option work? Tracking your expenses on paper is fine, especially if you've got the time. But it has its limitations.

In 1984, I went to study in Europe for a year. In addition to the cash I'd saved from working during summer vacation and my first two years of school, my mother and grandfather gave me a small stipend to help pay the cost of the year abroad. In exchange, my mother requested that I keep track of every "pence" I spent. My grandfather bought me a bound cash journal, something he used every week of his adult life to keep track of his financial portfolio.

Years later, my mother told me she didn't think I'd really do it. But I did. I wrote down every pound I spent during my year in Wales, down to the last pence. Every time I bought a *London Times*, the cost went into the journal. When I bought an old overcoat at an Oxfam store (the equivalent of our vintage clothing shops), I wrote it down. If I took a trip, bought a pack of gum, or picked up a round at the local pub, I put down how much I spent. Looking back, I am amazed that I was able to buy that old brown wool Oxfam coat for only £8, or about $10. (At the time, the English pound was worth about $1.25. During the year I was there, it fell to $1.05.) I have a strong recollection of the details of that year abroad, precisely because I wrote down every amount I spent and what the exchange rate was at a given time. By the end of the year, I had spent £4,374.35, which, at an average exchange rate for the year of about $1.20, came to $5,249.22. That princely sum (I was completely broke when I returned) included all trips, meals, lodging, clothes, haircuts, books, film, and film processing for the year, plus gifts for my family. The only thing it didn't include was school tuition and the cost of the dorm.

However, writing down every expense took a lot of time. I took my little red-and-black book everywhere with me, and wrote down expenses immediately so I wouldn't forget them. I saved receipts and entered those later if it wasn't possible to take the book with me. By the end of the year, the spine had collapsed, and my little book was being held together with rubber bands.

Here's what I learned from my year-long experiment of writing down everything I spent: It works. It also takes time, and I didn't have a lot of cash or expenses back then. Today, with a husband and two children, I live in a two-income household with many more expenses and a lot less time. Our monthly expenses look pretty typical for an average family of four (no dog!), and include things like a mortgage, doctor bills, insurance, and childcare. On the personal side, I'm having a good day if I can remember to pick up the kids at school on time, throw a load of laundry in the dryer on the way out, and take an umbrella in a downpour. Writing down every expense by hand wouldn't work that easily now. However, it *can* be done. As I said earlier, it will cost you less than $20 to set up your whole system. If you can't afford a computer or software, it's better to write down your income expenses and investments than not keep excellent track of them at all. After all, for thousands of years, people kept excellent track of these items on paper.

The method has some limitations. If you want to find a specific expense, you have to trust your memory and perhaps go back through years of pages to find it. If you want to compare how much you've spent, year to year, you'll need some additional time with a calculator. If you want to find a way to cut down your budget, you'll have to study what you spent week by week.

So there's your first option. A plastic storage box with hanging files from the hardware store, and a cash journal.

Option 2: A Computer

Your second option is to try electronic financial management software like Intuit's Quicken® or Microsoft Money®.

Computers are changing the face of everything we do. We can do two to three times the former amount of work with half the help simply because of the power of computer chips. For managing your money, a computer and software give you the tools of a professional. Not only will they help you track your daily expenses, but you can then look at those expenses on a daily, weekly, monthly, or year-to-date basis. The software can compare year-to-year totals with a keystroke. You can pull out a certain category of expenses—say, food—and see how much you spent on grocery bills each week, month, or year. You can pull out a certain department store, or restaurant, and see how much you've spent there in the past year. Or on travel. Or insurance premiums. You can balance your checkbook, keep track of cash received, run an amortization table for your mortgage, manage your stock portfolio, and keep track of how many miles you drive your car (useful if you can deduct them on your taxes). With Quicken®, you can even download your expenses directly into the companion tax preparation software, TurboTax®.

Basically, you can do everything you'd want to do when you analyze and track your personal finances. The cost? You can spend as little as $500 on a used computer or, for around $750, you can get a discontinued model at a computer superstore. You don't need all the newest bells and whistles to run personal financial software. They're typically designed for computers with a minimum of a 486 processor, or about what was considered top of the line in the mid-1990s. If you can afford one, you'll earn back your expense by being able to keep a much closer watch on your finances, and by finding ways to save its purchase price through eliminating some of the waste in your budget. (For tips on budgeting, check out Question 6.) In addition, if you purchase a scanner, you can scan in documents you need or want to save. A modem (which may come with your computer) will allow you to connect to the Internet and tap into virtually limitless amounts of free information.

Although you'll have to spend $500 to $1,000, you'll soon find that a computer is indispensable. As of 1998, nearly 50 percent of all households had personal computers, and more than 5 million households purchase them each year. More than 70 percent of the population had access to computers either at home or at work. This is the way of the future, and I'll go out on a limb here and suggest that if you don't decide to track your finances by computer today, you will do so within five years.

What are the limitations of personal finance software? If there's a blackout and you haven't saved everything, you could lose it. If you have saved everything, but your computer dies and you don't have your information backed up on a disk, you could lose it. If you don't have your software protected by a password, your two-year-old child could do some real damage. But that's about it. A small price to pay for the pleasure of using software to track expenses.

Option 3: An Accountant or a Money Manager

If you can afford the hourly fee, you could hire an accountant to track your expenses, write your checks, and manage your personal finances. Many famous actors and wealthy business executives do this. Some of the actors do it because they're financially irresponsible and would blow through $1 million faster than you can blink. The executives do it because they're so busy managing multibillion-dollar corporations they don't have the time to write personal checks (and their spouses don't want the job).

Hiring someone else to manage your cash sounds easy, but it's expensive. And, if you don't choose wisely, you could wind up with an accountant or money manager who blows through it, loses it, or steals it. Then you'd have to spend more money and time suing the money manager you chose, which would defeat the purpose of hiring someone in the first place.

Without a doubt, the best record-keeping device will be the one you actually use day in, day out. Choose a system that's easy to use—one that can expand to meet your needs as your financial life grows and changes shape. If you decide to go with computer software, think about all of the other things you can do with it—like electronic banking, and management of your stock and mutual fund portfolios—before you commit. You may not own stocks today, but you probably will someday. Software that can automatically track your stock portfolio might prove useful down the line. And once you've started using one brand of software, you're less likely to switch, even if someone else's software develops a cool feature you'd like to have.

Many couples divvy up their household responsibilities. Too often, however, only one spouse or partner handles the management of the family's cash. That may seem to work in the short run, but each spouse (or partner) should have a hand in how and where records are kept. While you hope and pray you'll grow old together, you should run your finances as if preparing for the worst. If your spouse or partner dropped dead tomorrow, would you know what to do? Would you know where everything is? If the situation was reversed, would your spouse or partner know? Dealing with an emotional tragedy is scary enough without adding on a financial disaster. When you set up your finances and start keeping records, make sure all of the adults in the relationship know how to do it, how to access the accounts, and where the important papers are kept.

QUESTION 2

WHAT KINDS OF FILES DO I NEED TO KEEP?

Human beings are born collectors. We collect everything from art, coins, crystal, and silver to faded Levis, beanie babies, baseball cards, and original Michael Jordan Nike basketball shoes. We also save memorabilia that have no intrinsic value whatsoever, like ticket stubs from a first date. Often, we save these things because of a misguided notion that they will be "worth something" someday, or that we'll need them in some desperate moment in the future.

Paper seems to accumulate faster than other things, and we hang onto it longer. We save letters and cards, our children's artwork and homework. We save our tax returns, old W-2s, and bank statements. Who doesn't have a stack of 20-year-old canceled checks sitting in the attic or basement? (Fortunately, most banks no longer send back canceled checks.)

When it comes to paperwork, there are some originals or copies that you need to keep around and others that you don't. The less clutter you have in your financial life, the more room you'll have to collect the things you really love. (You're not married to your old credit card statements!)

Here's a list of the important papers you should keep, why you need them, and when you can throw them away:

1. *Federal and state income tax returns.* Under current tax law, the Internal Revenue Service (IRS) may audit you for three to six years after you've filed your federal income tax return. Because you file annually for the *preceding* year, here's how the time frame works. You file in 1999 for 1998. The IRS may audit that return for up to three years after filing, or until the year 2002. If the IRS believes you've understated your income by more than 25 percent, your return could be audited until 2005. That's why most tax professionals recommend keeping a copy of your return for six years after you've filed it. However, if you intentionally fail to report income, or if you file a fraudulent tax return, there is no statute of limitations. The IRS could come after you ten, twenty, or even thirty years later.

Bottom line: Keep a copy of your final tax return in a file for at least six years, along with the attached W2s. If there are years for which you don't file a return, keep records showing that you didn't earn the minimum amount required to file in those years. If you use tax software to complete your returns, keep a copy of the file in your computer as long as you keep the supporting documentation. (Hint: Don't forget to print it out or save it on a disk when you sell or junk your old hardware.) Personally, I think your tax returns are important enough to keep every year, forever. In that way, you'll have a solid year-to-year record of your financial life, in case you ever need it. (If for no other reason, keep your tax records so you can impress your grandkids with how little you lived on when you were their age.)

2. *Investments information.* You need to know three things about your investments: (1) How much you paid for them, (2) how much you sold them for, and (3) what kind of annual returns you earned while you held them. When you buy an investment, you typically receive a written confirmation. If you trade through the Internet, your account statement will reflect the trade the next month.

Bottom line: Experts say you should hang onto your brokerage statements and other records pertaining to your investments until you sell them and report the capital gain or loss to the IRS. If there are annual capital gains or losses—for example, with some mutual funds or limited partnerships—you'll need the annual statements to file your returns. You may want to hold onto the purchase and sale documents until the six-year audit period expires.

3. *Nondeductible IRAs, paycheck stubs.* If you've been making periodic contributions to a regular IRA, or if you've started a Roth IRA or an Education IRA, there are certain tax records you should keep until you've withdrawn all funds from these accounts, to prove the amount of the nontaxable portion. (For more information on IRAs and their tax deductibility, see Chapter 13, Question 83: "What Are the Different Types of Retirement Accounts?") Paycheck stubs list important information, including your Social Security contributions.

Bottom line: Current tax law requires you to keep Forms 1040, 8606, 1099R, and 5498 for each year in which you made a contribution to your IRA accounts. Keep your paycheck stubs for the calendar year until you've received your W2 form (usually, in January) and checked it for errors.

4. *Insurance policies.* You'll buy many different types of insurance in your life, including homeowner's, life, medical, auto, disability, and liability. You may even purchase various insurance policies for estate tax purposes.

Bottom line: Keep the original insurance policy and signed contract for as long as you hold the policy. Once you cancel the insurance, you can throw out the documents about one year later.

5. *Trusts and other estate-planning devices.* Many individuals use trusts and other types of estate-planning tools to save on estate taxes.

Bottom line: You'll want to keep trust documents for as long as they're active.

6. *Medical records.* Current tax law permits you to deduct medical expenses in excess of 7.5 percent of your gross adjusted income. For example, if your gross adjusted income is $50,000, you may decuct the amount of medical expenses you paid that year in excess of $3,750. Unfortunately, this doesn't include medical insurance payments, which would easily put you over the top, but it does include dental and orthodontia costs as medical expenses.

Bottom line: After they've been settled by your insurance company, you should keep all your medical bills until the end of the year. If a claim isn't settled, or if you have a serious ongoing medical situation, you may want to keep the forms indefinitely, or until you've settled the claim. If you don't have enough medical bills to deduct any amount from your tax return, toss them after you file—and be glad you're in relatively good health.

7. *Credit card receipts and statements.* Once you receive your monthly statement listing your most recent payment and any items purchased (or returned) since the previous statement, you can toss out the credit card receipts for that month's activity. (If you have your own business, different rules apply.) Your credit card statement should also list any interest you have paid over the course of a year.

Bottom line: If you're fighting with a store about an erroneous charge, or waiting for a store credit, you should keep your statements until that situation is resolved. After you've closed out your year (for most people, that's December 31), you can toss all of your credit card receipts and statements. If you're using financial software, you can throw out your receipts after you've entered them. (If you ever need another copy of a credit card statement, most companies will provide it either free or for a small charge.)

8. *Household bills and receipts.* It would be nice if you could deduct the cost of food, heat, electricity, and diapers. Unfortunately, you can't. On the other hand, you may be able to deduct part or all of the cost of child care or school tuition.

Bottom line: After you've entered general household bills and receipts into your financial software or your expense book, you can pitch 'em. Keep child care receipts and tuition bills until you do your taxes. If you qualify for a tax deduction, make those receipts part of your permanent tax records.

9. *Canceled checks, ATM receipts, bank statements.* Few banks today still send account holders their canceled checks. Why? Because it's

easier and cheaper for the bank to put copies of the checks on microfiche and send out a statement with miniature photos of the canceled checks. Initially, there was a huge uproar from account holders who were used to receiving their canceled checks. Now, most people agree that keeping the statements is easier.

Bottom line: Keep copies of your account statements, for IRS purposes, at least three to six years, or forever (your choice). If you apply for a mortgage, the lender will often ask you to produce the last two to three years' account statements. Automatic teller machine (ATM) receipts should be kept until the transactions they document show up on your bank statement. (Be sure you rip up the receipts before you toss them, so no one can steal your numbers.) If you still get canceled checks, you can toss them after a year, except those that back up tax deductions or capital improvements. The bank keeps copies of the back and front of each check and can provide a print of a check for a small fee if the need arises.

10. *Mortgage, home equity loan, second mortgage, and property taxes.* Current tax law allows you to deduct interest paid on a first mortgage, a home equity loan, or a second mortgage up to $1 million spread over two homes. You may also deduct your property taxes.

Bottom line: Mortgage servicing companies will usually send you a year-end statement listing the amount of interest you've paid over the year. You'll need this statement and your property tax bills when preparing your income tax return. After you file your return, it should become part of your permanent tax records for that year.

11. *Home purchase/sale and capital improvements records.* When you sell your home, current tax law permits you to take the first $250,000 (up to $500,000 if you're married and both spouses meet the minimum requirements) in capital gains tax-free. The way you calculate capital gains is to add up the cost of purchase, the cost of sale, and the cost of any capital improvements (structural items like replacing the roof count; repainting doesn't). Then, subtract that number from the sales price. The answer is your profit (or loss).

Bottom line: Keep your purchase documents until you sell your home, and report the gain to the IRS. In addition, it's important to keep excellent records (including canceled checks if you have them) of the cost of any improvements you've made to the home over the years. You'll want to keep these documents as part of your permanent tax records for the year in which you sell your home.

Four of the most useful pieces of paper you can keep are: (1) an updated copy of your accounts and assets, (2) a living will, (3) a durable power of attorney for health care, and (4) a durable power of attorney for financial matters. Even if you keep extremely careful records, it's difficult to put your hands on everything at a moment's notice. Your "List of Accounts" should include the name, account number, contact person (if available), and phone number of every bank, mutual fund, stock, trust, and credit card account you own. List individual stocks, and note where the certificates can be found. List safe deposit accounts. You should also list insurance policies, policy amounts, where the policy and supporting documentation (if any) can be found, and phone numbers. Finally, list the professionals (including brokers, attorneys, or accountants) who have helped you with your financial life, and how to contact them. Put a copy of your updated list of accounts (you should update it at least once a year) with your important papers (including your will and trust agreements), and tell your closest relative or friend where it can be found in case of an emergency.

A living will is a document that expresses what kind of medical treatment you want in case of a life-threatening illness or emergency. You can purchase a living will at a stationery store, buy a book on writing one, use legal software to create one, or have an attorney write one up for you (see a copy of one used in the state of Illinois on page 438). Make sure you and your spouse each sign living wills, and then tell your closest relatives or friends what your living wills say and where they can be found in case of an emergency. Most importantly, make sure you give a signed and/or notarized copy of your living will to your doctor, so he or she is aware of your wishes in case of a medical emergency. Another alternative is to give a durable power of attorney for health care to a trusted friend or family member. You'll probably want to make your doctor aware of this assignment and possibly even give him or her a copy of the paperwork. If you are an organ donor, or would like to be one, make sure you fill out the appropriate paperwork. A durable power of attorney for financial matters will allow your agent to make investment decisions on your behalf should you become incapacitated.

12. *Airline ticket stubs, boarding passes, and frequent flier statements.* The only reason to save airline ticket stubs and boarding passes is to make sure you've been given the appropriate credit on your frequent flier account.

Bottom line: If you've been credited with the appropriate miles on your statement, you can toss out your ticket stubs and boarding passes (the only way you can prove you were actually on a particular flight). When you receive your new statement each month, you can toss out your previous statement. (If you prefer, save them for the entire year and toss them out at the same time.) If you belong to a gold, platinum, or other premium award level for an airline, you'll want to save the letters, upgrade stickers, and other information sent to you while your membership remains active. You never know when you'll need to prove that something was promised to you earlier.

13. *Warranties and receipts for big-ticket items.* You may get a ten-year warranty for your newly built home, a six-year warranty for your new car, a three-year warranty for your new laptop computer, and a one-year warranty on a new dishwasher. A home seller might provide you with a one-year home warranty on the old house you buy.

Bottom line: A warranty is only as good as the company providing it. However, you should save the warranty paperwork at least until the warranty expires or until you sell the item. If it gets damaged or stolen, the original receipt and warranty documentation might help you prove the value of the item, or its age, for insurance purposes.

DO I NEED A SAFE DEPOSIT BOX?

A safe deposit box is literally a fireproof box located in a vault at a bank. It is supposed to be a safe place to put important, irreplaceable documents (like a will, stock certificates, and insurance policies), valuables (like gold and silver coins or jewelry), and memorabilia (your grandparents' birth certificates, a videotape of your children when they were young).

Can safe deposit boxes be broken into? Sure. How often does it happen? Almost never. Is it a good idea to get a safe deposit box? Yes. Some people substitute fireproof boxes that they can take with them as they move from house to house, around the country. A fireproof box is good, but it can be broken into or stolen. And in a really bad physical catastrophe, like a flood, earthquake, tornado, or horrible fire, the box might be damaged or destroyed.

There are two negatives to a safe deposit box: cost and keys. You can get almost any size you want, but a safe deposit box can be costly. Charges run from around $30 per year to upward of $1,000 per year for the largest safe deposit boxes. (On the other hand, if you've got a small Renoir worth several million dollars, that might seem like an inexpensive way to protect your painting.) The other problem is that you need a key to get into a safe deposit box. Typically, you receive two keys. If you lose one of your keys, you'll have to pay the bank a fee when you stop leasing the box. If you lose both keys and need to get into the box, you'll have to pay the bank the cost of breaking into the box and putting in a new lock.

Check out the prices of safe deposit boxes before you head to the biggest bank in town to lease one. You might find a new bank offering free safe deposit boxes for life if you keep a minimum of $1,000 in an interest-bearing savings account. You could undoubtedly get higher interest on that money by throwing it into a money market account, but the difference in interest might be far less than you'd pay for the box itself. And, if a neighborhood bank makes the offer, the convenience might be worth it.

Safe deposit keys typically contain your box number, but not the name of the institution. That's to prevent someone from stealing the key and gaining access to your box. *Don't* label the key with where the box is located. (You'd be surprised at how many people write the name of the institution on the envelope that the key comes in.)

Budgets, Accounts, and Savings

HOW DO I CALCULATE MY NET WORTH?

What is your net worth? Quite simply, it's what you have minus what you owe. But what you have doesn't refer only to the cash in your checking account. Your net worth looks at *everything* you own in addition to your cash, stocks, bonds, and other investments: your home, with its furniture and furnishings; your clothes and jewelry; your cars, bicycles, and even the train set your grandfather built fifty years ago. It's the sum total of the value of everything you own, minus what you owe.

And what might you owe? You might have school loans, a car loan, a mortgage. You might also owe personal loans received from friends or relatives. Spend more than you make? You might have credit card debt.

Why would you want to pinpoint your net worth? To give you a snapshot of your financial life today, which becomes a point of comparison down the road. How much are you worth today? If you're worth $100,000 today and in ten years you're worth $200,000, you'll have seen your assets double in ten years, for an average annual return of about 7 percent. That isn't too bad if you're age 30 today. At age 40, you'll be worth $200,000; at 50, you'll be worth $400,000; and at 60, you'll be worth $800,000. Work another ten years and, at age 70, you could be worth $1.6 million. Increase your average annual return to 8 percent, and you'll be worth a whole lot more at age 70.

But we're getting ahead of ourselves. Let's start with some basic financial terms:

18

- *Assets are things you own.* Cash, real estate, jewelry, stocks, certificates of deposit, furniture, artwork, clothing, money market accounts, mutual funds, and other financial investments. Everything from your pots and pans to the sterling silver flatware your great-grandmother willed you.

- *Liquid assets are either held as cash or can be easily converted into cash.* For example, a savings account is a very liquid asset. All you have to do is go down to the bank (or the ATM) and withdraw your money.

- *Semiliquid investments are assets you can liquidate in a few days.* Stocks and bonds are good examples of semiliquid investments. You may take a hit because of the timing, but you'll have your cash in three days.

- *Illiquid assets, which might also be called investment assets, may take some time (and may cost you some money) to convert into cash.* For example, you may have $50,000 in equity in your house, but, to get your cash out, you'll either have to take out a home equity loan or sell your home. That can take some time, and may cost you some cash. Other examples of illiquid assets include limited partnership and some mutual fund shares.

- *Personal assets refer to your personal belongings,* such as furniture, artwork, jewelry, clothing, a car, and a boat.

- *Liabilities are debts that you owe,* including credit card debt, school and car loans, stocks you buy on margin accounts, money you owe to the IRS, and spousal or child support that you pay. Money you owe in your business (if self-employed) and items you purchased on credit or layaway (like a television, a refrigerator, or furniture) are also liabilities.

Remember, your net worth is the sum total of your assets minus your liabilities. The worksheet that begins on page 20 will allow you to figure out exactly what your net worth is on any given day.

When you know how much you're worth today, sit back and think about that number for a moment. Here are the tough questions you should ask yourself:

1. Am I surprised that my net worth is as much (or as little) as the number on the bottom line?

2. Should my net worth be higher, given the amount of money I'm earning each year?

This is the first opportunity you'll have in this book to get a good look at what you're worth. The worksheet is long and it may take you some time to get through it, especially the first time. But stick with it. The results are worth the effort. I've asked you to put down the approximate cash value of your assets. That may be tough to figure out, but take a guess anyway. If you have stocks or bonds, you may be able to calculate their worth by checking their listing in the financial pages of a newspaper. If you don't know how much something is worth, put down your best guess and come back to it later.

What You Own (Assets)   **Approximate Cash Value Today**

1. Liquid Assets

Cash _____

Checking account _____

   Acct. no. _____

Passbook savings account _____

   Acct. no. _____

Money market account _____

   Acct. no. _____

Other accounts _____

   Acct. no. _____

   Acct. no. _____

   Acct. no. _____

Treasury bills _____

Cash value of life insurance (all policies) _____

Other liquid assets _____

_____ _____

_____ _____

Total Liquid Assets _____

2. Investment Assets (not including retirement assets—see 3)

All stocks—current value

Stock _____   _____

   Shares _____   Value per share _____

Stock _____   _____

   Shares _____   Value per share _____

Stock _____   _____

   Shares _____   Value per share _____

Stock _____   _____

   Shares _____   Value per share _____

Stock _____   _____

   Shares _____   Value per share _____

Stock _____   _____

   Shares _____   Value per share _____

Stock _____   _____

   Shares _____   Value per share _____

Stock _____   _____

   Shares _____   Value per share _____

Stock _____   _____

   Shares _____   Value per share _____

Certificates of deposit   _____

Bonds   _____

Mutual funds

Name _____   _____

   Acct. no. _____   Shares _____

Name _____   _____

   Acct. no. _____   Shares _____

Name _____   _____

   Acct. no. _____   Shares _____

Name _____   _____

   Acct. no. _____   Shares _____

Limited partnership shares,
or investments   _____

Name _____

   Share (%) _____   Value _____   _____

Name _____

   Share (%) _____   Value _____

Business assets   _____

Business equipment   _____

Total Investment Assets   _____

3. Retirement Assets

Keogh Acct. no. _____

401K Acct. no. _____

IRA Acct. no. _____

Roth IRA Acct no. _____

Other Acct. no. _____

Other investment assets

_____   _____

_____   _____

_____   _____

_____   _____

_____   _____

_____   _____

_____   _____

_____   _____

Total Retirement Assets   _____

4. Real Estate Investments

[There may be some costs if you sell your house, just as there might be a minor cost if you sell your stocks or bonds. Don't worry about this now; or, if you want to be precise, subtract 7 percent from the price you think your home is worth today, to represent the approximate broker's commission and other costs of sale. Your actual costs of sale may be less, but we'll consider this the most expensive case.]

My house _____

Second home/Vacation home _____

Timeshare [Note: May not be worth what you paid]

Address _____ _____

Total Real Estate Assets _____

5. Personal Assets

Automobile(s) _____

Motorcycle(s) _____

Boat _____

Furniture/appliances _____

Artwork _____

Jewelry _____

Rare books/Antiques _____

Clothing _____

Other _____

Total Personal Assets _____

1. Liquid Assets   + _____

2. Investment Assets   + _____

3. Retirement Assets   + _____

4. Real Estate Assets   + _____

5. Personal Assets   + _____

Total Assets   = _____

What You Owe (Liabilities)   Amount

1. Mortgages

Mortgage on residence   _____

Home equity loan/Second mortgage   _____

Mortgage (vacation home)   _____

Total Mortgage Debt   _____

2. Credit Card Debt

Acct. no. _____   _____

Acct. no. _____   _____

Acct. no. _____   _____

Acct. no. _____   _____

Acct. no. _____   _____

Acct. no. _____   _____

Total Credit Card Debt   _____

3. School Loans

Undergraduate loan   _____

    Interest rate _____ Due _____

Graduate school loan   _____

    Interest rate _____ Due _____

Spouse's/partner's undergraduate loan   _____

    Interest rate _____ Due _____

Spouse's/partner's graduate loan   _____

    Interest rate _____ Due _____

Other school loan   _____

    Interest rate _____ Due _____

Total School Loans   _____

4. Vehicle Loans

Automobile loan no. 1 _____

    Interest rate _____ Due _____

Automobile loan no. 2 _____

    Interest rate _____ Due _____

Total Vehicle Loans _____

5. Miscellaneous Debts

Personal loans _____

IRS debt _____

Amount borrowed against life insurance _____

Amount borrowed from 401K, Keogh, IRA, or other retirement accounts _____

Loans from parents, relatives, or friends _____

Medical debts _____

Other debts _____

_____ _____

_____ _____

_____ _____

_____ _____

Total Miscellaneous Debt _____

1. Mortgages _____

2. Credit Card Debt   + _____

3. School Loans   + _____

4. Vehicle Loans   + _____

5. Miscellaneous Debts   + _____

Total Liabilities   = _____

Total Assets _____

Less: Total Liabilities   – _____

*NET WORTH   = _____

---

  * On financial statements, you'll often see a negative net worth expressed parenthetically, like this: ($3,500). It means -$3,500, or you owe more than you have.

3. Where are my largest liabilities? My key assets?

4. Have I spent myself into a corner, building personal assets instead of financial assets?

5. What are the big-ticket items I'm hoping to be able to afford in the future? Do I want to buy a house? Pay for my children's education? Their weddings?

6. What are my financial goals?

This last question is possibly the most important one you can ask. Why? The answer defines your need for cash and gives you something to focus on. It also helps you decide what kind of time requirements will frame your investments, which investments to choose, and when to shift your investment strategy. It defines your need for cash and gives you something to focus on. It's so important that I've dedicated the next question to defining your financial goals.

WHAT ARE MY FINANCIAL GOALS?

Susanne wants to retire and still spend money the way she does today. Chris and Roberta want to buy their first home. Sally Ann wants to live abroad for a year.

If I were to ask you how much money you need for your lifetime, you'd probably say you want to be "comfortable" financially; that is, you never want to think about the basics: being able to afford to go out to dinner, or to order in whenever you want to; buying new clothes when you need them; having the appropriate life and health insurance; paying your mortgage and taxes; allowing your children to choose any college they can get into; saving for retirement.

How much do you need for all that? Well, it depends. Some folks can buy their security for less than $100,000 a year. Others won't be satisfied with $1 million a year. Young people starting a career might say that if they earned $150,000 a year, they'd be rich enough to buy anything they want. The truth is, if we earn $150,000 a year, it will almost certainly *not* be enough because our tastes and our expenses tend to rise along with our income. If you're earning $40,000 annually today, $150,000 seems like the pot of gold at the end of the rainbow. And, if you lived on $150,000 as if you were earning $40,000, you'd quickly be a millionaire (the ultimate "rich" threshold for most Americans).

But saving in a vacuum is difficult. Most folks need financial goals to shape their spending and saving habits. You can have short-term goals ("I want a new stereo system" or "I want to go on vacation"), medium-term goals ("I want to pay for my children's education and weddings"), and long-term goals ("I want to retire when I'm 65"). And you can have lifelong goals ("To leave something to my children to make their lives easier after I'm gone").

Defining your goals is an important tool for tweaking your personal finances. It gives you something to dream about at night and something to work toward during the day. Later in this book, we'll talk about how to adjust your financial life as you achieve these goals and set others.

Use the worksheet on page 28 to start marking down some of your personal financial goals (and don't forget to put down when you'd like to achieve them).

Your age and where you are in the cycle of life should play an important role in determining your financial goals. For example, if you're age 25 and single, with no kids, and you want to start saving for your future progeny's college education, you'll have at least 19 years (a year for you to get married and conceive a child, plus 18 years before the child starts college). That's long-term saving. If you adopt a 10-year-old, you'll have only 8 years to save. That's medium-term saving. If you're age 25 and are beginning to save for retirement at age 65, you'll have 40 years, which will seem like a very long time. If you're age 50 and just beginning to save, you'll still have 15 years, but that won't feel quite so long-term, though the time frame meets the general definition.

HOW DO I CREATE A BUDGET THAT WORKS FOR ME?

QUESTION

6

When you know your net worth and decide on your short-, medium-, and long-term financial goals, it's helpful to figure out your cash-in/cash-out situation. In other words, how much do you spend each month? What do you spend your money on, day to day? Do you live within your means, or do you need a credit card to help balance the books at the end of each month?

WORKSHEET
My Personal Financial Goals

Goals

Time Frame
(Number of Years)*

1. _____ _____
2. _____ _____
3. _____ _____
4. _____ _____
5. _____ _____
6. _____ _____
7. _____ _____
8. _____ _____
9. _____ _____
10. _____ _____
11. _____ _____
12. _____ _____
13. _____ _____
14. _____ _____
15. _____ _____
16. _____ _____
17. _____ _____
18. _____ _____
19. _____ _____
20. _____ _____

*Time frame refers to how long you expect it will take to achieve your financial goals, or in how many years you might need the cash. Put down the number of years you think it will take. Short-term equals less than two or three years. Medium-term can refer to a three- to five-year time frame, or go up to ten years. Long-term usually means fifteen or more years to achieve.

Jill and Sam, with their two small children, are a fairly typical dual-income family. We were talking one day and they asked me how much house they could afford to buy. I quickly rattled off a number. They were amazed at how I had correctly guessed their income (I'd come within $1,000 or so). They didn't realize it, but their lifestyle (nanny, books, movies, dinners out, vacations, kids) had given them away. Life in a big city costs what it costs. If you live in New York or Los Angeles, your costs are about 25 to 30 percent more than in an average American city. If you live in a small town in Indiana, your costs are perhaps 25 to 30 percent less. But, on average, what you spend on food for a middle-class family of four in a given week isn't going to change much, no matter where you live. If you buy a new car, you'll pay virtually the same price coast to coast.

Ira and Sandra's Story

Money disappears like water in the desert. Here's a real budget for Ira and Sandra, two thirty-something homeowners who have two kids, an older house in the suburbs, and one paid-off car. They own their own sales business. This year was their best year ever, and they tried hard to stick to the spending level of their previous years, when their income was around $120,000.

Looking at his budget the bottom line initially disappointed Sandy, who wondered why they were spending so much time working for so little gain. Still, they had some bottom-line savings this year: $33,000 plus the $28,000 in retirement savings, which they won't be able to touch for at least thirty years. Add the two together and they're saving about 27 percent of their gross income. That's a fantastic number; most of us manage to save only 5 percent of our gross annual income.

Looking at it that way made Sandy feel a little better. In previous years, when the couple brought in $120,000, they managed to save about $8,000 a year by building up home equity with a fifteen-year mortgage, in addition to putting away $15,000 in their retirement plans. That's about a 19 percent savings rate, which felt tight because they didn't end up with any extra cash at the end of the year. What were they going to do with their windfall? Fix up their home, and put some money aside for their kids' college education.

(Note: Some of these budget items are assets, some are savings, and some are liabilities, but all are cash-out-the-door expenses. In other words, Ira and Sandra are definitely better off putting money into their Keogh for their future, but because they can't touch that money, they feel they aren't as far ahead as they'd like to be today.)

29

Income (after business expenses)	*$230,000*

Expenses	
Keogh contribution	$ 28,000
Federal income taxes	63,000
State taxes	7,500
Real estate property taxes	8,000
Insurance (medical, life, disability, auto)	15,000
Mortgage	23,000
Baby-sitting, preschool, programs for kids	25,000
Food (groceries, restaurants, take-out)	12,500
Clothing	5,000
Doctor bills (not covered by insurance)	2,000
Utilities	5,000
Vacation	3,000
Total Expenses	**$197,000**

Gross Income	$230,000
– Expenses	197,000
Net Savings	$ 33,000

Getting Out the Magnifying Glass

If you started at the beginning of this book and have already begun writing down what you're spending on a daily basis, you might be surprised to see that money you could be saving and investing is dribbling away from your fingertips. Sticking to your budget is important. But it's difficult to put together a reasonable budget, or see what you can cut, until you understand how you spend money, when you spend money, and on what you spend money.

When you see where you spend money, you can begin to find places to save it. That's the beginning of a workable budget that will put you in line to meet or exceed your financial goals.

The worksheet on pages 32–40 requires you to detail your income and your expenses. The idea is to see the relationship between what comes in and what goes out monthly and annually. Why should you be thinking about the details? Because that's where you'll find a great deal of your future savings.

Small change can quickly add up. If you use Quicken or Microsoft Money and you've begun to record your expenditures, create a report that will show you how your expenses ebb and flow over the course of a month. It may surprise you to see how quickly your small "never even think about it" expenses add up. Each cup of gourmet coffee can run you $3. Six cups a week is $18. If you buy it 50 weeks a year (minus two weeks of vacation), you've spent $900 a year on coffee alone. Do you smoke? A pack a day, at $3 per pack, sends $1,100 up in smoke. Do you eat lunch out every day? At $8 per lunch, that's $40 per week, and another $2,000 per year. If you put that $4,000 into a mutual fund earning 10 percent annually, it will double every seven years. You'll have $8,000 in seven years, $16,000 in fourteen years, $32,000 in twenty-one years and $64,000 in twenty-eight years. And that's for going just one year without coffee and cigarettes and brown-bagging your lunch.

Some of these items might be once-a-year sources of income. If that's the case, simply divide by 12 for a monthly entry. Likewise, you may have one-time expenses, like the cash purchase of a bicycle. Again, simply divide by 12 for a monthly expense. If your monthly expenses × 12 don't equal your annual expenses, you've made a mathematical error somewhere.

Biting Off More Than You Can Afford to Chew

If the last number on your budgeting worksheet is negative, you've got a real problem. You're spending more than you earn, and you need to find a way to redirect some of your expenditures and eliminate others. What should you eliminate? I'm not one of those "tightwad" experts who believe in living a pauper's existence in order to fuel a princely retirement. But I do think you should live *well within your means*, invest heavily for your future, and then spend the rest. If spending comes first, you will usually end up living too well, and your financial future or your security will suffer.

What should you cut? That depends on how badly your budget is in the red. If you've got a mountain of credit card debt to pay off at

(Note: This worksheet is also long, but I wanted to include everything that might possibly apply to your life. Take your time and go through it slowly. You may need to find receipts and look in your checkbook register to jog your memory.)

Income

Sources	Monthly Amount	Annual Amount
Your salary	_____	_____
Spouse's/Partner's salary	_____	_____
Second job salary	_____	_____
Third job salary	_____	_____
Self-employed income	_____	_____
Business income	_____	_____
Investment income	_____	_____
Dividends (stocks and mutual funds)	_____	_____
Interest income (bank accounts and bonds)	_____	_____
Cash gifts	_____	_____
Inheritances	_____	_____
Lottery winnings	_____	_____
Gambling winnings	_____	_____
Other	_____	_____
Subtotal—Income	_____	_____

Expenses

1. Household	Monthly Amount	Annual Amount
Rent/Mortgage payment	_____	_____
Condo/Coop/Homeowner assessments	_____	_____
Home upkeep and maintenance	_____	_____
Garden upkeep and maintenance	_____	_____
Utilities:	_____	_____
Electricity	_____	_____
Gas company	_____	_____
Telephone	_____	_____

Cellular telephone(s) _____ _____

Computer online services _____ _____

Cable TV _____ _____

Other _____ _____ _____

Groceries _____ _____

   Food (weekly menus) _____ _____

   Nonfood items _____ _____

   Take-out/Gourmet items _____ _____

Insurance _____ _____

   Health (premium, copayments, deductible) _____ _____

   Life _____ _____

   Disability _____ _____

   Renters'/Homeowners' _____ _____

   Automobile _____ _____

   Umbrella liability _____ _____

Other _____ _____ _____

Alimony/Child support _____ _____

Commuting expenses _____ _____

   Train/Bus _____ _____

   Taxicabs _____ _____

   Tolls _____ _____

   Gas _____ _____

   Car pool contribution _____ _____

   Auto repair/Maintenance _____ _____

   Other _____ _____ _____

Medical expenses _____ _____

   Hospital _____ _____

   Doctors/Practitioners _____ _____

   Dentist _____ _____

   Chiropractor/Physical therapist _____ _____

   Counselor/Therapist _____ _____

   Prescriptions/Over-the-counter drugs _____ _____

Clothing _____ _____

    Purchases _____ _____

    Dry cleaning _____ _____

House of worship contribution _____ _____

House cleaning service _____ _____

Other _____ _____ _____

Other _____ _____ _____

Subtotal—Household _____ _____

2. Taxes

(Note: Some local governments, such as New York City, require residents to pay a tax, on top of federal and state income taxes, simply for the privilege of living and working within their borders. Some foreign governments require their citizens working in the United States to pay taxes to their home country, above and beyond what they pay in U.S. federal and state taxes.)

	Monthly Amount	Annual Amount
Income taxes	_____	_____
Federal	_____	_____
State	_____	_____
Other government	_____	_____
Social Security (FICA)	_____	_____
Other _____	_____	_____
Property taxes	_____	_____
Capital gains tax	_____	_____
Sales tax	_____	_____
Subtotal—Taxes	_____	_____

3. Debt

(Note: Don't write in your monthly payments for items you charge to your credit card(s); you'll be accounting for those expenses in another area of the worksheet. For your credit card line item, just write in the additional interest and fees you're paying each month, the annual fee, if there is one, and any excess charges you pay, like late fees.)

	Monthly Amount	Annual Amount
Auto loan(s)	_____	_____
School loan(s)	_____	_____
Credit card debt(s) (interest only)	_____	_____
Loan(s) from parents or friends	_____	_____
Other _____	_____	_____
Other _____	_____	_____
Subtotal—Debt	_____	_____

4. Money Put Aside (for a rainy day or your future)

(Note: Write down what you are currently setting aside for savings and retirement. If you don't currently put away anything, write down what you'd like to save out of your current budget. Experts recommend an emergency savings account equal to six months' total expenses. That's a tough nut for many folks to crack, especially if they're also trying to save for their children's education or a house. If you have other relatively liquid, nonretirement assets (like a mutual fund or stocks you can sell) available in case of an emergency, you may be able to get away with having only two to three months' worth of expenses in this account. Also, if you are planning to buy your first home, setting up a house fund that is separate and distinct from your emergency reserve is a good idea. In that way, you won't be likely to raid one for the other.

	Monthly Amount	Annual Amount
Savings	_____	_____
Emergency savings	_____	_____
Your retirement account	_____	_____
Spouse's/Partner's retirement account	_____	_____
House fund account	_____	_____
Children's education	_____	_____
Children's wedding	_____	_____
Stocks, bonds, mutual funds, other investments	_____	_____
Other _____	_____	_____
Subtotal—Money Put Aside	_____	_____

5. Major Purchases

(Note: If you've already listed your car payments under debt, don't include them here. If you paid for your car in cash, or made a down payment, put that amount in this section. Include here only your vacation timeshare down payment, unless you paid for the timeshare in cash.)

	Monthly Amount	Annual Amount
Car (if paid in cash)	_____	_____
Boat	_____	_____
Motorcycle	_____	_____
Other vehicle _____	_____	_____
Computer	_____	_____
Furniture	_____	_____
Appliances (refrigerator, stove, freezer)	_____	_____
Electronic equipment	_____	_____
Vacation timeshare	_____	_____
Education (tuition and books)	_____	_____
College degree	_____	_____
Advanced degree	_____	_____
Fees for classes	_____	_____
Other _____	_____	_____
Other _____	_____	_____
Other _____	_____	_____
Subtotal—Major Purchases	_____	_____

6. Children/Family	Monthly Amount	Annual Amount
Aging parent contributions	_____	_____
Cash contribution	_____	_____
Nursing home	_____	_____
In-house care	_____	_____

Medical expenses _____ _____

Other _____ _____ _____

Sibling/Relative contribution _____ _____

Children _____ _____

   Diapers _____ _____

   Formula _____ _____

   Clothing _____ _____

   Day school/Preschool tuition _____ _____

   College/Graduate school tuition _____ _____

   Day care _____ _____

   Baby-sitters _____ _____

   Doctors _____ _____

   Prescriptions/Over-the-counter drugs _____ _____

   Games/Toys/Videos _____ _____

   Sporting equipment/Fees _____ _____

   Musical instruments/Lessons _____ _____

   Allowance _____ _____

   Hobbies _____ _____

   Furniture _____ _____

   Camp _____ _____

   Carpooling/Busing service _____ _____

   Lessons (extracurricular) _____ _____

   Tutors _____ _____

   Other _____ _____ _____

Other _____ _____ _____

Other _____ _____ _____

Subtotal—Children/Family _____ _____

7. Entertainment	Monthly Amount	Annual Amount
Movies	_____	_____
Books/Book clubs	_____	_____
Video rental	_____	_____
CDs/Tapes/Records	_____	_____
Restaurants	_____	_____
Breakfasts out	_____	_____
Lunches out	_____	_____
Dinners out	_____	_____
Theater	_____	_____
Concerts	_____	_____
Subscriptions	_____	_____
Newspapers	_____	_____
Magazines	_____	_____
Other _____	_____	_____
Subtotal—Entertainment	_____	_____

8. Recreation	Monthly Amount	Annual Amount
Sports events	_____	_____
Sporting equipment	_____	_____
Other sports expenses	_____	_____
Club memberships	_____	_____
Lessons	_____	_____
Classes	_____	_____
Other _____	_____	_____
Other _____	_____	_____
Other _____	_____	_____
Other _____	_____	_____
Subtotal—Recreation	_____	_____

9. Travel/Vacations

	Monthly Amount	Annual Amount
Transportation		
Airfare		
Trains		
Buses		
Car rental		
Boats		
Other _____		
Hotels		
Tolls		
Fees		
Food		
Gas		
Recreation		
Entertainment		
Package (prepaid excursions, cruises, or a safari)		
Other _____		
Other _____		
Other _____		
Subtotal—Travel/Vacations		

10. Miscellaneous

	Monthly Amount	Annual Amount
Gifts		
Postage		
Bank account fees		
Other _____		
Other _____		
Other _____		

Other _____   _____   _____

Other _____   _____   _____

Other _____   _____   _____

Subtotal—Miscellaneous   _____   _____

11. Self-Employed Business Expenses

(Note: You may deduct items that you use to run your business. For a list of items the IRS permits you to deduct, visit the IRS Web site at <www.irs.ustreas.gov> or get IRS documents faxed to you by calling 703-487-4160. You can also order informative brochures and booklets from the Government Printing Office; call 202-512-1800.)

	Monthly Amount	**Annual Amount**
Summary: All Expenses		
1. Household	_____	_____
2. Taxes	_____	_____
3. Debt	_____	_____
4. Money Put Aside	_____	_____
5. Major Purchases	_____	_____
6. Children/Family	_____	_____
7. Entertainment	_____	_____
8. Recreation	_____	_____
9. Travel/Vacations	_____	_____
10. Miscellaneous	_____	_____
11. Self-Employed Business Expenses	_____	_____
Total Expenses	_____	_____
Total Income (from page 32)	_____	_____
Less: Total Expenses	− _____	_____
Net Savings (Debt)	= _____	_____

16 percent plus, and you're not already doing so, you should cut up your cards, cut your expenses to the bone, and bring your lunch to work every day until you pay off the cards. On the other hand, if you've got a reasonable amount of debt at reasonable interest rates (say, a mortgage, car payments, and perhaps a school loan), and you're managing to save and invest, you can treat yourself to a few luxuries. I'm not giving you license to spend $1,000 on a ski vacation. Instead, you might buy a new CD ($8.95 on sale), or go out for a moderately priced dinner. Better yet, send off $50 to your mutual fund account.

Small Changes, Big Bucks

Small lifestyle changes can add up to big bucks. We've already talked about the gourmet coffee and the cigarette (or cigar) habit, and eating lunch out every day. Changing these habits alone add up to $4,000 a year in savings. Culture is expensive: Dinner and the theater for two people can quickly add up to $100 or more. Tack on the cost of a baby-sitter, and you're looking at another $50. Try saving the big night out for a really special event—say, a birthday or anniversary. On other Saturday nights, rent a video instead. Instead of spending thousands of dollars on a week in Hawaii, try vacationing at home, or somewhere within driving distance.

Only you will know what and where you can cut. When my husband, Sam, decided to open up his own law office, we took a look at

Cutting all the fun items from a budget hurts, and there's no getting around that. But once you start reining yourself in, the process of finding less expensive ways to do things becomes second nature. You'll feel enormously relieved and gratified when you see that you've been able to make a dent. A year from now, you'll find yourself making subconscious choices about spending that are foreign to your thinking today. As you become more focused on saving money, you'll become more appreciative of the small luxuries you allow yourself. Get to know the "leaner, meaner," "no pain, no gain" concepts at their best. The rewards—a healthier bank account, a more solid retirement, a paid-for college education, or a paid-off credit card or mortgage—are worth it.

COMMON SENSE

all the money we had frittered away by ordering take-out three nights a week. Each time we did that, it cost us at least $30. We were blowing about $100 a week on ordered-in food when we could've eaten well for a whole week on that amount of money. Needless to say, we cut the take-out to only about once a month. Now, eight years later, we order in Chinese or Thai food perhaps once every two months. We keep prepared pizza crusts in the freezer for evenings when we don't feel like cooking a regular dinner.

In life, few things weigh as heavily on the heart as a debt owed, particularly if you borrowed the money from a family member or close friend. When you have serious debt, you typically respond in one of two ways: (1) you go out and wantonly "spend, spend, spend" until you're completely out of credit, or (2) you feel enormous, crushing guilt every time you buy even the barest necessities. And sometimes you respond both ways. Getting your budget under control to the point where you can start to make a dent in your debt should be your top priority. It's much more important than buying that latest CD, eating yet another forgettable take-out dinner (I wish I could have back the $2,000 I spent in forgettable take-out dinners), or even seeing a top band in concert. A few years from now, if you concentrate on paying off your debt and creating a successful financial life, your heart and mind will be freer and clearer, and you will be in a position to do and achieve *much more*.

QUESTION 7

HOW MUCH SHOULD I SAVE EACH MONTH?

Saving money is relative. If your credit card debt is costing you a crushing 18 percent interest, putting $100 per month into a passbook savings account where you earn 2 percent on your balance really means you're spending more than you have to. The first step to saving money is to pay off your non-deductible debt as quickly as possible. Identify the loan with the highest interest rate first, and pay that off; then move to the next highest interest rate, and so on. (See Chapter 3, Question 17, for more ideas on consolidating your debt and paying it down.)

When you pay off debt before it's due, you're actually "earning" a rate of return on your money equal to the interest rate that the debt carries. Let me explain. If your credit card carries an interest rate of 16.9 percent, every dollar you prepay on that loan effectively earns 16.9 percent, thanks to the way interest is compounded. When you pay off your debt and start saving money for your retirement, that same compounding feature can turn $2,000 a year into hundreds of thousands of dollars thirty years from now. Prepaying your debt offers a guaranteed return, and it's one of the reasons why you should pay down all of your nondeductible debt first.

But let's say you've already paid off all your loans except your mortgage. How much should you save? If you're saving for your retirement, one school of thought says Social Security is going bankrupt, so save every penny you can. Others say, that how much you save depends on how old you are, when you plan to retire, what kind of life you plan to lead after you retire, and what rate of return you can get on your cash. If you're saving for goals that are a bit closer, like a college education, a wedding, or a down payment for a home, you'll have to assess the time you have and the return you can get.

Americans, as a rule, don't save much. In 1998, the average annual savings rate was 0.6 percent (6/10th of 1 percent) on an after-tax basis (or what's left after you pay the IRS). Of course, some people save more; most save less. Japanese workers typically save several times that. "So they'll retire with several times as much as I have." Hardly. The way compounding interest works, they might retire with eight to ten times as much as you have. Would you rather save an extra thousand dollars today and end up with an extra $200,000 when you retire?

It doesn't really matter how much you save, compared to, say, your Uncle David or your friend Susanne. What really matters is how much you're saving relative to the savings goals you've set for yourself. Earlier in this chapter (see Question 5), I asked you to make a list of your financial goals. Review that list, and estimate how much you think your goals cost. They will cost much more in thirty or forty years, as a result of inflation. That $35,000-a-year Ivy League education you want for your children could cost $75,000 a year, or more, by the time your infant is ready to enroll.

But as the cost of that education, or new car, or trip around the world grows, so do your savings—hopefully, at a faster rate than both inflation and the rising cost of a college education (between 5 and

7.5 percent a year). How much you save this month and next month (and every month until you retire) depends on what you want to purchase and when you want to purchase it.

First Things First

1. *Pay off your debt.* Start with the debt that carries the highest interest rate and work your way through all your nondeductible debt. These days, the only debt that is deductible is the interest paid on a mortgage or home equity loan.

2. *Make sure all of your insurance premiums are completely paid up.* You've got to protect yourself and your family.

3. *Put cash into a liquid emergency cash fund.* Experts recommend you set aside at least six months' living expenses, *just in case.* You can get away with a three months' amount if you have other semiliquid investments.

4. *Start saving toward your financial goals.* You don't have to make much each year. You just have to spend less than you earn and invest it wisely. If you're lucky, and careful, you'll wind up a multimillionaire.

Saving money can be as easy or as tough as you make it. For 50 cents, you can order a booklet called "66 Ways To Save Money," from Save Money, Pueblo, Colorado 81009. Written by the nonprofit Consumer Literacy Consortium, the booklet has tips that can help you save more than $1,000 without changing your lifestyle. A few of the tips: Find the long-distance calling plan that will save you the most money each month (some plans charge only 5 cents a minute if you call on Sundays); buy food in bulk at stores like Sam's Club, Price Club, and Wal-Mart; choose bank accounts with minimum balances you can meet easily, to avoid bank fees. (In Question 8, we'll talk about what kinds of accounts you should have, and where you should keep them to maximize your savings.) Some of my favorite ways to save money include: shopping the sales, raising the deductible on my insurance premiums, switching insurance policies, and sending in rebates.

How much will a single $100 investment grow over the years? This chart shows you how much you'll have, depending on the rate of return you achieve on that investment. To find out how much you'd have with a single $1000 investment, simply add a zero.

Days	Years	5.00%	6.00%	7.00%	8.00%	9.00%	10.00%
365	1	$105.00	$106.00	$107.00	$ 108.00	$ 109.00	$ 110.00
730	2	110.25	112.36	114.49	116.64	118.81	121.00
1,095	3	115.76	119.10	122.50	125.97	129.50	133.10
1,460	4	121.55	126.25	131.08	136.05	141.16	146.41
1,825	5	127.63	133.82	140.26	146.93	153.86	161.05
3,650	10	162.89	179.08	196.72	215.89	236.74	259.37
5,475	15	207.89	239.66	275.90	317.22	364.25	417.72
7,300	20	265.33	320.71	386.97	466.10	560.44	672.75
9,125	25	338.64	429.19	542.74	684.85	862.31	1,083.47
10,950	30	432.19	574.35	761.23	1,006.27	1,326.77	1,744.94

Days	Years	11.00%	12.00%	13.00%	14.00%	15.00%	16.00%
365	1	$ 111.00	$ 112.00	$ 113.00	$ 114.00	$ 115.00	$ 116.00
730	2	123.21	125.44	127.69	129.96	132.25	134.56
1,095	3	136.76	140.49	144.29	148.15	152.09	156.09
1,460	4	151.81	157.35	163.05	168.90	174.90	181.06
1,825	5	168.51	176.23	184.24	192.54	201.14	210.03
3,650	10	283.94	310.58	339.46	370.72	404.56	441.14
5,475	15	478.46	547.36	625.43	713.79	813.71	926.55
7,300	20	806.23	964.63	1,152.31	1,374.35	1,636.65	1,946.08
9,125	25	1,358.55	1,700.01	2,123.05	2,646.19	3,291.90	4,087.42
10,950	30	2,289.23	2,995.99	3,911.59	5,095.02	6,621.18	8,584.99

The worksheet shows how your money will grow if you put away $100 per month, or $1,200 a year. But the worksheet doesn't answer the one question on your mind: "How much will I need?" Economists look at everything in current dollar values. *If you'll need the equivalent of $50,000 in annual income in today's dollars when you retire in thirty-five years and your money earns only 8 percent, plan on saving enough (about $19,000 per year) to have more than $3 million saved.* If your money earns 10 percent a year (a hefty clip; the average return on the stock market), you'll need to save about $10,518 per year for thirty-five years to retire with the same amount of income.

Saving money and starting to take charge of your finances not only looks good on paper—it feels good. When you start to take control of your finances, you're taking care of yourself and your family, and the peace of mind you get from knowing you're doing the right thing will manifest itself in your ability to save even more and invest more profitably.

QUESTION 8
WHAT KINDS OF ACCOUNTS SHOULD I HAVE?

When I was little, my parents opened up a savings account for me at the First National Bank of Chicago ("First Chicago," as it was locally known; it was purchased by BancOne in 1998). Perhaps your parents did the same thing. The account was for birthday money, fees I earned from baby-sitting jobs, and the deposits for returning glass pop bottles to the store. Maybe once a year or so, I'd go downtown with my Mom or Grandfather for lunch. We'd head over to the bank with my enormous jar of pennies, have them counted, and then deposit the proceeds, along with whatever cash and checks I'd received, into my passbook savings account.

The best part was when the passbook was updated. The teller took my little passbook and stuck it into a machine that printed out all of the lines of interest owed since the last time the book had been updated. Ka-ching, Ka-ching. Ka-ching. In my head, I remember well the glorious sound of my money earning money.

What was I earning? Maybe 2 to 4 percent interest. Even in those days, it barely kept up with the rate of inflation.

But bank accounts aren't designed to be investment tools. They're merely portals through which your money passes. In other words, you should move enough money into your non-interest-bearing checking account to pay your bills each month, and that's about it. A larger reserve should be kept in a money market account, which will pay something on your money, maybe 2 to 4 percent. Not bad, but you could gain a couple of percentage points if you put your cash in a stock money market fund, like those found at Fidelity, Merrill Lynch, and other major brokerage and investment firms.

Here are the accounts you need:

1. *Standard checking account.* Make sure it requires only a low monthly minimum balance for free check-writing privileges.

2. *A money market account in lieu of a savings account.* You'll earn more money on your savings. This account does not have to be at the same place as your regular checking account. Indeed, you'll generally get a higher rate of return if your money market account is at a stock brokerage firm.

Add in different accounts, and life starts to get complicated.

In the future, you'll probably be able to get along with just the money market account, or some variation of it, because you'll be paying all of your bills from that account by computer. Many banks today offer electronic banking (and some firms will set up linked accounts outside of their own institutions). In the future, they all will. And even though a tiny percentage of folks will resist it (at least 10 percent of the population doesn't trust and won't use an ATM), the vast majority will discover how much easier it is than writing checks out by

A lot of folks ask me whether it's really worth it to open up a money market account at an investment house just for the extra percentage point or two. I suppose it depends on how you think. It's easy to call up my bank and order $1,000 transferred from my money market account into my checking account. But it's also easy to write a check from my "long-term storage" account at the investment firm, where, currently, it's earning close to 6 percent, and deposit it into my checking account so it's there when I need it. A little more work? Sure. But I'll earn nearly double the interest that I earn in my bank money market account. And why shouldn't I have that money?

hand. You'll save on the postage, and you'll earn interest on your money until the day it is transferred to pay your bills.

By the way, these accounts always cost something. That's how banks continue to show the profits that make them into takeover targets. Recently, I wanted to open up a checking account for a new company I started. I first went to my beloved First Chicago (now BancOne), where my family has been banking for nearly seventy years. I thought, "Hey, my regular business checking account is here; it will be easy to open up this account, too." It was easy. My banker sat with me as we filled out the paperwork. She told me that as long as I had a $5,000 balance, there would be no fees, but if I dropped below that amount, the fee would be about $10 per month. Each overdraft would cost $25.

I was in a hurry, so I signed up, deposited my $5,000, and took along the paperwork to read later. That afternoon, I realized I'd be earning zip on my money. The cost of that account? (Remember, the banker said as long as I maintained the minimum balance there'd be no fees.) The minimum balance would earn $250 per year at my "long-term storage" account across the street. But, to pay my bills, I needed to keep more than the minimum amount in the account, so the actual cost would be about $350 per year.

When I got home, I called my neighborhood bank for a price quote. (Opening extra accounts can complicate life, but there *are* reasons to have them. When this bank first opened, it said anyone opening a "founder" account would receive a free safe deposit box for life. So I put $500 into a non-interest-bearing account, and now receive a safe deposit box that I was previously paying $50 for. That's like earning 10 percent on your money each year. Not bad. Anyhow, this bank offers a few good deals.) When I called this time, I found out that I could open a similar business checking account for less than $10 per month. Hmmm. Would I rather spend $350 per year, or more, for the name and a little bit of convenience? Or would I rather spend less than $120 a year? Easy choice.

The Last Word

Years ago, banks just gave customers blank checks. After a while, they started charging for them. Then they started charging a lot. It galls me to pay $18 for a stack of 200 checks when I can pay $5 for 1,000 checks from a company like ChecksPlus (800-426-0822). I know it's only $18, and I know the cost of my business account was only about $350. But save $18 here and $350 there, and pretty soon you've saved enough to put $500 away in a Roth IRA or mutual fund.

The biggest misconception about money is that you go where you want to go financially by making tons of it. To the contrary, you'll get there by spending less than you earn. In fact, you can become rich simply by watching your pennies, taking small savings where you find them, and then putting them to work for you.

WHAT IS ELECTRONIC BANKING?

QUESTION 9

There's no mystery about electronic banking. Machines, instead of people, do your financial transactions. The concept has been around for a while. It started with wire transfers. Basically, a bank at one end would take the money to be wired, plus a fee, and credit the bank or institution at the other end with the wired amount. Think of all those Western Union commercials you've seen.

Actually, wire transfers are still around. But with the introduction of personal computers, high-speed modems, and the Internet, the hot term now is *electronic banking* or *e-banking*. Basically, you're moving numbers from one column to another. Want to transfer money between accounts? Call into your local bank, using its special software, and enter TRANSFER and the amount. Or, dial into your investment house and do the same thing.

The nice thing about electronic banking is that you can do it at any time of the day or night, and you don't have to actually deal with anyone else (except, perhaps, your sleepy spouse who can't stand the blue-green light from the computer monitor in the middle of the night). Right now, some banks charge a small fee of $5 per month to use electronic banking, but will waive other fees. In the future, those fees will probably drop as more banks offer electronic banking.

Is It Safe?

Safety is the biggest concern people have when they think about sending money through the Internet. Their fear is magnified every time they see a television or newspaper report about how 13-year-old computer geniuses have hacked their way into the Pentagon or are messing with Social Security numbers. I had second (and third) thoughts about trusting my retirement to a bunch of computer chips when one of the largest credit bureaus first offered credit reports on-line, and people started tapping in and receiving other people's credit histories. After all, how hard is it to learn someone's mother's maiden name? On the Internet, that might take all of five minutes, if you know where to look and are using a high-speed modem. The truth is, financial institutions spend plenty to make sure they have the best online security money can buy. And it's extremely unlikely anyone will be able to tap into your account and suck it dry. Users of electronic banking say its pleasures far outweigh any concerns they might have about security. It's nice to be able to have the mortgage check sent on the day it's due and be able to collect interest on your cash until the minute it's sent.

If you're worried about these sorts of things, you may want to wait a few more years until the Internet has been more thoroughly vetted. Until then, be sure you use permanent markers to write out any checks you send in the mail. Scam artists have been known to simply steal mail, slit open envelopes, and rinse the writing off of checks before writing them out to cash. High-tech or low-tech criminals will find a way, so protect yourself.

The Last Word

Should you choose a bank specifically because it offers online banking? In the not-too-distant future (meaning, before the next generation comes and goes), most folks will have a computer. Most will be tired of doing nothing but writing letters and playing Solitaire on their expensive computer systems. They'll be spending their time perusing the Internet and will undoubtedly end up banking and trading by computer. By that time, nearly every bank will offer some kind of online banking, probably for free. Today, you'll pay anywhere from $5 per month on up for the convenience of e-banking, and that may be worth it to you. I love being able to trade my retirement accounts online for a nominal amount, and having the accounts update automatically when I sign on. I wish I could move money with the same ease through my regular bank. I can, but I won't pay the $60 a year it costs because I can move money for free when I call my banker. If that changes, and even if it doesn't, I'll probably go online with my accounts within five years. When the convenience outweighs the cost, you should probably take the plunge. You'll have greater access to, and greater control over, your cash.

HOW CAN I MAKE THE BEST USE OF AN ATM?

QUESTION 10

True story of a five-year-old and his mother in a toy store:

"Mommy, I want to buy that toy."
"Sorry, darling, but we can't afford it."
"I know where we can get the money."
"Where?"
"The cash machine."

My good friend, Mark, has a bad habit he can't seem to break. Whenever he stops at an ATM, he pulls out only $20 to $40 at a time. He insists that's all he needs to meet his weekly needs. His wife also visits the ATM, and she pulls out about the same amount. It wouldn't be so bad, except that, by the end of the week, they don't have enough cash on hand to pay the baby-sitter, and someone has to run out again to get more money. Aside from being a colossal waste of time, his work check gets deposited at a bank that doesn't have many ATM machines. There's an ATM not too far away from his office, but nearly none is conveniently located near his home. So he and his wife typically end up pulling money from a cash machine owned by another financial institution, at a cost of $1 to $2 per transaction.

I suppose you could justify paying that kind of hefty fee if you were in a real hurry, no other options were available, and you were pulling out, say, $1,000 (about twice as much as most ATMs will allow us to withdraw in a single day). But the truth is, it isn't smart to spend that kind of money on a regular basis. If you withdraw $100 and pay an average of $1.50 each time, you're effectively paying a 1.5 percent tax on your money. That's quite a chunk of change, and it adds up. My friend Mark might be spending $5 per week on ATM fees, or about $250 per year.

The Bottom Line

ATMs serve a real purpose. Here are some ways to use them to the best of their ability:

1. *When you take out money, take out real money.* Figure out how much cash you go through each week (another good reason to budget), then visit an ATM weekly to take out the money you need. If you're worried that all that cash will burn a hole in your pocket, visit the cash machine on your way home from work, and then leave the money at home until you need it. Even if you already use an ATM that doesn't charge a fee, you're wasting valuable time with every visit.

2. *Use an ATM that doesn't charge a fee.* The worst place to use a cash machine? A casino. Not only are you taking money out to gamble, but you'll probably pay a $2 to $3 fee for the privilege. Bars are bad, and shopping centers—especially if the ATM is the only one around—can be worse. If you look around, you can usually find a machine that doesn't charge a fee. If a certain bank or financial institution owns an army of ATMs that are convenient to you (and charge a fee for nonmembers), consider opening an account there. In other words, bring the mountain to Mohammed.

3. *It's a cheap way to get money abroad.* If you're traveling abroad, using a cash machine to get local currency is often cheaper and more convenient than using traveler's checks, currency exchanges (particularly at the airport), or cash advances on a credit card. Before you leave, make sure your card works in the country where you'll be traveling, and transfer enough money into the account to cover your expenses while you're away. Take some traveler's checks just to be on the safe side; you may find yourself in a remote region that doesn't have ATMs.

4. *If you're really stuck.* Take out money wherever you are. Just be sure to keep track of your ATM charges in your financial software. The receipt may indicate you've taken out $101 rather than the $100 you've pocketed.

Credit and
Credit Reports

HOW DO I CHECK MY CREDIT HISTORY?

These days, almost everyone has one form of credit or another. We use credit cards to buy gas and food, charge department store items, and pay on layaway for furniture and appliances. I've often wondered whether how much people could be worth is tied directly to how much they can borrow. Having bad credit can hinder your ability to buy a house, refinance it at the best terms, or purchase a car. Good credit gives you access to the best interest rates and terms on all sorts of loans, from credit cards to mortgages. Someone who has excellent credit doesn't need the best terms and lowest interest rates as much as someone who has less-than-perfect credit—but such is the way of the world.

There are three major credit reporting bureaus whose sole job is to gather information about your spending and payback habits. They gather credit information on a daily, weekly, and monthly basis from credit card companies (American Express, Visa, MasterCard, Discover, and others), mortgage lenders, utility companies, department stores, banks, tax agencies, and court records, and sell that information to companies that extend credit to consumers—mortgage bankers and brokers, finance companies, and department stores.

When they receive information, credit bureaus combine it with what they already have, and update your file. If you pay off a loan or are late with your Visa payment, that information is entered into your file and made available to companies that purchase a credit history to check on your financial health. Credit reporting companies sometimes share their file information with each other, which would lead to the conclusion that all credit histories are created equal. Unfortunately, that isn't the case. Crucial data is often overlooked, numbers are transposed, people who have the same name have their credit histories switched, and so on. That's why you should check your credit at least once a year.

Your Credit Report

Your credit history is your financial autobiography. It lists your name, current and previous addresses, phone number, Social Security number, date of birth, current and previous employers. It may also have your spouse's name. The following information is listed:

- *Credit accounts.* Date opened, credit limit, loan amount, balance, monthly payment, and how you've made payments on the account (on time, late, or not at all).
- *Applicable public records.* Federal district bankruptcy records, state and county court records of tax liens and monetary judgments, and, in some states, overdue child support.
- *Credit inquiries.* List of companies that requested a copy of your credit report, and when.
- *"Statement of Dispute."* Consumers and creditors may make a 100-word statement explaining a credit problem or giving the factual history of an account. These statements are typically added to an account only after you've officially disputed its status, the account has been reinvestigated, and no one can agree on the account status. In other words, this is a last resort.

What doesn't your account include? Data about your race; religious, sexual, and political preferences; personal lifestyle; medical history; criminal history; or the names of friends and relatives.

Checking Your Credit History

Check your credit history at least once a year. If you suspect someone has stolen your credit history, check it out more often. If you've never checked out your credit history, you'll find it's easy to do, relatively cheap, and can save you a lot of anxiety and anguish down the line.

There are three major national credit reporting agencies: (1) Experian (888-EXPERIAN), formerly TRW Information Systems and Services; (2) Equifax (800-685-1111); and (3) Trans-Union (800-888-4213). Each charges approximately $8 (in some states, you have to pay tax on the $8 fee) to send out a copy of a credit report. If you call these numbers, a recorded message will tell you how to order. My guess is that soon you'll be able to order your credit report over the Internet. As we were going to press, Experian was still recovering from the black eye it gained when it first introduced access to credit reports via the Internet. The problem? People were getting other people's credit reports—a big "no-no."

You can get a free copy of your credit report if you've been turned down for credit. If you get turned down, ask the creditor (the bank, lender, or department store that denied you credit) which credit reporting bureau prepared the report. Call that bureau and obtain a copy of your credit report.

WHAT SHOWS UP ON A TYPICAL CREDIT REPORT?

QUESTION 12

If you receive a credit report, everything is revealed (or it's supposed to be). You'll see a list of your charge accounts, how much you owe on them, and whether you've been late paying your bills each month. You'll see tax liens, mechanics liens that have been filed against your home, court judgments, and public records (including bankruptcies). You might also find mistakes. Finally, your credit history includes a list of everyone who has requested a copy of your credit history in the past six months to a year. Why? If you apply for credit in a bunch of places at the same time, creditors get nervous that you're about to draw down on all of your available credit at exactly the same moment.

How much might that be? Open your wallet and take a look at how many credit cards you have. You might have a gas card or two (say, Amoco, Mobil Oil, or Shell), several credit cards (American Express, MasterCard, Visa, Discover—or perhaps two Visas from different banks), and a department store charge account. If you add up all the approved charge limits, you might easily have $25,000 to $100,000 in available credit! There's no trick to racking up credit cards; most of us are showered with several offers of credit each week. One woman kept track and reported that, over a year, she and her family received offers for *more than $1 million* in credit!

Reading a typical credit report can be tough, particularly if it shows a slew of "negatives"—industry jargon for the problems that show up on your account (like a history of late payments or a past bankruptcy). Here's a copy of a real credit report on pages 57–58 (the name and Social Security number have been removed).

What does a credit report contain? All kinds of information related to the different accounts you own, how much you owe on each one, and whether you pay on time. The individual whose credit report is shown has an excellent credit history.

Credit reports detail the creditor's name and account number, the date of the most recent information on the account, the date the account was opened, the credit limit, how much is owed and how much is past due, the minimum amount due each month, how many months you've had the account or owed a balance, how many times you've been thirty, sixty, or ninety days late in paying, and your current credit rating on a particular account.

The individual whose credit report is reproduced (in part) on page 57 has good credit, despite owing a huge amount of debt. The lender asked each of the major credit reporting bureaus to produce a credit score. The TRW Fair, Isaac Risk, the Transunion Empirica, and the Equifax Beacon scores for this individual were good enough to qualify for a home loan.

But some minor problems were noted. Each of the credit reporting bureaus commented that the proportion of revolving balances to credit limits is too high. The account has a few delinquencies, and there are a number of outstanding balances. Not all accounts have been paid as agreed, and there have been some recent credit checks. At the end of the report, it is noted that the credit report found no items of public record (such as liens, judgments, or bankruptcies) against the individual.

Despite these missteps, and with outstanding credit balances totaling $211,946 (including a mortgage), the lender has deemed this individual worthy of refinancing his or her home. (At the top of the report, you'll see that the cost of the credit report to the lender is $15. But the lender will turn around and charge you $50 to $75, or more, for each credit report pulled.)

On the other hand, the individual whose credit report is reproduced (in part) on p. 58 is in hot water with creditors. The three credit reporting bureaus concluded that the prospective borrower is in credit overload, and their credit scores (545 to 579) show it. Among the problems they noted are accounts that haven't been paid

Quality Credit Corp.

103 N. 11th Avenue, Suite 216
St. Charles, Illinois 60174
Phone: (630)377-2182
Fax: (630)377-3678

Prepared For:	NORTH SHORE MORTGAGE 576 LINCOLN AVE WINNETKA, IL 60093	REPORT TYPE: PREQUALIFYING REPORT		
000362		PRICE 15.00		

Report No.	Date Ordered	Requested By	Loan #	Prepared By	Date Completed	Repositories
					05/28/98	TRW,TU,EFX

Property Address:

APPLICANT				COAPPLICANT
		Name SSN/Age		

Marital Status: NOT DISCLOSED	Number of Dependents: NS
Current Address:	NOT SHOWN — RESIDED
Previous Address:	
Previous Address:	

	Present Employer	
	Since/Position Income Verified By	
	Previous Employer	
	Since/Position Income Verified By	

E C O A	Creditor Name Account Number	Date Reported and Method of Reporting	Date Opened	High Credit	Present Status		Terms	Historical Review				Current Rating
					Balance Owing	Past Due Amount		Months	30	60	90	

**** PREQUALIFYING REPORT ****

*** TRW FAIR, ISAAC RISK SCORE ***
00757 : A H K S
CURRENT BALANCES ON ACCOUNTS
NUMBER OF RECENT INQUIRIES
PROPORTION OF BALANCE TO HIGH CREDIT ON BANK REVOLVING OR ALL REVOLVING ACCOUNT
NUMBER OF ACCOUNTS DELINQUENT

*** TRW FAIR, ISAAC RISK SCORE ***
00735 : S A H K
NUMBER OF ACCOUNTS DELINQUENT
CURRENT BALANCES ON ACCOUNTS
NUMBER OF RECENT INQUIRIES
PROPORTION OF BALANCE TO HIGH CREDIT ON BANK REVOLVING OR ALL REVOLVING ACCOUNT

*** TRANSUNION EMPIRICA SCORE ***
+00766 : 001 008 010 018
EXCESSIVE AMOUNT OWED ON ACCOUNTS
TOO MANY RECENT CREDIT CHECKS
PROPORTION OF REVOLVING BALANCES TO REVOLVING CREDIT LIMITS IS TOO HIGH
FREQUENT DELINQUENCY

*** TRANSUNION EMPIRICA SCORE ***
+00757 : 010 001 008 018
PROPORTION OF REVOLVING BALANCES TO REVOLVING CREDIT LIMITS IS TOO HIGH
EXCESSIVE AMOUNT OWED ON ACCOUNTS
TOO MANY RECENT CREDIT CHECKS
FREQUENT DELINQUENCY

Page 1 of 7

57

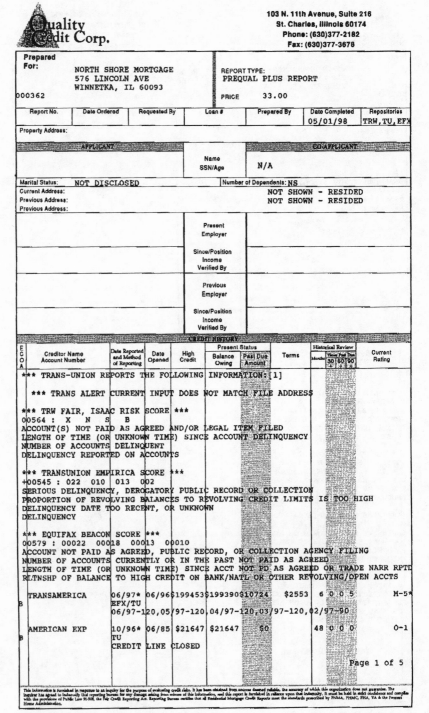

Source: North Shore Mortgage.

as agreed, or accounts on which the creditor charged off as a loss an amount owed. Several of the accounts are delinquent, there is a derogatory public record, and amounts have been turned over to collection agencies.

What does this debtor owe? On an old $199,390 mortgage with a monthly payment of $2,553, the individual paid late and was as long as 120 days past due five times. The credit bureaus report another mortgage for $213,872, taken out a year later, on which the borrower took out some additional equity and used it to pay off the old loan. Since then, payments have been late only three times.

There are other issues. This debtor has maxed out two American Express cards (to the tune of $21,647 and $15,135), and these credit lines have been closed. Another $36,353 is owed on three other credit accounts, and two collection agencies report paid collection accounts. TJ Maxx charged off $289 owed, though the individual eventually paid that debt. Several other charge accounts have been closed by the creditors.

There were three credit inquiries in a three-week period, though no accounts were subsequently opened. Finally, although you can't see it in the piece of the credit report we've replicated here, there is a long list of public records involving this individual, including several state and federal tax liens, one of which has not been released. For a lender, the two scariest things are mortgages that are paid late or foreclosed, or taxes that are not paid or are paid late.

> If you don't understand your credit report (not too tough to imagine, given how they look), you'll want to find someone who can explain what the report says. Your accountant or tax planner might be able to help, as might a mortgage lender. You can also make an appointment with a nonprofit credit counseling agency such as the Consumer Credit Counseling Service, which offers free or very low-cost help (as little as $9 per month) to individuals who are in over their head financially.

The Bottom Line

If you've got problems on your credit report, chances are they're in one of these categories:

- *Debt.* On a revolving or installment basis, you owe money. Debt stays on your credit report until you've paid it off. Then, it's noted as a paid-off debt.

- *Late payments.* You've missed paying your Visa bill and the next one appears with a past-due notice and a finance charge. You then send in your check. That's a late payment, and a history of chronic late payments concerns lenders. Late payments usually disappear from your credit history two years after they occur. You can make a late payment less important, however, by paying all of your bills on time and having a good explanation as to why you were late paying previous bills.

- *Bankruptcy.* Having a judge wipe your financial slate clean with the discharge of bankruptcy sounds like an easy way to start all over again. It isn't. If negative information is a gray stain, bankruptcy is a big black mark on your credit. Even after the bankruptcy has been discharged, it stays on your credit report for up to ten years.

- *Errors.* Because of the sheer volume of information being sent to credit reporting agencies, errors occur with alarming frequency. If you don't find and fix the errors, they'll come back to haunt you in the form of a lower credit score.

- *Repossessions.* If you buy furniture, jewelry, or appliances on an installment plan and fail to make a payment or two, these items can be taken back (repossessed) by the creditor until you ante up what you owe.

- *Accounts turned over to a collection agency.* If you fail to pay your bills and the creditor hires a collection agency to chase you down, that will get noted on your credit history.

- *Charge-offs.* If, after turning over your account to a collection agency, a creditor finally gives up on you, it will typically write off your debt as a bad loan. This is called a charge-off, and it will appear on your credit report.

- *Foreclosures.* If you own a home and fail to make your monthly mortgage payments, the lender will begin foreclosure proceedings to take back the house (a form of repossession).

- *Tax liens.* If you owe the IRS, every creditor will be told that fact when a copy of your credit report is printed. Tax liens stay on your credit report until you've paid them, and they will be noted as paid off for several years after that.

- *Too many credit inquiries.* It's perfectly normal to have a couple of inquiries, but twenty-five of them within three weeks will turn a few heads and possibly get you rejected by a future creditor. Credit inquiries stay on your credit report for two years, but creditors are particularly interested in the past six months.

- *Too much available credit.* Even if you owe nothing, you could get rejected for a loan if you have too much available credit. This is one of the easiest items to fix on your credit report.

HOW DO I FIX MY CREDIT REPORT?

QUESTION
13

Having excellent credit means you get the best rates for credit cards, a mortgage, and other loans you may need. Whether your credit has a few blemishes, or some major problems, you'll want to tune it up.

It may take some time to work out all of your credit problems. The road to excellent credit is paved with obstacles and frustrations. But there's nothing a "credit repair" shop (see item 8 below) can do for you that you can't do for yourself for free. Here are some steps you should take:

1. *Take stock of your current credit situation.* Start by ordering a copy of your credit report ($8 each) from each of the three national credit reporting bureaus, Experian (888-EXPER-IAN), Equifax (800-685-1111), and Trans-Union (800-888-4213). While you're waiting for them to arrive, use the budget worksheet in Question 6 (pages 32–40) to figure out how much you're spending on fixed living expenses and debt payments.

2. *Scrutinize your credit report.* When your credit reports arrive, look them over for errors. If someone else's debt has been posted to your account, dispute it. If you are listed as delinquent on several accounts, and you're current, provide copies of recent statements and canceled checks as proof. Look for other problems: too many credit inquiries, too much credit, or other inaccurate information. If you have a joint credit account and your partner has a credit problem, it could become your credit problem. If you lent your signature (cosigned a loan) and your partner is paying debt late (or not at all), you and your credit could be in real trouble.

3. *Fix your credit history errors.* Write letters to your creditors (send copies to the credit reporting bureau) and enclose documentation that supports your claims. To receive a brochure and sample letter on how to dispute faulty credit bureau information, write to the Federal Trade Commission, Correspondence Branch, Washington, DC 20580. The process of fixing credit errors is time-consuming, despite the fact that agencies are required to address disputes within thirty days.

4. *Pay off your debt.* One of the fastest ways to fix your credit is to pay off, or at least pay down, your debt as quickly as possible. If you're applying for a home loan, paying down your debt before you apply will make you a much stronger candidate.

5. *Freeze your credit cards.* If you're a spendaholic, make using your credit cards as difficult as possible. Cut them up, or put them in a bucket with water and freeze them. Don't put them in places where you might forget them. A shopaholic in New Mexico put her credit cards in a purse she wasn't using, stored the purse in a closet, and later gave the purse away without opening it or realizing its contents. Someone bought the purse at a thrift shop, took the cards, and charged $5,000 in purchases before getting caught. When the shopaholic got the call from the credit card company, she hadn't even realized her cards were gone.

6. *Cancel unused cards.* Remember that too much available credit can sink your credit history. Cancel unused accounts—in writing—and then ask the company to send you a confirmation that the account has been canceled. A few months later, double-check to make sure the cards have been removed from your credit history and not just labeled "inactive."

7. *Know when you need professional help.* If you're finding it difficult to create a workable budget or to put together a workout plan with your creditors, consider getting some free or low-cost professional help. The nonprofit Consumer Credit Counseling Service (CCCS), which has hundreds of offices all over the United States, offers free or very low-cost credit, debt, and budget counseling. Call (toll-free) 800-338-2227 for a referral to the CCCS office closest to you. One caveat: CCCS is funded by credit card companies and institutional creditors and may have a slight bias in its counseling. For

example, CCCS may urge you to settle on a workout plan rather than suggest bankruptcy, even if bankruptcy might be in your best interest. But a counselor will help you to come up with a workable budget, and may even have some leverage in getting creditors to accept what you're offering.

8. *Beware of credit repair companies.* If someone offers to fix your credit for a fee, run the other way. If someone offers to "erase" your bad credit history and give you "brand new grade-A credit instantly," run even faster, then call the nearest Federal Trade Commission office to report a fraud. Credit repair companies will charge you a fortune (even up to $1,000) to fix your credit, but they can't do anything you can't do for yourself—for free. Don't think anyone can wipe your credit slate clean. Only bankruptcy can erase your debts—and bankruptcy stays on your credit history for up to ten years.

9. *Make sure your workout payments are correctly reported.* After going through the hassle of setting up a workout schedule with a creditor, you don't want that creditor to report that you're not making the minimum payment. Be sure your workout payments are correctly recorded as paid on time and in full, so that your credit history improves.

10. *Get a secured credit card.* Whether you've been through bankruptcy or have had to cancel all of your credit accounts, you'll want to rebuild your credit history with a secured credit card. With a secured card, you put any amount from $500 to $5,000 into a bank account and the bank issues you a secured card for the amount deposited. You may "borrow" up to the level you have deposited, and as long as you pay it back on time, you will start to rebuild your credit. Eventually, the bank will offer you an unsecured card, which means your credit is good enough to borrow without pledging any money. It's a big step forward.

11. *Consolidate your debt, if you can.* If you consolidate your debts with a home equity loan, you may be able to use tax-deductible money with a lower interest rate to pay off high-interest-rate, nondeductible loans. That's the best situation. If you don't have any equity, or don't own a home, you'll want to consolidate your debt on a different credit card to take advantage of superficially low "teaser rates." These rates are very low for

six months to a year. At the end of that time, the rate bumps up. If you keep consolidating your debt every six months (before the rate changes) and use the difference to pay down the balance, you'll pay it off much more quickly than if you just pay the minimum amount each month.

12. *Keep your job.* Many folks don't realize that their employers are often listed on their credit history. Holding a job for a long time looks much better to a prospective lender than switching jobs every six months. Stay with your employer for a while. Job stability can only help your credit situation.

13. *Pay your spousal and child support on time.* It won't help your credit report if you make every Visa payment on time and in full but avoid paying spousal and child support. Remember, court judgments and tax liens are also listed on credit reports.

Divorce can be horrible, and an angry ex-spouse can easily inflict lasting damage on his or her ex-spouse's credit report. If you are considering divorce, cancel all credit cards and accounts held jointly. Otherwise, if your spouse starts to spend and then refuses to pay, the creditors will come after you. Even if the court says your spouse must pay his or her share, or is responsible for certain bills, as long as your name is on the account, you're stuck. Here's an unpleasant thought: You may have to pay off the whole bill just to save your credit history.

WHAT IS MY CREDIT SCORE?

One of the little known facts about the credit industry is that lenders treat your credit report as a running scorecard of your financial life. When you apply for a credit card, auto loan, or mortgage, lenders take your credit report and run it through a mathematical program called a "credit score." They assign points (positive *and* negative) to different information (called *tradelines* in industry jargon) in your file, to determine whether you're a good risk.

They look at your mortgages, personal loans, student loans, auto loans, and judgments; your credit card debt, payment history, total number of credit cards (and credit accounts), and level of debt (is it out of whack with your income?). Do you have too many credit inquiries? Do you have a checking and a savings account?

Currently, each creditor uses its own proprietary formula to see whether you pass financial muster, but the most common system was created by Fair, Isaac & Co, a San Raphael, California-based data management services and consulting company. Its credit scoring method, nicknamed "FICO," assigns you a credit score between 300 and 900. Most consumers score between 500 and 800. Each creditor determines which number will be acceptable.

The federal government hasn't yet seen fit to regulate credit scoring, so it'll be tough for you to know, until you've actually applied, whether you're going to have a problem getting approved for credit. If you have a lot of negative information on your credit report and you're applying for something big, like a home loan, chances are you're going to have problems. In that case, you're better off taking six months to fix your credit before you try again (see Question 13 for details on how to fix your credit history). Whatever you do, once you've been denied credit, don't keep applying without fixing your credit first. You'll just add more negative information to your credit history.

Credit laws are constantly changing, often to consumers' benefit. A recent change gives consumers a thirty-day window to shop for a mortgage. That means you can have thirty days for mortgage-related inquiries before a warning bell sounds. For all other loans, you now get a fourteen-day grace period. If you're buying a car, shop for your financing within fourteen days.

If you get rejected for a loan, it's hard not to take it personally. Still, buck up and ask the creditor why you're being rejected. You have up to sixty days to get a free copy of your credit report if you've been denied credit. Under the Equal Credit Opportunity Act (ECOA), the creditor must tell you why you were rejected, though there is no requirement to tell you the factors and points used in its scoring system. Use the information to clean up your credit or to improve weak spots. For example, if you're rejected because you've been at your job only a short while, wait until you've been employed there longer, and then reapply.

HOW DO I GET THE BEST DEAL ON A CREDIT CARD?

What kind of deal do you need? There are different ways to approach the use of credit and credit cards, and you need to ask yourself what's best for you.

Do you intend to pay off your balance each month? If the answer is yes, look for a card that gives you something for your business. The possibilities include:

- *Airline miles.* First Chicago Mileage Plus Bank Card Center (800-632-2505, but this may change with its BancOne merger), Citibank A/Advantage (800-359-4444), and American Express (800-528-4800), among others, usually offer a mile per dollar spent, plus a few thousand extra miles for joining up.

- *Discounts on cars and trucks.* All discounts are subject to change or elimination, but, as we went to press, the GM Card from General Motors (800-846-2273) still offered 5 percent on all purchases and transferred balances up to $500 per year (or $1,000 per year for their gold card) over seven years. Rebates can be used toward the purchase of GM cars and trucks. Volkswagen Visa (800-847-7378) also offered 5 percent up to $700 per year, as a rebate that you can use to purchase any Volkswagen vehicle.

- *Cash.* Discover Card (800-DISCOVER) gives you cash rebates that start at about a half percent per year and go up to 2 percent for certain amounts. GE Rewards MasterCard (800-437-3927) offers .05 percent rebate for charges of $2,000 or less per year, and up to 2 percent for charges of $6,001 to $10,000. Gas station cards like Exxon MasterCard offer 3 percent back on all Exxon purchases and 1 percent on non-Exxon purchases.

Which among these are the best bet? If you often need last-minute flight arrangements for a ticket priced at $1,500 or higher, and you charge or fly enough to give you at least one free ticket a year (at press time, this was 20,000 or 25,000 miles, which, at a mile for every dollar charged, is $25,000), then this is probably the way to go. But if you charged $25,000 on Discover Card, you'd earn back at least $500 and be able to buy a cheap plane ticket and have some spending money left over. With American Express, you can apply the miles to one of several airlines, or take advantage of some of their hotel specials as well.

You have to decide whether you're willing to pay for the privilege of getting points, or miles, or discounts. If you're going to pay $50 or $60 to carry one of these premium cards and will get only a minimum amount back, it's not worth it. Go with Discover Card, and get the cash back at the end of the year.

My husband and I have three credit cards:

1. A Citibank A/Advantage card. We pay about $60 a year as an annual fee, and because we charge a significant amount of business and personal expenses to that card plus travel somewhat frequently, we earn about two tickets a year.

2. A First Chicago Mileage Plus card. We pay no annual fee and we earn miles on United Airlines.

3. A Discover Card for the bulk of purchases and to take advantage of special monthly bonus chargeback awards.

All of our cards are paid off in full at the end of each billing cycle. The store credit cards we carry are Neiman Marcus (I like getting their fabulous Christmas catalog, and they take only American Express or their own store card), and Eddie Bauer, which awards points toward merchandise when we shop there. Everything else gets charged on a Visa or Discover Card.

If you're going to carry a balance, you should be much more interested in the interest rate and the fees charged by the card you're carrying. To find out which cards carry the lowest interest rate and terms, check out Bank Rate Monitor's Web site at <www.bankrate.com>, or RAM Research, P.O. Box 1700 (College Estates), Frederick, MD 21702; <www.ramresearch.com/carttrak/cardtrak.html>. You can also pay $4 and obtain a list of the lowest-rate cards from Bankcard Holders of America, 524 Branch Drive, Salem, VA 24153.

The initial interest rate period is important, but so is how much you're eventually going to be charged. To keep paying the least amount of interest, you should consolidate your debt, which means staying on top of which cards have the best rates and terms, and switching just before your interest rate bumps up (experts say you should be able to get the low rate for a year). (See Question 18 for more information.) It might even be worth paying a small annual fee (say, $25 or $35) to keep a long-term low-interest rate.

67

Sometimes, getting the best deal means not getting the worst deal. Here are some of the worst deals you can get on a credit card:

- Some banks charge as much as 4 percent to transfer a balance to another card. If you're carrying a $4,000 balance and want to transfer it, you could be charged as much as $160 for the privilege. Thanks, but no thanks.

- Some credit cards can raise rates on an existing customer's card to 24.9 percent if, in their judgment, the customer has too many other balances on too many other cards. Even if you pay on time, your rate could be jacked up until you've shown eighteen months of good payments. Sounds like a ball and chain to me.

- Credit cards are withdrawing their offers for buyer-protection plans, coverage of damaged or stolen merchandise, extended warranties, and car rental insurance. These haven't worked well. Read the fine print if you're expecting to make some use of these programs.

- Two-cycle balance calculations are getting more popular. If you don't pay in full each month, a card that calculates interest on the two-cycle month can kill you, interestwise. Two-cycle credit cards require you to pay in full two months in a row, or they reach back to eliminate the grace period between cycles. One-cycle cards look at each billing period on its own. For example, if you paid your $600 April bill in full, but only $300 of your $800 bill in May, a two-cycle method will go back and charge you two months' worth of interest in June, wiping out your grace period from May. Look for this in the (very, very) fine print.

- Some credit card companies charge interest from the day of purchase rather than from the day the merchant posts the transaction (which might be a few days later).

- If you pay your balance in full, you might get only a twenty-day grace period (or less). If you carry a balance, you might get twenty-five days (of course, you're paying interest that whole time). If the fine print doesn't say it, you should get a twenty-five-day grace period.

- Is it really a "no fee" card? Or is it just "no fee" for six months or a year?

- Some banks charge you an arm and a leg on top of insane interest rates. How much are you going to pay for a bounced check? Or a late payment? These penalties range from $5 to $25. If you need an extra copy of a bill or a transaction, you can pay between $2 and $5. Check out the obscure charges in the fine print.

- Is the interest rate fixed? Or is it a variable rate? You may think you're paying one rate, but it might adjust upward every month.

- Cards colored gold, platinum, titanium, or that special material used to construct the *U.S.S. Enterprise* are nice to have if you can get them. They usually allow you to charge more, and you may even gain extra perks. But you'll also pay higher annual fees, transaction fees, and extra charges, and maybe even a higher interest rate on balances carried. Some "gold cards" have eliminated their interest rate caps entirely. Could you conceivably pay 30 percent interest? Yup.

- If you're using the cash advance route, expect to pay through the nose for it, including interest charged from day one, transaction fees, and fewer, if any, protections. If you pay for casino chips or markers with a credit card, some companies will charge you as if you had received a cash advance instead of a service or entertainment.

The worst news of all is this: If you're paying off balances each month, you're probably going to see fees go up in the future. After all, banks must maintain their profit margins somehow.

Secured Credit Cards

A secured credit card is a way for you to rebuild your financial life. Basically, you deposit money in a special account that acts as collateral for your charge account. The bank gives you a card on which you can charge up to the amount you have deposited. If you don't have credit and are looking for a good secured card (see Question 13 for more information on secured credit), find a bank that will pay you interest on your deposit and that charges reasonable fees. Pay off the card on time and in full for six months in a row, and then ask the bank to update your credit information.

When searching for the best credit card deal, you'll have to wade through the fine print. Make sure you do before the interest starts ticking, or it could be an expensive lesson. Also, don't get lazy. If you're switching balances, the key to getting ahead is to switch before the interest rate goes up and before the fees kick in.

69

A lot of people feel empowered by switching to a lower-rate card with better terms. If you're just pulling your finances out of the muddy waters of debt, cutting up charge cards and choosing new ones can be a liberating experience. Just don't get carried away and start accepting every charge card offer your mail carrier brings by, or you may find yourself back in the same position you were in before.

QUESTION 16

WHAT IS THE DIFFERENCE BETWEEN A CREDIT CARD AND A CASH DEBIT CARD?

Banks are always introducing new "products" to make our lives easier. But you can bet your last dollar that if a bank didn't think it would somehow make money, it wouldn't be offering a product to you.

Credit cards allow you to borrow up to your credit limit, which usually exceeds the amount of cash in your checking account. You're not actually borrowing real dollars; you're borrowing the credit card company's money. In many cases, banks offer credit cards, so you're borrowing the bank's money. Cash debit cards are a cross between credit cards and checking accounts. You can pay for your goods and services with the cash debit card just as you would a credit card. But instead of borrowing the credit card company's money, the money comes directly from your checking account.

The good news is that you're paying for your goods and services with cash, not credit. Your cash debit card is also usually tied into your bank accounts so you can use it through ATMs (automated teller machines) to withdraw money. (One card, two functions!) The bad news is that if you pay off your credit card bill in full at the end of each cycle, you're using your money, not the credit card company's, to buy those goods and services. Many banks have a daily spending limit on cash debit cards. Even if you have $10,000 in your checking account, you may be able to withdraw only a few hundred dollars a day. (By the way, if you do have $10,000 in your checking account, go back and read Question 8 more carefully!) If you overdraw your account, the bank charges you additional fees. Actually, some banks charge as much as $.75 to $1.50 per transaction on a cash debit card—and it's your money!

Some cash debit cards don't offer the same purchasing protections as a credit card. With a regular Visa or MasterCard charge card, you'd be covered from ground zero if someone stole your card and bought a Mercedes with it. When first introduced, cash debit cards covered cardholders from about $50 on up *only* if a stolen card was reported within twenty-four hours. After that, you were basically on the hook for everything else. Today, some cards cover you from ground zero in case of theft, and some don't. If your card is stolen and someone taps your account, and if you bounce a check or two in the meantime because it takes your bank a few days to straighten out your account and give you credit, most banks will automatically refund your bounced check fees. They may not refund other fees you're charged, however. You'll have to read the fine print carefully.

Banks offer cash debit cards to lure folks away from using credit cards and to have them pay more fees to the bank. Great. What's in it for you? You might have easier access to the cash in your checking account—but so might thieves, who, at least in the short term, may not even need to use a PIN (personal identification number) to access your cash. And if your card is stolen, it can take weeks to get your money back. Also, credit cards offer a few advantages; for example, you're building up your credit (provided you're paying on time) because you're actually borrowing money. With a cash debit card, you're not. Also, because siphoning cash from your checking account is so easy, and you aren't carrying a check register with you, you might go overboard and start bouncing checks. You may not get all the consumer protection rights you would with a credit card company (in case that mink stole isn't really mink, or it was stolen within 90 days, or it never arrived from the store where you bought it). Finally, some airlines and car rental agencies don't accept cash debit cards (even if they have the Visa or MasterCard logo on them) because they aren't a measure of your creditworthiness.

The Bottom Line

What should you do? If you don't mind using two different cards (a credit card and an ATM card), and you pay off your credit card balance in full each month, you should probably keep doing what you've been doing. If you feel a credit card is too much of a temptation and you don't want to mess with checks, a cash debit card might be just the ticket.

Just remember: If your bank is pitching you on new "products" to use, it probably means the bank is going to be better off if you use those products than you are.

QUESTION 17

WHICH DEBT SHOULD I PAY OFF FIRST?

Debt drags you down. It weighs on your heart and mind as well as your wallet. To lighten your spirits (not to mention your bankbook), get out of debt as quickly as possible.

Pay off the non-deductible debt with the highest interest rate first. If your other debts have about the same interest rate, pay off those that aren't tax-deductible.

How do you know what your interest rate is? Your monthly statement should list the interest rate you're paying. Use the worksheet on page 73 to list all of your debts and their interest rates. When you've listed them all (including personal loans from your parents, relatives, or friends), organize the entries from highest interest rate to lowest, and start with a game plan. If your debt is primarily from credit cards, Question 18 gives some tips on consolidating your debt to a much lower level and then paying it off faster.

QUESTION 18

HOW DO I CONSOLIDATE MY DEBT?

I wish I could say I was the one who came up with the smart idea of consolidating debt on a cheap credit card, and then switching before the interest rate jumps. That idea was probably invented by a debt-ridden consumer at the end of his or her personal financial rope. As ideas rate, it's one of the best, and it's certainly a tool you should use in your bag of debt-defying tricks.

Consolidating Debt—How It Works

The strategy behind debt consolidation is to take up your fistful of credit cards, all with small balances on them, and consolidate the debt onto one card with a low introductory rate (by paying off all the

Credit Card or Loan	Amount Owed	Minimum Monthly Payment	Interest Rate

Remember, list each credit card separately, as well as your car loan, school loans, personal loans, mortgage, and any other debts you owe.

other balances with a cash advance from the new card). If you've chosen well, the card on which you consolidate your debt will give you a twenty-five-day grace period before starting to charge interest, and the low interest rate will stay low for at least a year.

You then take the savings each month between the old interest rate and the new (lower) interest rate, and apply that amount to the balance owed, to wipe out the balance as quickly as possible. Just before the interest rate jumps, you switch the balance over to a new card with another introductory balance and start all over again.

Even if you don't use your extra savings each month to make additional payments on the balance (but I strongly urge that you do!), you're paying less each month in interest, which should help ease your personal finance situation.

When you switch from card to card, there are some things to look out for. Choose a card that:

1. Offers you the twenty-five-day grace period. You can use that period of time to regroup and gather a little more cash to make the payment.

2. Doesn't charge a fee to transfer the balance. Owing an extra 2, 3, or 4 percent on your balance is the last thing you need right now.

3. Doesn't have a two-cycle balancing act. (See Question 15 for more information on two-cycle balances.)

4. Keeps the introductory interest rate for at least a year.

An Even Better Idea

Paying more than you owe each month is a very good idea. Depending on how much credit card debt you owe, you'll save thousands of dollars. If you pay half of what you owe on your credit card debt on a biweekly basis (that is, every other week instead of once a month), you'll save additional money without even missing it.

How does this work? Your credit card company is required to credit your payments the day they're received. With 52 weeks per year, you're actually making 26 biweekly payments, or about 13 months' worth instead of 12. The extra payments go toward prepaying your balance.

I can't stress enough the importance of paying down your highest interest rate first. Every dollar you prepay in interest effectively earns you a rate of return equal to that interest rate. So, if you're paying 18 percent interest on your credit card balance, every dollar you prepay effectively earns you an 18 percent return, or $1.18.

Marc Eisenson, a book author who publishes "The Pocket Change Investor,"* offers this example to show how much you'll save by making biweekly credit card payments. If you owe $3,500 on a credit card that charges 17 percent interest, your required monthly minimum payment could be anywhere from $70 to $105. If you only owe $70, your interest on the $3,500 would be $7,242.62, for a total tab of $10,742.60. That's more than three times what you charged. But if you pay half of the $70, or $35, every two weeks, *you can cut $5,000 in interest off the $7,242.62 you'll otherwise owe.* On top of that, you'll pay off your debt in seven years, rather than thirty. Now that's what I call significant savings.

Because you'll want to make sure your payments get to the credit card company every fourteen days, try to set up an electronic transfer, so the cash is automatically deducted from your checking account on the day you want. If you're writing checks, make sure you put your account number on each check. Send the check to the address on your credit card statement.

A Better Idea Even Than That

If you've got equity in your home, you may want to pay off your outstanding balances with a home equity line of credit. The interest rate should be low, and it's currently tax-deductible.

---

*This is an excellent quarterly newsletter filled with good advice on how you can get the best deals on things like credit cards and phone rates. A subscription costs $12.95 a year; call 800-255-0899, or write Good Advice Press, Box 78, Elizaville, NY 12523.

I'm often asked whether debtors should try to save something even while they're paying down debt. The answer most experts give is this: If you're paying down debt that carries a double-digit interest rate (say, 10 percent or higher), pay it down first before you start putting cash away for any other investments. Common sense tells us that unless you can guarantee a higher rate of return (minus taxes) than the interest rate you're paying (with after-tax dollars), you should pay off the debt. But sometimes we need to feel that we're building toward our future while paying off our past. If your financial ego needs a shot in the arm, take $25 or $50 each month and put it into a mutual fund or stock money market fund while you're paying down your balances. You'd probably save more money by paying down your credit card debt (at 18 percent), but the psychological benefits may outweigh the financial return. As you pay off higher interest rate debt and move to lower interest rate debt, keep adding anything you can to the money you're socking away. By the time you're done paying down your debt, you'll have a tidy sum to invest, or to use as a down payment or for closing costs on a home.

Cars and Trucks

I come from a long line of car keepers; that is, half of my family pays cash for their cars and then keeps them for a long, long time. My grandfather kept cars for ten years. My Uncle Rich has been known to keep a car even longer than that. The other half of my family are trader-inners. My father got a new car every couple of years. My mother drives her car a lot for business (and to visit her grandchildren) and is one of those consumers who is tough on vehicles. So, every three to five years, she gets a new car. My cousin's ex-wife went through two cars in the four years I knew her. I don't think I know anyone who gets a new car every single year—but perhaps you do.

Whether you were a car keeper or a trader-inner in my family, we didn't drive too much. We lived on the north side of Chicago, a city with fantastic and relatively cheap public transportation. So we took the CTA (Chicago Transit Authority) to school, to our after-school jobs, and to our summer jobs; to meet our friends, to go to the symphony or the theater, or to go out to dinner. Being only about four miles from the Loop (Chicago's central business district, so named for the century-old elevated train tracks that loop the oldest part of the city center), we tended to walk home a lot. (And, no, I'm not going to tell you that when I was a kid we always walked and it was always uphill. Chicago is about as flat as a pancake.) When I got to college, I walked or rode my bicycle everywhere.

I was 28 before I owned a car. My father-in-law gave my husband and me his old Volvo sedan, which was maybe six or seven years old when we got it. My three favorite things about it: (1) it was sky blue; (2) it had a seat warmer; and (3) it made it much easier to visit our friends who had moved to the suburbs and to haul home stuff from Home Depot when we were renovating our co-op apartment. On the other hand, it handled horribly in the winter—which always struck me as funny, given where Volvos are made—and during the two-plus years we had it, it was in the shop more often than not. It was probably worth about $8,000 when we got it. We managed to sell it to a Nigerian taxi driver a few years later for $5,500, about what we'd paid to the Volvo dealer to keep it running.

The most frustrating thing about the Volvo was that we had no place to park it. This, of course, was our own fault. We had bought a co-op apartment without a garage because we didn't have a car at the time and couldn't foresee ever needing one. (If you want to know more about that, and other real estate mistakes I've made along the way, you'll have to read my first book, *100 Questions Every First-Time Home Buyer Should Ask*.)

In May 1994, my husband and I bought our first brand new car, a black Honda Accord EX with a sun roof (Honda's marketing department calls it a "moon roof"; go figure!). As of this writing, we still have it. It hasn't given us a lick of trouble, rides well, and you should see all the stuff we can haul home from Home Depot and WalMart (Sam is an expert trunk-packer). By the time this book is published, it will have close to 50,000 miles on it. (One of my sisters, who bought an identical car minus the pinstripe, has barely 20,000 miles on hers. But she still lives in downtown Chicago.)

Our closest friends and family have bought or leased both new and used (excuse me, "previously owned") Volvos, assorted minivans, Saabs, Lexuses, Range Rovers, BMWs, Chevrolets, Hondas, Lincoln-Mercurys, and a few other cars I can't think of at the moment.

I say all this by way of introduction and bias. Having bought one new car in my life, I'm tempted to be buried with it. Barring that, I'd probably purchase a previously owned car that was still covered by the original factory warranty (more on this in Question 20). But I believe in buying rather than leasing (for almost all cases), and paying cash instead of financing, unless you get extremely low financing from the dealer as a special promotion.

My advice: Whenever possible, walk or take public transportation. It's good for you and for the environment.

QUESTION 19

SHOULD I BUY OR LEASE MY NEXT CAR?

If buying a home fulfills the American Dream, driving a new car may be the best way to show the world you've made it. So say the chieftains of hype.

Car companies spend hundreds of millions of dollars a year to convince us that we must drive a new car loaded with all the latest gadgets, styling, colors, and safety equipment. They encourage us to have our cars serviced by the dealer for superior maintenance. They produce gorgeous commercials that ooze style and substance, texture, and lots of leather. But these ads are really designed to get us within sniffing distance of that "new car" aroma. Is it just a coincidence that dealership service centers are positioned right in the middle of a shiny new fleet just begging for a test drive? How good are you going to feel about your clunker (which needs $500 worth of work, not to mention the thousands you could spend to fix all the dings that have accumulated during your years of ownership) when you have to brush by next year's model, all polished and shiny?

Not too good. And that's the whole idea behind new-car advertising and marketing. Approximately 15 million new cars and trucks are sold each year. At an average price of $20,000, that's hundreds of billions of dollars in sales that Ford, GM, and the other car companies feel the need to protect. And they'll protect their turf any way they can.

But this book isn't about Fortune 500 car companies' finances. They're doing fine. This is a book about your finances. And before you decide how you're going to acquire your new car (or preowned vehicle), I want you to stop and answer the three questions that follow here.

1. Do You Really Need a Car?

If you don't currently have a car, why do you want one? Do you need it to get to a job every day, or is it for weekend excursions, errands, and convenience? If you use public transportation to get to and from work every day, and you're looking for a car only for weekend errands and getaways, it will be far less expensive for you to rent a car every weekend of the year than to own one. That's right. You can actually rent a perfectly nice, brand-new car from a local car rental company every weekend of the year for less money than what it will cost to own a car. (See the worksheet, "Owning vs. Renting a Car," on page 84, for the cost comparison.)

If you have a car, do you really need to replace it? Is it worn out? Does it need costly repair work? Are you afraid that you'll get stuck on a highway somewhere in the middle of the night? Safety concerns are good reasons to replace cars.

2. How Far Do You Drive Each Year?

Without looking at the odometer, how many miles do you put on your car each year? 8,000? 10,000? 12,000? If you're like many Americans, you might easily put on more than 15,000 miles per year—perhaps much more.

How can that be when you only drive the car to the train and then do a few errands on the weekends?

Let's add up the mileage. Let's say you drive 5 miles each way to take the train to and from work. That's 10 miles a day, or 50 miles during the workweek. If you commute 20 miles each way to work, that's 40 miles a day, or 200 miles during the workweek. On weekends, you might drive another 100 miles to visit friends, do errands, go out to dinner, attend your house of worship, or visit family. Annually, let's say, you'll drive 1,000 miles on vacation.

During the week, in local driving, you cover 150 to 300 miles. Multiply those miles by 50 weeks (assuming two weeks of vacation a year) and you're putting on 7,500 to 15,000 miles a year. Add in your 1,000 vacation miles and you've logged 8,500 to 16,000 miles a year, and that's a conservative estimate.

If you don't believe me, and you can't remember the numbers on your odometer last January 1, here are two simple ways to figure out your average annual mileage:

1. Divide your current total mileage by the number of years you've owned your car:

$$\frac{\text{Total mileage}}{\text{Number of years you've owned your car}} = \text{Average annual mileage}$$

2. Pull out your receipts and reconstruct how often you bought a full tank of gas.

Depending on your car's fuel efficiency, whether you did highway or city driving, and whether you fill up when your tank is almost empty or at the quarter- or half-tank mark, you'll probably drive 250 to 350 miles on each tank of gas. If you fill up every week, you're probably driving an average of 250 to 350 miles per week, or 13,000 to 18,000 miles per year. That's a lot of driving. If you're in sales, or you commute a long distance to work each day, you might put on as many as 20,000 to 25,000 miles a year.

3. How Hard Are You on Your Car?

Do you eat or drink while you drive? Do you have young children? Do you have older children who borrow the car to drive their friends to the mall every afternoon? Do you go long periods of time without getting the car cleaned? Do you or your friends smoke in your car? Are you accident-prone? Do you think twice about opening your car door into another person's car in a crowded shopping-mall parking lot? Do you have your car's engine serviced regularly? How often do you change the oil?

Whether you're hard on a car or easy on a car is going to make a huge difference when it comes time to decide whether you should lease or buy. (We'll get to *why* in a moment.) It also helps you think about how long you can keep a car. The longer it's nice (even with old-fashioned styling) and running well, the longer you're going to keep it.

Leasing

Leasing a car has become almost a national pastime. In 1990, just a tiny fraction of those folks who drove a new car were leasing it. Most people bought a car the conventional way—a little money down, the rest financed at an interest rate of anywhere from 7 to 14 percent. Today, more than one-third of all new-car drivers are leasing their cars. Some experts project an increase to more than 50 percent early in the next millennium.

Why is leasing so popular? One possible reason is that car dealers and car companies have positioned leasing as a cheap way of always driving a brand-new car. They take out huge ads with headlines screaming: "Drive Away This Brand-New Lexus For Only $250 Per Month!!!" and it sounds pretty darned good, because drivers know that to buy a late-model Lexus would cost more than a year of tuition, room, board, and date money at Harvard University. Which would *you* rather pay: $45,000 for a brand-new car, or $400 per month for 36 months? A brand new Volkswagen Jetta would currently set you back about $18,000. Or, you could lease one, fully loaded, for $200 per month.

Dealers want you to say, "I'd rather pay the $200 a month and drive a fully loaded Jetta down the highway." (And if you find a deal that good, perhaps you should lease!) And so, to make it all seem more worthwhile, they'll hammer home the newest safety features, crash test results, CD player, tax benefits, and the fact that your new car will have a gizmo that will help police authorities locate it anywhere in the world if it gets stolen. Or something like that.

The Economics Don't Add Up

Their pitch sounds pretty good, but they won't tell you that you'll almost always end up paying as much, or more, to lease a car than to buy it. And get this: At the end of the lease, *you'll have nothing to show for it!* That's right. All that cash you've paid for your car comes to exactly zero. In fact, you may even have to pay the dealer to get rid of this car you don't own. ("Excessive wear and tear" could mean a few dings that have to be fixed, at a cost of $300 to $1,500.) On top of that, you'll spend time and money, over the course of three or four years, maintaining your leased vehicle. That's right. You'll change the oil every 3,000 miles ($20 to $25 a shot at the dealer's), change the tires ($100 per tire) when the tread wears down, do the required maintenance ($300 to $500 every 7,000 miles or as required by the manufacturer), and wash, wax, and vacuum regularly.

Think I'm exaggerating? In 1997, *Consumer Reports* compared the costs to lease or buy twenty-five of the most popular cars sold, from a Cadillac DeVille (invoice price, $35,183; manufacturer's suggested retail price, or sticker price, $38,445) to a Volkswagen Jetta GL (invoice price, $16,672; sticker price, $18,290). (For the most recent analysis, check out <www. ConsumerReports.org> or subscribe to the magazine.) *Consumer Reports* looked at a range of lease terms and compared them with the cost of ownership. In almost every case, the best purchase price was less than the best lease terms available. And when an average lease was compared with the best purchase price out there, the savings were *thousands of dollars.*

Consumer Reports made some interesting (and, I think, overly generous) assumptions on behalf of the leasing company. The three-year lease allowed you 15,000 miles per year (generous), and you disposed of the car when the lease ended. The magazine editors' formula built in a 3 percent "opportunity" cost for cash that you supposedly left in another investment instead of using it as the down payment for a car purchase. The magazine also assumed that if you bought your car with a four-year loan, you sold it after three years.

With all that, you'd still have saved nearly $1,000 by buying the Cadillac DeVille (best price) rather than leasing it (best lease). But if you compare the best purchase price with only an average lease, *you could have saved over $2,500 by buying the car.*

But I'm getting ahead of myself. Let's start by looking at how much it actually costs to own a car versus renting one on the weekends.

Owning versus Renting

Owning a car isn't cheap, despite the fact that most Americans of driving age own (or have access to) at least one car, and those who don't would like to join the majority. (This excludes car-less people who live in Manhattan. These folks do not pine away for a car; they dream of having their own limos and drivers. Meanwhile, they walk or use public transportation. But that's another story.) In fact, unless you use a car every day, it may be cheaper for you to rent a car every weekend plus two weeks of vacation a year.

In the worksheet on page 84, I'm assuming a $20,000 car, financed at 8 percent interest, with that cost to include tax, title, and all those nasty little purchasing charges. You get a four-year amortization, so this car will be yours at the end of the loan. When I list a range of average costs, I use the higher end for calculating the annual cost. Your actual cost may be lower, particularly if you buy a less expensive vehicle.

With that $2,617.12 in annual savings, you could open up a Roth IRA and enhance your retirement, fund your children's future college education (or weddings), or save for a down payment on a home.

Buying versus Leasing

When you need your car every day, the question becomes: Is it more cost-effective to lease a car or to buy one? Studies by *Consumer Reports* and similar sources say leasing is typically more expensive than buying, particularly if you're going to keep your car longer than three years. (The typical consumer keeps a car for about seven years, though that number has been falling as leasing has increased). And at the end of the lease term, you have nothing to show for all your spent cash.

How do you decide what to do? Let's start by defining a few of the most popular words and phrases in leasing jargon.

WORKSHEET
Owning vs. Renting a Car

Expenses of Ownership	Average Cost	Annual Cost
Monthly car payment	$488.26	$5,859.12
Oil change (every 3,000 miles or three months)	$20	80.00
Annual maintenance	$500–$750	750.00
Car wash/wax	$7–$12	48.00
Annual license	$30	30.00
Car insurance	$500–$1,500	1,500.00
Other (like an antitheft system)	$50	50.00
Total annual cost of owning a car		$ 8,317.12

Here are the costs of renting a car on weekends (Saturday and Sunday), plus two weeks a year for vacation use @ $50.00 per day (includes tax and insurance rider, but you might not need the rider if you carry a credit card that covers you):

50 weekends @ $100 per weekend	= $5,000	
2 weeks @ $350 per week	= $700	
Total annual cost of car rental	$5,700.00	
Total annual cost of owning a car	$8,317.12	
Less: Total annual cost of car rental	5,700.00	
Annual savings from renting vs. owning	$2,617.12	

The Language of Leasing—A Glossary

Acquisition or bank fee. The average fee you'll pay to the dealer at the start of the lease, typically, $300 to $400; not negotiable.

Annual mileage allowance. The number of miles included as part of the lease. Dealers will offer as few miles as they can get away with—perhaps as few as 10,000 per year, or 30,000 over a three-year lease. But some dealers will go as high as 15,000 miles per year if you negotiate with them. You'll pay anywhere from 10 cents to 50 cents for each mile you drive over the agreed-on limit, so think carefully about how far you drive, and then negotiate your mileage allowance.

Capitalized cost (sometimes called Gross capitalized cost). This is the price of the car that the dealer uses to construct the lease. It includes all the items and services that come with leasing the car. It's a crucial number, and it is negotiable.

Capitalized cost reduction. Your down payment—a negotiable amount. If you're trading in a car, the value of the trade-in should be applied to either the capitalized cost reduction or your monthly payments.

Closed-end lease. You return the car at the end of the lease and "walk away." But not before paying for your "end of the lease" charges, including excess mileage, wear and tear, and the disposition fee.

Disposal or disposition fee. You'll pay this fee if you opt *not* to buy the car at the end of your lease. It covers the leasing company's cost of moving, cleaning, and disposing of the car. It is sometimes negotiable, but you'll have to negotiate *before* you sign your lease agreement. (Don't forget: The dealer will charge someone an "acquisition fee" on the other side, too.)

Early termination fee. If you bring the car back early, the dealer has the right to charge you for all of your lease payments plus other fees for disposition, and so on. Or, the dealer may roll the termination fee into your next lease. Typically, this isn't negotiable. Expect to pay a hefty fee if you return the car before it's due back.

Excess wear and tear. The state of your car according to the dealer. Basically, the dealer can force you to pay for any repairs to the vehicle that he or she deems necessary to get it back into perfect shape. You will typically have to pay some amount, but know that your version of normal wear and tear will not be the same as the dealer's.

Even if you never drive the car during the lease term, something will undoubtedly turn up. Dealers have been known to use infrared sensors to detect microscopic chips in the windshield. Make sure the dealer spells out in writing, in the initial contract, what is considered to be *excess* wear and tear.

GAP insurance. This stands for *Guaranteed Auto Protection*, and you need it if you're leasing. This insurance will pay the balance on the lease and the early termination penalties if the car is stolen or totaled. Negotiate to have the cost included with your lease payments, not due upfront.

Inception fees. These are the upfront fees that the dealer will require you to pay: your first monthly payment, a refundable security deposit, Department of Motor Vehicles (DMV) fees, and possibly an acquisition fee. You'll have to come up with this upfront cash, even if you're getting a "no money down" lease. If you're paying a down payment, you'll have to add that in as well.

Lease charge/Lease rate, or Money factor. This is the complicated basis for dealers' calculation of lease payments. It's similar to an interest rate; you multiply the money factor by 2400 to approximate the annual percentage rate of your lease (see page 104 for an example of how the money factor works). It is not negotiable, and it differs from lease to lease, car to car, and company to company. Usually, it is not disclosed because car companies are not required to under Regulation M (see below).

Lessee. You, or the person leasing the vehicle.

Lessor. The leasing company, bank, or finance company that buys the car from the dealer and leases it back to you. The name of the lessor should be listed on the back of the contract.

Open-end lease. When you bring the car back, the dealer appraises the value of the car and compares it to the stated residual value in your lease contract. If the appraised value is less than the stated residual value, you make up the difference. If, by chance, the car has retained more of its value, the dealer pays you.

Purchase fee. This is a fee you'll pay in addition to the purchase option price (see below) if you decide to purchase your leased car at the end of the lease term. Typically, it's about $250 to $300 and it is negotiable.

Purchase option price. The price you'll pay to buy the car at the end of the lease. Typically, it's not negotiable, but it may be tied into the number of miles you're allotted each year. A car that's driven

15,000 miles a year will be less valuable than a car driven 10,000 miles a year.

Regulation M. The revised federal rules that went into effect at the end of 1997. Regulation M standardized and simplified leasing forms and language. It requires dealers to disclose all sorts of information, but it does not require them to disclose the money factor (also known as the lease charge or lease rate).

Residual value. How much the car will be worth at the end of the lease term. Typically, this is not negotiable.

Sales tax. In most areas, a lease is considered the same as a purchase, so you'll pay sales tax on your "purchase." That's one reason to think carefully about where you purchase or lease your vehicle. You might pay 7.5 percent sales tax instead of 8.75 percent, depending on where you buy or lease your car. And when you're talking about a $20,000 car, saving 1.25 percent means saving $250.

Subvented lease. A lease that's subsidized (typically, by the auto manufacturer) in order to get rid of a certain kind of car. Subvented leases can be exceptional deals, and they are often the only way that leasing may be cheaper than owning, especially if you plan to finance your purchase rather than pay cash.

Term. How long the lease lasts. Generally, you won't want to get a lease for longer than three years. Too many things can start to go wrong with a leased car in its fourth or fifth year, and the likelihood that you'll get some nicks and dings increases.

The Federal Trade Commission (FTC) regulates car leases. For more information, you might want to check out a guide called "Look Before You Lease: Keys to Vehicle Leasing." It's available from the FTC by calling 202-452-3244, or you can pull it off the FTC Web site at <www.bog.frb.fed.us/pubs/leasing/guide.htm>.

Now that you know the jargon dealers will throw at you, let's look at the differences between buying a car and leasing.

When you buy a car, you purchase exactly what you want and you negotiate how much you're going to pay for it. You may pay cash, or you may take out a loan. If you take out a loan, you'll make monthly payments of principal and interest (like a mortgage), until the car is paid off. Typically, the car will be worth about 50 to 60 percent of the price you pay by the time a four-year loan is paid off. Sometimes, high-end cars like an Infinity or a Lexus, or a popular vehicle such as a Jeep Grand Cherokee, will keep more of their value. But if you expect that, four years down the line, your car will be worth only slightly more than half of what you pay, you won't be disappointed.

Leasing a car is quite different from renting a car from a company like Hertz or Avis. When you rent a car, you pay a daily, weekly, or monthly fee plus sales tax. When you lease a car, your payment consists of three parts:

1. The amount of the car's depreciation in value during the time of your lease.
2. Interest on a loan for the entire cost of the car.
3. All the add-on charges, including sales tax, an acquisition fee, the down payment, and license and registration fees.

The price of the car, called the *capitalized cost* or *cap cost* is where you start. The residual value is the leasing company's estimate of the vehicle's value at the end of the lease. The difference between the cap cost and the *residual value* is the depreciation.

If you were buying a car, you would ferociously negotiate the sales price, and perhaps it would be as little as $500 above the dealer's *invoice price* (what the dealer pays for the car), and well below the manufacturer's suggested retail price (MSRP), also known as the sticker price. With a lease, you have to do the same kind of negotiation. (For a further discussion of how to negotiate the purchase or lease of your vehicle, see Question 21.) The lower the cap cost, the less depreciation you'll pay and the lower your lease payments.

The depreciation counts for the biggest chunk of your lease payment. Here's how it works. Let's assume you're leasing a $35,000 car that will be worth $18,000 at the end of your three-year lease. The depreciation (difference between the cap cost and the residual value) is $17,000. Divide that number over a three-year period and you'll pay $472.22 per month for the depreciation.

Interest on the money you're borrowing is the next chunk. Remember: You're borrowing enough cash to pay for the entire cost of the car, which is $35,000. In addition to paying interest on the $35,000 you're borrowing to pay for the car, you also pay interest on the depreciation. Does it seem like you're paying twice? Well, that's leasing. To continue with our example, you take the net cap cost (which, in our case, is $35,000) and add the residual value ($18,000) to it. Multiply that sum ($53,000) by the money factor (also known as the lease factor), which is a strange number brewed up by the leasing company. To get the approximate interest rate, multiply the lease factor by 2400. (To get a lease factor or money factor, divide the interest rate by 24.) In our example, the net cap cost ($35,000) plus the residual value ($18,000) equals $53,000. If the lease factor is 0.00375 (roughly equivalent to a 9 percent interest rate), multiply $53,000 by the lease factor and you'll get a monthly finance charge of $198.75.

Another major line item is the sales tax. Most states and cities treat leasing the same as buying. In effect, you're paying sales tax on $35,000 in our example. Multiply the sales tax (we'll use 8.5 percent) by the price of the car and divide by the number of months.

Depending on the price of the car you're leasing, you may also be charged a luxury tax.

The worksheet on page 90 shows how our numbers add up.

Pros and Cons of Leasing

Now that you understand the mechanics of leasing, you need to analyze whether this approach is good for you. Study the lists of the pros and cons of leasing, then decide whether you might or might not want to do this.

Reasons Why You Should Lease

1. You get to drive a brand-new car every year, every other year, or every third year. You take advantage of all the newest safety features, bells, and whistles the manufacturers come up with. Besides, the neighbors are impressed.

2. For short periods of time, leasing may cost approximately the same as purchasing a vehicle. If you'll only own your car for two or three years, leasing may cost the same. If you plan to keep your car longer, owning is usually less expensive.

3. If you plan to purchase a very expensive car, and you drive it more than 50 percent of the time for your business, certain tax deductions may be more favorable with leasing than if you buy the car. (The IRS sets depreciation limits for a car purchase, and even if your car is a more expensive make and model, you can't go over the IRS limit for depreciation.) If you own the car long enough, you might eventually catch up, but, in the first few years, you'd lag behind. For example, if you bought a car in

WORKSHEET
Ten Steps to Figuring Out Your Lease Payment

Depreciation:

1. Gross capitalized cost (also known as cap cost)	$ 35,000.00
2. Cap cost reduction (also known as the down payment)	-0-
3. Net cap cost (Step 1 – Step 2)	$ 35,000.00
4. Residual	$ 18,000.00
5. Depreciation (Step 3 – Step 4)	$ 17,000.00
6. Lease term (in months)	36

Monthly Depreciation Charge (Step 5 ÷ Step 6)   **$ 472.22**

Finance Charge:

7. Finance base (Step 3 + Step 4)	$ 53,000.00
8. Money factor (approximately 9 percent*)	0.00375

Monthly Finance Charge (Step 7 × Step 8)   **$ 198.75**

Sales Tax:

9. Sales tax rate (8.5 percent assumed)	0.085
10. Total sales tax (Step 3 × Step 9)	$ 2,975.00

Monthly Sales Tax (Step 10 ÷ Step 6)   **$ 82.64**

Monthly Depreciation Charge	$472.22
Monthly Finance Charge	+ $198.75
Monthly Sales Tax	+ $ 82.64
Estimated Monthly Lease Payment	$753.61
Annual Payment	$ 9,043.32
Three-Year Lease Total	$27,129.96

*To get the approximate annual percentage rate (APR) of your lease's money factor, multiply the money factor by 2400. To turn an interest rate into a money factor, divide the interest rate by 24. To convert 9 percent into the equivalent money factor, divide .09 ÷ 24.

1997, the depreciation deduction for 1997 (first year of ownership) would be $3,160. For the second year (1998), you could depreciate $5,000. For the third year (1999), you could depreciate $3,050. And for the fourth and succeeding years, you could depreciate the car $1,775. (I don't know why these numbers aren't more evenly scaled.)

For a leased car, you can generally deduct whatever your lease payments are. However, you must add back into your income the offset rental deduction for each year during which the car is leased. That reflects the fact that the lease is composed of several different parts, and the IRS is attempting to distinguish between them, and not give you a deduction for, say, sales tax. The bottom line: If you drive an expensive car for business, and you trade in your cars frequently, leasing may be a better deal. (But that's assuming you're getting a great deal on your lease. If you get taken to the cleaners on your lease, buying will always be a better deal, despite the tax advantages.)

Reasons Why You Shouldn't Lease

1. Leasing is typically more expensive than owning, particularly if you're going to keep the car for more than four years. Do the numbers. If you get a bad lease, owning could be cheaper from the second year.

2. Leasing is more complicated than buying. Dealers have a whole bunch of ways to increase your costs without your noticing (see Question 22).

3. You may owe a ton of money when you bring the car back. You'll owe for "excess wear and tear" (the dealer's definition, not yours), including dings and dents you may consider normal in a three-year-old car. And, you'll owe anywhere from 10 cents to 25 cents for each mile over the allotted number.

4. You don't own your car. That means you don't have any rights of ownership. You can't sell it if you get into financial trouble and can no longer afford it. And you'll pay a hefty termination fee if you bring the car back early.

5. You'll spend good money maintaining a car you don't own. It will still need regular maintenance, like oil changes, tire replacements, servicing, washing, and waxing.

6. If you lease a lemon, your state may not cover the car under its automobile lemon laws. In a handful of states, leased vehicles are specifically exempt from lemon laws. In other states, the law is silent on leased vehicles, which might mean you're in for a fight with the dealership if something goes wrong.

7. Your down payment serves only to reduce the gross cap cost, and ultimately your monthly payments. It doesn't create any equity in the vehicle (unlike a down payment for a house).

8. Leases can be restrictive. They may tell you where you can and cannot drive. You may not be able to take the car out of your area, or your state, for more than thirty days. You may not be able to drive it into Canada or Mexico. If you move to another state, the leasing company may have the right to terminate the lease, or you may need its consent in writing.

9. Insurance costs might be higher. You'll need GAP insurance, and you may need liability insurance not just for your leased vehicle, but for all the cars you drive. The leasing company may also try to sell you other insurance you don't need. Your car registration costs may be higher for a leased vehicle.

The Bottom Line

If you want to drive a shiny new car with all the available bells and whistles, and trade it in every year or two, you'll probably want to lease. You may also be reading the wrong book. This book is for people who want to take hold of their personal finances and improve them. Unless you get a phenomenal deal, leasing isn't going to help you do that; it may, in fact, set you back. Short term, it looks like a great option. But let's look at the long-term picture.

Long term, the cheapest way to go is to buy a car for cash. If you can't manage to swing the whole price in cash (few people can), then put down the biggest payment you can afford, get the best interest rate you can find, and prepay your loan. Each dollar you prepay cuts down the term of your loan and saves you from paying interest that isn't tax-deductible (only your mortgage interest is tax-deductible).

Once you own your car, keep it in top-notch condition—not to hold its value, but to keep it running for as long as possible. If you want to get ahead financially, one of the best ways to do so is to buy your car and keep it for as long as you can. If you can keep each of your cars for ten years, and pay them off as quickly as possible, one financial adviser estimates you'll be able to retire five years sooner (if that's your goal). Or, you'll be able to save for your children's education or build your dream house, or realize whatever long-term plans you've made. The point is, if your means are limited, you'll have to make choices. Buying or leasing is one choice. The next decision is whether to buy or lease a new or a preowned car.

Gerhard's Story

In 1991, Gerhard leased a Jeep Grand Cherokee, which, he says, was the best and cheapest deal he ever did. An International business consultant and a tough negotiator, he got the cap cost reduced and eliminated the early termination fees. In addition, Chrysler was trying to push the Jeep Grand Cherokee, so the money factor on the lease was equal to an interest rate of about 1.9 percent. Gerhard's total payment was $289 per month.

But no deal is perfect. The car turned out to be a lemon. It handled badly, and it spent more time in the shop than on the road. After twenty months of a three-year lease (and $5,780 in payments), Gerhard returned the car to the dealership. Lo and behold, the Grand Cherokee had become so popular that its residual value was $2,000 *higher* than the dealer had stated. In addition to allowing return of the car and charging no early termination fees, the manufacturer sent Gerhard a check for the difference in the residual value of the car. Amortized over the twenty months Gerhard had used the car, the cost was just $189 per month to lease. It was, as Gerhard puts it, one of the great car deals of his lifetime.

With that in mind, he turned around and leased another car, a Chrysler LHS. This was also a subvented lease, with Chrysler offering 0 percent interest. The deal was good, though not nearly as good as the Jeep deal.

But by 1995, when Gerhard went looking for a third car, the leasing climate, in his view, had changed. He realized that dealers were making leases far more complicated than they had to be, and not as many desirable car leases were being subsidized. He says he hasn't seen a lease worth signing, though he occasionally looks through the car ads in the Sunday paper. For a lease to work for him, he says, the interest rate needs to be about 4 percent or less, with no other fees built into the price.

His latest car? He bought a red Volvo station wagon.

93

QUESTION
20

SHOULD I BUY OR LEASE A PREOWNED VEHICLE?

If buying or leasing a new car is prohibitively expensive, or if you're just looking around for the best deal on four wheels, you'll probably want to consider buying or leasing a used (also known as preowned) vehicle.

Buying a preowned car can be a smart move. A brand new vehicle, the saying goes, loses one-third of its value the day you drive it off the dealer's lot. That's a bit of an exaggeration, but the steepest decline in value *is* in the first few years of ownership. If you get a car that has already had a big chunk of its value depreciated, at least you're not paying for it. A two-year-old car is typically still under the manufacturer's warranty. If you buy a preowned car that was previously leased, you'll probably find it's in great shape. To minimize all the end-of-lease costs for excess wear and tear and excess mileage, drivers tend to take good care of their leased vehicles.

Buying a preowned vehicle is such a great deal that the number of preowned cars sold in a year recently surpassed the number of new cars sold. Some of that shift can be attributed to consumers' getting more savvy about their money, but the real reason is leasing. Manufacturers and dealers push leases, and after two, three, or four years, those leased cars get turned back in. They have to go somewhere.

There are three places to find a good preowned car:

1. *Dealerships.* Dealers who lease cars usually offer preowned or preleased vehicles. You'll pay top dollar for one of these cars, but they're usually in good shape, have been given the once-over by the dealer and his or her mechanics, and may even come with an extended one-year warranty, just in case anything goes wrong. The price is negotiable. Look for "factory certified" cars if you're going for the high end. They're supposed to be cherry-picked and put through a long factory checklist of repairs and maintenance to ensure they're in top condition.

2. *Superstores.* A new trend in buying or leasing a preowned or preleased car is to go to a used-car superstore. They don't exist everywhere yet, but you'll find them in many of the major metropolitan areas. Typically, superstore cars are priced reasonably, but prices may not be negotiable. On the other hand, you don't have to go searching through the thousands of cars parked on the lot. The vehicles are organized, by size and type,

in a computer system that any salesperson on the lot can access. You can call and ask about a particular car or simply walk in.

3. *Private owners.* A third source for used cars is the people who bought them new. There are good deals to be had by buying them directly, but you'll have to take the initiative. Car owners typically don't give warranties on vehicles.

What kind of deals are to be had? Wendy's story is a perfect example.

Wendy's Story

When Wendy lived in cold, snowy Chicago, she drove an old red Jeep. It had a zip top, a pull-out radio, and doors she didn't bother locking. When she got a job in Los Angeles, she sent her stuff on ahead and drove the car out. She had been about to sell it in Chicago, and had been told it would be worth about $1,800.

Although it was a problem in Chicago (zip tops aren't the greatest thing in wet weather), her Jeep was the hottest thing going in Los Angeles. She spent some time polishing it up, bought some new floor mats, and placed an ad in the local paper. The Jeep looked great. She got a lot of calls. Within a week, she sold it for $3,500.

But now she needed wheels. She shopped around and finally whittled her selections down to two choices: (1) a brand-new, fully loaded Volkswagen Jetta or (2) a three-year-old, fully loaded, black BMW sedan. The BMW came with everything, including a 6-CD changer, a pop-out space for a pair of shades, a secret locking mechanism (to keep the car from being stolen), an alarm system, black leather seats, and an engine that purred. Plus, the BMW had only about 35,000 miles on it (low for cars in Los Angeles and for BMWs in general), had been well kept, and was only halfway through the manufacturer's warranty. Both cars were priced just over $20,000. The BMW had been returned early from a lease by a movie industry guy who was hot one day and unknown the next.

What should Wendy do? No contest. The Jetta would be worth about $12,000 in three years. The BMW, if maintained, would be worth approximately $18,000. Wendy went with the BMW, which released in her a race-car mentality that had been previously unseen. She took out a five-year loan from her credit union and paid it off in eighteen months. Now she's sitting pretty in a car she aims to keep for a long time.

Other folks have found buying or even leasing a preowned car or truck to be a very good deal. On the verge of divorce, Madeleine didn't want to spend a lot of cash, but she needed a reliable vehicle that looked good enough for a date and yet was hefty enough to cart around three kids, their friends, and a dog. She ended up buying a two-year-old formerly leased Toyota Land Cruiser. It looked brand-new and she hasn't had any trouble with it in the past three years. Mark regularly buys old SAABs. He tries to find them with about 60,000 miles on the odometer, and drives them until they have logged about 160,000 miles. Ruth leased a Toyota that had been previously leased from the same dealer she's worked with for twenty years. She pays almost nothing for the lease (the depreciation is only $3,000 over two years, instead of $18,000, and interest rates are low), and she intends to buy the car when her lease is up. Knowing that going in, she negotiated a favorable pickup price.

Leasing a Used Car

Leasing a preowned car isn't nearly as common as leasing a new vehicle. Although it's going to be cheaper, you're still going to have to negotiate a tough deal on a complicated contract. Buying still makes more sense, but check out the costs for yourself. Just remember, two brand-new Honda Accord EXs are exactly alike. But once a car rolls off the dealer's floor and into its owner's life, maintenance, accidents, and mileage make each car a little different.

How Good a Deal Is a Preowned Car?

Take the word of a new-car salesman: "Everyone wants to buy a new car because it's an emotional decision. But if you're going to buy a car, buy a preowned car. If you can find a used car that's only one or two years old, you can get a really good deal. Cars take a huge hit in value that first year. The only trouble is, it's hard to find a car that's only a year or two old."

What about the potential problems of a used car? "It's a roll of the dice," he says. "You've got to take the good with the bad. Try to get a bit of history with the car," and see how the owner took care of it. Make sure you take a preowned car to be checked out by a mechanic before you buy it. The $100 or so that you spend will be well worth it if you can steer clear of a lemon.

Reliability should be a primary consideration. Consider checking out the most recent *Consumer Reports* (www.consumerreports.com) annual questionnaire that evaluates 200-plus models of cars and light trucks going back eight years.

> If you buy a preowned car from a dealer who sells other vehicles from the same manufacturer (for example, a preowned Toyota from a Toyota dealer), you can ask the dealer to run the vehicle identification number (VIN) through the computer. It should pull up any warranty repairs made to the vehicle. You can also get a title report on the car you select, which will show problems like odometers that have been turned back, patched-up salvage cars, and returned lemon-law cars.

I told you at the beginning of this chapter that I bought a brand new Honda in 1994. We plan to drive it until it wears out, which it currently shows no sign of doing. But the next car I buy will probably be at least two years old and still under factory warranty.

HOW DO I NEGOTIATE THE BEST DEAL?

QUESTION
21

You've decided that you need to buy or lease a car. Whichever you choose (and if you're really concerned about your finances, you'll decide on preowned versus new), you're going to want to get the best deal. No sense paying more than you have to. There are other things to do with your money.

Here are the basic steps to take in order to negotiate the best deal.

Buying a New Car

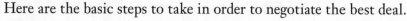

1. *Decide what kind of car you want.* If you don't know what you want, you can't possibly negotiate for the best deal. Knowing what you want also means knowing what kind of options and extras you want and need. Do you need power steering and power windows? Do you need a CD system? Cell phone? What about windshield tinting, rust protection, or a seat heater?

2. *Make sure you have a backup.* If you fall in love with a car and decide there is only one model that you can live with, you're going to put yourself at the mercy of the dealer. The savvy strategy is to come up with a second model that you'd be perfectly happy with. For example, when we were deciding to buy, we chose a Honda Accord. But we would've been completely satisfied with a Toyota Camry. Similar styling, similar make, similar driving and crash survival statistics, similar pricing. We ended up with a Honda, but knowing that we could've had a Toyota strengthened our negotiating position by allowing us an out.

3. *Learn the invoice price.* The invoice price is how much the dealer paid for the car. But invoice prices can be inflated. You also need to find out whether there are any factor-to-dealer incentives, rebates, or holdbacks. *Consumer Reports* offers a New Car Price Service (www.consumerreports.com). For $12, *CR* will send you the information you need by fax or mail. *Automotive News* (another magazine) also offers current information on incentives and rebates. The sticker price (also known as the manufacturer's suggested retail price) is the price the dealer wants you to pay. You should also find out the dealer's price for all of the options and extras available with the car. If you're going to put in a lot of these features, it may be cheaper (and will certainly involve less haggling) to simply upgrade the car to the next level.

4. *Shop around.* These days, once you've decided on the exact car you want, and on the options you want and need, you can shop around for the best price on the Internet, or in newspapers, or on the good old-fashioned telephone. Look for dealer ads and be sure to read the fine print. Then, call the dealer, describe what you're looking for, and ask what the best price is. You'll already know what the invoice price is; expect to pay $300 to $500 above the invoice price. The sticker price may be $2,000 to $10,000 above the invoice price, so knowledge is power. If the dealer tells you that a car that is the color you want and has the extras you want is unavailable, keep calling until you find one in stock. Or, make concessions you can live with for the price you want, like settling for hunter green instead of black, red instead of blue. Generally, you'll get a better price from a dealer who already has inventory on the property that

he or she wants to get rid of, although you can order from the factory.

5. *Be a tough negotiator.* At some point in time (although perhaps not, if you're working through the Internet), you'll actually have to go into the showroom and do the deal. The dealership's "business manager" might try to foist several unnecessary and costly extras onto you in the name of a good deal. Resist them. You don't need undercoating, rustproofing, fabric protection, an extended warranty, windshield etching, and so on. Stick to the model you requested, loaded with the options and extras you prefer. Ask to see the car and to take it for a test drive before settling down to do the hard-core negotiations. (Consider taking the test drive and then going away for a day or two to whet the dealer's appetite for the deal.)

6. *Be prepared to walk away.* Unfortunately, there *are* bad-apple dealers, and the "bait 'n' switch" lives on. You might get a dealer to agree to something over the phone, think you have a deal, and suddenly find, when you get to the showroom, that the deal doesn't exist. If you can't get your terms in writing, you don't have a deal. On the other hand, there are dozens of other dealers who will be willing to sell you the car you want at the price you want to pay. And, knowing you have a second choice that would be acceptable will give you the strength to turn around and walk out the door if you can't get the deal you want for a particular model.

7. *Be reasonable.* Dealers expect to make some money—it's their living. But they don't have to go to town on you. Be reasonable. You will reach a point in your negotiations where no one will go lower. Then, you need to make two decisions: (1) Are you going to buy this car at this price? and (2) From whom are you going to buy it? Recognize that if you're only interested in a really hot model, you're going to have to give more. For example, negotiating on the new Volkswagen Bug when it came out in 1998 might have been tough, especially when dealers were getting thousands of dollars above the sticker price for each car.

8. *Recognize the dealer's profit motive.* Dealers make money in all kinds of ways: the difference between the invoice price and what they get you to pay; all the extras and options they can tack on; and the servicing they will do for the car. If you end up leasing the car, all kinds of hidden profit may be tacked on that

you may never know about (despite the new Regulation M rules). You can even say, "Hey, I know you want to make some money here. Let's make a deal we both can live with."

9. *Be savvy about your trade-in.* If you have a car you want to trade in on your new model, don't even mention it until you have already locked up the deal for your new car. You want to have already agreed on a price, options, and so on. Once that's done, you can negotiate the sale of your existing car (that's what you're doing—selling your car to the dealer). Start by knowing how much it's worth ($10 from *Consumer Reports* <www.consumerreports.com> or you can buy the Blue Book). You can then sell it to the dealer you're buying from, or another dealer, or privately. But simply allowing the dealer to give you the "trade-in" value on your old car may mean you won't get the very best deal on your new car.

Sharon's Story

Sharon went to buy a new car. She wanted to sell her old car to the dealer. But the dealer talked her into "trading in" her old car, which was worth about $15,000. She bought the former year's model at the end-of-the-year sale, and its price was "dropped" from the sticker price of $40,000 to $36,000. Sharon was credited only $12,000 for her trade-in, the dealer said, because she got a better price on her new car. Sharon was happy. But the dealer is the one who should've been overjoyed. With the rebates and incentives, his $40,000 car cost him only $32,000. He earned $4,000 on the car sale and another $3,000 on the trade-in. True, Sharon had to come up with only $24,000 out of pocket for a $40,000 car. But if she had negotiated a better deal, she might've gotten away with paying only $19,000 for the same vehicle, after the trade-in.

Best Time to Buy?

The best time to buy a new car is early in the new-model year (August or September) when you are buying last year's model. During the rest of the calendar year, look for deals at the end of a month, or in December. The dealers will be trying to make their numbers look good and to get cars off their lot to meet quotas or bonus levels.

Negotiating Your Lease

Car dealers and leasing companies make leasing a car a much more convoluted and complicated experience than it needs to be. They do this to confuse you. They believe that by pulling the proverbial wool over your eyes, telling you how difficult and complicated the arrangement is, you won't try to understand it. That will leave the door open for the dealer to add all kinds of excess junk fees into your lease agreement. The dealer will get you to focus only on your monthly payment, and you'll never know what hit you.

How complicated is leasing? Here's what a senior attorney from the Federal Trade Commission (FTC) had to say about car leasing and Regulation M:

> Federal law requires that dealers disclose the actual dollar amounts for the rent charge before you sign your lease. But that [lease] isn't going to tell you what is the actual figure (money factor) the company used. . . . This isn't a standardized calculation. The Federal Reserve decided not to impose a rate calculation. They looked at the issue and decided it was a complicated issue because the residual value could be manipulated. [They felt] the result would be unreliable. There is no one single way of calculating [the interest] . . . and you can't really figure it out from the lease contract.

When a senior attorney from the FTC, which helped put together the recommendations for Regulation M, can't explain how the money factor works and why companies aren't required to disclose it, how is anyone else supposed to understand?

The important goal with a lease is to figure out exactly how much you're going to pay and what that means in terms of your personal finances. If you can afford to pay $300, that's great. But wouldn't you rather pay less if possible? If you tell a dealer that you can afford $300 per month, I guarantee you'll walk out with a lease for $300 per month (or even a bit more—"After all, you forgot to figure in tax, license, and so on," the dealer might say). But if you negotiate the lowest price for your car, and try to understand where the dealer is going, you might end up with a much better bottom line.

With that in mind, start your negotiations for a leased car as if you were buying a car. Find out the invoice price for the model and options you want. Don't forget to check factory rebates and incentives to the dealer. Then, check the newspapers for lease deals. Call the dealers and try to get information over the telephone. Typically, they'll deliver one of the following lines:

1. "I don't have all the numbers in front of me."
2. "I can't find my calculator."
3. "The residual prices are different for each car. I can't figure it out in my head."

They will then invite you into the showroom for a conversation. Ask them to fill out the government form that discloses all of the information required by Regulation M. Ask them what the money factor is. Some dealer might surprise you and actually disclose it.

Next, you need to analyze your own lease payment. The worksheet used for an example earlier in the chapter is repeated on page 103 in a blank form. Use it to calculate your own numbers.

Calculating the Money Factor

If you can't get the dealer to divulge the money factor, the worksheet on page 104 will help you to closely approximate it. Start with the total monthly payment (minus taxes and license fees) and subtract the monthly depreciation. Everything else is basically interest. Add the net capitalization ("cap") cost to the residual value. Divide this number by the amount of interest you will pay per month. That's the money factor. Multiply the money factor by 2400 to get the interest rate.

Caveat Emptor

When you're leasing a car, dealers have more than a few tricks up their sleeves. In Question 22, I'll explore some of the more common scams and bad business practices. Here are some good negotiating tips:

1. *Make sure you see (and read) the deal in writing before you sign.* Regulation M requires the dealer to make certain disclosures. Request the disclosures, and then put a "freeze" on the transaction until you can take the disclosures home and analyze them. If the dealer won't do that, or threatens to make the deal go away, walk. Otherwise, you could wind up in trouble.

Depreciation:

1. Gross capitalized cost (also known as Cap cost) $ _____

2. Cap cost reduction (also known as the Down payment) $ _____

3. Net cap cost (Step 1 – Step 2) $ _____

4. Residual $ _____

5. Depreciation (Step 3 – Step 4) $ _____

6. Lease term (in months)

Monthly Depreciation Charge (Step 5 ÷ Step 6) $ _____

Finance Charge:

7. Finance base (Step 3 + Step 4) $ _____

8. Money factor [see the next section]

Monthly Finance Charge (Step 7 × Step 8) $ _____

Sales Tax:

9. Sales tax rate (8.5 percent assumed) $ _____

10. Total sales tax (Step 3 × Step 9) $ _____

Monthly Sales Tax (Step 10 ÷ (Step 6) $ _____

Monthly Depreciation Charge	$	_____
Monthly Finance Charge	+ $	_____
Monthly Sales Tax	+ $	_____
Estimated Monthly Lease Payment	$	_____
Annual Payment	$	_____
Three-Year Lease Total	$	_____

WORKSHEET
Calculating the Money Factor

1. Total monthly payment (minus taxes and license fees) $ _____

2. Monthly depreciation   – $ _____

3. Total monthly interest   = $ _____

4. Net cap cost $ _____

5. Residual value   + $ _____

6. Principal base for interest payment   = $ _____

7. Divide Step 3 by Step 6 (for money factor)   = $ _____

8. Multiply Step 7 × 2400 (for interest rate)   = $ _____

2. *Make sure the deal that you have gets translated accurately to the paperwork.* Some bad-apple dealers substitute numbers on the lease, and fan the paperwork so you see only the signature line. Make sure you take the time to read the final paperwork thoroughly. Don't leave or sign until you do. (And don't let the dealer feel bad about missing his kid's graduation or after-school soccer game, or a junior league meeting. If he or she doesn't have the time, offer sweetly to work with someone else.)

3. *Don't agree to put down a down payment, if you can help it.* When you're leasing a car, the down payment only serves to reduce the capitalization cost of the car, which does lower the monthly payment. But you'll never see that money again.

4. *Make sure all of the other provisions, such as the early termination fees and other costs, are written into the contract.* Otherwise, they're not valid.

5. *It's perfectly all right to play one dealer against the other.* And if at any time you don't feel comfortable, simply put the pen down and walk out.

When I was writing this chapter, I wondered why the interest on a lease is calculated this way. Why does the lessee (you) have to add the cost of the car (net capitalization cost) to the residual and, in effect, pay interest on 1½ times the cost of the car? The first answer I got was: "Depreciation." That extra amount is the allowance for depreciation, and you're paying interest on that to the dealer. But that doesn't make sense. The biggest part of a lease payment is the depreciation (which you're paying for in full). The next answer I got was: "It's an extra fee, like private mortgage insurance for people who are risky borrowers and can't afford the entire 20 percent down payment." That doesn't make sense either. You *own* a house; leasing a car is like renting it. And, with a lease, you're putting down exactly what the dealer tells you to put down (a throwaway sum designed to lower your monthly payments). The only answer that makes sense is this: It's an excellent way for the dealer to make more money. By not having to disclose the money factor (and giving you an easy way to compare the true cost of the lease), and by charging you interest on 1½ times the true cost of the car, the dealer is padding his or her profit—at your expense. If I ever get another answer, I'll put it in the next edition of this book.

The Bottom Line

When you decide to buy or lease a car, only you know what you can truly afford. This book aims to get you to the point where you can afford what you want: college education for your kids; help with their weddings; your own retirement. A car is about getting from here to there safely. I've also known exceedingly wealthy people who drove a Chevrolet, a Ford Taurus, or a Toyota, and never spent more than $20,000 on their car. I've known people who live from paycheck to paycheck but leased an Infinity or a $50,000 Range Rover.

You have to decide what's right for you and your family. Once again, here's how I see things:

- If you can, walk, ride a bike, or take public transportation.
- If you need a car, buy a preowned one that's still covered by the factory warranty and hasn't had any major rebuilding.
- If you can afford it, pay cash. If you have to, finance the car the least expensive way possible. Consider using a home equity loan, which is tax-deductible.
- If you find an incredible, once-in-a-lifetime deal, like Gerhard's—$3,700 to lease a Jeep Grand Cherokee for twenty months (approximately $189 per month)—then lease. It's far less than you would have paid to own.

QUESTION 22

WHAT LEASING SCAMS SHOULD I LOOK OUT FOR?

I've talked a little bit about bad-apple dealers; there are plenty of them out there. Even some of the honest ones can make you feel a little queasy. While conducting interviews for this chapter, one of my researchers, Colleen, came up against a few folks who displayed an appalling lack of sensitivity coupled with some pretty naked discrimination.

But so it goes in the real world. Fortunately, there are people like Florida Attorney General Robert A. Butterworth, whose office spent years investigating scams and fraud in the car-leasing world. Here, according to the Attorney General's office, are some of the most offensive things going on. Be careful!

1. *Pockets-of-profit scam.* A dealer may not disclose enough information for you to make an informed decision. Although Regulation M requires specific disclosures, if you're not looking out for them, you won't even miss them. If you don't have everything disclosed, you won't know what's being charged.

2. *The flip.* You spend hours negotiating the purchase of a car. After reaching an agreement, you go into the finance and insurance (F&I) manager's office, where the F&I guy will try to renegotiate the price. The F&I guy will then introduce the concept of leasing. If you agree to lease the car, the F&I guy will totally ignore all of the agreed-on price and concessions, and may even ignore the promised trade-in allowance. The price then gets bumped up, without your even realizing it.

3. *The trade-in.* If you know the allowance for your trade-in, but not the gross capitalization cost (which, under Regulation M, must be disclosed), the dealer can raise the gross cap cost higher, so that it more than offsets the trade-in allowance. Or, the dealer may agree verbally to a certain amount for the trade-in, but will then put a lesser amount on the paperwork (read your paperwork!). Or, the dealer will agree to what you want and put "N/A" (not applicable) alongside it on the paperwork, which you won't notice because you're exhausted from hours of negotiating.

4. *Cash and rebates.* Dealers can discount your cash by raising the gross cap cost. Dealers usually insist that consumers apply the rebate to the lease rather than get a check back. By raising other costs and fees, the rebate gets absorbed like cash.

5. *Clipping coupons.* Dealers issue coupons that are supposed to be credited to the transaction. But they may not be.

6. *Payoff on trade-ins.* The payoff is presented to consumers as being higher than it might really be, just to get you in the door.

7. *Big bank fees.* These are junk fees that the dealer adds to the transaction to bloat his or her profit. Referred to as "acquisition" or "administrative" fees, they may range from $200 to $940. The consumer may be told that these fees are fully paid to the leasing company when a percentage may actually be returned to the dealer as a kickback.

8. *Extended warranties and car care service plans.* The dealer says these are free, but in reality, their cost has been added to the

gross cap cost of the car. On the contract, the dealer writes "N/A" in the space for the price of the warranty or car care service plan.

9. *Delivery, advertising, dealer preparation, and other fees.* These fees are added to the price without the consumer's knowledge or consent. In another twist, the taxes and fees are overestimated, and the dealer pockets the extra amount. Or, the dealer might charge tax on the security deposit.

10. *The right rate.* The dealer may tell the consumer he or she is getting a certain interest rate, when, in fact, the interest rate is higher. Or, the consumer will be told there is no interest rate, only a money factor (multiply the money factor provided by 2400 to get the interest rate).

11. *Misrepresenting the residual value.* On the residual value line of the contract, "N/A" is filled in and the consumer is told this means "national average." Or, the residual value is represented as the amount of money that the consumer will get back at the end of the lease.

12. *Equity.* Consumers are told they are building equity in the vehicle, as if they were buying it. They are also told the down payment goes toward the equity and they will get it back.

13. *Get out of the lease free.* Consumers are told there are no charges for early termination. Not so.

14. *Right of rescission.* Consumers are told that they have a three-day cooling off period and can return the car within three days without any problems.

15. *Multiple security deposits.* Consumers are told if they put down an amount that is five times the amount of the security deposit, they can buy down the interest rate. The rate, however, is not reduced.

16. *Insurance required.* Dealers tell consumers they must have term life, disability, credit life, unemployment, or payment interruption insurance in order to lease a vehicle. Or, they are told they get this insurance for free, when the premium is built into the car price.

17. *False options installed.* Lease contracts will indicate an option that isn't on the vehicle, even though the consumer is charged for it. When the car is returned and the option isn't there, the consumer is charged again.

18. *Excess wear and tear.* Dealers accept a returned vehicle and tell the consumer there is no charge for excess wear and tear. Months later, the leasing company sends a bill and the consumer can't defend himself or herself because the vehicle's condition when returned cannot be proven. (Hint: Take pictures of the inside and outside of the vehicle in order to prove its condition at the end of the lease. You might want to date-stamp your VHS tape or photographs by including the front page of a current newspaper.)

19. *Excess mileage.* Consumers will have to initial lots of changes on a standard lease contract, including a lower mileage limitation. You might think (or be told) you're getting higher mileage if you don't read the paperwork. Or, the dealer might forge your initials.

There are other variations on these scams; watch out for them. Leasing is big business, and if it weren't enormously profitable to car companies, they wouldn't push it as hard as they do. Attorney General Butterworth's office analyzed thousands of car leases and found that individual consumers had been bilked anywhere from hundreds to thousands of dollars. Some people who thought they were buying a car ended up with a lease. Don't let this happen to you.

The Bottom Line

If you suspect you are being taken advantage of, or find that you have been a victim of a leasing fraud, contact the Federal Trade Commission (Washington headquarters is at 202-326-2222) or your state Attorney General's office.

5

Insurance

When you think about the word "insurance," what pops into your mind? Protection. More specifically, trying to protect yourself from the financial devastation caused by the physical catastrophes and calamities of this world: earthquakes, floods, fires, serious illnesses, accidents, and deaths.

But that kind of thinking can lead to all sorts of trouble. For example, you could wind up paying for coverage you don't need, or think you're covered when you're not. You might then say, "If there's a chance that I won't get what I need, no matter how much I pay for it, I might as well just forget it." Or, "Let's talk about this later." Or, "What does this have to do with my personal finances?"

Insurance is an important, if sometimes expensive, piece of your personal finances. Having the right kinds of insurance—from good medical, disability, automobile, and homeowner's insurance coverage to medi-gap, long-term care, and even travel insurance—can make a huge difference in both the quality of your life and the contents of your wallet.

Without insurance, paying for medical care might cost you thousands of dollars every year. Having a baby without complications can cost $6,000 to $10,000. With complications, the bill might start at $20,000. If you face a serious illness, such as cancer, or need a heart transplant, or spend some time in intensive care, the experience might bankrupt you—even if you have $1 million in the bank.

What about homeowner's (also known as hazard) insurance? If your house goes up in smoke and you don't have homeowner's insurance (or *enough* homeowner's insurance, as we'll talk about later in this chapter), you could wind up broke. A serious car accident or a visitor's fall on your front steps can have the same result.

The idea is to find a way to get the insurance you need, to protect you in the ways you want to be protected, at a price you can afford. This chapter covers the most important things to know and think about.

WHAT BASIC INSURANCE COVERAGE SHOULD I HAVE?

QUESTION 23

Everyone has different needs when it comes to insurance. If you have children or other people dependent on your income, you may need life insurance. Even without children or a spouse, you may need disability insurance. If you own a home and have a mortgage, your lender will require you to have at least a minimal amount of home or hazard insurance. If you have a car, your state will require you to have automobile insurance. If you are concerned about not being able to afford a nursing home when the time comes, you may want to purchase long-term care insurance. The only type of insurance *everyone* needs is health insurance.

Let's take a quick look at the various types of insurance and what they might be able to do for you. (These are the basic types you'll probably consider purchasing at some time in your life. In Question 30, I list others that you may or may not need down the line.)

Life Insurance

Life insurance is a misnomer. It should really be called death insurance because it pays out upon the death of the policyholder. The idea behind life insurance is that the proceeds from a policy will support the health and welfare of those who survive the deceased.

Life insurance comes in a variety of flavors, including term, whole life, variable whole life, and others. Each type of life insurance has its own strengths and weaknesses, and each serves different needs. (See Question 24 for more information on life insurance.)

The most important thing to remember about life insurance is this: If no one depends on your annual income for food, clothing, and shelter, you may not need it, unless you're using it in certain estate-planning situations.

111

Health Insurance

You may feel perfectly fine today, but at some point in your life, you'll need to see a doctor. And, you'll need health insurance from a company that pays its bills.

According to the Health Insurance Association of America, more than 165 million Americans under age 65 received private health insurance reimbursements in the past year. The most recent statistics available as we went to press indicate that the numbers of medically uninsured Americans are on the rise. An additional 37 million nonelderly Americans were covered by health insurance from publicly financed sources, including Medicaid, the Civilian Health and Medical Program for the Uniformed Services (CHAMPUS), or the Civilian Health and Medical Program for the Department of Veterans Affairs (CHAMPVA). More than 41 million Americans, including about 17 percent of those under age 65, did not have any private health insurance at all. Many of these are children.

If you're lucky, you get affordable health care insurance through your employer, your spouse's place of employment, or a nonprofit trade group for your profession. If you're self-employed, you might have to buy insurance yourself—which can be incredibly expensive—but you may currently deduct a portion of the cost of purchasing health insurance on your federal income tax return. Soon, you may be able to deduct all of it.

To some extent, it's a letters game—PPO, HMO, and so on—but the most important thing to remember is this: If you don't have this insurance and you get really sick, the sucking sound you'll hear is the extraordinary cost of health care, from $26 for an aspirin to $15 for bandages. Your wallet will empty faster than you can say, "Where do I sign?" (See Question 25 for more details.)

Homeowner's Insurance

If you own your own home and you have a mortgage, your lender will require you to have enough homeowner's insurance to cover the mortgage balance should your house be destroyed (by fire, storm, tornado, or other catastrophe). In some flood-prone or earthquake-prone areas, your lender may require you to purchase seperate insurance to cover these disasters, or others.

But that won't begin to cover your real losses. One of the mistakes homeowners often make (we'll talk about this more in

Question 26) is undervaluing their property and underestimating the true cost of replacing not only the house, but all of their personal property that may be lost as well, including furniture, artwork, clothing, and appliances. Another mistake is not knowing exactly what your policy covers.

Renter's insurance is for people who rent instead of own. It covers loss of personal property and, if you cause the damage, liability. Unfortunately, most folks who rent don't realize they need renter's insurance (or even that it exists) until after they've had their home or apartment consumed in fire or broken into.

Disability Insurance

The basic problem with life insurance is that it doesn't pay until after you're pronounced dead. It won't help you if you're critically injured in an accident and unable to earn a living.

Short-term and long-term disability insurance can step in and help. The benefits kick in after a certain period of time has elapsed— a month or two, or even a year. Disability insurance provides you with a portion of your income while you're unable to work, and it can go a long way toward saving you from eating up your assets.

Some companies provide their employees with short-term and long-term disability, but many do not and you may have to purchase it separately. Also, people in some professions, such as writers and editors, aren't necessarily covered by all disability policies (you have to prove that the disability prevents you from being able to work). (See Question 27 for more details.)

Automobile Insurance

If you drive a car, you had better be insured. Most states require drivers to be insured for at least a minimum amount of damage caused by the insured (liability coverage). (Not every individual who drives a car is insured, as plenty of accident victims have discovered.)

You should have insurance as a car owner, and so should everyone else who drives your car. But that doesn't mean you have to pay through the nose for it. More than any other kind of insurance, you can change what you pay by choosing a different type of car, raising the deductible, choosing a different type of coverage, and keeping the keys from your teenager. (See Question 28 for more details.)

Special Policies

Other types of insurance include credit life or mortgage insurance, dread disease insurance, umbrella liability insurance, trip insurance, medi-gap insurance, and long-term care insurance. I'll talk about those in Question 29. But the basic kinds of insurance—life, health, home, disability, and auto—will see you through most of the catastrophes in your life—which, as you'll recall, is why you buy them.

Four Basic Questions

Before you run out to your local insurance agent's office, checkbook in hand, ask yourself the following four questions, to help determine whether you really need to spend the money.

1. *Can I afford the loss?* If you can cover the cost of fixing a problem, you probably don't need the insurance. For example, if you buy a piece of high-tech equipment, such as a stereo system or a computer, you may have been offered extended warranty coverage. (Automobile manufacturers offer this as well.) Unless you can afford to toss your purchase away if you get a lemon (if the store won't exchange it), an extended warranty might be an option. You should also compare the cost of an extended warranty or service agreement with the annual maintenance costs of a mojor purchase—for example, a central air-conditioning system. If the price of the warranty is too high, you may be more willing to shoulder the risk.

But could you afford to pay for a total hip replacement surgery? To replace your car if it's wrecked in a crash? To rebuild your house?

2. *Am I getting enough coverage?* Make sure that your basic types of insurance provide enough coverage to get you through your life. Today, having a ceiling of $1 million in medical benefits probably won't be enough. You'll want to make sure you have at least $2 million to $5 million in total coverage. Are there exclusions and limitations for certain surgeries, for certain types of diseases, for experimental treatments? Are prescription drugs covered?

Buying dread disease policies is a little like gambling. Unless your entire family has breast cancer, for example, why would you try to get a policy that covers only one particular disease? Many experts feel that if you have proper health insurance, these types of policies aren't necessary. You'd be better off spending your cash to buy a decent basic medical health insurance policy with coverage for major medical problems.

3. *Am I duplicating coverage I already have?* If you already have a life insurance policy through your employer, do you need an additional policy? If so, do you need as much as you're planning to buy? Should you take out insurance when you rent a car? If you already have automobile insurance, your policy might cover you for any car you drive, including a rental. Some credit cards offer automatic supplemental car insurance (and extended warranties for certain items purchased with the card) that cover you when you're renting a car.

You should also ask yourself why you need the additional coverage. If you're single, with no dependents, you probably don't need life insurance. If you're fabulously wealthy, you may want it for estate-planning purposes. Or, if you anticipate having a family down the line, you may want to lock in a low rate today, for a long period of time.

4. *Am I getting the best deal I can?* Want to buy a car, take out a mortgage, buy airplane tickets, or paint your house? You'll have to shop around for the best price. So why do so few people actually take the time to shop around for the best insurance at the best possible price and terms?

Probably because insurance is complicated and takes some time to understand. Too many folks simply rely on what their agent tells them. You may be getting excellent advice, but your agent typically has a financial interest in your decision. There are sources that will help you be certain you're getting the best deal.

Getting the Best Deal

As with anything you buy, getting the best deal on any kind of insurance means shopping around. These resources should be tapped for all kinds of insurance, not just life insurance:

- At the Insurance News Network (www.insure.com), you'll find excellent information on different types of insurance programs—including auto, health, home, life, and annuities—and ways to check out the financial health of various companies. You'll also be able to find the latest news about different insurance companies. Be aware that insurance companies (and other corporations) advertise on this Web site.

- For good prices on low-load, level-term policies, Quotesmith (www.quotesmith.com or 800-556-9393) has a database of 159 insurance companies.

- Insurance Information Inc. (800-472-5800) will make its database of 600 insurers available to you. The charge is around $50 for five or more quotes, and you are asked a dozen health questions. Other quote services to try include: Wholesale Insurance Network (www.win.com or 800-808-5810); TermQuote (800-444-8376); SelectQuote (800-343-1985); InsWeb (www.insweb.com); and QuickQuote (www.quickquote.com).

- InsureMarket (www.insuremarket.com) is run by personal finance software giant Intuit and has a decent calculator.

- Charles Schwab & Co. (800-542-LIFE) and Jack White & Co. (800-233-3411) offer good information and low costs. You might get a free quote online, but be prepared to pay something for some of their services.

- Among individual companies, Veritas (a direct-to-consumer subsidiary of Ameritas Life Insurance Corp. (www.veritas.ameritas.com or 800-552-3553) and USAA (800-531-8000) are low-load insurance companies that sell direct to consumers.

- If you want a fee-only personal financial advisor who can help you go over your insurance choices, expect to spend $250 to $1,000. Call the National Association of Personal Financial Advisors (800-366-2732). Fee for Service will also help you find an advisor to help with your life insurance choices (800-874-5662).

Taking the High Road

If you're using whole life insurance or credit life insurance as a financial planning tool, think through the idea before you sign the papers, and perhaps consult a financial planner or accountant. If you're disciplined enough, you may reach your goal more quickly by investing the money you set aside for the insurance premiums each year.

For example, *credit life insurance* (also known as *mortgage life insurance*, not to be confused with *private mortgage insurance*, or *PMI*) will pay off the remaining balance due on your mortgage or credit cards when you die. This is a particularly expensive type of insurance, especially because you're covering a declining liability (you pay off a portion of your mortgage balance or credit card balance each month, and that portion gets larger as you get closer to the end of your loan). If you're worried about paying off your mortgage, you'll be better off with a cheap *term insurance* policy (the insurance pays you the stated amount if you die within the term, which is typically one year). Then, your heirs have the right to do what they want with the money: invest it, use it for daily living expenses, pay for college education, or pay off the mortgage. The same arrangement applies to flight insurance (if your plane crashes, your beneficiary will collect on the policy and may then sue the airline and settle for an "undisclosed" sum of money).

There are exceptions to everything, of course, and there are real reasons to buy all of these types of insurance. Let's take a closer look at the basic types of insurance you'll probably need at some point—and the people who sell them.

A Word about Insurance Agents

Before we get too much further along, I want to talk about insurance agents, both good and bad. The insurance industry is gearing up to take advantage of the cost savings of selling insurance online (and, hopefully, passing on those savings to the consumer) or through toll-free numbers, but much of the insurance sold in America today is sold by agents.

Like the car leasing industry, the insurance industry is shrouded in secrecy because insurers know the more confused and scared people are, the faster they'll sign on the dotted line. With convoluted answers to basic questions like "How much life insurance do I need?" bad-apple insurance agents might have you coughing up more than you can afford.

Some insurance agents work for a particular company and only represent policies sold by that company. Other agents act as brokers for a number of different companies. The only way to know your agent's role is to ask.

The way insurance agents operate is somewhat similar to the way homes and cars are sold. Most homes are still sold by real estate agents, and most cars are still sold by car salespeople, and a percentage of the sale is the sellers' commission. Insurance agents also take a commission on each policy sold, as well as a smaller commission if the policy is renewed.

There are great insurance agents, horrible ones, and a bunch who are just mediocre. Unfortunately, agents make their living by selling policies, and unethical agents may try to sell you more insurance than you need, or put you into the wrong insurance policy simply because they will earn more money (sometimes, substantially more money) on the commission.

If you find a good, honest, knowledgeable insurance agent with whom you develop a good rapport, and who seems to have your best interests at heart, by all means work with him or her to plan all of your insurance needs. My grandfather, Paul, to whom this book is dedicated, sold disability insurance to farmers and businesspeople in the Chicago metropolitan area for the last ten years of his professional life. He was well loved and successful because he sold his clients only what they needed, and he explained policies in a way that made sense to individuals who didn't think about insurance more than once every few years.

Unfortunately, there are bad insurance salespeople who will try to take advantage of you. In this chapter, I'll highlight some of the more common unethical or illegal things they do. I want you to recognize these people when they cross your path. In the last chapter of this book, I talk about how to find good professionals to help you. Information on how to recognize a good insurance agent can be found on page 160.

QUESTION 24

HOW MUCH LIFE INSURANCE DO I NEED, AND WHAT KIND OF COVERAGE SHOULD I BUY?

Figuring out how much life insurance you need is surprisingly simple. You can use the worksheet on pages 122–123, or go online and use one of a dozen or so calculators. Each major insurance company now has a Web site, and most of these offer life insurance calculators.

But be careful. As part of the research for this book, I went online and ran sample numbers through five different calculators. Each one came out with a different amount for the insurance needed in my made-up example. Why? Because each calculator uses a different set of financial assumptions. One assumes that your cash will grow at 5 percent, another at 8 percent. One estimates that your monthly expenses will be only 70 percent of what they are today, another estimates 75 percent. One calculator projects that college education expenses will grow at 7 percent a year, another allows you to put in whatever growth rate you think is accurate. Each of these differences can affect the final life insurance recommendation.

The best life insurance calculators tell you what their assumptions are, or they allow you to input your own assumptions. They also address immediate expenses, short-term expenses, and long-term expenses. Immediate expenses are designated as the costs of burial and of maintaining the home until your estate is settled. This includes creation of an emergency fund (three to six months' worth of expense cash, above and beyond what is needed). Short-term expenses apply principally to people whose spouses, partners, or children depend on their annual income for food, clothing, and shelter. Short-term expenses include costs of child care and other home and family-related care (laundry, cooking, lawn work, car repairs, home maintenance). If a stay-at-home spouse or partner dies, you'll need income to pay outsiders for all the maintainance and care that person provided. If you're the major breadwinner, you'll need enough cash for your spouse or partner to live on while he or she gets through the first year and decides what to do. If you don't want your spouse or partner to ever have to work outside the home, you'll need enough insurance to replace your income for the rest of his or her life. Long-term expenses include children's college fund, and retirement money. Will your spouse or partner pay off the mortgage in one lump sum, or continue to make monthly payments? Your spouse or partner might need money for training to reenter the workforce. You might need a boost to your entertainment budget for you and your children and for you as a single adult.

Here's the bottom line: You're trying to buy enough insurance so that if you die, or your spouse or partner dies, the remaining person will have enough money to replace the lost income. You'll also want enough cash to pay for funeral expenses, as well as any other immediate expenses such as probate. Some people may want to factor in the amount of cash they'll need for their children's education. If you don't have kids, and your spouse or partner works, you may not even need life insurance.

Cost of Living

What's it going to cost you to live? Go back to Chapter 2 and look at your monthly budget. If your spouse or partner dies, what expenses will be eliminated? Will you spend less on food? If you provide money to pay off the mortgage in full if you die, you can deduct the monthly mortgage payment from your future monthly expenses. Clothing? Transportation? Education? Will you spend more on yourself? On clothes? On dating? If your spouse stayed at home and cared for your children, how much will it cost you to have the best child care money can buy? Will someone else shop for groceries and clothes? Are you going to want to treat your kids and yourself, to help get past the loss of your spouse or partner and the children's parent?

My mother and father only fought about one thing: insurance. My father, an attorney, didn't think he needed to do anything about it. My mother, who stayed at home raising my sisters and me, felt he should do something—just in case. Because he was in a small private practice where the senior partner was several decades older than the other partners, everyone focused on getting clients and building the business rather than on insurance and retirement. Those items could wait. After all, if anything was going to happen, it would happen first to the aging senior partner, right?

That was the thinking until my Dad suddenly dropped dead of a heart attack a month after his forty-ninth birthday. It was a wake-up call for everyone who was connected to my family. Suddenly, life insurance and retirement accounts took on a renewed urgency. Fortunately for us, my mother kept at my Dad, and we received some life insurance proceeds when he died. Unfortunately, at that time, the federal government taxed insurance proceeds as earnings. I still remember my mother writing a huge check—more than my father had ever earned in a year—to the government. A year later, that tax law was changed. Today, spouses can inherit an estate tax-free. But even with the estate money, which seemed like such an enormous sum back then, my mother lived in fear that she wouldn't be able to provide for us. My mother went back to work, changed careers (she was formerly an art teacher) and became one of the top-selling real estate agents in the Chicago metro area. Still, it was years before that particular fear subsided.

It's Never Enough

How much is enough? Don't fool yourself. No matter how much life insurance you buy, it will never replace the loss of a parent, spouse, or partner. You could buy a $5 million policy, but it will never give you the comfort and warm hugs you need after a long day at the office or a bad day at school. If you had unlimited money and could buy a huge life insurance policy, you might not need it at all. The point is: Your life insurance should cover what you need to live and, if you can afford it, what you'd hoped to give your family down the line.

> If you end up with a negative number on the following worksheet, you already have enough life insurance—possibly, too much. Or, you might be underestimating your final expenses. The one thing calculators don't do is give your spouse or partner and children an improved standard of living as the years go on. Eventually, if you and your spouse or partner have the chance to build a life together, you'll hope to do better as the years go on—that is, decrease or eliminate your debts and increase your standard of living. Internet calculators tend not to project any improvement, so be mindful of just getting "enough" insurance. A hundred thousand dollars might meet your loved ones' needs today. But, in 25 years, even growing at a respectable 8 percent, it might not give them what you'd hoped it would.

What Kind of Insurance Should I Buy?

Now that you know how much life insurance you need, you have to decide what kind to get. You have two basic choices: *term* and *cash value*. Everything else (including *whole life*, *universal life*, and *variable universal life*) is a variation on cash value insurance.

Let's start with a few definitions.

1. *Term insurance* covers you for a fixed amount of years (called the *term*). A policy is usually for a one-year term and is renewable. *Level* or *guaranteed level* term insurance means the premium you pay is fixed for a stated number of years, usually five to thirty years. An *annual renewable* term means you may renew, but the premiums will probably go up as you get older. If you die during the term, the insurance company pays out the death benefit to your beneficiaries. When the term of the policy is up, you can drop your insurance, renew it, or (if your policy permits), convert it to a permanent insurance product (whole life). Why would you want to convert? You

Figuring Out Your Household Income Shortfall

A. Current Monthly Household Income $ _____

B. Future Monthly Household Income $ _____

    Surviving spouse's income $ _____

    Social Security* $ _____

    Pension (monthly) $ _____

    Other income $ _____

C. Household Income Shortfall (A – B) $ _____

D. Current Monthly Expenses $ _____

E. Surviving Spouse's Expected Monthly Expenses* $ _____

    Regular expenses $ _____

    Retirement $ _____

    Extras $ _____

F. Monthly Household Income Shortfall (B – E) $ _____

G. Annual Income Shortfall (F × 12) $ _____

H. Lifetime Shortfall (G × Number of Years)** $ _____

Figuring Out Your Total Additional Expenses

I. Survivor's Future Expenses† $ _____

    Additional child care $ _____

    Debt repayment $ _____

    Mortgage payoff $ _____

    College tuition $ _____

    Emergency fund $ _____

J. Survivor's Final Expenses‡ $ _____

K. Total Future and Final Expenses (H + I + J) $ _____

Figuring Out How Much You Have

L. Assets

Investment portfolio $ _____

Retirement accounts $ _____

Real estate equity
(current value minus mortgage) $ _____

Life insurance proceeds
(what the surviving spouse would receive today) $ _____

Other assets $ _____

Total assets $ _____

M. Amount of life insurance needed (K – L) $ _____

---

*Some experts (and calculators) assume that when a spouse or partner dies, your remaining monthly expenses will be only 70 to 75 percent of what they were. But that assumes no change in your standard of living. Every family hopes that, as the years go on, they will be able to do more because they're earning more. So, before you decide you can give up your spouse's car, what happens when your baby-sitter needs a car to take your kids to the doctor's office while you're at work? You may not need to buy work clothes, but you might want to take the family on a nice vacation once a year, to really bond. Be sure to factor in possibilities like these. When you go back to dating, there will be "extras" like baby-sitting (if you have young children), entertainment, and perhaps new clothes. If you're going to provide insurance money to pay off the mortgage, don't forget to subtract the monthly mortgage payment from the total regular expenses.

**The lifetime shortfall is your annual shortfall multiplied by the number of years that you'll need the extra income. Typically, experts recommend you anticipate these extra expenses until your youngest child is through college. However, if advanced degrees run in your family, these extra-costly years may continue.

†Future expenses are sometimes hard to figure. Your emergency fund should equal at least three times your monthly future expenses. A year of private school or college tuition could top $30,000 a year. (See the college tuition calculator on page 274 for assistance in planning for your children's future college tuition.) There are less expensive choices, but if you have two kids, you might need $250,000 to cover the future cost of their college education.

‡Final expenses include funeral services. The average funeral costs about $5,000. Most experts say to double that, to be on the safe side. If your spouse or partner dies intestate (without a will) or if the estate has to go through probate, tack on another $10,000 or more for legal fees, depending on the size of your estate.

might wish to continue your insurance for its coverage or for estate-planning purposes. If you're in poor health, it may be your only option, because you won't have to submit to another physical exam. Term insurance is simple, easy to understand, and relatively cheap. Experts believe it's right for about 95 percent of everyone applying for life insurance.

Problems: Term insurance is great, as far as it goes. You're gambling that you will die within the term. The insurer is gambling that you won't. If you hold term insurance long enough, one day you will be right. But that isn't the point. You're buying catastrophic cost coverage: enough term insurance to cover the annual income lost when a spouse or partner dies. If you have young kids and you die, or your spouse or partner dies, you've got twenty or more years of big expenses ahead of you. If your kids are grown and out of college, you may not need any life insurance, unless you're using it for estate-planning purposes. (See Chapter 14 for more information.) Finally, when you're done, you're done. If you don't die within the term and you decide not to renew the policy, there's nothing to show for your premiums, except relief that you're still on the planet.

2. *Whole life insurance* (also called permanent insurance) combines the death benefit with a savings component. It's broken down into two parts: (1) the mortality charge (the part that pays for the death benefit) and (2) a reserve (the savings component that earns interest). As you get older, the cost of the death benefit rises (true if you buy any kind of life insurance). The amount of cash you're putting into the reserve early in the life cycle of your whole life policy helps pay for the increase in the mortality charge as you get older. In addition to interest, the reserve might receive an annual dividend, depending on how many policies have been paid out and how well the insurer has invested the premiums it has received. The *cash surrender value* (also known as the *cash value*) is what you'd get if you cashed in your policy today. You can typically get it in cash or in paid-up insurance.

Problems: Agents tout the savings or investment opportunities with whole life or cash value policies. And the charts and policy illustrations an agent will show you will likely promise you big returns. But read the fine print: they may be projecting an 11 percent or 15 percent annual rate of return. Their returns are based on the stock market. If the stock market generates an average annual return of 30 percent, things will be rosy. But should the market return 3 to

5 percent for ten years, watch out. You could end up owing money to keep the policy in force. Whole life is expensive, so buying enough coverage may be tough if you're on a tight budget.

3. *Universal life insurance* also combines insurance with a savings or investment component. The savings component is called an *accumulation fund*. It earns interest and goes to pay the higher cost of the mortality charge as you age. The big pitch here is that as long as you pay enough to fund the mortality charge, you can skip payments if your funds dry up. And, if you contribute enough to the accumulation fund early on, and your rate of return is pretty good, it may be enough to pay the premium later on.

Problems: If you don't pay enough early on, the shortfall could come back to haunt you. You might pay a lot more later, at a time when you thought you'd be done paying. If you drop the policy, you may have to pay a surrender charge (which could be steep).

4. *Variable life and variable universal life insurance* also have the savings/mortality charge combination. When you choose where your savings will go, you have a number of different investment choices. Think of it as putting your money into a bunch of different mutual funds, all administered by the insurance company (which takes a management fee on top of your premium commissions). If you're feeling risky, you can put your savings into a stock fund. If you're more risk-averse, you can choose something less aggressive. Variable life insurance has fixed premium payments; in other words, you must pay each premium. Variable universal life insurance has flexible premiums, like universal life.

Problems: If you choose to put the savings component into a stock fund and the market tanks, you'll lose a portion of your investment account, and the insurer may ask you to pay additional cash to keep the policy in force. If you're on a tight budget and wouldn't be able to tap your savings for a huge chunk of money on short notice, this isn't for you.

Term or Cash Value?

Should you go with term or a variation of cash value insurance? The answer depends on what you're trying to do. If you're young (20s, 30s, or early 40s), if you want to cover your major expenses while your kids grow up and go through college, and if you're investing money for your retirement separately, term insurance may be the best and cheapest way to go. If you're in your 40s and 50s and have young children, buying enough term insurance may cost about the same as some cash value policies. If you're in your 50s, 60s, and 70s, you're probably better off making other investments, unless you're looking into estate-planning vehicles.

If you're planning on getting life insurance from one company and keeping the policy for at least twenty years and maybe even thirty or forty years, if you want the enforced savings and investment, and if you have a cash reserve to dip into in case the insurer's rosy projections of growth don't quite hold up, cash value can make sense over the very long run.

But getting out sooner can cost you an arm and a leg. According to the Consumer Federation of America, consumers lose about $6 billion every year by cashing in whole life insurance policies prematurely. Why so much? Think about how a home loan works. In the early years of a thirty-year loan, you pay almost all interest and virtually no principal. Somewhere around fifteen to eighteen years, your interest-to-principal ratio balances out. During the last few years of the loan, each payment consists of almost all principal and virtually no interest. Likewise, the first few years of a cash value insurance policy's premiums go to pay the hefty commissions earned by your agent and the fees the insurer takes (none of these is currently required to be disclosed, but you can always ask the agent how much they are and what the premium pays for during the early years of the policy).

If you consider buying a guaranteed level term policy, say, for twenty years, review the policy to verify that the rate is indeed fixed for each year of the twenty-year policy. Sometimes you'll find the rate is fixed only for the first five years, after which it will surely rise.

As you get older, your needs may change. Years before, you wanted lots of life insurance to protect against an untimely death. You may have different needs now that your children are grown, educated, and married, with families of their own. Reassess your insurance needs every year or so, to make sure you're still getting the best coverage for where you are today, at the best price.

The Tax Do's and Don'ts of Cash Value Policies

One topic you'll hear about (mostly from insurance agents) is the amazing tax benefits you'll get from a cash value policy. As long as you *never cash in the policy*, you can reinvest the dividends tax-free. You can trade among the different policies' funds without worrying about capital gains taxes. And, you can borrow most of the cash value as a tax-free, interest-free loan that you never have to pay back. When you die, your heirs receive an income-tax-free (not estate-tax-free) benefit minus any "loan" amount. However, if you cash in the policy, expect to pay capital gains tax on your investment gains.

Should you go for a variable universal life policy? Experts agree on the following criteria:

1. You need more life insurance.
2. You will keep the policy for the rest of your life.
3. You can afford to "overfund" the policy by putting in far more than is required.
4. You have already maxed out on other tax-favored retirement accounts.
5. You won't need to "borrow" money for at least ten and preferably twenty years.
6. You are in good health (so the premiums are relatively low).
7. You have the time to closely monitor your investments.
8. You are an aggressive investor willing to put your money into a riskier stock fund rather than a more conservative choice.

Variable universal life insurance may then be an excellent choice for you. (Just be sure to pick a top-rated insurer so the company will outlast you.)

To me, that's a lot of up-front requirements. Considering that whole life policies typically cost as much as *ten times* more than a term policy (nope, you didn't read that wrong), I'd rather buy enough term insurance and then invest the rest separately. In that way, if I'm going to invest in mutual funds, I won't have to pay a management fee twice (first, to the mutual fund company, and second, to the insurance company through which I'm investing my accumulation account). That doesn't mean a cash value policy isn't right for you. Some folks find the idea of investing and buying insurance to be downright appealing. And some people will want to buy a whole life policy and invest separately as well. But before you make your decision, get a professional evaluation of your particular situation. For about $40, the Consumer Federation of America will evaluate two different policies for you. (Write to: CFA Insurance Group, P.O. Box 12099, Washington, DC 20005.)

Caveat Emptor: Buyer Beware

If you have a cash value policy that already has cash built up, you may be a target for *churning*, a nasty little trick bad-apple insurance agents (who might represent well-respected companies) might pull in order to get another huge commission from you. What they'll do is call you on the phone and tell you your policy just isn't any good, or your insurance company isn't any good. But they have the answer for you. They'll put you into a new cash value policy, and so on. Uh-huh. What they really do is take the cash value built into your old policy and use it to fund the new policy, which it will for a while. Eventually, everything catches up and, in a worst-case scenario, you could owe thousands of dollars and have nothing to show for it.

Jeanne and William's Story

Jeanne and William's life insurance agent told them they could increase their life insurance from $30,000 to $150,000 at no extra cost. Their $77.50 monthly premiums would stay the same, provided they surrendered one of the two policies they had. They didn't realize the agent would take out a loan on the other policy to pay for the new policy. After five years, the cash ran out and Jeanne and William had to make payments on the loan or risk losing the policy.

The Bottom Line

If an arrangement sounds too good to be true, just assume it is. You'll save yourself from throwing away thousands of dollars and from the heartbreak of finding out that you've been duped.

Things You Should Know

Here are some facts that may help you avoid problems with buying, renewing, or using your insurance policies.

1. *Insurance companies are not required to disclose information about their commission structure and fees.* But you should know that 55 to 100 percent (or more) of your first cash value policy's premium will go to pay fees and commissions. Approximately 35 percent of your annual term insurance fee (a much lower amount than a cash value policy premium) will go to pay fees and commissions.

2. *Churning, also called* twisting, *continues to plague the industry.* With churning, unscrupulous agents from small and large companies might suggest you cancel your existing policy and replace it with a new one, drawing down your cash value (called "juice" in industry jargon) to pay for it. (Remember, cash value policies make the most sense if you hold onto them for a long period of time.)

3. *Many consumer advocates in the insurance arena believe current state regulations (insurance is regulated at the state level) are inadequate.* They allow bad-apple agents and anticonsumer practices to slip through the cracks more easily.

4. *Consumers often fall for unscrupulous agents and practices because they think they're savvy and they trust the agent with whom they're dealing.* Worse, many consumers can't tell a good insurance policy from a bad one. In recent surveys, only one-third of those surveyed knew that term insurance delivered the biggest bang for the buck. Only 14 percent knew the *surrender value* is the best measure of the current value of your cash value policy. One-third thought it was the death benefit. Forty percent of those surveyed thought the agent's commission on a policy was 10 percent of less. Don't be afraid to ask questions until you understand exactly what the agent is telling you.

WHAT TYPE OF MEDICAL INSURANCE SHOULD I HAVE?

As I said earlier, medical insurance is the only kind of insurance everyone needs at some time. And that statement makes the first question (Should I get medical insurance?) a no-brainer.

The type of medical insurance you get depends largely on your financial wherewithal, special medical needs, selectivity regarding the doctors you see, and whether your employer gives you a choice. Do you like to choose your doctors? Or, would you be happy with a selection from an HMO? What if all the doctors you see just happen to be affiliated with an HMO? Would that make a difference to you?

The main focus of this book is to help you figure out how to organize your financial life and create wealth. But while you're busy creating all this wealth for your future, you need to take care of your own physical health and that of your family. If you don't take care of yourself physically, you'll have no one to spend your money on (and trust me, I do believe in spending). Being good to yourself physically translates into feeling good about your life, no matter how much money you have. I'm not suggesting you bankrupt yourself in order to have the most expensive medical care. It may not be any better than your local HMO, and it may have the same doctors affiliated with it. But you should be comfortable with your doctors and able to tap into specialists if you need to.

The Three Privates

Today, there are three basic types of private medical insurance:

1. *Indemnity plans* are set up as fee-for-service. You get something done, you pay for it. Typically, there are no restrictions on care, and the plan coverage kicks in when you reach a certain deductible. Unlike an HMO, you (or the doctor's office) will have to bill the insurance company. The very nice thing about indemnity plans is that you choose the doctor you see and you can seek second opinions or specialists anywhere in the country. On the other hand, it's the most expensive way to go, and not every employer offers this plan.

2. *Preferred Provider Organization (PPO) or Point of Service (POS)* plans are considered hybrids. You have an opportunity to choose your own doctor, but you may have to pay extra fees if you go outside of the network. These plans are cheaper than indemnity insurance because the doctors, hospitals, and other

providers of care have agreed to accept lower fees from insurers for their services. But they're typically more expensive than an HMO plan. One big plus: If you have a PPO and want to see a specialist or get a second opinion, you can do so without needing your primary HMO physician's official referral. If you have a POS plan, you will still need a referral.

3. *Health Maintenance Organizations (HMO)* have received their share of good and bad publicity during the 1990s. On the plus side, they offer routine checkups, baby well-care, preventive services, and lower out-of-pocket costs. When you visit doctors, you may have no payment or a small copayment, like $5 or $10. Many HMOs offer dental care and a very low maximum charge for medication. Some cover alternative care, such as chiropractic services. But the HMO is firmly in control of your health care choices. You must see doctors in the network, and you can see a specialist only if you're referred to one by your primary HMO physician. The specialists you're referred to will always be within the plan, which limits your ability to seek outside opinions. Some treatments may be considered too "experimental" by the HMO, even though they've been shown to be effective. If you're healthy or if you have young children, HMOs can be a good way to go. But it's tougher if you're really sick or have a serious or chronic illness.

Having good medical insurance is one of those things that can make you feel really good about your money. But having the best medical insurance you can afford doesn't always mean buying the most expensive plan. Depending on where you live, you may be able to get an HMO or PPO plan that covers every doctor you'd want to see. Many of these plans now extend to include hundreds or even thousands of doctors in their networks. Many private teaching hospitals have become affiliated with other local and community hospitals, bringing their doctors into a major network. Ask to see the doctor lists for each type of medical plan before you sign up.

Which plan is right for you? That depends on your health, how important choice-of-doctor is to you, whether all the doctors you'd ever want to see are in your local HMO or PPO network, and what options (if any) your employer provides.

Choosing the Right Plan

Medical insurance can be complicated. Each plan type typically can be customized with deductibles and copayments. *Read the fine print carefully.* You may be covered under a group policy (typically, through your job or the job of a family member) or an individual policy (if you're self-employed or if your company does not offer group policies).

If you get a choice of health coverage at work, you may be allowed to join or change health plans once a year during an "open enrollment" period. Typically, once you choose a plan, you must keep it for at least a year. Your benefits office will be able to explain the medical plan choices your company offers, and what they mean for you and your family.

If you can't afford individual coverage, check into unions, professional associations, trade associations, or social or civic groups. These often offer health plans for members. Insurance brokers may be able to find special policies for you. Some states provide insurance for very small groups or the self-employed.

If you're self-employed, you can deduct a portion of the cost of medical insurance on your 1998 tax return, and in future years you may be able to deduct the entire cost. If you have to pay for medical insurance privately, it may be worthwhile to start a small home-based business so that part, or all, of the monthly premiums will be deductible.

Other Options

If you're over the age of 65, or you have certain disabilities, you may qualify for *Medicare*, a federal health insurance program. You can find out more about Medicare by calling your local Social Security office or your state's Office on Aging. *Medicaid*, a joint federal–state health insurance program run by your state, covers some low-income people (typically, children and pregnant women) and disabled individuals. For more information, call your state's Medicaid office.

The Health Insurance Portability and Accountability Act

A *preexisting condition* is a medical condition that has been diagnosed or treated before you join a new group health plan. Before the passage of the Health Insurance Portability and Accountability Act (which went into effect on July 1, 1997), a health insurer could make you wait a specified amount of time before covering you. Now, if you've been covered by insurance during the past twelve months, a new insurer cannot refuse to cover you, nor can it force you to accept a waiting period when you join a new group plan.

What's Covered?

As with so many other things in life, medical insurance is all about details. Basic catastrophic care is covered, but before you sign onto a plan, ask what's covered, what the exclusions are, what the limits of coverage are, and who the doctors are. Find out how the plan handles these items:

- *Deductibles and out-of-pocket expenses.* What does the plan allow?
- *Physical exams and health screenings.* Is there well-care for babies, children, and adults? Are immunizations for children covered? What about Pap smears and breast exams, including mammograms?
- *Care by specialists and referrals to specialists.* Who makes the decisions?
- *Hospitalization and emergency care.* Do you have to call before you come in?
- *Prescription drugs.* Are they free or is only a portion of the cost covered? Are you required to use generic drugs?
- *Vision care and dental services.* Are routine checkups covered?
- *Mental health counseling, psychiatric services, and psychotherapy.* Is your psychotherapist or psychiatrist required to file periodic reports on you to your health insurer?
- *Services for drug and alcohol abuse.* Is there help for smokers who want to quit?

- *Obstetrical-gynecological (OBGYN) care and family planning services.* Are birth control pills covered? What about abortions? Do you have to pay for maternity coverage separately? When does it kick in?

- *Physical therapy and other rehabilitative care.* Is there a fixed limit on treatments?

- *Home health care, nursing home admission, and hospice care.* What are the limits?

- *Chiropractic or other alternative health care such as acupuncture and holistic treatments.* Is the insurer among those who have begun to give these methods a fairer shake?

- *Experimental treatments.*

- *Coverage for college students, older children, elderly dependents, and family members who travel frequently for work or pleasure.*

- *Overseas travel or coverage for an insured who travels abroad frequently.*

A most important factor is how you feel you're being treated by your medical insurer. As we discussed at the start of the chapter, each plan has trade-offs in terms of cost, coverage, and services. Only you can decide which compromise you're willing to make. Think about referrals, convenience of care, access to doctors and hospitals, cost, and the paperwork involved. Do you want to keep receipts and file claims? Compare services, choices, locations of doctors and hospitals, and costs. Finally, choose a quality insurer that has a reputation for paying its bills. You may still have trouble getting a claim paid from time to time, but the process should be orderly and the insurer should be responsive. Your state's Department of Health or Insurance Commission can explain your plan to you in detail. *Report cards* generated by the insurance company might include satisfaction survey results and other information on quality; how many people join or leave the plan each year; and the average waiting time for an appointment.

Getting the Best Care

Getting the best care means taking responsibility for your health. Here are some things you should do.

First, check out your doctor. Make sure he or she ranks right up there. Ask the plan administrator and medical offices for information on the doctor's training and experience. Basic information on doctors is available in the Directory of Medical Specialists (available at your local library). Go to the American Medical Association (AMA) free service on the Internet for information about member doctors (not every doctor belongs to the AMA). The address is <www.ama.org>. Is your doctor board-certified? For a listing of any registered complaints or disciplinary actions taken against the doctor, call your state's Medical Licensing Board. Other complaints against your insurer may be on file with your state's Department of Health or Insurance Commission.

Stay informed. Read your health insurance policy and member handbook. Ask questions if you don't understand something. If your plan has a magazine or newsletter, it can be an excellent source of information on how the plan works or on policy changes. Be proactive. Ask your doctor about regular screenings to check your health. Keep asking questions until you understand the answers, and don't be afraid to take notes when you're at a doctor's appointment. Keep track of your health. Log any symptoms so that you'll have details ready when you talk to your doctor. Set up health files for family members at home.

Finally, if you're not happy, change doctors or insurers. Again, you have to take responsibility for your own health care and that of your family. If you're not happy with the level of service you're receiving, make a change. Services will never be perfect, but you need to feel protected in this area so that you can get on with the rest of your life.

For More Information

Here are some sources of additional information. When you call or write, be sure to ask for any new publications that may address your concerns.

"Checkup on Health Insurance Choices" and "Questions to Ask Your Doctor Before You Have Surgery" are available from the Agency for Health Care Policy and Research. Write to Publisher's Clearinghouse, P.O. Box 8547, Silver Spring, MD 20907, or call 800-358-9295.

"Consumer's Guide to Health Insurance" is available from the Health Insurance Association of America, 555 13th Street, NW, 600 East, Washington, DC 20004-1109, or call 202-824-1600.

"Guide to Health Insurance of People With Medicare," "Your Medicare Handbook," and "Managed Care Plans" are available from the Health Care Financing Administration, 7500 Security Boulevard, Baltimore, MD 21244-1850, or call 800-638-6833.

"Putting Patients First" is available from the National Health Council, 1730 M Street, NW, Suite 500, Washington, DC 20036-4505, or call 202-785-3910.

"Managed Care: An AARP Guide" is available from the American Association of Retired Persons, 611 E Street, NW, Washington, DC 20049, or call 202-434-2277.

"Choosing Quality: Finding the Health Plan That's Right for You" is available from the National Committee for Quality Assurance, 2000 L Street, NW, Suite 500, Washington, DC 20036, or call 800-839-6487. The Web address is <www.ncqa.org>.

QUESTION 26

HOW MUCH HOMEOWNER'S INSURANCE OR RENTER'S INSURANCE SHOULD I HAVE?

If you own a home and you have a mortgage, your lender will require you to carry a minimum amount of homeowner's insurance on your property. But even without that requirement, you should carry homeowner's insurance. The amount you carry should cover the cost of replacing your home and your contents *today*, not when you bought them 5, 10, 20, or even 25 years ago. If you rent, you should

Condos and co-ops have different types of insurance because the property's common elements must be covered separately: a hallway, an interior staricase, elevators, the roof, a laundry room, or landscaping in common areas. Typically, co-op or condo associations will hold a building insurance policy that covers the common elements of the property and will satisfy your lender. But don't be confused. This policy does not cover you. You will still need a separate policy that meets your lender's requirements as well as your own.

carry renter's insurance that would cover the cost of replacing your personal possessions if they become damaged, stolen, or destroyed in some kind of catastrophe.

What kind of homeowner's insurance is available? The insurance industry offers this assortment:

Type	Coverage
HO2	Most perils, except floods, earthquakes, war, and nuclear accidents.
HO3	All known perils (with a few exclusions).
HO4	Renter's insurance. Similar in scope to HO2, but geared toward renters rather than owners.
HO6	Homeowner's insurance for condos and co-ops.
HO8	Special insurance for older homes, but rarely used.

Deciding on the Right Coverage

In some ways, homeowner's insurance is the easiest type of insurance to purchase. You basically decide (1) what you want to cover and (2) how much you're willing to pay as a deductible amount on any claim. These items will dovetail into a policy that's right for you.

Start by deciding which perils you want to cover. A *peril* is the calamity from which you're trying to protect yourself. The perils most commonly covered include:

- Fire or lightning.
- Windstorm or hail.
- An explosion.
- An aircraft or car ramming through the wall or ceiling of your home, or damaging walkways, lawns, a pool, or other features of your property.
- Smoke.
- Vandalism and other malicious mischief.
- Theft.
- Glass breakage (when a window is smashed).
- Falling objects; damage from weight of snow, sleet, or ice; collapse of building(s).

- Sudden and accidental tearing apart, cracking, burning, or bulging of a steam or hot water heating system or of appliances for heating water.
- Freezing of plumbing, heating, or air-conditioning systems and/or household appliances.
- Sudden and accidental damage from artificially generated currents to electrical appliances, devices, fixtures, and wiring (TV and radio tubes are not included, if you happen to have an old one lying around).

Floods, earthquakes, and mud slides are never covered on a regular homeowner's policy. A "riot of civil commotion" may or may not be covered. If you want coverage, you'll have to purchase separate insurance to cover each of these risks (see pages 143–144). A "land disturbance" may or may not be covered. What about a chemical or paint spill? Damage from wild animals? Backed-up sewers and drains? Blood stains? Scorching without fire? What about the additional living expenses you'll have to pay if your home is demolished and must be rebuilt? Be sure to ask.

When comparing policies, you'll want to look at the deductible, the items or conditions covered, and what type of coverage you're buying. *Replacement insurance* guarantees that the insurer will pay for the cost of replacing the home as it exists today, up to the amount of your coverage. *Guaranteed cost replacement* coverage guarantees to

Replacement cost insurance for contents may reimburse you only for the actual, depreciated value of the items. If you paid $2,000 for a sofa ten years ago and the insurance company says it's worth only $1,000 today, you'll have to cough up the extra cash to buy a new one, even though it may cost $3,000 to purchase another one just like it.

Pay attention to your insurer's cost-per-square-foot calculations. Your insurance company might estimate that replacing your home will cost only $60 per square foot. In reality, only the cheapest construction methods cost that little. Replacing your home the way it is, with all the tile, hardwood floors, wallpaper, marble, and granite you may have will cost much more. A more realistic estimate is $90 to $125 per square foot, depending on where you live. For a high-end home, expect to pay upward of $150 per square foot.

rebuild your home no matter what the cost and has a rider built in to allow for inflation. A *cash value* policy will reimburse you based only on your property's current market value—not what it would cost to build it new. Today, guaranteed cost replacement has been somewhat limited. Insurers might only pay to rebuild your home up to 120 to 125 percent of your policy amount. It's up to you to stay on top of how much it will cost to rebuild your home.

Other Sorts of Coverage

Some places call it *code-and-contention* coverage; others call it *building code* coverage or an *ordinance-and-law* rider. Whatever its label, what you're after is the cost of meeting new building codes that may have gone into effect after your home was built and to which any newly built homes are subject. If you lack code coverage, your insurer will probably pay only what it would cost to rebuild your old home to its former status, and you'll pay the rest to bring the house up to code. Some companies include code coverage in their basic policies, but if you don't ask, you won't know.

If there have been changes in zoning, you may be out of luck unless you have zoning coverage. For example, suppose you live in a beach house and the zoning law has been changed to prohibit any new development on the beach. If your home burns down, you might find yourself unable to rebuild on your site. That's where zoning insurance kicks in. It ensures that you can rebuild where you want to go. The policy should state that you can build your exact house, no matter what the cost, on a different lot. Otherwise, choose another policy.

You should also have a policy that covers the cost of replacing your foundation. (Seems obvious, but some insurance companies don't include it.) A *personal articles rider* is the official name for extra coverage

Pictures speak louder than words. If your home is destroyed, the last thing you'll want to do is try to prove what you owned and when you bought it. Use a video camera to record everything in your home. Make sure you date it by showing a current newspaper in the screen, and then go around your home, inside and out. Back up the video with close-ups of jewelry, furs, rugs, and fine art. Put the tape, the photos, and any appraisals in a safe deposit box outside your home.

139

of your expensive jewelry and fine art. Make sure you have current appraisals to support your claim. And, don't forget home office coverage. If you run a business out of your home, you'll need a rider to cover that business.

What They Want to Know

When you contact an insurance agent to get a homeowner's insurance policy (or if you do it over the Web), you'll need to provide some basic information about your home. Here are some of the questions you'll be asked:

1. What is the complete address of your home (or the home you'll be buying)?

2. What is your home made of? (Homes with exteriors of aluminum siding or shingles are typically considered to be made of wood.)

3. Is your home one story? Two stories? Split level? Other?

4. How many rooms are there?

5. What is the listing price of your home? What was the purchase price?

6. How old is your home? When was it built? What kinds of major improvements has it had (a new roof, or new mechanicals)?

7. What is the square footage of your home? (Multiply the length by the width and then multiply that number by the number of livable stories. Typically, attics and basements don't count).

8. How far away is the nearest fire department? The nearest fire hydrant?

9. Does the home have security devices, including smoke detectors, alarm systems, security lighting, deadbolt locks, or carbon monoxide detectors?

10. Is your home located on a flood plain?

11. Are there other structures on the property (a garage, guest house, or cabana)?

12. Do you own a dog?

13. Do you have any valuable jewelry, fine art, furs, antiques, or silverware on the premises? Do you typically keep large

amounts of cash in the house? (You may need special insurance riders to protect these items.)

14. What kind of deductible do you want to pay? (The higher the deductible, the lower your premium.)

15. Do you have a business on the premises? (Typically, homeowner's insurance policies either don't include a home-based business or have extremely low coverage. If you have a business based at home, you may want to purchase a home business rider or a rider for your computers and other electronic devices.)

16. How much liability insurance do you want? (Typically, homeowner's policies include a certain amount of liability coverage. But in these litigious times, you may wish to carry increased coverage.)

By knowing the answers to these questions, you'll speed up the time it takes to find the best deal.

Discounts and Deductions

Although homeowner's insurance is getting more expensive (a direct result of a spate of disasters in recent years, when insurance companies took huge losses), there are ways to cut down on your costs. If you move or refinance, you might be tempted to poke around and see what else is out there. If you've got a good record, you should find plenty of options. You might even cut your premium by as much as 35 to 50 percent. Here are some ideas:

1. *Shop around.* Once you have insurance, you'll be tempted to stay the course unless something happens, but you may be able to lower your premiums simply by shopping around. If you can't lower them, at least you'll feel good knowing you got the best deal. Direct writers of homeowner's insurance include American Express (800-535-2001), Amica (800-242-6422), GEICO (for auto, home or boat insurance, 800-841-3000), and USAA (800-531-8100). They do their selling over the phone and if you qualify, you'll save, big time, on the commissions. Even with a great policy, you might be able to drop your premium further with one of the ideas given here.

2. *Raise your deductible.* Some insurance companies will drop you if you make more than two claims in a year. Make sure your

141

insurance covers you for the catastrophes, and plan on picking up the cost of the everyday expenses. Raising your deductible from $250 to $500 might enable you to shave 12 percent off your premiums. Raise your deductible to $1,000 and your savings may double.

3. *Tout your improvements.* If you've put on a new roof, and it's made of a flame-repellent material, you might've earned yourself a discount. A new plumbing system, new wiring, or a new heating system might also qualify.

4. *Get connected.* A home security system might qualify for a small discount of 3 to 5 percent. But connect it to the local police and fire station, and you might lower your premium by up to 15 percent annually. If you put in a sprinkler system or smoke detectors, you might get smaller discounts.

5. *Grow old.* If you're over the age of 55, you can probably get a discount.

6. *Educate thyself.* Your insurance company may offer an education program or brochures that will allow you to lower your premium after you've attended or read the material.

7. *Buy your home and auto policy from the same insurer.* Some companies that sell homeowner's, auto, and liability coverage will take 5 to 15 percent off your premium if you buy two or more policies from them.*

8. *Insure your home, not the land it sits on.* If a tree falls in your backyard, chances are it won't hurt anything except the grass. So, don't include the value of your land when figuring out how much homeowner's insurance you need.

9. *Stop smoking.* The Insurance Information Institute says smoking accounts for more than 23,000 residential fires a year. Quit. Not only will you save on your homeowner's insurance, but you'll probably save a bundle on health insurance (and health-related costs, not to mention the cost of the tobacco products you won't have to buy over your lifetime).

10. *Find out whether group coverage is an option.* Professional, non-profit, and alumni organizations often offer discounts for association members.

---

*Some states don't allow discounts on premiums. Why? Most likely it's because the state insurance lobby is strong, and deductions lower the insurers' profits. Ah, politics.

11. *Stick around.* If you've kept your coverage with the same insurer for years, you should ask for special consideration. Some companies will give discounts of up to 6 percent if you've been a policyholder for six years or more.

12. *Look around.* Your home is an appreciating asset, but some items in your home are depreciating as the years go by. If you've purchased special riders for certain items, you may be able to reduce your coverage if they've lost their value. If you've sold items covered by riders, inform your insurance company so the riders can be removed from your policy.

13. *If all else fails, move.* According to a study by the nonprofit Insurance Research Council, it costs insurers 42 percent more to cover losses in a city than to settle claims for those who live five miles outside the city limits. City dwellers may be paying double the amount that nearby suburbanites pay for their insurance. But before you put your urban home up for sale, consider this: The cost of the 6 percent sales commission you'll likely pay to sell your home would more than make up the difference in city-vs.-suburb insurance premiums for a long, long time.

Floods and Earthquakes

If you live in a flood plain (check with the local municipality for flood plain information), your lender will require you to have flood insurance. You can only buy flood insurance from the federal government, although most agents sell the policies. The average annual cost is about $300 for $100,000 worth of coverage, and the maximum limit as this book went to press is $250,000 for the structure of your home and $100,000 for the contents. Finished basements are not covered by federal flood insurance policies, except for basics like the washer, dryer, furnace, and air-conditioning units. You'll take a loss on any damaged carpeting and wood paneling, not to mention items you may have stored, in your basement. The cost of your policy depends on the value of your home, construction costs, and where your home is located. If it's close to a shoreline, you'll pay a lot more money for your policy.

Flood insurance is about the cheapest kind of insurance you can purchase, and it's well worth the few hundred bucks you'll spend. Your regular homeowner's insurance won't cover anything if you get flooded because its considered to be a rising body of water, and that includes an 18-inch rainstorm. (If your basement floods because your sump pump failed, your regular insurance company will probably pay. Ask your insurance agent.) Still, only 20 percent of folks who live in a flood plain have flood insurance. For details and referrals to agents, call the Federal Emergency Management Agency (FEMA; 800-427-4661) or check out the agency's Web site <www.fema.gov>.

Earthquake insurance, unlike flood insurance, is offered through private insurers, typically as added coverage (called an *endorsement*). But the recent spate of earthquakes has made this insurance very difficult to buy and relatively expensive. This helps to explain why only about 10 percent of homeowners living in earthquake areas actually have earthquake insurance. You can purchase earthquake insurance through your insurance agent, though it is not available everywhere (by law, insurers in California must offer earthquake insurance). The cost depends on where you live, whether you are close to a fault line, what type of home you have, and whether the structure incorporates modern antiearthquake technology. In some areas that are highly seismic (except California), earthquake coverage may not be available at any price.

Some Final Thoughts

When putting together your final homeowner's policy, don't forget these items:

1. *College may not be covered.* Some policies cover your kid's stuff when he or she is away at school. Some don't. Be sure to ask. For a few extra dollars, you can get a rider that will fully cover Junior, plus all the hot-shot computer equipment he's bringing with him, from things that happen in a college environment.

2. *Make sure your stuff is fully insured.* Most policies will give you half the face value of any item you must replace. If you have a $300,000 homeowner's policy, most insurers will pay up to $150,000 for you to replace your personal belongings. If that's not enough, investigate additional coverage to fill the gap.

3. *Under the umbrella.* The general liability portion of a regular homeowner's policy is pretty small. Consider getting additional coverage that will give you an overriding umbrella liability policy—just in case.

SHOULD I HAVE DISABILITY INSURANCE?

QUESTION
27

First, some facts:

- Approximately 100 million working Americans are not insured against the risk of a catastrophic disability.

- Doctors, lawyers, and corporate executives typically have coverage. Nearly 80 percent of all doctors have it.

- If you're a 40-year-old white-collar worker, there's a 20 percent chance that you'll have some sort of disability that will last longer than 90 days.

- The leading causes of disability are: psychiatric ailments (including drug and alcohol abuse, and stress), cancer, accidents, illness, a heart condition, and back problems.

- Insurers cap most group policies (the kind you'll get from your employer) at $5,000 per month, or $60,000 per year.

- Disability insurance can be incredibly expensive.

- Your insurance agent will make a bundle on you, earning 40 to 80 percent of the first year's premium plus 10 percent of your annual premiums thereafter.

Should you buy disability insurance? The answer lies in how much cash you'll get from your job, from Social Security (if you qualify), and from your own resources should something bad happen.

Most employers offer some short-term sick leave—a few weeks, or even a few months, depending on how long a newly disabled person has worked for them. Some states require most employers to offer disability benefits for up to twenty-six weeks. In California, the duration for disability benefits is a year.

No long-term disability benefit is required, but about half of all mid- to-large-size employers provide disability benefits that last up to five years. Typically, group benefits (if you have them) will replace up to 60 percent of your salary, to a ceiling of $5,000 per month. No insurance company will insure you above 80 percent of your predisability salary, so if your company is giving you 60 percent and you qualify for Social Security disability payments, you might already be covered. Even if there is a slight discrepancy, you might more than make that up by drawing on your own savings or your retirement income.

Who qualifies for Social Security disability payments? Everyone who contributes to Social Security is covered, but to qualify, you must prove that you're unable to do any job, located anywhere in the United States. That's a fairly tough standard—much tougher than the private disability insurance you'll buy. In addition, you're only covered if your disability is expected to last at least 12 months. And if you receive payments from other government programs (including the Veterans Administration, workers' compensation, civil service, military programs, and government pensions), your Social Security disability payments could be slashed or eliminated.

If you become disabled, you might be able to draw income from: group coverage (for eligible employees); workers' compensation (if you suffer an accident or illness at work); Veterans Administration (for qualified veterans only); civil service pay (federal or state employees); black lung program (for miners); state vocational rehabilitation programs; group disability coverage from a union; auto insurance (if your disability stems from a vehicle accident); private insurance (including credit or mortgage disability insurance to meet your monthly debt payments); Supplemental Security Income (SSI) and Medicaid (for those with very low income and limited assets); and your own investments and savings.

Use the following worksheet on page 145 to help calculate how much income you could expect to receive if you became disabled tomorrow. Include money you'd get from your current disability coverage or from savings. "How Long?" refers to how long the benefit will last. If you have short-term disability insurance, it might kick in after a week but last only a year. Your goal should be to make sure you're covered from the start of a disability, or shortly thereafter.

Insurers will cover you for a total of only 60 to 80 percent of your predisability income. If your current employer covers you for 60 percent of your predisability income and you qualify for Social Security benefits for another 10 percent, you would be able to qualify for only an additional 10 percent of your monthly salary. Insurers won't cover you for a higher percentage of your salary because they don't want to encourage you to stay out of work if you're able to return. And don't expect to collect anything more, even if you have duplicate insurance. When you file a claim, your insurance company will quickly track down your other available benefits and reduce your claim accordingly.

WORKSHEET
Disability Income

From Where	Monthly Amount	Waiting Period	How Long?
Sick leave*			
Short-term*			
Group long-term*			
Social Security			
Other government programs			
Investment income			
Savings			
Spouse's income			
Other			
Total			
Current monthly salary			
Current monthly disability benefits			
Disability income shortfall			

*These are disability benefits from an employer. They do not apply to those who are self-employed.

Before you rush out and buy a disability policy, think about whether your spouse or partner earns enough—or could earn enough—to get you through your disability without yet another insurance premium to pay.

Think It Through

If you decide you do need private disability insurance, pay attention to the following items on the policy:

1. *Definition of disability.* Are you buying an *own-occupation* (pays if you can't work at your specific job), *any-occupation* (pays if you can't work at any job your education and training qualify you for, from the insurer's perspective), or *income replacement* policy (covers the difference between what you earned prior to the disability and what you now earn doing a different job). Consider whether your policy has *residual coverage* (the difference between your former salary and current salary, if you can now work at your job only part-time) or *partial disability coverage* (not as good; it pays you a fixed amount of the benefit for a limited amount of time). For the policy to kick in, do you have to be completely disabled? Partially disabled? Who determines what you're really able to do? Does your policy have *presumptive disability* (you are presumed fully disabled and entitled to full benefits if you lose your sight, speech, hearing, etc.)?

2. *Size of benefits.* Typically, you are limited to 60 to 80 percent of your predisability income. Higher-paid workers tend to get less.

3. *When the payments start.* With private insurance, you typically get to choose when to begin your payments. (Your employer will select it for the group policy.) The longer you wait, the cheaper the policy. You can choose to wait only thirty days before coverage kicks in, but you'll pay a heck of a lot more than someone who chooses a waiting period of 180 or 365 days.

4. *When they stop.* You can buy insurance that will pay for a year, two years, five years, to age 65, or throughout your lifetime. But because disability insurance is designed to replace your earned income, you may not need it after you hit your golden years. Still, the whole point of insurance is to protect against a

catastrophe. Think about the worst-case situation: What happens if you're never able to go back to work?

5. *Cost-of-living adjustment (COLA).* Do you want your disability payments to keep pace with inflation? Financially, you'd probably be better off taking the difference in the two premiums and investing it.

6. *Can the policy be canceled?* With a *noncancelable* policy, as long as you pay your premiums on time, the insurer can't raise your premium and can't dump you. A *guaranteed renewable* policy means you'll be automatically renewed but you might get hit with an increase. *Optionally renewable* or *conditionally renewable* policies may be renewed at the insurer's discretion.

7. *When do the premiums get waived?* Once you file a claim, you may be able to stop paying your premium. Find out if that arrangement is available with your policy.

8. *What happens after?* Is there an option to buy additional coverage without evidence of insurability at a later date? What happens to your policy once you've filed a claim, recovered, and gone back to work?

If you buy private disability insurance, you receive the benefits tax-free. If you receive disability from your employer, you'll pay tax on the proceeds. Social Security disability payments are also taxed, if your income is over the limit.

Trimming the Expense

Disability insurance is expensive enough without adding in everything under the sun. Before you write the check, consider these money-saving alternatives:

- *Don't buy more coverage than you can collect.* Insurers will pay out only after they've made sure you're not already maxed out from other insurers or government programs, and no one will cover you for more than 60 to 80 percent of your predisability income.

- *Don't add on all the perks.* Experts say the cost-of-living adjustment isn't worth the extra money you'll pay (an additional 4 to 40 percent). You'll pay more for the rider than you'll ever get back in income.

- *Take an exemption.* Even if you have a specific medical problem, like a bad knee, you can insure around it by taking an exemption. It's cheaper than trying to cover all your medical baggage.

- *Convert your policy.* If your employment situation changes, or if you plan to retire sooner than you imagined, adjust or eliminate your policy. Changing from a policy that pays out for life to one that ends at age 65 will save you big bucks. Take it down another peg to a five-year policy and you'll save even more.

- *Join an association.* If you're self-employed, you'll have more trouble getting a disability policy—even though you may need it more. Consider joining a nonprofit association in your profession that offers various insurance programs.

- *Shop around.* Low-load (low, or no, agent's commission) disability policies are available directly through some companies, and on the Internet. See the "Insurance Resources" section in Question 24.

If you can't qualify for disability insurance, consider upping your savings. If you don't end up using your nest egg to cover your income in case of a disabling injury, you'll have more for your retirement.

QUESTION
28

WHAT KIND OF AUTO INSURANCE DO I NEED AND HOW CAN I BUY IT FOR LESS MONEY?

If you drive a car, you need automobile insurance. Where you live, how old you are, what you drive, and your driving history are important factors that will affect how much you pay for coverage.

Even if you live in the suburbs (you'll pay less for coverage than city dwellers), are over age 25 (under 25, you'll pay a much higher premium), drive a boring car (fast cars bring you a one-way ticket to higher premiums), and have a great driving record (no moving violations in the past three to five years), you'll still pay a chunk of change for your car insurance. Why? Auto insurance prices are climbing for a bunch of reasons:

- *The cost of repairing cars has skyrocketed.* Replacing high-tech goodies like fuel injection, antilock brakes, and on-board computers adds to the total cost.

- *A larger number of cars are written off as a total loss.* Why? Because it's too expensive to fix them. The Alliance of American Insurers did a study and found it would cost more than $81,000 (not including labor!) to totally rebuild a 1992 Cadillac De Ville sedan, far less than the cost of purchasing a new one today.

- *Medical bills related to accidents are up.* Between 1982 and 1992, the cost of doctors' services rose 195 percent, compared to 145 percent for the Consumer Price Index.

- *Auto insurance claims are on the rise.* And more people are suing each other, which means insurance companies spend more on legal defense against personal and commercial liability claims.

- *Auto theft is on the rise.* Some insurance companies will give you a discount if you use a theft-prevention device.

- *Cars cost more money.* In fact, they're more than twice as expensive as they were ten years ago, so buying enough insurance is more expensive.

Pieces of a Puzzle

Auto insurance is based on a series of components, including *liability, medical payments, uninsured/underinsured motorist,* and *collision and comprehensive* coverage. Here's what each one means:

- *Liability.* If you hit someone and that person sues you, liability insurance protects you against claims for medical expenses, lost wages, pain and suffering, or property damage. Given our litigious society, you'll need bodily-injury liability coverage of $100,000 per person and $300,000 per accident, at a minimum. Property-damage liability coverage should be around $50,000. If you've got assets to protect, you may want to increase your liability coverage. But if you've bought an umbrella liability policy for $1 million (see Question 29), you may not need to raise the liability ante on your auto insurance.

- *Medical payments.* If someone gets injured in a crash, there's going to be a bill to pay. Medical coverage pays that bill, regardless of who is at fault (although your medical insurance may kick in as well). In states with *no-fault* insurance laws, you can buy *personal injury protection,* which means you pay for your injuries and the other driver pays for his or her injuries.

151

- *Uninsured/Underinsured motorist.* If you get hit by someone who isn't insured, this coverage pays out. Experts usually say you should get coverage equal to your liability coverage.
- *Collision and comprehensive.* This part of your insurance pays for fixing or replacing your car if it hits another car or object, or it bursts into flames, is stolen, or is damaged by other noncollision causes. How much you pay depends on how big a deductible (the portion you pay before your insurance kicks in) you're willing to take. Your costs will be higher if you choose a $250 deductible than if you choose a $500 deductible.

What Your Insurance Company Won't Tell You

If you're the kind of person who gets into a lot of accidents, you probably think your smartest choice would be to go with the lowest deductible possible. But what your insurance company won't tell you is that no matter how much you claim per accident, your rate may rise on a fixed scale based on the number of claims, not the dollar amount. If you get into a fender bender that costs $500 to fix, your rate will rise as much as if you totaled the car. What should you do? Consider taking a higher deductible (in case of a catastrophic accident) and paying to fix the small dents yourself.

Lowering Your Cost

The rate you end up paying for automobile insurance depends on how you combine the different coverages we just discussed. Here are some ideas on how to lower your total rate:

1. *Shop around.* Hundreds of insurers offer automobile insurance in every state. Check with some big companies, some direct-to-consumer companies, and some online insurance resources. (See the "Insurance Resources" section in Question 23.) But make sure the insurer you choose provides quality service and pays its claims.
2. *Increase your deductible.* The easiest way to lower your cost is to raise your deductible. Increasing your deductible from $250 to $500 might reduce your collision and comprehensive cost by 15 to 30 percent.

3. *Rethink your coverage for an older car.* If a car is worth less than $1,500, you may want to drop collision and comprehensive cost coverage.

4. *Buy a different car.* Hot cars cost more money to insure than quiet, dependable, steady ones.

5. *Drive less.* Many insurance companies will give you a break if you drive less than 7,500 miles per year.

6. *Move to suburbia.* It costs less to insure a car if you don't live in a large city.

7. *Ask about high-tech discounts.* If you've got antilock brakes, automatic seat belts, or air bags, you might get a discount.

8. *Keep your record clean.* Speeding tickets and accidents mean higher insurance rates. If you've been accident-free for at least five years, you can request a discount.

9. *Ask for other discounts.* If you're over age 50, have had a driving training or defensive driving course, have antitheft devices in your car, get good grades if you're a student, or have a child going to college, you may be eligible for a decrease in rates. You may also get a discount if the same company insures all of your vehicles, or your home.

WHAT OTHER KINDS OF INSURANCE DO I NEED?

QUESTION 29

Out of money yet? A family of four (without major medical coverage through work) could spend upward of $15,000 per year on premiums for just the insurance basics: life, medical, home, automobile, and disability insurance. If that isn't enough to give you a heart attack, there are other types of insurance competing for your dollars. Should you bite?

Whether or not you do depends on how old you are, how sick you are, and how scared you are that certain things will happen to you. If you're worried that all the assets you're going to work so hard to accumulate will disappear in a three-year, $240,000 stay in a nursing home, then *long-term care* (LTC) insurance may be for you. Fortunately, most insurers won't even sell it to you until you hit age 50. By then, you may not need to carry as much life insurance; your kids may be grown and out of the house, so your auto insurance premium will drop—as might your health care costs. But coverage doesn't

153

come cheap, and you may find your total insurance costs heading north as you pay for two long-term care policies.

Then there's *Medicare Supplemental* insurance, known informally as *medi-gap* or *MedSup*. It pays for all the stuff that Medicare doesn't cover. Want to go further? The American Association of Retired Persons (AARP) offers seniors extended coverage that pays a daily benefit for each day they're in a hospital. It can be used to pay for a private room, or for other costs not picked up by other insurance.

An *umbrella liability* policy will boost your general liability coverage to $1 million or more. If you've got assets to protect, and you get sued, you'll be happy to have extra coverage.

And there's more. Here is a quick look at some of the other basic types of insurance available to you. For more information, check out online sites like those provided by the Health Insurance Association of America <www.hiaa.org>, American Association of Retired Persons <www.aarp.com>, and Insurance News Network <www.insure.com>.

Long-Term Care (LTC)

If your parents ended up in nursing homes and you're terrified this will be your fate, *and* if you have substantial assets you don't want to deplete, LTC coverage may be for you. Experts say that 40 percent of Americans over age 85 will need some long-term care, and with everyone living longer these days (a baby born in 1999 has an excellent chance of seeing the year 2100), your odds just went up. Nursing home care can cost anywhere from $40,000 to $80,000 a year (in 1998 dollars). Home care can cost $1,000 to $1,500 per month (1998 dollars). Medicaid will only kick in when your money is nearly depleted, though your spouse may be allowed to keep some assets.

What do you need to know? For some readers, long-term care may be a long way off. But you should know that some LTC benefits may be taxed; others are tax-free. Rarely do nursing home stays last beyond five years (but that could cost you $400,000 in today's dollars), so get a policy that covers you for a minimum of three to five years (consider lifetime coverage if you have a family history of Alzheimer's or other diseases that are debilitative but progress slowly). Nursing home or home health care benefits shouldn't be limited to skilled care. The policy should: cover Alzheimer's disease; have an inflation-protection option (there are several versions); include an outline of coverage that allows easy comparison with other policies, plus an LTC "shopper's guide" (required by law), a guarantee that the policy cannot be canceled, declared nonrenewable, or terminated because you get old and sick, a thirty-day no-obligation cancellation period, and no requirement that you have to first be hospitalized or receive nursing home care, in order to qualify for benefits. Try to get a policy that will allow you some benefits even if, at some point, you can no longer afford the premiums. Experts say you shouldn't spend more than 5 to 7 percent of your income on LTC premiums.

Medi-Gap or MedSup

Medi-gap insurance supplements your Medicare benefits, reimbursing you for things (prescriptions, for example) that Medicare doesn't cover.

What do you need to know? The time to enroll in a medi-gap plan is when you join Medicare (which is available for seniors only). There is a six-month "window" during which new Medicare enrollees can buy a medi-gap policy regardless of health problems. After that, they are required to have medical screening and may be denied. Currently, ten medi-gap programs are offered, labeled A through J; J has the most comprehensive benefits (and is the most expensive). Shop around; rates vary. For more information, check out the Social Security Administration's (800-772-1213) free booklet, *Guide to Health Insurance for People with Medicare*, an annually updated directory of agencies providing free counseling on Medicare and medi-gap insurance.

Umbrella Liability

Also known as extended personal liability insurance, this offering protects you from the huge awards juries tend to hand out these days (the awards that "send a message"). Your automobile and homeowner's insurance policies carry some general liability, but it's usually limited to $300,000 or less. Umbrella liability coverage of $1 million or more can help you preserve some, or all, of your assets in case a jury decides to use you to set an example.

What do you need to know? Umbrella policies protect you and your family from claims stemming from *personal* activities. Job-related activities aren't covered. (If you have a home office, you'll need business liability protection.) Premiums are relatively cheap—$100 to $200 for $1 million in coverage—but make sure the policy covers attorneys' fees.

Collector's Insurance

Have you built a room to house your collection of Beanie Babies or model trains? If you have, or if you own any type of collectibles worth a considerable amount of money, you may want to think about insurance to protect them.

What do you need to know? Insurance companies tend to tailor specific policies to personal collections, but prices and specialties vary widely, so shop around. If a separate policy is too expensive, consider increasing the insured-contents coverage on your home policy, if your insurer will allow it.

Trip Insurance

Going on a big trip? Your first thought might be to get trip insurance. But unless you've paid a big nonrefundable fee for a special charter trip to somewhere exotic, or have expensive airline and/or cruise ship tickets, your out-of-pocket loss may not be so steep as to require trip insurance in case you have to cancel your vacation plans.

What do you need to know? Trip insurance can be very expensive and may place specific limitations on your ability to cancel your trip and receive a full or nearly full refund. Read all of the qualifying literature first, and don't forget the fine print.

Health or Liability Insurance for Travelers

If you travel extensively, travel abroad frequently, or choose dangerous or exciting adventure travel (like climbing Mount Everest), you may be advised to purchase extra insurance above and beyond what you currently have.

What do you need to know? If travel insurance is offered for free, don't refuse. But before you pay for coverage, check out what your own health and auto insurance and credit card will and won't cover. (Many cards offer holders additional protections and insurance.) The company may pay for a hospital to set your broken leg, but will it pay for a medical helicopter to pick you up at one of the Mount Everest base camps? Also, make sure you understand exclusions and requirements for collecting your benefits. Experts recommend dealing with a reputable company that specializes in travel insurance.

Mortgage Life or Credit Life Insurance

"You can make sure your home stays in your family, without forcing your loved ones to face potentially crushing debt." So goes the pitch for mortgage life insurance, which promises to pay off your mortgage when you die. Credit life insurance promises to pay off your credit card bills in case you die in debt. Are these insurance policies really as good as they sound? In short, no. Mortgage life and credit life insurance policies are relatively expensive, and they protect a declining liability: you're paying off part of the principal with every debt payment you make to a mortgagor or credit card company. You're paying more to insure a smaller payoff as each year goes by.

What do you need to know? If you're worried that your family won't be able to afford your mortgage after you die, buy cheap term life insurance. Then your heirs will have the full amount of the policy to do with as they please.

Safe Deposit Box Insurance

Putting irreplaceable documents like stock certificates, wills, and expensive jewelry in a safe deposit box located in an institution is supposed to be safe enough. But for some folks, that's not quite safe enough. Couldn't someone break into the bank's vault, drill through the lock, and steal your valuables? Yes; it has happened to major banks. Or, your bank's vault could be damaged in a flood or natural disaster. If you're really worried, safe deposit box insurance could be for you.

What do you need to know? If you want coverage from your bank, ask for it in writing, and then be prepared to have the contents of your box inspected every time you go into it. Your homeowner's or renter's policy may insure the contents of your box up to a small limit, like $2,000, but you may be able to buy a rider that will provide more coverage.

Car Rental Insurance

Every time you rent a car, the rental agent will put a list of optional coverages in front of you and encourage you to sign up. Not so fast. Typically, car rental insurance is expensive and can add as much as $10 to $20 per day for coverage.

What do you need to know? First, see what your current insurance policies and credit cards (don't forget business or corporate cards) offer by way of car rental protection. If you don't own a car, don't have automobile insurance, and don't have a credit card that provides you with decent coverage, you should probably sign on. Ditto if you're traveling in a foreign country, particularly Mexico. (If you ever get into a car accident in Mexico, don't exchange insurance information and drive away and expect to resolve it later. Insurance adjusters representing everyone involved in an accident often come directly to the site to evaluate the cars, and you can spend all day waiting for them to arrive, inspect the cars, negotiate the settlement, and issue the report. Several years ago, while the respective insurance adjusters worked out a settlement, my husband and I had a particularly delightful lunch in Cuernavaca, Mexico, with the driver of a Chevrolet suburban who had run right over our Volkswagen Beetle. Yes, he paid.)

Cancer Insurance

As we discussed earlier, you can buy a dread disease policy to cover a specific illness, but it's a little like gambling on whether you're going to get the disease. Experts say the policy is expensive, particularly in light of how much you'd actually get back.

What do you need to know? Specific illness insurance doesn't make a whole lot of sense; your regular medical policy will generally cover you.

Children's Life Insurance

Should you buy a life insurance policy on your child? If your child is an actor who brings in the bulk of the family income, then perhaps you should consider it.

What do you need to know? Instead of buying variable policies, put an equivalent amount into growth investments you can use for your child's future college education.

Adoption Insurance

For a couple planning on adopting a child, there's nothing worse than the birth mother's changing her mind about keeping her child.

If you've laid out big bucks to support that mother emotionally and physically, you could have nothing to show for your investment in her care.

What do you need to know? Few insurance companies offer adoption insurance, and even if it is available, you may not want to spend the money for it. Are you out $5,000 or $50,000? Typically, the minimum purchase is for $5,000 worth of coverage, for which you might pay $750 to $1,000.

Child Support Insurance

If the supporting spouse loses his or her job, this insurance will pick up the slack. But it's expensive, and there are a lot of situations where it won't pay out.

What do you need to know? Coverage typically lasts four months, and you should expect to pay a fair hunk of cash for it. After three years, you'll have paid in more than 40 percent of your expected premiums, experts say.

Wedding Insurance

No, it doesn't provide you with a new bride or groom if yours run off. And, if that does happen, the policy won't even cover the non-refundable deposits you've put down for the room and the band. But if there's a death in the family, or the about-to-be-happy couple gets arrested, and the ceremony is postponed or canceled, it will pay out.

What do you need to know? Only a few companies offer this expensive insurance. Read the fine print before you sign on.

Pet Insurance

Several years ago, a few companies introduced the concept of insuring the medical health of your pet as a way to cover increasing veterinary bills. Is it worth the money? If your pet needs a major operation, you could be out a couple of thousand dollars.

What do you need to know? A typical premium is $100 per year, and the average claim paid is just over twice that. Unless your animal needs catastrophic care, the costs might be lower than you think.

159

Broadway Ticket Insurance

For $5 per ticket, you can buy insurance that allows you to cancel two days in advance, in writing.

What do you need to know? Even with seats approaching $75 per ticket, this seems a little ridiculous.

If you've got life insurance and end up with a terminal illness, like AIDS, you may need cash before you die. A *viatical settlement* allows you to sell your life insurance policy to a company and receive a percentage of the proceeds today, when you need them. The big catch is this: You'll get only a fraction of what the policy is worth, perhaps 25 to 40 cents on the dollar, or $25,000 for every $100,000 in life insurance. Your heirs receive nothing. That cash might help you live well for whatever time you have left, but you may not have the strength it takes to complete the negotiations, so enlist the help of your spouse or partner, attorney, or accountant. Before you sign anything, find out whether you can receive an *accelerated benefit* directly from your insurance company. You may be able to purchase a rider that allows terminally ill people to cash in on their policy before they die, and collect up to 95 percent of the face value of the policy.

QUESTION 30

HOW DO I CHOOSE A GOOD INSURANCE COMPANY?

Major insurance companies are rated by their financial strength, how quickly they settle claims, and the amount of cash they've set aside to pay claims. Check your local library or the Internet for ratings by A.M. Best, Moody's, Standard & Poor's, and Duff & Phelps Credit Rating Company. The Dalbar Ratings (800-296-7056) of insurers measure consumer satisfaction with sales methods, service, and communications. Look for it at your local library. You can access some of these reports, and others, from the Insurance News Networks site <www.insure.com>.

When choosing an insurance company, you want to make sure it will be there when you need it. Getting the cheapest insurance isn't worth it if it means you have to go with a brand-new company with no claims-paying or financial history.

Real Estate

6

This chapter is designed to pinpoint the ways in which real estate relates to your personal finances. You'll get some of the basics here; for more in-depth information on buying or selling a home, please check out my earlier books: *100 Questions Every First-Time Home Buyer Should Ask*; *100 Questions Every Home Seller Should Ask*; and *10 Steps to Homeownership: A Workbook for First-Time Buyers*.

SHOULD I BUY A HOME OR SHOULD I RENT?

QUESTION 31

For most of us, the home front shapes up like this: You rent, you own, or you live with your parents.

Which category do you fit into? If you're living with your parents to save up for a down payment and your financial future, you're doing fine—but you're postponing the inevitable. Eventually, you're likely to want to move out on your own. When you do, you'll have to choose to either rent a place or buy a home.

Which way should you go? Ultimately, the difference between deciding to rent and deciding to purchase a home depends on where you are in your life—financially, personally, and emotionally.

Here is some information to consider when you're deciding where to go.

Financial Issues

- *Income.* If you don't have enough money coming in each month, you'll never qualify for a home loan. A regular stream of income—whether from a job, an inheritance, or lottery winnings—

combined with excellent credit, will put you in the driver's seat when you apply for a mortgage.

- *Cash for a down payment.* Even with today's super-low down payment loans, you'll still need enough money to cover a 3 to 5 percent down payment. In addition, lenders require you to have a certain amount of cash on hand as a reserve, so you don't spend your last cent at the closing and put yourself at risk financially. Finally, you'll want to have some savings above and beyond this outlay, so you can add some finishing touches to the home you eventually buy.

- *Credit, credit, credit.* As we discussed earlier in the book, having good credit is extremely important. The first thing a lender will do is pull a copy of your credit report for information on the types and amounts of debts you owe today and have owed in the past, and how you repaid those debts. Can you get a loan with lousy credit? Sure. But you'll end up with a mortgage interest rate that makes your credit card interest rate look like a bargain. Lots of people with bad credit rent until they've had some time to clean up their debts. Usually, you'll have better luck in the mortgage market if you let a year's time push your bad credit into the more distant past.

- *Tax time.* Studies show that homeowners tend to vote more often than renters, keep their property in better shape, and participate more in their community. In addition, when the U.S. economy generates at least 3.5 million existing home sales, there is a distinctly positive effect on the economy. As this book went to press, existing home sales seemed sure to surpass 4.7 million in 1998. For all of these reasons, the federal government continues to support homeownership with terrific tax breaks. Not only can you deduct your mortgage interest and property taxes on your federal income tax form (provided you have enough deductions to itemize, which most homeowners don't), but if you've lived in your home for two of the past five years, you can take all profits on the sale of your home (up to $250,000 per sale for single homeowners, and up to $500,000 if you're married) tax-free. And you can take this tax benefit once every 24 months. Renters get zero tax breaks on their federal income taxes, but some states give renters a tax break too.

- *Job security.* Having a good job is important. But lenders like to see stability, so they'll look at your job history over the past few years and ask for pay stubs and account statements. If you're self-employed, the standards are even stricter. Lenders will want to see your signed federal income tax forms.

Personal Issues

- *Job insecurity.* Even in the best of economic times, there are still companies that will lay off large numbers of employees because of sales slowdowns or mergers. If you're working for one of these corporations, and you're on (or may be on) the hit list, looking for a home should be way down on your priority list. By the same token, if you don't like what you're doing, and you're looking to switch career paths rather than just make a lateral move, you'll want to rent for a while. This gives you the flexibility to make a change that's good for you in the long run, without worrying about wrecking your credit if you fail to make a monthly mortgage payment.
- *Moving around.* If you're not certain where you want to live, or if you're on the brink of a career move to another state, consider renting for six months or a year, until you find the place that's right for you.
- *Neighborhood "know-nos."* If you're in a new town and don't know where you want to live, don't rush out to buy the first place you see. Buying in a neighborhood you know nothing about is one of home buyers' major mistakes. Consider renting in a neighborhood until you know whether you want the folks who live near you to be your permanent neighbors.

Emotional Issues

- *Life changes.* Do you know where you're going to be in five to ten years? I'm talking about your personal life. Are you single? Dating around? In a committed relationship? Married? Kids on the way? Married with children or an aging parent who lives with you? When it comes to buying a home, where you are today isn't nearly as important as where you'll be in five to ten years.

• *Settling down.* Homeownership isn't just about owning a home. In its best incarnation, it's about settling down and sinking roots into a community. Are you prepared to take the time to find the right home, maintain it, keep abreast of the changes in your neighborhood, and fight those who might have a negative impact on your home's value? Homeownership requires work. Renting requires writing a check. If you're not ready to be a homeowner, rent until you are.

There's an old joke in real estate that if you're single and want to get married, you should buy a studio apartment. Within six months of closing, you'll be in a long-term relationship, wondering where you're going to live and how you're going to sell your studio without losing your shirt. Bottom line: If you can't imagine where you'll be in five years, rent until your vision of your future becomes a little less cloudy. (Or, buy something big enough for two, three, or more.)

Ken and Debbie's Story

Ken and Debbie, two professionals, bought a two-bedroom condo just as they were getting married. They could afford the condo and wanted to stay close to the city until they were ready to move to the suburbs and start their family. They bought a two-bedroom unit because they figured it would be easy to sell and they could certainly accommodate a baby there for a year or two.

That was before they found out twins were coming. Suddenly, their two-bedroom condo started to seem small. They still wanted to live in the city for another two years, and they considered buying a three-bedroom condo for two years, and then selling it to trade up to a single-family house in a nice suburb. Another option was to rent a three-bedroom apartment.

The final option, which I told them I thought was the best and cheapest for them, was to stay in their two-bedroom apartment while the twins were small, then jump directly to a house in the suburbs. While they'd give up perhaps a year of city life, they'd save a ton of money on the costs of moving and the costs of sale (the broker's commission alone would eat up 6 percent of the proceeds).

The Two-Step

Sometimes, no matter what you do, you'll need to make a short-term interim move. It could happen if you take a job in another state, or if you sell your home before you find one to buy. If you're wondering whether to wait to list your home until you've found one to buy, the answer is easy: Don't wait. If you've got a buyer for your home at the price you want, take it and rent until you find what you want.

That's what my husband and I did. We had our old place listed for a year before we finally received a decent offer. Even though we didn't know where we wanted to live, we accepted the offer, set the closing date, and went house hunting. We came upon the house we now live in, and it was for sale, but we couldn't agree on a price with the owner. We signed a lease, rented for six months, and waited a few months more before going back to the owner and asking him to make a deal. By the time we went back, his life and attitude changed and he was ready to move. We spent six months living in a high-rise building in downtown Chicago, overlooking Lake Michigan, Grant Park, and the city skyline. It was a fabulous experience we'll never forget.

> If you know you'll be living in your new home for only a short period of time (say, less than five years), consider renting in an area where you'd never buy. The experience may change you in ways you never imagined.

HOW MUCH CAN I SPEND ON A HOME?

QUESTION
32

The answer to this question depends on three things: (1) how much you earn, (2) how much you have saved (or plan to save) toward a down payment, and (3) where interest rates are. Other incidental ingredients make up the home purchase pie, but let's examine these three first.

Annual Income

For conventional loans (not government-backed loans like those from the Federal Housing Administration (FHA) or the Veterans

Administration (VA), lenders like to see home buyers who meet certain debt-to-income guidelines. They want your overall debt (credit card, auto, school, and so on) to be no more than a fixed percentage of your income. The guidlines are set so that people don't buy more house than they can comfortably afford. The traditional ratio is 28:36: lenders will allow you to spend up to 28 percent of your *gross monthly income* on your home expenses (including your mortgage, property taxes, and insurance), and up to 36 percent of your *gross monthly income* on all of your debt (including your home expenses plus car loan, school loans, and credit card debt). The part about *gross* monthly income is important. After you subtract taxes, your take-home pay is substantially less and your mortgage payment is a substantially larger portion of your take-home pay. If you earn $60,000, your gross monthly income is $5,000. That means you could spend up to $1,400 (28 percent) on your mortgage, taxes, and insurance, and up to $1,800 (36 percent) on all of your debt. If you have no other debt, you could spend that much on your mortgage. Out of your take-home pay, which, at $5,000 gross, might be $3,600, that $1,400 actually feels more like 40 percent, not 28 percent. If you had $1,800 per month in debt, it would eat up half of your take-home pay.

Down Payment and Closing Costs

In the past decade, lenders have basically reinvented the mortgage loan by introducing a number of new takes and spins that have opened up the homeownership door to millions of home buyers. The benchmark for down payments used to be 20 percent. If you didn't have 20 percent in cash ($20,000 for each $100,000 of purchase price), forget it! There wasn't a loan you could get. Today, you need to put down only 3 percent on a home. Some lenders will even do zero-down loans, and a tiny percentage will lend you 125 percent of your purchase price. (These loans can be extremely expensive and carry credit-card-type interest rates.) In addition to your down payment, you once had to have 4 to 7 percent of your purchase price put away to cover closing costs, like points (a point is one percent of the loan amount) and fees. Today, you can get a *no-point, no-fee* (also known as "*no cost*") loan. Your interest rate will be a little bit higher, but you can close on your home with little or no cash. (Study after study shows that scraping together the cash for a down payment remains a first-time home buyer's biggest problem.)

Interest Rates

Interest rates can throw the whole game in your favor, if you play them right. If they're low, you can spend a lot more money on a home than if they're high. In the late 1990s, interest rates are as low as they've been in thirty years: at, or under, 7 percent for a thirty-year fixed-rate loan. (Indeed, for most of the 1990s, interest rates for the thirty-year fixed-rate loan have been in the 7 percent range.) Contrast that to the early 1980s, when interest rates topped out at 18 percent. What's the difference in spending power? Let's look at home buyers who have $60,000 annual income. They can spend a maximum of $1,400 per month on their mortgage, or go as high as $1,800 if they have no other debt. Subtract insurance and property taxes of $400 per month, and you're left with $1,000 to $1,400. At 7 percent interest rate, the maximum mortgage they can afford is $171,428.57 on the low side ($1,000 per month) or $240,000 on the high side ($1,400 per month). If interest rates were at 18 percent (as they were in 1982), spending levels would drop to $66,666.67 on the low side ($1,000 per month) and $93,333.33 ($1,400 per month) on the high side.

Don't forget to include a line on your worksheet for your property taxes and homeowners' insurance premiums. Figure these will be 2 to 3 percent of the cost of the home, although they might end up costing more (or less), depending on where you live. Lenders will subtract estimates for these items from the amount they'll allow you to borrow. Condominiums, co-ops, townhomes, and even some single-family home developments have monthly or annual assessments you'll have to pay. If you're considering purchasing in a development with a monthly or annual maintenance fee, be sure to include that in your calculations, or you could be off just enough to break your heart.

The worksheet on page 169 will walk you through the steps a lender takes to calculate how much loan you can afford. The calculators you'll find on the Internet will take you through the same approximate computation.

Prequalification and Preapproval

The easiest way to figure out how much you can afford is to get *prequalified* or *preapproved* for a home loan. Any local lender or national lender (via a toll-free number), and many Web sites, can do this for you. Getting prequalified for a loan means a lender has crunched your numbers and has figured out how much you can afford. Getting preapproved takes the process several steps further. The lender has you apply for the loan, verifies your documentation, and then gives you a written confirmation that you are approved for a loan up to a certain amount, provided that your home *appraises out* in value. ("Appraising out" means the lender has sent out an appraiser, or done an electronic appraisal, to verify that your home is worth what you're paying for it.)

The main benefit of getting preapproved for your loan is that it makes you a strong buyer. With a written confirmation, you may be able to make an offer as if you were a cash buyer, rather than someone who has a financing contingency. And in a very hot market, where many buyers are vying for only a few homes, that's a big plus.

RESOURCES

The last time anyone counted, there were more than 30,000 real-estate-related Web sites. To locate these, and to zero in on mortgages, visit the International Real Estate Digest <www.ired.com>, Yahoo! <www.yahoo.com>, or other portals on the Internet, or go to the real estate sites on American Online or MSN (the Microsoft Network).

To get additional information about the mortgage process, visit Fannie Mae <www.homepath.com> or Freddie Mac <www.freddiemac.com>. To check out rates, visit Bank Rate Monitor's site <www.bankrate.com>. To apply online, try a couple of different

Note: Remember that interest rates and how much you can borrow form an inverse relationship. The lower interest rates fall, the more you can borrow. Also, there are special first-time buyer programs that will allow you to put nothing down and will stretch the lending ratios to 36:41 (up to 36 percent of your Gross Monthly income can be spent on your mortgage; up to 41 percent can be spent on total debt). To play around with these ratios, substitute .41 for .36 in Step 2.

1. Gross monthly income from all sources   _____

2. Multiply by .28 (28 percent) or .36 (36 percent)   × _____

3. Subtract your current monthly debt service:

    Credit cards   _____

    Car loan(s)   _____

    Charge accounts   _____

    School loans   _____

    Other personal debt   _____

    Total debt service   − _____

4. Subtract homeowner association, condominium, or co-op assessment, if any   − _____

5. Maximum mortgage payment   = _____

6. Subtract real estate property and insurance tax escrow   − _____

7. Net mortgage amount   = _____

8. Multiply by 12 (months in a year)   × _____

9. Annual mortgage payment   = _____

10. Divide by current interest rate   ÷ _____

11. Total amount of mortgage   = _____

12. Down payment and closing cost cash added   + _____

13. Approximate amount you can spend on a home   = _____

approaches. Visit sites like Intuit's QuickenMortgage <www .quickenmortgage.com>, Microsoft HomeAdvisor <www.homeadvisor.com>, and HomeShark <www.homeshark.com>. These sites get a whole bunch of the top lenders together and essentially ask them to bid on your business. Also visit a lender's direct Web site (like Country-wide Home Loans <www.countrywide.com> or Chase Manhattan <www.chase.com>, and a mortgage broker such as Homeowners Finance Center, one of the earliest mortgage brokers to take loan applications on the Web <www.homeowners.com). You'll start to get a feel for rates by testing all of the waters.

After you've scouted out everything on the Net, give a call to a local mortgage broker or banker for a hands-on comparison and reality check of what you found online. You may be surprised to discover you can get a cheaper loan from your neighborhood lender than you can online.

With 30,000-odd real estate-related sites on the Internet, I haven't visited them all. And the Internet is changing every day. The lenders I've cited are large, well-funded companies that should show up at your closing. But make sure you talk to someone, at least on the telephone if not in person, before you sign loan documents. And, if you have any questions, talk to a real estate attorney before you get too far down in the process.

The Bottom Line

Being able to afford something means being able to sleep at night. The bottom line is: You don't necessarily have to spend everything your lender says you can afford (which I like to call *underbuying*). If it feels like too much money out the door each month, even if you know you're getting a huge raise next year that will make things more comfortable, don't do it. Peace of mind is worth a lot more than losing sleep over whether you'll ever be able to take your spouse or partner out to dinner, or buy your kids presents on their birthday, or take the family on a vacation.

WHAT KINDS OF TAX BREAKS EXIST FOR HOMEOWNERS?

As I said earlier, the federal government encourages homeownership. From a political point of view, homeowners typically vote more regularly than renters. They also take better care of their property and are more likely to get involved with their neighborhood. At the end of the 1990s, there were more than 67 million homeowners (roughly 67 percent of 100 million households in the country). During President Clinton's term in office, pressure has been put on Congress and on Fannie Mae and Freddie Mac (leaders in the secondary mortgage market) to find ways to expand homeownership. One result was the expansion of lending ratios and loan programs to encompass more marginal first-time buyers. Another was an expansion of tax breaks available to homeowners.

Here are the three major federal tax breaks for homeowners (you may be entitled to other tax breaks in your community):

1. *Mortgage interest deduction.* One of the biggest tax benefits to homeowners who qualify is the mortgage interest deduction. The federal government allows you to deduct from your gross earnings the mortgage interest you pay annually, which lowers the amount of income on which you pay taxes. You may deduct mortgage interest up to $1 million, for either a primary residence or a second home. You may also deduct the mortgage interest you pay on a home equity loan or an equity line of credit up to $100,000. But, to actually benefit from this tax perk, you must be able to itemize the deduction on your federal income tax return.

2. *Real estate property taxes.* Another tax deduction centers around the real estate property taxes you pay to your local government. You may deduct those property taxes from your gross income, and the adjustment to your gross income lowers the amount of tax you pay. If you don't itemize on your federal income tax form, this benefit will be lost to you.

3. *Tax-free capital gains.* The biggest boon to homeowners since the introduction of the mortgage interest deduction was the Taxpayer Relief Act of 1997, which changed the way sellers compute their capital gains profit on their home sale and, consequently, the amount of tax they have to pay on that profit.

The Act eliminated the one-time, $125,000 tax-free exclusion available to individuals over the age of 55, as well as the twenty-four-month rollover replacement rule. Formerly, to avoid paying capital gains taxes, a seller had twenty-four months to purchase a new home for the same price (or a higher price) as the home that was sold. According to current tax law, homeowners may now take up to $250,000 in capital gains (up to $500,000 if married) tax-free when they sell their home at least twenty-four months after purchasing it. To qualify, you must have lived in your home two out of the past five years. If you have to move sooner than two years, you may take a portion of your capital gains tax-free. Finally, you may take a $250,000 (or $500,000) tax exclusion once every twenty-four months.

How much does the mortgage interest deduction really help? It depends. It will only help you if you itemize on your federal income tax form. Approximately 60 percent of homeowners take the standard deduction, typically because it is more than the mortgage interest they pay. If you itemize, then the higher your tax bracket, the greater the mortgage interest deduction benefit. For example, if you are in the 15 percent bracket, you will save approximately 15 percent of every dollar you paid in mortgage interest, above the standard deduction. If you're in the 28 percent bracket, you'll save 28 cents on the dollar. Conversely, the tax bracket you're in helps you determine the interest rate you're really paying on your loan. For example, if your interest rate is 7 percent and you're in the 15 percent bracket, the real interest rate that you're paying (after the tax deduction) is 5.95 percent. If you're in the 28 percent tax bracket, your real interest rate would be even lower: 5.04 percent.

Home Office Deduction

If you have a home-based business, you may be entitled to a *home office deduction*. You are permitted to deduct the percentage of the mortgage and household expenses you pay for the portion of the home you use regularly and exclusively for your business, whether it's one-twentieth of your home or one-half. The deduction also allows you to depreciate the portion of your home that is used exclusively and regularly for business.

The problem is that when you sell your home, you must pay back the depreciation, and then pay capital gains taxes on the profit percentage that you claimed for the regular and exclusive use of your business. If you claimed that your business occupied 20 percent of your home, and you have a profit of $100,000 when you sell, you'll owe the IRS capital gains tax on the $20,000 that represents your business profit. There may be ways to get around this, however. Check with your tax preparer for more information.

WHAT ARE THE BENEFITS AND THE DANGERS OF COSIGNING LOANS?

QUESTION 34

Buying a home is increasingly expensive. And as housing economists know so well, for every rise in the price of homes, a group of home buyers gets priced out of the market.

Low interest rates certainly help more people to qualify for a home loan, but interest rates won't always be low. Another popular way to qualify to buy a home is by sharing someone's buying power. It's called *borrowing a signature* or *lending a signature*, or *cosigning*. The concept is also used for renting an apartment, buying a car, or getting a first credit card.

Melanie's Story

After college, Melanie bounced around from job to job, but spent money as if she was working on Wall Street. She soon maxed out her credit cards and was pumping hundreds of dollars each month into paying off her thousands of dollars of credit card debt and interest. By the time she paid off her debts, she realized she couldn't get any credit card companies to give her another credit card. Because her parents didn't want her to be without a credit card in case she got into financial trouble, they cosigned a new charge account for her, putting their own credit on the line. Unfortunately, Melanie hadn't learned her lesson and, with a new $4,000 limit burning a hole in her pocket, she went shopping. Soon, she maxed out that card, too. Because she still didn't have a job, she decided not to pay anything on the bills, even the $75-per-month minimum.

One day, her father tried to get his own credit limit increased before a business trip. He was soundly rejected, even though he paid his own bills on time. Why? Because he had cosigned his daughter's credit card and she didn't pay her bills. Melanie's parents' credit was severely blemished by their daughter's irresponsibility.

> ### *Carole and Marco's Story*
>
> When Carole and Marco wanted to buy their first home, a $120,000 two-story bungalow in California, they went to Marco's brother and his wife and asked them to cosign the loan. The two families agreed to share the house and expenses, with the understanding that, a few years later, they would pool their money again and buy Marco's brother and his wife their own house.
>
> Five years later, both families are living in their own homes, down the street from each other. Their credit is intact, and each couple is able to make the respective mortgage payments.

Cosigning: A Major Risk

How much is a signature worth? If it's Monet's and it's on a painting called "Water Lilies," it may be priceless. If it's yours and you cosign a loan for a relative or friend, your signature could be worth everything you own—your home, bank accounts, stocks, possessions, and good credit history.

There are pleasures in cosigning a loan for a close friend or relative. It feels good to give a deserving person a leg up and then watch that person grow financially strong enough to stand alone. On the other hand, there may be some serious consequences for you if that person topples and falls.

Most folks don't realize that cosigning a loan makes them entirely responsible for paying off the debt if the landlord, credit card company, or mortgage lender is not paid by the primary borrower. In other words, if your best friend cosigns your loan and you fail to make the mortgage payments, the lender will turn to your friend and demand those payments. If your house burns down and you don't have enough homeowner's insurance to cover the cost to rebuild the home or pay the amount owed on your mortgage, your friend's pockets had better be plenty deep.

If you cosign for a home purchase, your name will go on the title as an owner of the property. Your credit report will list the mortgage as a debt, and if your cosigner gets into financial trouble, your cosigner's creditors could come after everything you've worked hard to build.

What can you do? If you don't want to say no, think these questions through carefully:

1. *How well do you know the person?* Is it your brother who's asking, or a friend you don't know all that well? Is this someone you can rely on to come through?

2. *Ask to see a copy of the borrower's credit report.* What kinds of credit problems does your friend or relative have? Is this purchase going to be a repeat performance and mess up your excellent credit?

3. *Will you need to borrow money in the near future?* If you lend your signature, it might be more difficult for you to go out and get your own mortgage or auto loan.

4. *What kind of lender will you be?* Will you be constantly harping on your friend or relative to see whether the bills and mortgage have been paid? Or will you relax and not think about it? Losing the ability to sleep at night is one excellent reason to decline to cosign a loan.

If you cosign a loan for your children and then you die, the amount of the loan may be seen (for IRS purposes) as a part of your children's inheritance, and they may then owe inheritance taxes on it. The IRS's position is that your children would have been unable to get a loan without your signature. But if your estate is, or will be, worth more than $600,000 (or the current inheritance tax-free amount), you'll want to make sure you've properly prepared your estate. (See Chapter 14 for more information.)

WHICH TYPE OF MORTGAGE SHOULD I CHOOSE?

QUESTION
35

Shopping for a loan is like shopping for plums in midsummer. There are yellow ones, tiny red ones, fat black ones, tart green ones, shiny purple ones, and ones that look green on the outside but are bright red on the inside. Plums are grown in northern Michigan, in Latin America, and, organically, in northern California. Which plums are right for you? Are you cooking with them, baking with them, or eating them raw? Your choice may depend on the cheapest price, the best taste, or the specific variety needed for a recipe. Bottom line: Although they're usually best in the heart of the summer, if you're willing to pay, you can buy good plums year-round, from just about anywhere in the world's temperate or tropical zones.

Mortgages also come in a variety of shapes and sizes, and you have the ability to choose a loan that suits your particular needs. You can get it with or without points, fees, and costs. You can get a fixed-rate, an adjustable, or a hybrid loan. There are about a half-dozen basic types of loans which can be altered, adjusted, or prepaid so that you can get 'em the way you want 'em.

Before we discuss the basic types of home loans, you should know what an *amortization schedule* is. When you take out a loan, you pay the lender monthly installments of principal and interest. In the beginning of the loan term, you pay almost all interest. When you're halfway through the loan, your payments are relatively balanced portions of principal and interest. By the end of the loan, you're repaying almost all principal.

The schedule of payments of principal and interest is called the amortization schedule. Typically, it has a thirty-year or fifteen-year length because most mortgages are given on those terms. You can alter this schedule by adding a little bit extra, called a *prepayment*, to each loan payment. Prepaying your loan even a little means you'll save thousands of dollars over the life of the loan, and you can prepay most mortgages. Just watch out for prepayment penalties. (In Question 56, I discuss prepaying and when it might be a good idea.)

Here are the basic loan types you're bound to run across during your search for a mortgage:

- *Fixed-rate mortgage (FRM).* The granddaddy of them all, the fixed-rate mortgage, was the first real mortgage to be introduced after World War II, and it remains the most popular, especially when interest rates are low. The rate is rock-steady; you know exactly how much you're going to pay each month for the entire life of the loan. A fixed-rate mortgage comes in thirty-year, and fifteen-year lengths, although you might be able to find one at a twenty- or forty-year length. (Stay away from forty-year loans. For the extra $50 per month you might save on a $100,000 loan, it will take you twenty years to start building up some real equity. Instead, consider an adjustable rate mortgage.)

- *Adjustable-rate mortgage (ARM).* This mortgage has variable interest rates; they fluctuate according to the financial index or benchmark to which they are tied. Some indexes move slowly, others change quickly. Some ARMs adjust monthly, semiannually, annually, or every three or five years. ARMs are typically used when interest rates are high because the starting rate is so much lower than the thirty-year fixed-rate mortgage (FRM). The initial rate (also called the *teaser rate*) is sometimes two points below a fixed-rate loan, but the ARM will adjust upward, typically a point or two, each time the loan adjusts. On typical ARMs, the interest rate may rise only five or six points over the life of the loan. In a given year, however, the amount the rate may rise is capped at one or two percentage points. The rate could never go from 5 to 10 percent overnight (although you'll want to read the loan's fine print just to be sure). Over the years, research has shown that folks who got ARMs tended to pay less for their loans than buyers who chose fixed-rate mortgages. ARMs are riskier, because the rate could go up, but if you're planning to stay seven years or less, you should probably choose some sort of ARM. Lenders commonly offer semiannual, annual, and three-, five-, seven-, and ten-year ARMs. The rate is fixed for the first period. The mortgage either adjusts once per term, or it converts at, say, the seven-year mark into a one-year ARM (a 7/1 loan, in which the interest rate is fixed for the first seven years after which the loan converts to a one-year ARM), after which it adjusts annually.

- *Hybrid loan.* Hybrid loans include 3/1 (pronounced "three-one"), 5/1, 7/1, and 10/1 loans. Hybrids take the steadiness of a fixed-rate loan and marry it to the slightly riskier nature of an ARM, for an interest rate slightly below a fixed-rate mortgage but above a true ARM. *Two-step* loans from Fannie Mae do the same thing. The most common forms of the hybrid loan are a 5/25 ("five-twenty-five") and a 7/23 ("seven-twenty-three"). These loans carry an interest rate that is fixed for the first five or seven years. Then the loan converts into either a one-year ARM (adjusts annually) or a fixed-rate loan, typically at a higher interest rate than might otherwise be found on the open market. The starting interest rate is lower than a standard thirty-year loan, but it is amortized on a thirty-year schedule. In other words, you'll have paid off the loan in thirty years, but your payments may vary from year to year.

- *Balloon loan.* A balloon loan is typically a short-term loan (three, five, seven, ten, or fifteen years in length). During that time, you typically make regular payments of principal and interest on a thirty-year amortization schedule. But at the end of a ten-year balloon, you owe the remaining balance of the loan in a lump-sum payment. Sometimes, balloon loans are arranged as "interest only," which means you pay only the interest on the loan and owe the entire principal at the end of the loan term. Balloon loans were the original American mortgage. Why would anyone want them today? They still tend to carry a lower interest rate than a thirty-year fixed and even some two-step loans.

- *Negative equity loans.* This type of loan isn't too popular anymore, mostly because home buyers (and lenders) have realized what a lousy deal it is. With a negative equity loan, your mortgage and interest payments are fixed at a dollar amount that doesn't equal all the interest you owe on your loan. The interest that you don't pay back is added on at the end of your loan and could significantly add to the amount you owe. When interest rates were 18 percent, people liked negative equity loans because they could buy property at a lower monthly payment than was available with a thirty-year fixed-rate mortgage. But the introduction of the 5/25 and 7/23 has rendered negative equity loans obsolete.

- *Graduated payment loan.* This is another form of loan that has gone the way of the wooden wagon wheel. A graduated payment loan is a stepped-payment mortgage that starts out with a below-market interest rate, but the rate increases a certain number of percentage points each year until the loan levels out at a higher interest rate. The loan is calculated on a thirty-year amortization schedule, so that you pay it off in thirty years.

- *FHA loan.* A government-backed Federal Housing Administration (FHA) mortgage is often called "the first-time buyer's loan" because it offers an expanded debt-to-income ratio, an extra-low down payment mortgage, and financing for those with, shall we say, less-than-perfect credit. Most conventional lenders can issue FHA loans, and, in recent years, they have come up with cheaper alternatives for buyers with little or nothing to put down and not-so-great credit. One nice thing about FHA loans is that if you get into trouble regarding your payments, you can ask your lender for "forbearance": the lender has to arrange a special repayment program while you get back on your feet financially. Many lenders will tell you that this is "impossible," but if you have an FHA loan, they are required by federal law to help you.

- *VA Loan.* Veterans of the United States armed forces are entitled to a wide variety of benefits, including the opportunity to get a zero-down-payment home loan backed by the Department of Veterans Affairs. The VA started the program at the end of World War II. Since 1945, more than 13 million veterans have obtained loans worth more than $360 million. Not having to put down cash is a boon, but VA loans carry interest rates fixed by the VA (which may be higher than conventional loan rates). If you actually want a zero-down loan, you'll have to pay extremely high fees. And, of course, only qualified veterans can apply. You are eligible if you served ninety days of wartime service in World War II, the Korean Conflict, the Vietnam War, or the Persian Gulf War, and were not dishonorably discharged. You are also eligible if you served between six and twenty-four months of continuous active duty from 1981 through today, and were not dishonorably discharged. Check with your local VA office for more details on eligibility.

- *Biweekly mortgage.* With a regular mortgage, you make twelve monthly payments per year. With a biweekly mortgage, you make twenty-six payments, one every other week, or the equivalent of thirteen monthly loan payments per year. A biweekly loan allows you to pay down the principal faster and save thousands of dollars in interest. The problem I have with biweekly mortgages isn't the concept; I think you *should* prepay your loan to some degree (see Question 56 for a further discussion of prepaying a loan). What I don't like are the lenders who'll charge $500 to $800 to set up a biweekly schedule for you when you could do it yourself for free. Also, once you're tied into a biweekly schedule, you have to make those payments *or else.* Better to set up your own schedule. (Again, see Question 56 for tips and suggestions on prepaying.)

- *Shared appreciation mortgage.* There are nonprofit housing organizations around the country that sometimes offer special programs for first-time buyers. With a shared appreciation mortgage, the housing organization will offer an extra-low interest rate, or will give you part of the cash for the down payment. You make the monthly mortgage payments and get all the tax benefits, and when you sell your home (if you sell), you pay them a share of the profits. Community Development Block Grant money is typically used to help make up the difference between a low-to-moderate-income family's resources, and what the lender wants to see on the balance sheet.

- *Very low down payment and zero down payment loan.* FHA loans were invented to help folks who didn't have enough cash saved for a 20 percent down payment. Over the years, the down payment threshold has fallen sharply. When conventional lenders saw that borrowers weren't really defaulting all that often with only 3 percent down, they leaped into the fray and began offering super-low down payment mortgages, too. In 1998, the final barrier was broken. Bank of America (which, in 1998, merged with Nation's Bank) offered a specialized zero down payment loan to borrowers who met certain income restrictions, Freddie Mac also announced it would back a new zero-down program that will be available nationwide beginning in 1999. As soon as other lenders and investors in the secondary mortgage market see that the default rate isn't sky-high, I believe they'll offer other zero-down programs for first-time buyers.

- *125 percent loan.* As we move toward the year 2000, lenders are falling all over themselves to lend money—even to folks who probably shouldn't borrow it. If you're in need of cash, some lenders may be willing to lend you 125 percent of the value of your home. As always, beware of lenders that appear to give you something for nothing. The deal behind the 125 percent loans (some lenders will go as high as 130 percent) is that you get a regular 80 percent loan at the going rate, then a 20 percent loan at a slightly higher rate, and then the top 25 percent of the loan at an outrageous, credit-card-level rate. On top of that, you'll pay high fees and points. If you're really in a jam, this may be the cheapest way to borrow money. But here's an important caveat: *Although you can typically deduct mortgage interest paid up to $1 million per year, the IRS believes the extra 25 percent above your home's value is a personal loan, not a home loan. A tax ruling early in 1998 seemed to indicate that the IRS would disallow the deduction for any amount above your home's current value.* (Consult with your tax preparer for more details.)

- *Construction loan, and other loans that let you fix up your home.* There are 125 percent loans that are fully deductible. If you want to borrow money to renovate your home, you may be able to borrow up to 125 percent (or more) of your home's value, if you plan to use the extra 25 percent in cash to fix up your home and if, when you're finished, your home will be worth at least what you're borrowing. First-time buyers should check out Fannie Mae's Web site <www.fanniemae.com or www.homepath.com> for more information on these special mortgage/renovation loans, called 203K loans. Construction loans require you to have plans in hand. An appraiser will then estimate what your home will be worth when it's completely finished, and you will be allowed to borrow based on that number. Unfortunately, you could wind up with a problem if the appraisal is off and you can't borrow enough money to build what you want.

Choosing the Right Loan

The first issue to deal with is timing, and then you have to consider points, costs, and fees. Before you apply for a home loan, think through your answers to the following questions:

1. *How long am I planning to live in my home?* If you're only going to be there five to seven years, there's no reason for you to get a thirty-year fixed-rate loan. You'll save thousands by getting some form of ARM, such as a 5/1 or a 7/1, and you'll still have the same degree of stability with payments for as long as it's going to matter. If you're going to be there ten or fifteen years, or longer (i.e., "I'll die in this house"), then a fixed-rate loan of some length is probably a good idea. If you can afford the payments, go with the fifteen-year loan. You'll save more than half the interest on a thirty-year loan for the same amount.

2. *Do I want to pay points and fees?* A point is one percent of the loan amount. Traditionally, you pay points and fees in cash up front to get a lower interest rate. With the creation and popularity of *no-point, no-cost* loans, you can choose to pay a slightly higher interest rate (typically ¼ to ½ points higher than the published rate) by not paying anything in cash when you close on your loan. Or, you can essentially *buy down* your interest rate by paying points and fees. When should you pay points? Points are fully deductible in the year you purchase your home, or you may deduct them over the life of the loan. If you're refinancing, you may only deduct them over the life of your loan. If you're closing in the middle of the year and want to maximize your deductions for that year, and you have the cash, you may want to pay points. If you're going to be in this home forever

181

(or thirty years, whichever comes first), you may also want to buy down the rate with points. The only way to know is to do the numbers. Take a paper and pencil and figure out how much you'll save each month with the lower rate. Then add up the months until you've "paid off" the buy-down. If you pay it off in eighteen months or less, it's probably a good idea.

3. *Am I a risk taker?* You'll ask yourself this question any number of times as you read through this book, and for each set of circumstances (budget, retirement, real estate), the answer may be different. For financing, if you're a risk taker, you might want to go with an ARM, perhaps a 3/1, and then bet that rates will be as low or lower in three years, and you'll refinance. Or, you can do what my friend Ron did: refinance your one-year ARM every year with a no-cost loan, and get the bonus rate each year. Either way, you're getting a super-low rate, paying perhaps a point (or more) less than your neighbor with the thirty-year fixed-rate loan. Then again, one day, interest rates may rise and you'll change your mind about fixed-rate mortgages.

Unless a lender's fee covers something real (i.e., an out-of-pocket expense for the lender), its only use may be to pad the lender's bottom line. For example, the lender may pay $2 to $15 per credit report pulled, but you'll pay $50 to $80 to have yours handed to you. Or, you'll be charged a document preparation fee for preparing the loan's closing documents, but the information is already in the computer. In the same vein, "underwriting" is what lenders *do:* they underwrite—that is, approve and process—loans. So an "underwriting fee" on top of your other fees seems redundant. If you spend enough time on the Internet or the telephone with a handful of lenders, each will understand you're a serious borrower and your business is something they want. This is the time to really negotiate your fees and costs. Once you apply for the loan, and sign the application, it's too late. And, be certain everything you've agreed to orally ends up written on the application you've signed, or you're out of luck.

Seller Financing

Seller financing can be a great way to go. The seller acts as the bank (as far as you're concerned, there is no difference) and will typically

WORKSHEET
Comparing Loans

Expenses	Loan A	Loan B	Loan C	Loan D
Loan type				
Interest rate				
Loan term				
APR				
Monthly payment				
ARM index				
Interest rate caps:				
Each adjustment period				
Lifetime				
Discount points				
Origination points				
Application fee				
Credit report fee				
Document preparation fee				
Processing fee				
Appraisal fee				
Tax service fee				
Underwriting fee				
Flood insurance certification fee				
Courier charges				
Title insurance:				
Lender's policy				
Special endorsements				
Recording assignment of mortgage				
Other fees				

give you the market rate without charging you extra points and fees. For sellers who don't need lump-sum cash and have thoroughly vetted the buyer, seller financing can provide an excellent steady stream of income.

If you want to buy a home via seller financing, look for a home owned by folks who probably won't need the cash from the sale to finance the purchase of their next home. Your best bet is elderly homeowners who are moving to a rental apartment or vacation home they already own, or a seller who rents out the property. Ask your real estate agent to look for sellers who meet the seller-financing criteria.

The Bottom Line

If you don't choose your lender well, and you get hammered by junk fees and costs, it almost doesn't matter which loan you choose. Before you sign a loan application:

1. *Learn everything you can before you apply for a loan.* The Internet is a great resource. Check out the "Resources" section of Question 32 before you apply. Read other books. Pick up the free pamphlets local lenders offer. Go to a free first-time-buyer seminar. Ask a lot of questions. There's good inforamtion all over the place.

2. *Make sure you understand the different types of loan programs being offered.* Ask questions, and use the worksheet on page 183 to compare loan choices on an apples-to-apples basis.

3. *Negotiate points and fees before you sign the application.* Make sure what you've agreed to orally with the lender is in writing. Once you've signed, negotiation time is over.

WHEN SHOULD I REFINANCE MY LOAN?

Years ago, the refinancing rule went something like this: If interest rates dropped 2 percent or more below the rate on your loan, you should refinance. In that way, your savings would pay off the costs within two years, and you'd reap the benefits of lower rates.

Today, with the popularity of no-point, no-fee, no-cost loans, you should consider refinancing if the no-cost loan rate drops below the current interest rate on your loan. The catch is: You have to look at the no-cost rate, not the general interest rate that's often quoted. That rate is usually ½ point higher than the general rate (a point is 1 percent of the loan amount) because of the fees and costs built into the interest rate. Some lenders will also allow you to fold your closing costs back into the dollar amount of your loan and get the very best rate they offer. This is a good deal, particularly if you'll be refinancing or selling in the near future.

If you are going to pay points when you refinance, you should know that you must amortize and deduct them over the life of the loan. Points paid when you purchase a home are entirely deductible in the year you closed on your home purchase. However, if you sell your home or refinance again the year after you initially refinance, you may deduct your unused points at that time.

Prepayment Penalties

Refinancing has become so simple, and so popular, that a writer in the early 1990s coined a phrase to capture the soul of those gluttons for punishment who are in a near-continuous cycle of refinancing: "Refi-junkies." These folks are always scoping out new interest rates, gathering together their information, and applying for or being approved for a loan.

They may be onto something. People are refinancing so often that it has started to affect the way lenders securitize loans. Lenders know, when you take out a thirty-year fixed-rate mortgage, the odds are you'll get a new loan within five to seven years because you're either selling or refinancing your home. But with the steadily low interest rates of the late 1990s, folks have started refinancing every one or two years, which changes the profit margins for these lenders. In 1998, some homeowners refinanced three times within an eight-month period as rates dropped.

In an effort to bring some steadiness back to the lending industry, some mortgage lenders are reintroducing *prepayment penalties*—fees that you'll have to pay if you refinance your loan before a certain number of years has elapsed. (Prepayment fees are illegal in some states. check with your real estate attorney for more details.) Some prepayment penalties kick out after a year; others, after four years. If a lender adds a prepayment penalty to your loan, you'll typically get a lower rate. But before you sign on, make sure you understand exactly what the prepayment penalty is, and what it will cost you if you are forced to refinance your loan, sell your home, or otherwise pay off your loan. In some cases, you may pay as much as 2 to 4 percent of the loan amount.

QUESTION 37

SHOULD I TAKE OUT A HOME EQUITY LOAN?

In its 1998 National Housing Survey, Fannie Mae, the largest mortgage investor in the secondary market (Fannie Mae buys loans from lenders who give mortgages to consumers, thereby providing the lenders with more money for new loans), asked consumers about home equity loans. Twenty-five percent of Baby Boomers (born 1946 to 1964) currently have home equity loans, compared to slightly more than 19 percent of Generation Xers (born 1964–1974). Both groups agree on one thing: Home equity loans are great vehicles for renovating homes and paying off debts.

What is a *home equity loan?* It is simply a second mortgage that you take out against the cash value (called *equity*) you've built up in your home. In effect, you pledge your home as collateral for the new home equity loan (just as you did when you took out your first mortgage).

Why would you want to take out a home equity loan?

1. *It's tax-deductible.* You may deduct the interest paid on a home equity loan up to $100,000 per year.

2. *You can consolidate your debt.* If you've got credit cards and other sky-high interest-rate loans, you may want to reduce your monthly payments. Use your home equity line of credit to pay off your other nondeductible loans.

3. *It's a ready source of cash.* You can use the money for anything, including paying for a college education, home improvements, a new car, or even polo ponies. There are few, if any, restrictions on the use of home equity loans.

How Does Your Equity Grow?

Equity accumulates in one of two ways: (1) each time you make a monthly mortgage payment, the principal portion of your payment helps build up your equity in your home; and (2) your home appreciates in value.

For example, if you paid $100,000 for your home and put down 20 percent, you'd have $20,000 in equity. After five years of mortgage payments, you'd probably have added another $3,000 in equity by paying down your mortgage balance. However, during those five years, your home's value may have appreciated. If you sold today, you'd collect $120,000. Now you have $43,000 in equity in your home ($20,000 down payment, $20,000 in home appreciation, and $3,000 in mortgage balance paid).

Lennie and Gene's Story

After many years of renting in the San Francisco area, Lennie and Gene finally saved up enough money to buy a house. It was 1991, and people were getting fired left and right. A lot of them put their homes up for sale, and prices dropped.

Lennie and Gene bought a house from sellers who had been recently fired (in a neat turn of fate, they ended up renting Lennie and Gene's apartment). The house needed some fixing up, which Lennie and Gene did themselves.

The house was on the fringes of an up and coming neighborhood, and as the years started to roll by, the neighborhood improved and prices started to rise. Lennie and Gene started with about $25,000 in equity in the house—about 10 percent of the purchase price. By 1993, their home had risen another $25,000 in value, so they had $50,000 in equity. By 1995, the house had jumped another $50,000 in value, so they had $100,000 in equity. By early 1998, homes on their block were selling for $250,000 to $350,000 more than they had paid for their home, giving them an estimated $285,000 to $400,000 in equity.

When they went to get a home equity loan to fix their carport, they were stunned to see that their house had more than doubled in value since 1991.

Although many homeowners' equity rose at a stunning rate during the 1990s (particularly during the latter half of the decade), Lennie and Gene really lucked out with their timing. Their home equity had soared, and so, in turn, did their net worth.

Tapping Your Home Equity

The nice thing about having home equity is that you have access to a sizable source of tax-deductible cash should you need it (and can afford it). There are three ways you can tap into your home equity:

1. *Refinance your existing mortgage.* If you want to take cash out when you refinance, lenders will hold you to 75 or 80 percent of your home's current value. But if your home has doubled in value, this could be a significant source of funds.

   Why do it? You'll have only one mortgage payment (other options require more than one), and you'll be able to take advantage of the lowest interest rates available.

   Why not? If you need to refinance for more than 80 percent, you're looking at getting both a new first loan and a home equity loan. If that's the case, you would be better off getting a home equity loan or line of credit in the first place.

2. *Get a home equity loan.* Also called a second mortgage, a home equity loan allows you to tap up to 85 or even 90 percent of your home's value. You'll get the cash in one lump sum, and start paying interest on it from day one.

   Why do it? It gives you all the cash you need, and it's tax-deductible.

   Why not? If you're borrowing cash to pay for your kids' education, or for a long-term renovation project, there's no sense in paying for money you're not going to use immediately—unless, of course, you find an investment that will more than pay the costs of borrowing the cash.

3. *Get a home equity line of credit.* Sometimes referred to as an *equity installment loan*, the lender approves you for a home equity line of credit up to 85 or 90 percent of your home's value and then hands you a checkbook. You incur no interest charges until you actually write a check to pay for something.

   Why do it? Like a home equity loan, a home equity line of credit is tax-deductible, and if you're paying for a home renovation, it's handy to be able to write the checks as they're needed.

   Why not? If you're not careful, the temptation to dip into the home equity checkbook can leave you in the lurch when the time comes to pay for a big-ticket item, like a car, home improvement, or college education.

Typically, lenders stretch your debt-to-income ratios when you apply for a home equity loan. If you can borrow up to 36 percent of your gross monthly income for all debt, including your first mortgage when you buy a home, a lender might let you stretch as high as 45 percent—or more!—when you get a home equity loan. But be prepared to pay off any other liens against your property (including second mortgages, construction or home improvement loans, or other home equity loans) before you get approved.

Getting the Best Deal

Shopping for a home equity loan is a lot like shopping for a first mortgage. You'll need to price it out. What can you get if you pay points and fees? If you pay nothing up front? Then, you'll need to compare the interest rate, points and fees, and loan types, and try to get each lender to bid for your business.

You can get a home equity loan with a fixed interest rate or with an adjustable rate tied to an index. The loan can have a variety of different lengths, from short-term (one to five years) to long-term (typically, fifteen to twenty years). Many home equity loans are balloon loans: you pay either principal or interest on a thirty-year amortization schedule for the length of the loan, and then ante up the rest in cash on the last day of the loan term. On some loans, you'll pay interest only; on others, you'll pay a combination of interest and principal.

Interest rates are all over the map for home equity loans. You might pay slightly more (perhaps a half point or so) than the going thirty-year fixed-rate loan, or you may be charged prime plus one to two points. If the prime lending rate is at 7 percent and your home equity loan is pegged at two points above prime, you could be paying 9 percent for your cash. If you have poor credit, you might have to settle for a more expensive option.

Like first mortgages, most home equity loans have a "due on sale" clause. If you sell your home, you'll have to pay off both your home equity loan and your first mortgage at the closing.

Start by checking out the going rate for home equity loans in your area. You can go online to Bank Rate Monitor <www.bankrate.com>, and then look through the advertisements in the real estate section of your local newspaper. Call the lender who holds your current mortgage, and check out your bank's rates. Credit unions typically offer their members some of the cheaper loans around.

If you don't like what you see, keep looking. Many financial institutions offer home equity loans and lines of credit, so you probably won't go begging for programs to evaluate.

If you're only going to borrow money for the short term—say, until you've received a couple of year-end bonuses—you'll probably want to look into a variable-rate home equity loan or line of credit. In that way, you'll benefit from the introductory rate and probably pay less than if you opted for a fixed-rate loan.

Read the Fine Print

The proverbial saw, "If it sounds too good to be true, it definitely is," applies to home equity loans, too. Here are some caveats:

- *Keep your eye on the loan amount.* Your lender may not tell you how much you'll owe each month; the exact amount depends on how much you borrow. But you will be told how to calculate how much you should be paying. The calculation may read: "5 percent of the outstanding balance." If you've just written a check for $5,000 from your home equity line of credit, you'll owe $250 at the beginning of the next month.

- *Don't get sold a home equity bag of tricks.* Some lenders may promise you fixed monthly payments even with an adjustable rate loan. How is that possible? It's an old version of a negative amortization loan. If the rate goes up, your payment stays the same, but the extra interest you'd normally owe gets tacked onto the back end of the loan. You could wind up owing money just when you thought you'd made your last payment.

- *Credit card, anyone?* Some lending institutions will give you a home equity credit card rather than a checkbook, and will specify no minimum amount that can be spent. (Other lenders insist that home equity line of credit checks be written for no less than $500.) That's pretty dangerous, particularly if you're using your home equity loan to pay off high-interest-rate credit card debt—even if the amount is tax deductible.

- *Beware any lenders bearing gifts.* Way back when, bankers and lenders gave out toasters to lure customers. Today, you might get air miles or discounts on cars for using certain credit cards (see Question 15). Some lenders will co-brand their home equity loan programs to give you a discount on a car if you get your car loan from the home equity lender. Fine and dandy, but look at the fine print. You may be paying a sky-high interest rate for the car, plus a higher rate, points, and fees on the equity loan. You might be better off shopping around for the best deal and negotiating separately for your new car or truck.

The Bottom Line

As the 1990s end, the mortgage market has taken a huge leap forward. More than $1 trillion worth of loans were completed in 1998, the market's third record year in a row. Lenders had tons of cash and were competing heavily for borrowers. That's the best situation for you to be in if you're shopping for a mortgage or home equity loan. Make sure you check out all your options and negotiate for the best deal before you sign the paperwork. You could save yourself thousands of dollars.

WHAT DO I NEED TO KNOW IF I'M GOING TO OWN A SECOND HOME?

QUESTION
38

For a number of years, home ownership experts have been predicting a boom in second-home ownership. The reasons for this optimism are simple: The most likely ages of people who buy a second home are: 55 to 65, then 45 to 55, and then 65 to 75. The Baby Boom generation hit age 50 during the mid-1990s (led by Boomer poster child President Clinton, who had his fiftieth birthday while in office), and are now heading into the years when they are most likely to buy second homes.

According to the most recent U.S. Census estimates (which are years out of date), approximately 6 percent of American households own a second home. But other estimates are higher. Some observers see second-home ownership approaching 10 percent, especially if all of the time-share units sold during the 1990s are included.

The real boom in vacation homes probably hasn't hit yet. When it does, it's likely to last well into the first couple of decades of the new millennium. Why? Because the main crunch of Baby Boomers will hit age 50 in 2007 and the last of them will reach age 50 in 2014, smack in the middle of the best second-home buying years. One economist, David Weil of Brown University, projects that Baby Boomers could buy second homes until 2023 (a Boomer born in 1964 would be 59 in 2023, just in the middle of the peak second-home buying years). And, because the majority of folks who purchase second homes eventually retire to them, it could go even beyond that.

We're living longer, and healthier, and we're much more active in retirement than we used to be. Shuffleboard used to be the game of retirement. Today, we're much more likely to be skiing, roller-blading, and mountain biking in our golden years. Vacation homes provide the entertainment and recreational opportunities we'll have time for after we retire. Typically, these home sites are located within 150 miles of our principal residences, a reasonable driving distance for family and friends who will visit. The most obvious reason for growth in the vacation market? Money. The 1990s boom in the stock market fueled a tremendous growth of personal wealth. All of that cash has to go somewhere, and, for many people, the focus is on home: home improvements, and everything from time-shares in Mexico to weekend cottages on a lake or farmhouses on real acreage.

It also helps that there have been thousands of stories of stunning appreciation in the vacation market. In Aspen, Colorado, a two-bedroom, two-bath condo at The Gant could've been bought for $45,000 when it opened twenty odd years ago. In 1998, you'd have been hard-pressed to purchase one for less than $650,000. In 1990, a couple paid $250,000 for eight mountaintop acres in a resort development that was then far beyond the edges of Colorado's Vail Valley. Today, the land alone is worth close to $1 million, and with the 6,000-square-foot house they built, the value of the whole property is probably close to $3 million. That's quite a ten-year return on an investment.

What do you need to know? Here are some tips if you decide you have to have a second home:

1. *All locations won't appreciate 1,000 percent over ten years.* Some second homes will be great investments, but you should buy

your second home because you want to *use* it. Still, if you want to buy a home that will appreciate, all the regular home-buying rules apply: Buy the cheapest house on the best block and fix it up; buy in the best neighborhood you can afford; and make sure that plenty of activities, shopping, and culture are nearby. The site should be easily reachable, and the area should be relatively crime-free (the last thing people on vacation want to worry about is whether their mountain bikes will be stolen).

2. *Buy a home you're going to use.* Unless you're really buying it to rent out (and you've done the numbers), buy a second home you're going to use. If you're not sure how often you'll use a second place, try renting a home or a condo for a season. See how often you get there, and decide whether that's really where you'd want to own property. Don't fool yourself into thinking that if you owned it you'd visit more frequently. (And don't forget, every weekend you're at your second home is a weekend you're not with friends and family in your own neighborhood. Your kids won't get to their friends' birthday parties, and you may miss some special events. But if you regularly go to your weekend home, you may make new friends there.)

3. *Easy access.* Two-thirds of second homes are located within 150 miles of an owner's primary residence. The best second-home locations should take no more than four to five hours to reach, whether you drive all the way there, or drive to the airport. If it's too far, or too expensive to get to, you won't use it.

4. *Diversions and recreation galore.* Don't choose a second-home location because there's nothing to do and you think you're going to totally relax. Find a place that has a lot to do, preferably year-round. In recent years, the Hamptons (a group of towns on the tip of Long Island, New York) have stretched the visitor/renter season (formerly Memorial Day to Labor Day) from Easter to Thanksgiving by introducing cultural events like film festivals and traveling shows that give people something to do when the weather won't cooperate. At a minimum, you should have access to water (a small lake or river will suffice) and open space for summer or warm climates, and outdoor and indoor activities for cold-weather areas.

5. *Security is important.* Second-home owners want to feel that they can walk outside without worrying about their personal safety. Many city-dwellers want a place where their kids can

193

run free and be safe. For Baby Boomers, safety is right on top of the list, and that doesn't mean buying a house with a top-notch alarm system. In fact, if you have to have an alarm on your second home, it may not be the right location.

6. *Planned growth.* Some of the most successful second-home locations are now completely built out, like Hilton Head, South Carolina. But others, like New Buffalo, on Lake Michigan in the southwest corner of Michigan, have grown a huge amount in the past decade. Whether you look for a place that hasn't been completely developed or one that's already been completely filled in, make sure the town has a plan for its development. Many Americans end up retiring to their second homes, and they'd rather retire to a place that has a sense of order and community than to a hodgepodge of stuff and styles.

7. *Play the margins.* If you can't afford to buy the place next door to Steven Spielberg in the Hamptons, perhaps you can find a place on the edge of town, away from the water, that needs some fixing up. Buying on the edge of a resort town or development can yield impressive returns down the line. Remember the couple who bought on the edge of Vail Valley. Today, there are developments much farther down the road, and they're considered close in.

8. *Are there celebrities?* Never underestimate the value of star power—even the local variety. When the fact that Chicago's former mayor, Richard M. Daley, and his family had vacationed in Grand Beach, Michigan, for a number of generations, interest (and prices) in the area swelled. That's nothing compared to how much some celebrities have done for Aspen, Telluride, the Hamptons, and Palm Beach (the playground for the rich, royalty and Donald Trump).

9. *Tax trap.* There's good news and bad news here. The good news is: You can deduct the interest paid on your mortgages up to $1 million for first and second homes. The bad news is: If you make money buying and selling a vacation home, you'll have to pay taxes on it. On the other hand, if you sell your primary residence and take your $250,000 (or up to $500,000) capital gains exclusion, and then move into your vacation home (and live there for two out of the past five years), you may be able to sell that home and take another $250,000 to $500,000 in tax-free capital gains.

WHAT IS A REVERSE MORTGAGE?

QUESTION
39

A *reverse mortgage* is a way of allowing homeowners age sixty-two and older to tap into their home equity to help finance their retirement. It's called a reverse mortgage because, instead of paying the lender each month, the borrower receives either a lump sum or monthly payments from the lender. The payments can continue until you've used up the allotted equity in your home, or for the rest of your life. And, you have no obligation to repay the cash until you or your heirs sell your home.

This cash doesn't come cheaply. The points and fees to originate a reverse mortgage are steep, and not every senior who qualifies is going to get a good deal. In fact, if you end up paying off your reverse mortgage within a couple of years, you could wind up paying points, fees, and other costs equal to 50 percent of the amount you received!

But there is a specialized group of homeowners for whom a reverse mortgage can make sense. To start with, you (and your spouse, if you own your home jointly) must be sixty-two years of age, or older. (If you're much younger, perhaps you'll consider this for your homeowner parents or grandparents.) Next, your home must be virtually or completely debt-free. You won't be paying back this loan in your lifetime, so there is no income or credit requirement to qualify. And, you can roll into the loan the points and fees you'd pay, so almost no cash is required to close on the loan.

The most important thing to know about a reverse mortgage, however, is that it should be your last resort. A much better option would be to simply sell your home and move somewhere less expensive, invest the proceeds from the sale of your home, and live off of them. But some seniors adamantly refuse to move from homes they've lived in for thirty, fourty, or even fifty years, even though they don't have enough cash coming in to maintain the home and buy food and medicine. A reverse mortgage may be a good option in this case.

If you have the cash flow to qualify for a traditional home equity loan, or if you need only short-term cash, don't choose a reverse mortgage. It's like paying for your retirement with credit cards.

Just the Facts

You and all coowners of the property must be age sixty-two or older. (If you coown with your kids, you may be out of luck.) Your home must be your principal residence, that is, you have to live there more than six months per year. For a federally insured Home Equity Conversion Mortgage (HECM), your home must be a single-family house, a two- to four-unit building, or a federally approved condominium or planned unit development. For Fannie Mae's version of a reverse mortgage, called "HomeKeeper," your home must be a single-family house or a condominium. Co-ops and mobile homes typically don't qualify for a reverse mortgage. Finally, if you have any debt, you must pay it off before getting your reverse mortgage, or use a cash advance from the reverse mortgage to pay it off. If you can't qualify for enough cash to pay off your debt, you won't be able to get a reverse mortgage.

Typically, your reverse mortgage will be limited to between 50 and 80 percent of your home's value, up to the current Fannie Mae loan limit (in 1998, it was $227,150, but this number adjusts upward every year or so). How much you can get depends greatly on your age, the value and possibly even the location of your home, and current interest rates. The oldest homeowners living in the most expensive homes when interest rates are low will get the most money. Finally, how much you get varies tremendously from loan program to loan program. It's entirely opposite from the conventional mortgage market, where, by and large, a thirty-year fixed-rate loan carrying a 7 percent interest rate will have just about the same monthly mortgage payment no matter which lender you choose.

You can have your reverse mortgage paid to you in one of three ways:

1. *Immediate cash advance.* You receive a lump sum, paid at closing on the first day of the loan. If you choose a cash advance, you'll get no other money from the lender.

2. *Credit-line account.* As with a home equity line of credit, you can take a cash advance whenever you choose, until you use up the funds available to you. With a *flat credit-line account* (available through Fannie Mae's HomeKeeper), you have a certain amount, say $50,000, against which you can draw. With a *growing credit-line account* (available through an HECM), your

available credit grows over the years. The increased amount is based on current interest rates.

3. *Monthly cash advance.* You can have a monthly check sent to you for a specific number of years, for as long as you live in your home, or, if you use the loan to buy an annuity, every month for the rest of your life.

You may also opt to have the cash distributed to you in any combination of these three ways. If you have a loan against your home that you haven't paid off, you would have to take a lump sum large enough to pay off the loan at the closing.

It's Payback Time

A reverse mortgage has to be paid back when the surviving borrower dies, sells the home, or permanently moves away (has not lived in the home for twelve months in a row). You may also have to pay back the loan if you fail to pay your property taxes or homeowner's insurance premiums, or do not keep up your home.

How much will you owe? All of the cash advances you've received, plus interest on them, plus all of the fees associated with closing the loan (if you haven't already paid for them in cash). Reverse mortgages typically are adjustable rate mortgages (ARMs) pegged to an index that changes monthly. Unlike traditional ARMs, where the rate is capped at 5 or 6 percentage points above the starting rate, a reverse mortgage interest rate may be capped at *12 percent* above your starting rate.

What does this mean? If the interest rate on a conventional thirty-year fixed-rate mortgage is 7 percent, a reverse mortgage's starting interest rate might be 8.75 percent, which means the interest rate would never climb above 20.75 percent, under Fannie Mae's guidelines.

You might owe a little beyond this as well. If you choose the *equity share* reverse mortgage under the Fannie Mae HomeKeeper loan, you and your heirs have committed to pay the lender an amount equal to as much as 10 percent of the value of the home when it is finally sold. Other non-Fannie Mae lenders might charge you as much as 50 percent of the value of the home as a premium. Why choose an equity share loan? You'd get access to more cash up front. The difference on a Fannie Mae HomeKeeper loan could be significant. But if you sold your home for $227,150, you'd owe the lender an additional $22,715 on top of all of the other fees, charges, and equity borrowed.

If there's any money left after you sell the home and pay off the costs of the sale and the reverse mortgage, your heirs get to keep it. On the other hand, you can never owe more than your home is worth. So even if you receive monthly checks until you're 120, and your home declines in value, and you've borrowed more than the home is worth, you'll still end up at zero when you pay off the loan and have no other liability.

Truth-in-Lending

The federal Truth-in-Lending law requires all mortgage lenders to disclose all costs associated with a loan, as well as the projected annual average costs. For a regular mortgage, you'll see an APR, or *annual percentage rate*, which is the average annual cost of your loan, once all the fees, points, and other costs are built into it.

Reverse mortgage lenders are required to provide you with the *total annual loan cost (TALC)*, which shows you what the single, all-inclusive interest rate would be if all of the points and fees you'll pay were built into the interest rate. In lender jingoism, TALC is the APR for reverse mortgages. But unlike an APR, TALC rates do not assume you take all of the loan on the first day. Most reverse mortgage borrowers get their cash monthly over a long period of time.

Because you're going backward instead of forward, TALC rates can change based on the length of time you keep the loan and the rise in your home's value over time. Your percentage rate could be 18 percent (or as high as 50 percent) if you keep your loan for only one year. If you keep that same loan for thirty years, your TALC could drop to as low as 2 percent.

The Bottom Line

Any way you cut it, reverse mortgages are an expensive way to get money. You'll use up your equity, which many seniors see as their only legacy to their children. And once that's gone, you'll either have to sell your home or be a financial burden to your children. If you're looking for a monthly check, you'll have the added burden of using your reverse mortgage cash to purchase an annuity. (See Question 69 for more information.)

On the other hand, if you're bound and determined to stay in your home until you die, this may be an option worth exploring. The best place to get information is the National Center for Home Equity Conversion (NCHEC). You can find NCHEC on the Web at <www.reverse.org> (don't type <www.reverse.com> or you'll end up at a Web site of a mortgage brokerage that offers reverse mortgages), or write to NCHEC, Room 115, 7373 147th Street, Apple Valley, MN 55124. NCHEC offers software that can help you compare reverse mortgages to each other. NCHEC will also evaluate different reverse mortgage proposals for a fee. You can get additional information by calling the Department of Housing and Urban Development (toll-free: 888-466-3487) for a referral to a lender, or check out the list of HUD-approved counseling agencies on the Internet <www.hud.gov>. Fannie Mae's Web site <www.fanniemae.com> also offers a useful palette of information, but bear in mind that this source is pushing its HomeKeeper loan and does not discuss all of the options available. You can also get good information on reverse mortgages from the American Association of Retired Persons (AARP) Web site <www.aarp.org>. Look for their pamphlet, "Home Made Money," or write to the AARP Home Equity Information Center, 601 E Street, NW, Washington, DC 20049.

When it comes to money, plenty of lowlifes are just waiting to take advantage of you. Reverse mortgages are complex and expensive. If you're not familiar with them before you start shopping around, you could easily fall into the wrong hands. Steer clear of companies that will charge 5 to 10 percent of your loan amount to guide you to the proper loan. You should meet with at least two different lenders to see what the charges would be for a reverse loan.

A lot of seniors decide they're not moving from their home, and that's that. But it could end up being an extremely expensive choice that doesn't completely fill the gap. Please consider all the costs involved for you and your family before ruling out selling and living off the proceeds of your home. Independence is a fine thing, as long as you can afford to pay for it. Before you make a decision about getting a reverse mortgage, talk to your financial planner, and at least two or three financial counselors approved and sponsored by HUD in your area. Their advice is independent and usually is free.

QUESTION 40

HOW SHOULD I HOLD TITLE TO MY HOME?

How you hold *title* to, that is, the ownership of, your assets is important. If something goes wrong and one spouse or partner is sued professionally, how you and your spouse or partner own your home can mean the difference between having to sell it to pay off a judgment, and being allowed to live in it. Your ownership of your home and other assets can have important estate considerations as well.

Common Ways to Hold Title to Property

For now, let's focus on the ways in which you can hold title to your home. Unfortunately, all things aren't equal for spouses and for couples who are unmarried. But the time to think this through is before you buy. Here are some ways you may hold title to your home:

- *Individual.* If you're a single person, your options for holding title to your home are rather limited. You may hold title to your property as an individual. In a few states, you may hold title in a land trust (see the next section).

- *Joint tenancy.* Joint tenancy with rights of survivorship is the most common way married couples hold property. You each own the property as a whole. If you or your spouse dies, the deceased person's share in the property is immediately transferred to the surviving spouse. You share and share alike in the entire property. This type of tenancy is only for married couples.

- *Tenancy in common.* Tenancy in common allows each party to own a piece of the property separately. For example, you may own 40 percent, your spouse or partner may own 40 percent, and your parents may own 20 percent, but you may each use and enjoy the whole property. You cannot be restricted to just the 40 percent that you own. And, you may sell your share of the property to anyone you choose, as though you were selling stock in a corporation. Tenancy in common is available to married couples or unmarried partners.

- *Tenancy by the entirety.* Tenancy by the entirety is similar to joint tenancy with rights of survivorship. But both spouses in the marriage must agree to the title arrangement before the property is subject to one spouse's creditors. Neither spouse may do anything that would create a claim or lien on the marital property, and as long as the couple is married, the interest of each spouse is protected. For example, if one spouse is sued, the creditors could not attach a lien to the residence because each spouse owns the whole property. The creditors would have to wait until the marriage is severed, or the other spouse consents to the claim, or the property is sold. Once the property is sold, a claim may be attached to the proceeds. Tenancy by the entirety is not available in every state, and it is only for married couples.

Less Common Ways to Hold Title to Property

- *Land trust.* A *land trust* is a legal creation in which the sole asset in the trust is the property you are buying, and you are the beneficiary of the trust. At one time, a land trust might have been used to obscure the identity of the beneficiary. Today, that veil has been lifted. If permitted in your state, and few do, land trusts are available to individuals, two or more buyers, and married couples. Children may also be the beneficiaries of a land trust.

- *Qualified personal residence trust.* This is an estate-planning move that allows you to discount the future value of a home and save yourself gift and estate taxes. You set the term of the trust, and you place your home into it. You're allowed to live in the home for the term of the trust. The beneficiaries of the trust (your heirs) will receive the home when the term of the trust expires. (For more information, see Chapter 14.)

- *Living trust.* A revocable living trust is one way to pass assets from one generation to another and avoid probate, but it won't help you minimize taxes like an irrevocable trust will. You set up a trust and then transfer assets, such as your home or stocks, into the trust. You may name beneficiaries and leave a list of instructions for the trustee who will administer the trust. For many people, trusts take the place of wills. Also, living trusts aren't public documents, so the privacy is appealing. (For more information, see Chapter 14.)

- *Family limited partnership.* By creating a partnership, parents can pass along pieces of their property to their children (or anyone else) by making them small limited partners of a partnership that owns the property. Limited partners don't manage the property or have an active role in it, and that can discount their share of ownership, resulting in lower estate and gift taxes when the property is transferred. (For more information, see Chapter 14.)

• *Charitable remainder trust.* If you have a lot of assets and feel inclined to give some away (and collect the substantial tax benefits that go along with giving), you can set up a charitable remainder trust. By placing property in a trust for charity, you can sell it tax-free, without worrying about paying capital gains tax. You may then use the proceeds of the sale to set up an annuity that pays you (or another beneficiary) an income for the rest of your life. Upon your death, the remaining funds go to the named charity. (For more information, see Chapter 14.)

If you're unsure about the best way to hold title to your property, ask a real estate attorney or an accountant to explain the ins and outs of each type of ownership. There may be some very real reasons to go one way or another, and you should be thoroughly informed before you close on your home.

Although you may want to share title equally with your spouse, if you have financial assets that exceed $1.25 million (rising to $2 million by 2006), holding property as joint tenants may not be an economically savvy choice. Estate taxwise, it may be better for you to own the property on your own or place it into a trust. Emotionally, it may be difficult for you and your spouse to accept an unequal ownership of assets. Your financial planner can help you work through the various options.

Taxing Taxes

A truism: In life, only two things are certain—death and taxes.

WHAT ARE THE TAX BASICS I ABSOLUTELY HAVE TO KNOW?

QUESTION 41

Let's start by talking about the Internal Revenue Service (IRS). The IRS is the federal government body responsible for assessing and collecting taxes. The IRS comes under the wing of the Department of the Treasury.

Here are the three most important things you need to know about the United States system of taxation:

1. Uncle Sam gets a piece of everything you earn.
2. The more you earn, the more taxes you pay.
3. You are within your rights to find and implement any legal way to reduce your tax burden. It's called *tax avoidance*.

Paying taxes has become increasingly complex over the years. Some members of Congress favor a simpler method—that is, eliminate all income taxes in favor of a national sales tax. Others argue that a national sales tax isn't fair because lower- and middle-class households

> If you purposefully misrepresent your earnings in order to pay less in tax, you are committing *tax evasion*. The penalties for tax evasion include interest, penalties, and, possibly, jail time.

203

consume a larger percentage of their income than upper-middle-class or upper-class households and would end up paying a proportionately larger share of taxes.

While Congress debates the issue, the average American spends a longer amount of time each year on filing his or her income tax forms. Even when using the 1040EZ form, taxpayers need time to think about what the IRS is asking for on each line and then supply the exact information that is required.

As your life gets more complicated (children, debt, a bigger job, a second home), paying your taxes takes longer and longer. You'll pay a large chunk of your income (anywhere from 15 to 39.6 percent) in federal taxes (not to mention what you pay in state and local taxes), so it's worth spending some time investigating how you might be able to lessen your tax load.

Remember, tax avoidance is perfectly legal. Tax evasion is not.

Most of us don't have a PhD in taxation. However, the government says it is our responsibility to learn enough about the federal income tax system and tax law to be able to file our returns. If you aren't certain that you know enough to file your own taxes, hire a professional to help you. See Question 99 for information on hiring the right tax professional.

Deciphering the Jargon

Let's face it: Tax talk is almost incomprehensible to those who don't practice in the tax field. The text looks and sounds like English, but when the words come together, they form sentences that make little sense to the average person.

Here is a glossary of important definitions you should know.

Adjusted gross income. Your total income, reduced by: contributions to retirement accounts, alimony payments, and certain other exclusions.

Capital gain. A profit made on the sale of stocks, bonds, real estate, or other assets.

Capital loss. The loss taken on the sale of stocks, bonds, real estate, or other assets.

Deferred compensation plan. Employees may put a limited portion of their pretax earnings into a deferred compensation plan, like a 401(k) plan or a Keogh plan. The earnings are excluded from tax calculations, and they grow tax-free until the funds are withdrawn during retirement.

Dependent. An individual for whom the taxpayer provides over half of the support for the calendar year. This person could be a child, spouse, relative, or nonrelative living as a member of the taxpayer's household.

Dividend. A distribution of cash or additional stock shares to shareholders of a corporation.

Estimated tax payments. If you are self-employed, or have significant dividend income or investment income in addition to your regular salary, you must make tax payments based on the estimated tax you'll owe at the end of the year. Your estimated tax payments must equal either 100 percent of the tax you paid in the previous year or 90 percent of your total tax for the current year.

Exemption. From your adjusted gross income, you may take an exemption for yourself, your spouse, and any dependents. The exemption is basically money excluded from taxation.

Filing status. A declaration as to your personal status (married, single, separated, with or without dependents). Your filing status will determine your standard deduction, the tax rate table you'll use to compute your tax liability, and the deductions and credits to which you're entitled.

401(k) plan. A defined contribution plan for employees. Some companies do not offer this plan, but if yours does, you may contribute any amount up to a maximum set by the government and indexed to inflation. For the 1998 and 1999 tax years, the 401(k) limit is $10,000 (you have to earn much more to be able to put that amount away). As an additional benefit, some employers match employees' contributions up to a certain dollar limit or percentage.

403(b) plan. A retirement plan offered by certain religious, charitable, or public organizations. It operates much like a 401(k) plan.

Individual retirement account (IRA). An account to which any individual who earns income may contribute up to $2,000 per year.

The contributions are tax-deductible, and the earnings grow tax-free although they may be taxed upon withdrawal.

Keogh. A retirement plan (named for its originator) for employees of unincorporated businesses or self-employed individuals. A contribution of up to 25 percent of earned income, to a maximum of $30,000, is allowed.

Penalty. A fine levied by the IRS. You may pay a flat dollar fee or a fee based on an interest charge for: unpaid (miscalculated) taxes, failure to pay taxes; failure to make estimated tax payments; failure to make federal tax deposits; or late filing.

Roth IRA. The Tax Relief Act of 1997 created a Roth IRA, which allows nondeductible, after-tax contributions of up to $2,000 per year. As long as you hold the IRA for at least five years, the distributions are tax-free. In addition, you are not required to make a minimum contribution each year, and there is no age limit for additional contributions.

Standard deduction. If you decide not to itemize your deductions, or if you can't, you may opt for the standard deduction, an amount set by the government and indexed for inflation.

Simplified Employee Pension (SEP-IRA). This is a type of pension plan used by small businesses. The employer's contributions are excluded from the employee's taxable salary. They may not exceed 15 percent of the employee's salary or the current dollar amount set by the government ($30,000 in 1998), whichever is less.

Savings Incentive Match Plan for Employees [SIMPLE]. A pension plan for employers with 100 or fewer employees (who earn at least $5,000 per year). The employer must match the employee contribution, which is limited to a dollar amount that is indexed for inflation. (The 1998 contribution limit for employees was $6,000.)

Social Security. Under the Social Security Act of 1935, the federal government established the Social Security Administration, which now provides retirement benefits based on earnings over a period of years, disability income to individuals who qualify, and Medicare for individuals and their spouses.

Tax audit. A formal examination of your tax return by IRS auditors.

Tax bracket. A range of income for which a certain level of taxes must be paid. The higher your income, the higher your tax bracket, and the more tax you pay.

Tax credit. A dollar-for-dollar amount subtracted directly from the taxes you owe.

Tax shelter. Investments entered into for the sole purpose of lowering your tax burden.

Taxable income. Your gross earnings minus deductions and exclusions.

Wash sale. If you sell stocks at a loss and then purchase them back again within thirty days prior to or after the sale, the transaction is called a wash sale.

Withholding. An ongoing deduction from your pay that is sent by your employer, on your behalf, to the IRS.

Withholding allowance. One withholding allowance is available for each personal and dependent exemption that you're entitled to take. You may take additional exemptions to compensate for deductions and credits you plan to use. You may change your withholding allowances during the year if your income will be higher or lower than you predicted.

Figuring Out Your Taxable Income

If you have an employer (you are not self-employed), your taxes will be deducted or withheld from your earnings. After completing your tax form (the one due on April 15), you might owe a little more, or you can expect a refund four to six weeks after filing. If you're self-employed, you'll subtract your business expenses from your gross income, and, if your estimated tax installments have not covered the amount you owe, you'll mail the balance with your return.

The formula for figuring out your taxable income is fairly simple. Use the worksheet on pages 208–209 to help you calculate it.

Nontaxable Income

It may seem that every incoming dollar will be taxed, but that's not exactly true. Some types of income are nontaxable: accident and health insurance premiums paid by your employer; accident and health plan proceeds; allowances received by dependents of members of the armed forces; "combat zone" military pay; most disability payments; disability pensions from the Veterans Administration; federal

WORKSHEET
Your Taxable Income

Income Source		Annual Income
Wages and salaries	$	_____
Tips	+ $	_____
Back pay or bonuses	+ $	_____
Unemployment benefits	+ $	_____
Interest income	+ $	_____
Dividends	+ $	_____
Profit (or loss) from trade or business	+ $	_____
Net capital gains (or losses)	+ $	_____
Rents or royalties	+ $	_____
Profit or loss from partnerships	+ $	_____
Trusts, estates, and S corporations income	+ $	_____
Pensions and annuities	+ $	_____
Taxable Social Security benefits	+ $	_____
Alimony (if you're receiving it)	+ $	_____
Cancellation of debts	+ $	_____
Gambling winnings	+ $	_____
Government payments to offset farm losses	+ $	_____
Miscellaneous reimbursements	+ $	_____
Whistleblower awards	+ $	_____
Jury awards, punitive damage awards	+ $	_____
Prizes	+ $	_____
Buried or sunken treasure found	+ $	_____
Some Stipends	+ $	_____
Other	+ $	_____
Other	+ $	_____
Other	+ $	_____
Total Gross Income	= $	_____

This is the basic formula for figuring out your taxable income.

Adjustments to Income	Annual Amount
Alimony (if you're paying it)	$ _____
IRA or Keogh plan contributions	+ $ _____
Self-employment taxes	+ $ _____
Total Adjustments To Gross Income	= $ _____
Total Gross Income	$ _____
Total Adjustments to Total Gross Income	– $ _____
Total Adjusted Gross Income	= $ _____
Standard Deduction or Itemized Deductions	– $ _____
Personal Exemptions	– $ _____
Total Taxable Income	= $ _____

income tax refunds (you've already paid tax on these); some fellowship awards and scholarships in degree programs; capital gain on the sale of your home (up to $250,000, or $500,000 for married couples; you pay capital gains tax on gain in excess of this amount); gifts received (the giver pays any taxes owed, even on cash gifts of over $10,000); interest received from "tax-free" municipal bonds (you may owe state and local taxes); life insurance proceeds paid on the death of the insured (you'll pay no income tax, but estate taxes may have to be paid out of that money); living expenses paid by an insurance company while damage to your home is being repaired; monetary damages you receive for personal injury or disability; pensions and annuities for personal injuries, sickness, or disability during active service in the armed forces; foster care payments; strike benefits; veterans' benefits; and worker's compensation benefits, among others.

Keeping Track

As we discussed in Chapter 1, it's up to you to keep the records you may need in case the IRS wants proof of the deductions, credits, or exemptions you're taking. You can use the following lists to help track your income and expenses for the year (and prove to the IRS that your deductions are legitimate).

Income Records	*Expenses Records*
W-2, W-2P, and/or 1099 forms.	Sales slips, invoices, and receipts.
Pay stubs.	Canceled checks
Bank statements.	Credit card statements and/or
Brokerage statements.	receipts.
Mutual fund statements.	Proof of alimony paid.
K-1 form (for partnership	Charitable contribution receipts.
activity).	Mortgage interest statements.
IRA distribution statements.	Real estate tax payment receipts.
Pension distribution statements.	Home closing statements.
	Home purchase/sale documents.
	Proof of mortgage payments and
	insurance premium payments.
	Copies of state income tax returns.

How Much Do I Have to Withhold from My Salary?

If you work for a company, the government requires your employer to withhold a portion of each paycheck to meet your federal income tax obligation. You can control how much is withheld by changing the number of *withholding allowances* you take. You're responsible to the IRS for paying as you go, so you should periodically check your withholding to make sure you're paying the right amount. If you're paying too much, you can reduce your withholding. If you're paying too little, you can increase your withholding to make up the difference.

You may take one withholding allowance for each personal and dependent exemption that you expect to declare on your tax return. Additional allowances can be included if you expect your deductions and credits to reduce the overall tax you're planning to pay. Don't take extra withholding allowances if you don't need them. (See Question 45 for information on penalties for underpayment of taxes.)

Deductions

A *deduction* is a subtraction from adjusted gross income. Among the best deductions for homeowners are the mortgage interest and the real estate taxes paid on their home during the previous year. If your deduction exceeds the standard deduction (which every taxpayer is entitled to take), you should consider *itemizing* your deductions. When you itemize, you individually list your deductions on Form 1040, Schedule A.

You may benefit from itemizing your deductions if:

- Your out-of-pocket medical and/or dental expenses exceeded 7.5 percent of your adjusted gross income.

- The total of the interest you paid on your mortgage or home equity line of credit plus your property taxes exceeds the standard deduction.

- You had significant employee business expenses that were not reimbursed.

- You had large casualty or theft losses that were not covered by insurance.

- You contributed money, or other assets, to charity.
- You paid state income taxes and this amount, along with other deductions, exceeds the standard deduction.

Some tax deductions (and/or credits) are limited or eliminated as your income level rises. By the same token, as your income rises, you need more deductions to lower your total taxable income. If you get into this situation, you may want to ask a tax planner to help you identify other ways of legally lowering your total taxable income.

Ten Facts You Need to Know

Here are ten facts about Uncle Sam's Internal Revenue Code that you should know.

1. *A few good deductions can help.* If you can itemize, you'll get the most bang for your buck from the deductions for mortgage interest, property taxes, and home equity loan interest. You may deduct from your taxable income the interest paid on $1 million worth of loans on a first or second home plus the interest paid on a home equity loan of up to $100,000. Interest on school loans is now also deductible in some cases. And if your deductions need pumping up, consider prepaying your January mortgage interest and your next year's property taxes by December 31.

2. *Some things are no longer deductible.* Personal interest of any sort, including credit card interest and car loan interest, is no longer deductible. When you pay 24 percent on your credit card debt, that's after-tax cash.

3. *Credits are more valuable than deductions.* A *credit* reduces your taxes dollar-for-dollar. A $1,000 credit means you'll pay $1,000 less in taxes. If a child care credit is $480, you reduce your taxes by $480. A *deduction* reduces your adjusted gross income. If you're in the 28 percent bracket, a $1,000 deduction will save you $280.

4. *Municipal bonds generate tax-free income.* The interest earned on "tax-free" municipal bonds (typically put out by a municipal

body) is exempt from federal taxes. If you live in the state where the bonds are issued, you can typically escape state and local taxes, too. You may earn less interest on your money than in other investments, but the savings on taxes can make up for some of that. (See Question 42 for more detailed information.)

5. *Tax-sheltered retirement accounts grow faster than other investments.* When earnings are eaten up by taxes, there's less left on which compounding can work its magic. For example, if you contribute $2,000 to an IRA growing 6 percent tax-free, in 20 years, your $40,000 worth of contributions would grow to $73,571. In a money market fund earning 6 percent, your $2,000 investment would grow to $60,429 if you were in the top tax bracket. With the new Roth IRAs, you put in cash that's already been taxed, but your contributions grow tax-free, and as long as you hold the IRA for more than five years, you may withdraw your earnings tax-free. (Again, see Question 42 for more information.)

6. *The top capital gains rate has dropped.* If you hold onto your investments for at least eighteen months, you'll pay only 20 percent in capital gains if you're in the 28 percent tax bracket (or higher), or 10 percent if you're in the 15 percent tax bracket (or lower).

7. *Home sellers are in the clear.* As we discussed in Question 33, home sellers may take up to $250,000 (up to $500,000 if married) in tax-free capital gains. You may take this tax-free exclusion once every twenty-four months, as long as you have lived in the house for two of the past five years. And if you meet other criteria, you may be able to make your second home into your primary residence after you sell your home, and exclude that property's capital gain from taxes as well.

8. *Deductions should be itemized only when they exceed your standard deduction.* The standard deduction rises slightly every year. Take a look at your deductions. If they are higher than the standard deduction, you should itemize your deductions on your income tax form. If not, take the standard deduction. Many taxpayers take the standard deduction, eliminating the potential benefit of the mortgage interest and home equity interest deductions.

9. *When calculating the cost basis of your home, decorating doesn't count.* You can tack on the cost of a new roof, or structural additions

but, in the eyes of the IRS, painting and wallpapering don't substantially add to the value of your home. But if you repaint your interior within 60 days of closing, you may be able to adjust your basis to include the repainting as a cost of sale (plus, a willing buyer may pay you thousands more for your home).

10. *If you need more time to file your taxes, you can get it.* Anyone who needs more time can get a four-month extension from the IRS by filing an extension request form before April 15. If you need more time beyond the August filing date, you'll have to prove that you have a valid reason for not being able to file by the extended deadline, and you must pay what you think you'll owe in taxes. If, by the time you file, you figure out that your actual taxes are higher, you'll owe interest on the previously unpaid taxes, plus a possible penalty.

> Writing your check correctly could save you problems later on. Use indelible ink and make your check payable to "Internal Revenue Service" rather than "IRS," which could be changed if someone illegally intercepts the check. Make sure you note on the check your Social Security number and the tax that your payment is intended to cover (for example, "1998 1040 Taxes"). If you leave something to chance, you may be unhappy with the result.

WHAT ARE SOME WAYS I CAN REDUCE MY TAXES?

As we just discussed, your goal is to take advantage of everything that will allow you to reduce your tax liabilities. The first step is a thorough assessment of your income tax situation. Make sure you're meeting your tax obligation through your withholding and your estimated tax payments, or a combination of both.

Here are some of the most popular ways you can reduce your federal income taxes:

- *Tax-deferred retirement plans.* Whether you have access to a 401(k), a 403(b), a regular IRA, or a Keogh plan, making the most of your tax-deferred retirement plans is the fastest way to build for your future and reduce the amount of taxes you pay today. Why? Because every dollar you put into a retirement account today reduces this year's taxable income. You may be limited in how much you can contribute to a particular plan, but you have at least postponed the taxes on that income. On the down side, you have restricted your ability to use that money until you retire. (Most folks should pump every dollar they can into a tax-deferred account. For more information on tax-deferred retirement plans, see Chapter 13.)

- *Flexible spending accounts.* Employers often offer flexible spending accounts, also called "cafeteria plans," which allow you to put a certain amount of pretax dollars away to pay for medical, dental, or dependent care expenses that are not otherwise reimbursed, such as coinsurance payments or a nanny's wages. Because these are pretax dollars, they effectively reduce your taxable income. On the other hand, these plans are usually headlined "Use It or Lose It." If you don't spend everything in your account by the end of the year, you lose the cash.

- *Mortgages and home equity loans.* Every dollar you pay in interest on mortgages (up to $1 million) or on home equity loans (up to $100,000) is tax-deductible. The higher your mortgage interest, the lower your taxable income (if you qualify for itemization).

- *Timing is everything.* You can accelerate your deductions by playing around with dates. Make one additional mortgage payment this year instead of next. If you want to boost your deductions for next year, close on your home on January 2 (or the first business day after the New Year's holiday), and you can deduct points paid on your next year's taxes. You may also be able to push income into the next year, which lowers your tax obligation for this year.

- *The tax consequences of investing.* Different types of investments offer various tax advantages. Some of the best include: municipal bonds; U.S. Treasury bills, notes, and bonds; U.S. savings bonds; investment real estate; annuities; and stock. Each of these investments has pros and cons. Your dividends from a municipal bond, for example, may be tax-free, but the interest rate you earn may be lower than from other sorts of bonds.

- *Sell at a loss.* If you're planning to sell a stock in which you have a huge capital gain, consider pairing the sale with a different security in which you have a loss. In that way, you can offset your gain with a loss and perhaps pay less, or nothing, in capital gains taxes. If you still want to hold the stock that's down, consider selling for tax purposes and then repurchasing the stock thirty-one days after you sell. If you repurchase the stock before the thirty-first day, the IRS's "wash sale" provision will disallow your loss. Under current tax law, you may sell a security at a loss to offset ordinary income. The limit allowed is $3,000 per year.

- *Shift some income to your children.* Up to age fourteen, children pay tax on income over $1,400 (for 1998) at your marginal tax rate. (The first $650 in investment income earned is generally tax-free.) That's the so-called "IRS kiddie tax." At age fourteen, children pay based on how much they earn, just like anyone else. If you transfer assets to your children, you may pay less tax. On the other hand, your child will have control of those assets. On significant gifts, you may have additional gift taxes. You may give anyone a gift of up to $10,000 per year without triggering the gift tax.

- *Increase your charitable giving.* If you paid a few thousand dollars for a painting now worth millions, you may be able to donate that painting to charity at its appreciated value, and use that value as a deduction against your current tax obligation. In addition, you owe no tax on the appreciated value of the asset. However, the sky is not the limit. If you give cash, you can deduct the full amount of your contribution up to 50 percent of your adjusted gross income. If you're giving more than that, you can carry forward the unused portion of the deduction for the next five years. If you still haven't used it up, it's gone. If you're giving appreciated assets, the maximum you can deduct is 30 percent of your adjusted gross income. If you need more time than that, consider pledging your donation over ten or twenty years. That effectively allows you fifteen or twenty-five years in which to maximize your deduction.

- *Roll It over.* If you leave your job, are laid off, or are fired, and you have been contributing to a retirement account, you may take your contributions (as well as any matching proceeds that you are entitled to, based on your years at the company) and roll them over directly into an IRA without having to pay a tax. If you do not have the funds transferred directly into an IRA account, you'll be assessed a 20 percent penalty. You have sixty days to enact the transfer without triggering the penalty. And, you may make one tax-free rollover per year per IRA account. If you are rolling over a traditional IRA to a Roth IRA, however, you will have to include the amount of your IRA with your gross income and pay taxes on the amount transferred.

- *The costs of investing.* If you itemize, you may deduct a portion or all of the costs associated with making your investments, including investment counseling fees, telephone fees, clerical assistance fees, office rent, and travel expenses.
- *Mutual fund maneuvers.* If you decide to sell your mutual funds, selling earlier in the year may give you an unexpected tax break. Funds typically pay dividends or capital gains at the end of the year. Selling before the distribution means you'll have pumped-up appreciation, on which you'll pay a maximum of 20 percent (just 10 percent if you're in the 15 percent bracket). If you sell after the distribution, you'll have received the dividend, which is added to your income. True, your capital gain will be lower, but you'll pay a higher tax on the extra income.

Employee Business Expenses

If you spend money on job-related expenses that are not reimbursed by your employer, and, if they exceed 2 percent of your adjusted gross income, they may be deductible on your tax return. These expenses, which must be "ordinary and necessary" under the Internal Revenue code include:

- Entertainment expenses.
- Travel expenses for your job.
- Automobile and transportation expenses for your job, including going from a home office to another location.
- Business gift expenses (limited to $25 per business gift per tax year).
- Office in the home.

Self-Employed Business Expenses

If you are self-employed, you may deduct regular business expenses against your gross business income. These expenses include everything from hiring employees and purchasing office equipment and supplies to paying legal fees, rent, postage, telephone, and utility bills. There is even a home office deduction.

To cut down on your hefty self-employment tax (you make double the contribution, one as employee and the other as employer), consider stacking purchases and payments in a single year, to lower your tax bite.

Marriage Penalty

There's a distinct contradiction between the United States' goal of self-perpetuation (which is all about getting married and having children) and the IRS tax code, which penalizes folks specifically because they're married instead of living together.

The so-called "marriage penalty" is based on the differences among the three ways you can file a return. You can file (1) as an individual, if you are single; (2) separately from your spouse, if you are officially separated; and (3) jointly if you are married.

Tax experts say that the marriage penalty can sometimes be a marriage bonus. The tax obligations for married couples filing jointly are often less than for individual filers, especially if the couple has unequal incomes. For example, if one spouse earns $75,000 per year and the other spouse earns $20,000 per year, their joint return might generate a lower tax than if they filed separately. But when each spouse has a roughly equivalent income, the joint return imposes a penalty instead of a bonus. Follow this rule of thumb: If the lower income is within 70 percent of the higher income, you'll probably encounter the marriage penalty.

In about sixty provisions in the tax code, filers' tax liability depends on whether they are married. The most common areas of discrepancy are in tax rates, the standard deduction, and the earned income tax credit. Marriage penalties are also inherent in the taxation of Social Security benefits, limitations on capital losses, and the home mortgage interest deduction.

How much is the marriage penalty costing you? One accountant figures the average marriage penalty is no more than $1,000; others say it can run much higher.

What You Can Do

There's no way to completely erase the marriage penalty, but here are some tactics for possibly reducing your liability:

1. *Take all the deductions and exemptions to which you're entitled.* Take advantage of the child tax credit, the dependent care credit, and, if applicable, the deduction of interest on student loans. Medical deductions might include prescription birth control pills, a vasectomy, and psychiatric treatment.

2. *Consider other new programs that might help.* These include the HOPE Education Credit, Lifetime Learning Credit, Education IRAs, or qualified state tuition programs.

3. *If you're divorcing or are already divorced, think through who gets the exemptions, credits, and deductions relating to your children.* This is especially important if there is a large gap between the high and low wage earners' income.

4. *If you're adopting, there may be relief.* A new law provides a significant credit for expenses associated with the adoption of a child. There is an exclusion for costs covered by the employer.

5. *Max out on your retirement contributions.* Not only will this help you when you retire, it might help you with this year's taxes. (See Chapter 13 for more information on retirement plans.)

Many folks feel it is a privilege to pay taxes in a country that works harder than any other at protecting the rights of its citizens. And, they're happy to pay what they owe. But that doesn't mean you have to feel good about paying *more* than you should. Make sure you take advantage of every tax break to which you're entitled.

WHEN DO I HAVE TO PAY MY TAXES?

QUESTION
43

Whether you're single or married, separated or divorced, employed by a company or self-employed, the magic date is still April 15 of the calendar year. Your federal and state income tax returns are due on (or must be postmarked by) April 15 of the year following the year that's subject to tax. For the 1998 tax year, your IRS tax return is due on April 15, 1999. For the 1999 tax year, your IRS tax return is due on April 15, 2000.

Uncle Sam doesn't wait that long to get his hands on your cash. Individuals employed by companies have taxes withheld from each paycheck, and self-employed individuals must pay estimated taxes on the fifteenth day of the fourth, sixth, and ninth months of the taxable year, and the first month of the year following the taxable year. In English: For the taxable year 1999, you'll owe estimated withholding taxes on April 15, 1999 (when your income tax forms for 1998 are due), June 15, 1999, September 15, 1999, and January 15, 2000.

Why aren't the payments spread out more equally? Historically, it's unclear, but Mark Luscombe, principal tax analyst at CCH, Inc., a tax information publisher, believes that the dates were set because they offer individuals the best opportunity to assess where their business is going that year. By the first payment on April 15, they have had three months to see the year's pattern. June 15 is almost midway through the calendar year. September 15 offers a decent opportunity to look at the first three quarters. January 15 is past the winter holidays and the year-end date when many businesses close their books for the calendar year and tabulate their year-end income. Today's computers allow us to push a button and glean these numbers from the data entered throughout the year. But when this system was set up, calculations were done by hand, and payments were sent through the U.S. mail, so a couple of weeks were needed for end-of-year tallying and reporting to come through.

How Much You Have to Pay

The IRS wants to get its cash from you in fairly equal installments. If you are an investor who has a steady stream of income each month, your tax will be easy to calculate, and you'll pay the IRS your estimated taxes in fairly equal installments. If your income varies from month to month, you'll calculate your income each quarter. Your estimated tax payments must be filed with Form 1040-ES, Estimated Tax for Individuals. (See pages 231–232 for ways to contact the IRS.)

If you can't get your estimated amount to the penny, don't worry. Your estimated payments must be equal to at least 90 percent of what you'll owe in the current year, or 100 percent of your prior year's taxes. If you paid the IRS $20,000 in taxes the previous year, but you're not sure how much you're going to earn this year, you can pay estimated payments of $5,000 each and be in good stead with the IRS. If you see your income rising through the year, increase your later payments as needed.

If you earn income that exceeds $150,000 for married couples filing jointly, or $75,000 for single taxpayers, your estimated payments during 1999, 2000, and 2001 (for tax years 1998, 1999, and 2000) must be 105 percent of the previous year's payment. If you paid $20,000 in taxes in 1998 (for the 1997 tax year), your estimated tax payment must be at least $21,000 in 1999, or 90 percent of what you will owe. For the taxes paid in 2002 (for the 2001 tax year), your estimated tax must be 112 percent of the previous year's tax, or 90 percent of what you will owe. And for taxes paid in 2003 (for the 2002 tax year), it's 110 percent of the prior year's taxes. And so on.

Bear in mind that IRS rules and regulations change frequently, which is why I haven't included information on many of them in this book. Congress has come down pretty hard on the IRS in recent years, and is trying to shift the balance of power a little bit away from the IRS and back to the people. We'll see whether it works.

Refunds

If you overpay the IRS, you get an income tax refund, usually within four to eight weeks after you file. If you file electronically, you should receive your refund more quickly. Getting an income tax refund is nothing to smile about. You've just given Uncle Sam an interest-free loan. Some people call refunds "enforced savings" (I know an attorney who is completely delighted to get her refund every year), but there are better ways to save cash. (One way is to have funds withdrawn from your earnings and deposited directly into a mutual fund account before you ever see your paycheck.)

The idea is to end up even, or owing the government only a bit more cash. If necessary, adjust your withholdings at work so that you end up just about even. If you are self-employed, consider reducing your estimated payments, unless you plan to use the "refund" as your first estimated tax payment.

If you've made estimated tax payments but end up owing the IRS a few extra dollars on April 15, don't forget that you still need to pay, when you file your return, your estimated tax for the first quarter of the current calendar year.

If you underpay during the year (or forget an estimated tax payment), you can make up for it. Go to your employer in, say, October, and ratchet up your withholdings for the final two months of the year; or, increase your next estimated tax payment. (In Question 45, we'll talk about what happens if you don't pay your taxes.)

The Nanny Tax

After Zoe Baird lost her chance of being the U.S. Attorney General because she didn't pay her estimated withholding taxes for her domestic employee, everyone became aware that, yes, it is illegal to hire undocumented workers, and it is even more illegal to pay them, or any workers, under the table. Paying your cleaning lady under the table may save you a few hundred or thousand dollars in taxes, and may save her the same amount (if she even earns enough to pay taxes), but what you're really doing is keeping her from later claiming Social Security benefits to which she might be entitled, had she been paying into the system all these years.

Taxes are owed for all domestic workers who earn more than $1,000 per year. You may file Schedule H with your 1040 form, and pay FICA (Social Security and Medicare) and FUTA (unemployment) taxes once a year.

If you're not running for public office, you're not a public figure, and no one tattles on you, you might get away with hiring undocumented workers or not paying the appropriate taxes for your help. Whether you do or don't is up to you, but there could be other ramifications if you don't pay taxes for your domestic help. Attorneys who do not pay these taxes, for example, could be disbarred and lose their license to practice.

QUESTION 44
WHAT ARE MY CHANCES OF GETTING AUDITED?

If you open up your morning newspaper (or online news channel) and read the horror stories stacking up in congressional hearings, you might get the impression that the IRS has been out to get you (and all taxpayers). Going through an audit sounds downright unappealing.

You may know someone who has been audited, but odds are it will never happen to you. On average, less than 2 percent of the individual returns filed are audited by the IRS. That's a pretty small number, and it gets whittled down further because it includes any form of contact from the IRS, including letters asking for more documentation or additional explanations. The true number of audits conducted by the IRS is probably less than 1 percent.

In addition, all returns are not treated equally. Those who file in the lowest and highest income ranges get audited more frequently. For example, if your income is less than $25,000 per year or more than $100,000 per year, your chances of being audited are more than double the chances for taxpayers earning between $25,000 and $50,000 per year. The group most often audited earns more than $100,000 per year, yet only 2.85 percent of individuals in this group received any form of contact from the IRS. That's down dramatically from 1988, when 11.41 percent of high-income individuals were contacted.

Are there other ways to protect yourself? It may sound silly, but consider moving. If you file at the IRS Central and Midwest Regional Centers, the IRS considers you less likely to cheat than those individuals who file at its Western and Southwestern Regional Centers. Or, you can work for someone else. If you're self-employed, your chances of receiving a note from the IRS go up as well.

Here are a few things you can do to possibly lower your odds of being audited:

- *Include all your family's Social Security numbers.* All Social Security numbers must be entered for any children claimed as dependents on your return, even if your newest bundle of joy was born on December 31. Make sure you note the Social Security number of an ex-spouse receiving alimony or a child receiving child support payments.

- *Don't make math mistakes.* Spend time recalculating your return. A computer tax program can really help out here (unless you type in wrong numbers!).

- *Copy numbers correctly.* The IRS receives copies of W-2 and 1099 forms, and will expect your numbers to match the numbers already received.

- *Include all forms.* Depending on the deductions you take, you may need additional forms. For example, if you make a noncash contribution worth $500 or more, you must report that donation on Form 8283 for noncash charitable contributions.

- *Receipts, receipts, receipts.* Keep your receipts, records, and letters regarding all deductions, including charitable contributions (charities must now send you a letter or a receipt acknowledging your donation), medical expenses, and business expenses not reimbursed by your employer. Once you sort your receipts, you can toss out what you don't need to prove your deductions. If you can't prove a deduction, it may be disallowed.

- *Write a letter.* If there's something funny about your return, be proactive and explain it. Tax experts say a short letter explaining a situation can often avoid an audit.

- *Keep your receipts and tax records for at least three years.* After that time, your chances of being audited are reduced. To be on the safe side, keep a copy of your return plus the attached documentation for six years (which is how long the IRS may pursue you) or for life. There is no statute of limitations for the IRS if it believes you willfully misrepresented your income on a tax form.

Nearly 100,000 individuals never collect tax refunds totaling more than $60 million each year. That's because the checks are returned to the IRS as undeliverable. If you move, send the IRS Form 8822, Change of Address. Or, you can choose to have your refund deposited directly into your bank account.

Your Rights as a Taxpayer

Yes, there is a Taxpayer Bill of Rights. You have a right to privacy, a right to representation during an audit, and a right to appeal an IRS decision.

When dealing with the IRS, remember that your rights to privacy and confidentiality are still valid, and that you may refuse certain requests from the IRS for additional information. The IRS may not disclose to anyone the information you give them, unless it is authorized by the law. You also have the right to know why the IRS is asking for certain information, how it will be used, and the consequences if you fail to provide it.

Your right to representation cannot be stripped away from you, and you may choose to be represented by an attorney, your tax preparer, an enrolled agent, or yourself. You don't have to be at the initial interview, but if you go, someone may accompany you and represent you. If you are considering recording on tape any meeting with the IRS agents during your audit, you must give the IRS ten days' notice in writing. The attorney–client privilege has been extended, in noncriminal cases, to anyone licensed to practice before the IRS.

Recent changes in IRS law have created a separate liability for "innocent spouses"—people who unknowingly signed a false return or were coerced into signing. Under the new law, taxpayers who can prove they were "innocent spouses" are liable only for taxes on their own income. Previously, they were responsible jointly and separately (the IRS could go after them for payment of taxes owed, even if they knew nothing about what was on the return).

Other recent changes in tax law have shifted the burden of proof to the IRS. Previously, it was up to you to prove that you filed correctly. Now, the IRS must prove that you didn't. To qualify, the taxpayer must maintain records, cooperate with the IRS, and be worth less than $7 million.

Interest and penalties will be waived if the IRS fails to contact you about a dispute within eighteen months of filing. After 2004, interest and penalties will be waived if the IRS fails to contact you within one year of filing. Other penalties may be reduced as well.

For more detailed information about your rights, see IRS Publication 1, "Your Rights as a Taxpayer," and IRS Publication 17, "Your Federal Income Tax." If you get an audit letter, you'll certainly want to read both of these publications.

If you receive a letter from the IRS, or an invitation to come in and chat, take a deep breath before you do anything. Most of these notices can be resolved quickly and easily, if you simply provide additional information. New tax rules that were recently signed into law prohibit the IRS from doing random audits simply to check how their internal mechanisms are working. That's right, the IRS used to choose, at random, people who had nothing wrong with their return, and put them through the wringer. They can't do that any more. If you do receive a letter, take out your return and try to sort through the problem yourself or with your tax preparer. Then, armed with your documentation, place your call to the IRS office that contacted you.

QUESTION
45

WHAT HAPPENS IF I DON'T PAY MY TAXES?

If you don't pay your taxes or you file incorrectly, you can wind up in a heap of trouble. You can ruin your credit, end up owing thousands of dollars in interest and penalties, have your wages garnished and your property seized and sold, and possibly end up in jail.

Correcting Your Return

If you file incorrectly or discover a computation error after you have sent in your return, you can file an *amended return,* which is simply a tax return that has been corrected. You should detail what changes have been made and why. An amended return doesn't always mean you'll owe more taxes. You might discover that you failed to take advantage of some deductions and credits and actually owe lower taxes.

Consider filing an amended return if you failed to report some income, claimed deductions or credits you should not have claimed, did not claim deductions or credits that were available to you, or chose the wrong filing status.

Failing to File

If you fail to file a tax return, or you pay less than you should, the IRS has these tools at its disposal to "encourage" you to pay any taxes due:

- *Interest on taxes owed.* If you haven't paid the right amount of tax, the IRS can levy both interest and penalties. Interest (the current rate charged is the federal short-term rate plus three percentage points) is levied from the time the payment should have been made until the payment is made. And, because the federal short-term rate changes monthly, you could have a variety of interest rates being levied on your underpayment, which can make it difficult to calculate the tax.

- *Accuracy penalty.* If you paid on time but made an accounting error or didn't read the rules correctly, you may owe an accuracy penalty, which is 20 percent of the underpayment that is attributed to negligence or disregard of the rules. The accuracy penalty typically goes into effect if you underestimated your taxes by 10 percent or more. If you owed $20,000 but paid only $15,000, you'd owe interest on the $5,000 underpayment from the time it should have been paid until the time you pay it, plus a $1,000 penalty.

- *Intent to commit fraud.* You can be penalized for negligence or for making mathematical mistakes. But if you *intend* to pay less than you owe, and you try to cover up your excess income, the government can recommend criminal prosecution and penalties. In addition to fines and interest payments, you could wind up in jail.

How the System Works

The IRS can't collect what it's owed if it doesn't realize you haven't paid in full. There are folks who escape the IRS system by never filing taxes, by working for cash, and by not doing anything that might attract the IRS's attention. However, if you've filed a return before and have a Social Security number, you're in the system and the IRS looks to receive a form from you each year.

If the IRS doesn't receive a tax form, or if it comes in with a different name on it, the IRS might start an internal procedure that tracks down folks who should have filed but didn't. That might result in a letter assessing a penalty and interest or inviting you into the IRS field office for further discussion.

If you filed, but not on time, the IRS computer might kick out your file for further examination. That might result in a computer-generated letter that reflects the calculation of what wasn't paid on time, the tax that's due, and any interest or penalty charges that apply. If you agree with the letter and pay the amount stated, everything might end there. Or, if you have documentation that proves that the computer made a mistake (or the human who entered information into the computer made a mistake), that might also be the end of it.

There's nothing like a letter from the IRS to make your heart start pumping.

> ### Jennifer's Story
>
> Jennifer lives and works in the Midwest. She and her boyfriend had a child but never married (they now live in separate states). Jennifer kept her maiden name, and she gave their son his father's name.
>
> She has filed taxes for years with the help of the same person at a tax-preparation shop. One year, a different person assisted her. That person assumed that her son had her name, and not a different last name.
>
> The IRS computer spit out her return and generated a letter saying that she owed an additional $2,000 in taxes because she claimed to have a son who didn't exist. Because her son's name on the return didn't match his Social Security number, the IRS canceled him out of the return.

Fortunately for Jennifer, a simple call to the IRS office listed on the letter, followed by furnishing additional information and documentation, proved that there was, in fact, an error on the return. The additional tax owed was removed.

If you don't agree with what's in an IRS letter, you can present information and documentation and insist that the IRS correct a mistake. If you get a letter and don't respond to it, or if the IRS thinks there's evidence of additional problems with your return, your file might be turned over to the collection division, which might initiate an audit procedure. You might be asked to come into an IRS office and meet with an IRS representative to discuss why you filed your return the way you did. Consider going into that meeting with an attorney and your accountant, or an Enrolled Agent.

If things get worked out at the audit or examination, great. You're done. If, however, you choose not to show up to resolve things, you may either pay the tax and then claim a refund, or appeal your decision and go to Federal Tax Court or a district court.

Tax Court

Most of the decisions in Tax Court favor the IRS, but some tax experts believe that's because taxpayers frequently file frivolous tax-protester-type cases. Taxpayers often represent themselves. But when everything is factored in, most people agree that Tax Court isn't especially pro-IRS. You may get a more knowledgeable handling of the case than in District Court, where the judge may have limited knowledge of tax law.

If you don't like the verdict you get at Tax Court, you may appeal the decision all the way to the U.S. Supreme Court—if you can afford the attorney fees.

District Court

District court is a regular court, not a special court for tax disputes. If you believe the IRS ruling that you're protesting is improper, you may be better off in District Court, some experts say. You may be raising a constitutional argument, which will be heard with different ears than in Tax Court. Tax Court is supposed to give a fair reading of the tax law, but may not be as receptive to other arguments.

A disadvantage of going to District Court is that you must pay the tax before you argue your case, and then try to collect monies back from the IRS if you lose. Tax Court allows you to postpone payment until after you've exhausted your appeals. As in a Tax Court case, you may appeal a District Court decision all the way to the U.S. Supreme Court.

Working It Out with the IRS

From time to time, the IRS will host its version of a "Get Out of Jail Free" day: if you step forward and pay your back taxes owed, plus the interest and penalties due, there will be no further action from the IRS. You may even be able to negotiate a reduction in or elimination of interest and penalties, or a payment plan that will keep everyone happy. The IRS intent is to bring wayward taxpayers back into the system. If you've fallen behind in payments or have skidded out of the IRS system, and you want to get back in, you may find the IRS more than willing to work with you. Contact a tax attorney first, however, to map out your strategy.

Scams and Such

Have you ever received a letter or e-mail message like this?

> The Founding Fathers of the United States of America wrote our Constitution, Bill of Rights, and Declaration of Independence to set us FREE from TYRANNY and TAXATION. Our Founding

Fathers did not want our government to make you pay INCOME TAXES. If you study the Constitution, and the IRS tax laws, you will find that paying income taxes is not mandatory. It is based on a voluntary system. The LAWS and the SUPREME COURT and the IRS have ruled that Federal income taxes are VOLUNTARY and FILING A RETURN IS NOT REQUIRED in many cases if you properly VOLUNTEER OUT OF THE SYSTEM AND THEIR JURISDICTION.

"Our tax system is based on a voluntary assessment and payment and not on distraint." Supreme Court Ruling, Flora v. U.S., 362 U.S. 145.

It is very EASY and LEGAL to volunteer out of the IRS tax system, but you must know the EXACT PROCESS REQUIRED to do this simple task. If you don't know the correct way to do this, you could be FINED $500 by the IRS.

If you will spend just $35.00 we will send you our report: "BEAT THE IRS & PAY NO MORE."

Nobody has ever failed.

—Internet offering via e-mail, July 1998

There are folks who, if you pay them a modest fee (anywhere from $35 to $1,500), will supposedly teach you how to circumvent the IRS and opt out of the taxpaying system. They will tell you that the Constitution doesn't permit taxation on U.S. citizens, and that they've made these arguments in court . . . yadda, yadda, yadda.

The truth is, you *do* need to pay your taxes. These folks are running a scam and, in some cases, they're running from prosecution. Don't waste your time or your money.

QUESTION
46

HOW DO I FILE ELECTRONICALLY, AND HOW DO I CONTACT THE IRS?

As more and more people use personal computers to keep track of their finances, demand should also grow for electronic tax preparation software. The IRS has been slowly expanding its capacity for electronic filing of tax forms, but it was tough going in the early years. Those who were first to file electronically often found that their tax forms and refunds were mucked up. With interest in electronic filing growing, Congress has demanded that the IRS ramp up its computer equipment to make it easier to file electronically. The initial technical expenditure will be high for the IRS, but tax experts believe that the long-term investment will be worth it.

Even if you don't use a computer or tax-preparation software, you can still file electronically. The IRS has joined up with several companies to provide electronic filing (also known as e-file) options for individuals and tax professionals. If you're interested in filing electronically, you may contact one of the following companies for more information:

- Drake: (800) 890-9500. Internet address: http://www .drake-software.com
- H&R Block: (816) 753-6900. Internet address: http://www .hrblock.com
- Intuit: (800) 224-0991. Internet address: http://www.intuit.com
- Universal Tax Systems: (706) 624-4214. Internet address: http://www.securetax.com

Electronic filing is fast but it isn't inexpensive. These companies will charge you a fee for processing your electronic tax return. If you're expecting a refund, you should receive it more quickly if you file electronically than if you send in your handwritten or typed tax forms. The cost of filing online is not terrible but it might eat up a large percentage of your refund check. Decide ahead of time how much you're willing to pay to receive your check quickly.

At a 1998 meeting of technology providers and real estate professionals, Scott Cook, chairman of Intuit (creator of TurboTax), said he envisioned a time in the near future when he would "sit down on April 15, and electronically pull together all of the information I need for my taxes, then electronically file all in the space of a prime-time television commercial break."

We're not there yet, but we will be soon. One of these years, those frantic April 15 late-night drives to a post office will be nothing but a distant memory.

TAX HELP AND RESOURCES

The IRS is loaded down with information for consumers. The problem is, you may find some of it incomprehensible. Still, for more information, you can go to the IRS Web site <www.irs.ustreas.gov> and find tax forms and publications, tax information for individuals and businesses, information on tax changes, taxpayer help and education, information about other IRS electronic services, answers to frequently asked questions, "plain language" summaries, full text of regulations, statistical studies, and newsletters and press releases.

231

When downloading documents from the IRS Web site, or receiving faxed forms, be sure you have the right year. More than one taxpayer has gotten strung up by downloading outdated forms. Check the date at the top!

Here is some other useful information about the IRS:

- *Free tax help.* Call 800-829-3676 to order Publication 910, which describes year-round services, tax-time assistance, and frequently requested publications.

- *Volunteer tax help.* The IRS offers Volunteer Income Tax Assistance (VITA) and Tax Counseling for the Elderly (TCE), which provide specially trained volunteers to prepare basic tax returns. Call your local IRS office for more information.

- *Problem resolution.* If you have a problem that hasn't yet been resolved, the Problem Resolution Program (PRP) might be able to help. Call your local IRS number and ask to speak to someone involved with this program.

- *Direct deposit.* The fastest way to get your refund is to have it deposited directly into your bank account. You can do this whether you file electronically or not. Make sure you check the direct deposit option on your return.

- *File by phone.* You can file your return by telephone with Tele-File. If you qualify, you simply pick up the telephone and enter the tax information the computer program asks for. You must stay on the phone until you receive a confirmation number, or the filing will not be valid. To receive a TeleFile booklet, call 800-829-3676.

- *Check out your local post office or library.* Often, your local post office or library will carry some blank tax forms during the tax season. This might save you a trip to your local IRS office when the time comes.

- *Faxes and CD-ROMs.* The IRS will also fax forms to you; call 703-487-4160. You may order a CD-ROM of tax forms from the Government Printing Office by calling 202-512-1800.

- *More information.* Another helpful toll-free number gives listeners recorded tax messages; some are in Spanish and English. Call 800-829-4477.

Marriage, Partnership, and Children

8

WHO SHOULD HANDLE THE FINANCES IN OUR FAMILY?

In our society, the topic of money is even more intimate than sex. If you're like most folks, you and your friends will more readily swap stories about past relationships than talk about how much you earn. Your parents probably never sat down with you and talked about how much money the family had. Yet they (finally!) told you about the birds and the bees. Given that money rules our society, our cultural reticence is ironic. Sex is used to sell everything in our society, from beer cans to technology. Imagine what our national savings rate would be if sex was used to sell personal finance.

Have *you* ever sat down with your friends and talked about how much each of you earns? Compensation, withholding, and retirement contributions are hardly the stuff you'll hear bandied about in a restaurant or bar, or at a ball game. Rather than discuss what you earn or save, you're much more likely to talk about what you spend—how much those new CDs cost, the bottom line on your vacation package, or what you spent on your last car. You might compare notes on how much it really cost to buy your home, or how quotes vary on the interest rate to refinance your home. But most of us are completely uncomfortable telling people what we're worth and how much we make.

And yet, we're very, very interested in what everyone else earns! *Newsweek* puts out an annual issue of what people earn in particular job categories, and it flies off the magazine stands. *The Wall Street Journal* and *Parade* magazine also publish an annual salary review. Many trade publications publish salary ranges for jobs within their industries. Our society celebrates wealth, tracks the riches of our richest citizens (most people know that Bill Gates is worth billions of dollars), and has created thousands of instant "millionaires" through state lottery games in which the odds are at least 14 million to 1.

When we're so completely consumed by the subject of money, why not talk about it? Money—your money, not money in the abstract—is the last bastion of privacy in a world where even the most private acts get a full public airing.

I can understand why you might not want to talk about money publicly. But what about in the privacy of your own home? Do you and your spouse or partner talk about money? More couples than you can imagine never talk about money. They don't talk about it before they get married or while they're married; then they leave it to the divorce lawyers to talk about after they separate.

Jorie's Story

Jorie was a highly successful computer salesperson who earned more than $100,000 a year. After she married and had her son, she quit working, and she and her husband divided up the responsibilities: he would for earn a living, pay the bills, and make sure the financial stuff was taken care of. She would keep the home running and raise their son. Later, when she started a home-based business, she only ran the finances for that business, leaving the household finances to her husband. "I've never even asked him what he earns in a year," she said.

Maybe it works for them—but maybe it doesn't and she won't admit it. Not knowing about your spouse's or partner's finances leaves you vulnerable to some pretty nasty surprises down the line. Some people are shocked to learn that their spouse has horrible credit and is thousands of dollars in debt. When you marry, your and your spouse are joined financially from that point on. (If you're living with someone and you are not married, the law treats you as unmarried partners, and your credit is not joined.) If your spouse has bad credit and you have perfect credit, you may not qualify for a mortgage because of your combined credit report.

Who should handle the money in the family? You and your spouse or partner should do it together. You should each have a turn at recording how much you spend, so you know where the money goes. You should each have a turn at paying bills, so you know how much it really costs to finance your lifestyle. And each adult member of the family should know what you have, where it's located, and how to get to it.

Did you marry for love or money? Either way, relationships work best when each person knows what's really going on behind the scenes. You and your spouse or partner should be able to talk about *any* subject without blushing, including money. One CPA's client handled all of the money while his wife stayed home and took care of the kids. She charged things left and right without consulting him, and since he didn't want to deny her anything, he didn't tell her that their financial resources had been devoured by years of material consumption. Slowly, they fell deeper and deeper into debt, and one day woke up to a heap of trouble. When she found out, the wife felt awful, and said, "If I'd only known. Why didn't you tell me?" To which the husband could only shrug, "I wanted you to have it all."

Starting Out Right

The time to get your money management organized is when you start out. Once you've made the decision to form a household, you should have an open, frank discussion about money. Here are twelve issues you and your spouse or partner should discuss with each other:

1. *How much do I have? How much do you have?* If you've never thought about money and stocks before, this could be an eye-opener. You should include everything: the balances in your checking and savings accounts, the penny-filled jars in the basement, the stock your Aunt Ruth gave you when you were born, your retirement accounts, and your personal property, including jewelry, cars, and real estate. You may find that you have more than you'd imagined.

2. *Are you a spender or a saver?* In Aesop's fable about the ant and the grasshopper, the ant worked hard all summer and stored away enough food to survive the winter. The grasshopper lived for today and starved to death when the cold weather came. Are you the kind of person who lives (i.e., spends) for today? Or do you put money away for rainy days or retirement?

3. *What do you spend your money on each month?* Even people who save money have to spend some amount on food, clothing, and shelter. What else do you spend money on? Do you buy a whole wardrobe of clothes or just the minimum? Do you buy

235

CDs or books each week? Do you have the newspaper delivered? Do you go out for dinner during the week? Are you a season ticketholder for the opera, a theater group, the ballet, or a particular sports team? Are your telephone bills large or small? Do you travel a lot? (If you don't know where your money goes, check out the budget in Chapter 2 for some ideas.) Do you spend frivolously or cautiously?

4. *Do you know approximately how much things cost?* While in office, former President George Bush was amazed that grocery stores were using scanning devices. He was also amazed at the price of bread. Do you know what a loaf of bread costs? What about a gallon of milk? A tube of toothpaste?

5. *How do you feel about discount stores?* Are you happy to be buying the same thing but at lower prices? Or, do you hate fighting the crowds, finding space to store items that you've bought in bulk, and clipping coupons?

6. *Do you know how much your current credit card bill will be?* Do you keep track of what you spend (either written down or in your head)? Or do you literally charge ahead?

7. *Do you know how much money is in your wallet right now?* Some folks know to the penny, and some folks don't have a clue.

8. *Do you know how much total debt you owe and how much you spend on interest in a given month?* If you're combining money and expenses, you may have twice the debt to pay off. Thinking this through early will help you develop a plan of action.

9. *What kind of billpayer are you?* Do you pay on time, or only when the phone company starts sending red notices? If you pay on time and your honey pays late, will this drive you to distraction? What about people who pay just at the due date, or who fail to keep enough money in their accounts? Have you ever sent a credit card payment by overnight mail so it got there on time? (I have.)

10. *What kind of giftgiver are you?* Do you do expensive gifts or tokens of affection? Are you paying off Christmas bills with your tax refund? Do you exchange gifts with family and friends or just family? What kinds of gifts would you like to receive?

11. *What are your dreams? How do you want to live in the future?* Unless you've inherited a substantial sum, or won the lottery, you'll need to work to pay off your present and create a future. How many children do you want? How do you feel

about financially helping aging parents and other relatives? Would you want them to live with you if they needed to? Some people are willing to sacrifice their future to live well today. Some people want to sacrifice now for some measure of comfort down the line. How you and your spouse or partner dream about the future and plan to pay for it can be a telling sign of your long-term compatibility.

12. *What would you cut in order to live on less?* These days, few workers spend their careers with the company that initially hires them. It's also possible that one or both of you might lose your job at some point. If you have to economize, where will you do it? Where will your spouse or partner cut? What if you decide one of you should stay at home with the kids? Will you both be willing to make the necessary adjustments without resentment?

It is important for each spouse or partner in a relationship to have a turn at paying the bills, but one of you may be better at it than the other. If that's the case, you may want to assign that specific job (paying bills) to one person. However, that doesn't relieve the other person of the responsibility of knowing what the numbers are, where the family assets are invested, and how to get them if need be. Managing your financial life is an important task, and each of you deserves a stake in how it goes and grows. To feel really good about your money, you need to have a handle on what you have. Every six months (or more frequently) you and your spouse or partner should sit down and go through the numbers: what you have, where you have it, and how much more or less it's worth than the last time you reviewed it. This is the time to take stock and make decisions about what you should do.

Whether you've already combined your finances or are about to, it's important to know where you stand with respect to the ownership of, and use of, money. Spend the time it takes to reach a meeting of the minds about your financial future. Almost everyone goes through some financial stress during their lifetime. If you don't work out some of these issues ahead of time, and give yourselves a firm financial foundation, your relationship could be the casualty.

237

QUESTION
48

HOW DO WE DETERMINE WHETHER IT MAKES FINANCIAL SENSE FOR ONE OF US TO STAY HOME WITH THE CHILDREN?

If you can afford to do it and you feel good about it, staying at home with your children is a wonderful option. But many folks have trouble figuring out whether they can afford it and whether the arrangement is really worth it. Here's one mother's story.

Kathy's Story

When Kathy and her husband were first married, she was the big bread-winner in the family. She earned two-thirds of the household income. Her commute to work wasn't bad—about forty-five minutes door to door. But when her company moved to the other side of town, her commute went up to almost an hour and a half each way, or three hours per day. She needed to switch trains twice and then walk a fair bit to get there.

As she rose in the business, her hours grew. Pretty soon, she was leaving the house at 7 A.M. and returning around 7 P.M. When she and her husband decided to start a family, she worried about what her hours would be, and wondered how she'd feel about leaving the baby.

She took three months' maternity leave, and then hired Bonnie, a highly skilled nanny who cost about half of Kathy's salary, or one-third of the family's income. After deducting her transportation expenses and clothing expenses, not to mention taxes, Kathy began to see that she was netting only about $5,000 per year, after work expenses were figured in. For that money, she realized it wasn't worth seeing the baby less than two hours per day plus weekends.

She quit her job and dismissed the nanny. Later on, she started a successful consulting practice from her home. She trades babysitting days with a neighbor, and has someone help out in the home once or twice a week, so she can get out and have meetings with her clients.

Kathy's experience worked out well for her, but sometimes a father must play Mr. Mom. Scott pursued his doctorate while caring for his two children. He was his kids' soccer coach, Cub Scouts leader, and head lunchmaker. His wife, an accountant, went back to full-time work after each maternity leave.

The worksheet on page 239 will help you figure out what you're netting after household and job-related expenses. Compare all of the benefits you receive from working—salary, insurance, sickpay, and

Should You Work or Be a Full-Time Parent?

Income

Gross monthly income	$	_____
Taxes	– $	_____
Employer-paid medical insurance	– $	_____
Other deductions	– $	_____
Pay docked for days missed in excess of time allowed	– $	_____
Net Monthly Income	= $	_____

Costs (Monthly)

Child care (including taxes, if applicable)	$	_____
Transportation to and from work	+ $	_____
Business clothing	+ $	_____
Dry cleaning (for business clothes)	+ $	_____
Nonreimbursed business expenses	+ $	_____
Lunch and/or dinner when working	+ $	_____
Office gift and/or party contributions	+ $	_____
Gardening service*	+ $	_____
Cleaning help*	+ $	_____
Other costs	+ $	_____
Total Monthly Costs	= $	_____

Net monthly earnings	$	_____
Total monthly costs	– $	_____
Net earnings	= $	_____

*Don't include these costs if you plan to stop hiring cleaning help and your gardening service once you leave your job.

retirement contributions—versus the cost of paying someone else to watch your child. No worksheet can quantify the emotional charge you get from either working or being a full-time parent. This worksheet merely attempts to help you work through the hard numbers.

"Net earnings" is how much you're making after you subtract the expenses of working, income taxes, and child care. But the "net earnings" line may or may not tell the whole story. Does your job provide your family with medical, disability, and life insurance benefits? If you stop working and your spouse's job can't provide these benefits, you'll have to pay these costs out-of-pocket. Retirement account options for stay-at-home spouses are still extremely limited. You may invest $2,000 in a Roth IRA or a regular IRA. (If you start a business at home, as Kathy did, you may be able to pump up your retirement savings through a defined benefits plan, such as a Keogh.)

The bottom line is that it may be much more expensive (now and in the future) for you to quit working and stay at home, than to stay employed and bear the expenses of full-time child care. On the other hand, who's going to give your children the love and attention you or your spouse can? It's a tough choice, and there's a different right answer for every family.

Here are some things to think about:

- *Will I have to buy insurance?* Medical, dental, disability, and life insurance can be costly to replace, particularly because large employers get breaks not available to the rest of us, and they typically pick up some, or all, of the cost. Can your spouse's insurance cover you? If you and your partner are unmarried, this option is probably not available to you, though your partner's health insurance may cover any children you have together.

- *Will I contribute to an IRA or Keogh account (if I set up a home-based business)?* If you deposit the maximum (currently $2,000) into an IRA, that will be change out of your pocket. And, it may not come close to replacing the retirement cash you were able to put away at your job (or the amount your employer contributed, if any).

- *Will I still need help?* Many full-time parents still have cleaning help, or a gardening service, and they hire baby-sitters to watch the kids while they shop, workout, or have a day off.

- *Will I lose a child care tax credit?* Even families with relatively high incomes can take advantage of the child care tax credit to offset the cost of baby-sitters or day care programs.

Why You May Not Want to Quit

There are valid reasons why you may not want to quit, even if you'd save money by staying at home. If you have a serious or chronic illness and you're currently covered by your employer's insurance programs, you might have problems switching to your spouse's plan. Or, if you're not married, you may not be able to find decent coverage.

Some people just want to work. They feel challenged and excited by the day-in, day-out problem solving that work brings. One new mom recently said she felt stifled at home. If that's the case, you'll want to do something to feel as though you're making a contribution. If the economics don't work out for you to hold a full-time job outside the home, look into things you can do from home, while raising your children. A part-time business started when your children are young might grow into a full-time, money-making empire when they start school and you have a little more time to yourself. Finally, consider doing some volunteer work while you're at home, to refine your skills or develop new ones. In that way, you'll be ready to reenter the job market. If you work for a company, look into the possibility of working from home a few days a week. If you're on site with your children, even if a baby-sitter is there, you may feel connected to both your children and your job. Sometimes you just need a change.

HOW DO I TEACH MY CHILDREN ABOUT MONEY? WHAT GIFTS SHOULD I GIVE THEM?

"Teach your children well . . . ."

—*Crosby, Stills, Nash, & Young*

I've always wondered why you can't take a course in college called Personal Finance 101. Perhaps there is such a course, but I never found one while paging through my course books. In truth, college is too late to begin teaching someone about personal finance fundamentals and the benefits of compounding. Too many college kids today have credit card debt, no savings, and car loans, not to mention school loans. They've mortgaged their future for the pleasures of a Spring Break trip. High school students get a taste of reality if they hold a part-time job, such as bagging groceries or baby-sitting, and then are responsible for part of their expenses, such as a date night or a new outfit to wear to a big dance.

But high school students already have attitudes about money that might be difficult to dispel, including: "All you have to do is ask Mom or Dad for it." Grade school might be a good time to start teaching the value of money. But I think the best time is when children are curious enough to ask what it is and be fascinated by it. Many children start to show a curiosity about money around age two or three. (At about this age, my son, Alex, started to ask to hand the waitress my credit card to pay for dinner and started collecting change he found around the house and putting it in a jar.)

We pick up a lot of what we know and feel about money from our parents. If they're ashamed of money, we may be ashamed. If they're big spenders, we may end up as spenders. On the other hand, if our parents spent themselves into trouble, we may end up with a Depression-era mentality, always fearing that the "repo" man is at the door.

Starting Out

If there's a money gene, it hasn't been discovered yet. Studies have shown that more than 82 percent of Americans learn about money and finances from their families. That means the financial environment we create for ourselves can feather our children's financial nest. And eventually, most of us do wake up to the fact that money doesn't grow on trees.

No matter what kind of financial values you try to instill in your kids, your efforts might not matter if they have a credit card in their pocket and they know that you'll bail them out if something bad happens. In preparing this chapter, Amy, one of my researchers, and I talked to a couple dozen twenty-somethings from all over the country. Some came from wealthy families, some from poor ones. All had at least one credit card in their wallet, and most were paying off credit card debt. Read what they had to say about money, and about the financial values their parents tried to give them.

Dave's Story

When he was ten years old, Dave's dad paid him for doing odd jobs around the house, and encouraged him to put this money in a savings account. He still has this account and has added to it for the past eleven years. At age sixteen, he opened a checking account. "This was a very exciting day because I remember that my dad gave me money to open it. I felt older and like I had come to a turning point in my life."

Many of Dave's jobs through the years have been unpaid, but they were rich in experience. When he had jobs that paid, he spent half of his earnings and saved the rest. Dave is on his way to medical school, and will leave debt-free, thanks to his parents' and grandparents' footing the bill. His big concern for the future: Earning enough money to buy nice things.

Bridget's Story

"I've always had a problem saving and still do," says Bridget.

As a child, she used her allowance money to buy candy, magazines, and books, and to go to the movies with her friends. She's still treating herself. She currently has two credit cards. One is for items her parents have agreed to pay for in advance. The other feeds her spending habits. She recently returned from a vacation in Cancun, Mexico, and is now facing a credit card balance that is five times the amount of money she really has. She's a little troubled by this, but glad she took advantage of the opportunity to have a vacation. "I know I just have to work harder to get the money to pay it off." And yet, this card never seems to get paid off. She barely manages to pay the minimum each month.

Some of Bridget's other money secrets include using her ATM card regularly, but paying a fee each time. If she's honest with herself, she knows it's because she's too lazy to switch banks. Money dribbles out of her fingers even as she faces paying off several large school loans. On the other hand, fresh from a well-known private college, she has landed a good job with an excellent company, and her prospects for income are sky-high.

"I've just started to realize the value of money and how important it is to think about finances [for the] future," she says. "I've been terrible with day-to-day budgeting but, come next fall, when I start work and have a lot of real expenses, I hope this will change."

243

Beth's Story

Beth received $5 per week for doing odd jobs around the house when she was young. But she only got her money if all of her chores were complete. She feels this taught her a good work ethic. Her parents also established a savings account for her. "I loved to see the numbers go up in the passbook, so I put more money into my account," she said. "Now I go in shifts of spending and being frugal. Especially now, I feel like I have my whole life to save. I do think of my future, and saving for my kids' future, but for now I want to live comfortably and not deny myself the little comforts."

Beth uses ATMs to get money, and she laughs because her mom won't use one. Her mom insists on writing a check for "cash" at the bank because using an ATM is too tempting. To Beth, writing a check just takes too much time and seems almost antiquated, given the technology that's available.

"I think a lot of how you relate to money is because of how you were brought up. For instance, my parents only have one credit card, and they use it only for emergencies. My grandparents were frugal people who saved every penny and invested a lot. We didn't even know the extent of it until my grandmother died. I think a lot of how you're raised rubs off on you and [helps define] your own spending and saving habits."

Kyle's Story

"I worry about not being able to make ends meet for the first few months of my time in the real world. I've been dependent upon my parents for such a long time, but I am really looking forward to claiming full financial independence. I think our generation has seen our parents work so hard for money at the expense of so much else. It's a [priority] for me to find a job that makes me happy and pays enough to live. If I don't take chances at this point in my life, when will I? I worry most about my college credit card debt, and having enough money to start my life and furnish my first apartment."

To combat the never-ending debt cycle, Kyle started using his bank check card rather than whipping out his credit card. "I recently read that investing now, while I'm in my twenties, instead of later, when I'm in my thirties, could mean hundreds of thousands of [extra] dollars down the road. I'd really like to invest, but I just don't have the cash right now."

Cindy's Story

Cindy's parents put her on a clothing allowance, starting in ninth grade. At the end of the summer, her mother would go through her closet, throwing out old and worn clothes and assessing what she needed for school. Her mom gave her a list of items she needed, and a sum of money to purchase them. (It's called budgeting.) Sometimes it went well, and sometimes it didn't. "A lot of times, I'd mess up and spend $50 on a shirt and then realize I didn't have enough for the other shirts I needed," Cindy says.

With all this training, you'd expect Cindy to manage her money well today. Unfortunately, it hasn't worked out that way. "I'm not frugal," she admits. "I've had credit card debts for the past two years, and every month I only pay the minimum. I do not have savings, and I spend whatever I get." Cindy's parents bailed her out of one credit card problem, when she'd charged over $800. "Credit cards are so tempting. It's amazing! I know I'm paying four times more in interest. It's a terrible habit, but come graduation, I'll get money from my grandparents and parents and use it to pay off my bills."

Her parents have done without a lot of things in order to send their three kids through private schools. Cindy thinks this is important, but, at the same time, she wants to be able to buy what she wants, live in a nice place, and take weekend trips with her friends at the drop of a hat.

All of these men and women have good basic values. And perhaps their naïve attitudes about money can be forgiven as a folly of youth. After all, when you have your whole life ahead of you, it's easy to psychologically disconnect from a tomorrow that won't arrive for forty-five or fifty years.

11 Ways to Teach Your Children Well

Here are eleven things you can do to help your children develop a sense of awareness about money and the power it holds:

1. *Give an allowance.* Make sure it's age-appropriate and covers regular expenses, such as school lunches (if they're not brought or paid for separately) and transportation (if your child uses public transportation). Allowances should be given for being part of the family, but they should come with the

requirement that your children keep up their end, including making their beds, keeping their rooms clean, emptying the dishwasher, setting the table, helping out with dinner or food shopping—whatever you think are the normal chores associated with keeping the family going.

2. *Pay for work performed above and beyond.* Occasionally asking your thirteen-year-old to baby-sit his or her younger sibling may or may not be above and beyond his or her regular chores. But if you ask for a regular Saturday evening commitment, which means your child cannot accept other baby-sitting assignments, you may want to consider paying for that service. The same thing goes for cutting the grass, or other jobs around the house. You want your child to understand that he or she deserves to get paid for a job that's outside normal responsibilities. And, consider an occasional bonus for a job truly well done.

3. *You pay for the basics, they pay for the extras.* A regular allowance should include a little bit of cash outside the necessities, so that your child learns how to make choices about spending. But he or she should work (either for you or someone else) for the extras. Any cash received should be divided into three piles: savings, spendable cash, and a donation to a charity or your house of worship. (Unless your child is really raking it in, you may want to leave aside the issue of taxes for the moment.)

4. *Give gifts of stocks or mutual funds, then teach how to follow these investments.* Most children receive more toys than they have time to play with. But a gift of stock (perhaps a stock that relates to children in some way, like Disney or a sports team) or a mutual fund is a gift that keeps giving, and may even help defray college tuition costs when the time comes. Encourage grandparents or godparents to follow your example. Teach your children how to follow these investments, and add to them along the way.

5. *Open a savings account.* Children like to see things grow and change. Money growing in an account may be intangible, but they'll understand if you relate it to their piggy bank's getting heavier and heavier. When they're old enough, open a checking account.

6. *Teach them to keep a written record.* As soon as they're ready, have them record what they spend, what they earn, what they save, and what they give away. When they're computer literate, show them how to input their expenses and savings into a money management program such as Quicken or Microsoft Money.

7. *Require thank-you notes.* If someone gives them a gift, time and money were spent, and a prompt thank-you note should follow. A gift that is unacknowledged devalues both the gift and the act of giving.

8. *Don't bail them out.* Nearly every college student we talked to had a credit card, and more than two-thirds of them had credit card debt. Don't give your child a credit card with the understanding that you'll bail him or her out every time. If the card is for emergency use only, make it known that you'll pay the bill only in true emergencies.

9. *Toss away the cigarettes and booze.* Even if you smoke or drink, try to teach your children that smoking and drinking (especially in excess), in addition to being bad for health, are incredibly expensive. A two-packs-a-day habit will cost you more than $2,000 per year, or more than $100,000 over your lifetime. Two beers a day at a local bar will set you back even more. If you invest that money instead of smoking or drinking it away, you'll retire a multimillionaire.

10. *Have high expectations.* If you let your children know you expect them to be responsible about money, chances are they'll absorb this message and rise to the occasion. They won't always make the right decisions about money, but they'll at least know what they *should* be doing.

11. *Give it away.* Giving money away is one of the best lessons you can teach your children. Years ago, my late stepfather, Leon, told me he gave $5 to every legitimate nonprofit organization that sent him a letter. He gave more to those charities about which he felt strongly. I was only twenty when I met him, and his actions made a huge impression on me. I don't give to every organization that sends a form letter, but I spread out my giving to a large number of charitable organizations. Besides writing a check, let your children see you giving your time to help those less fortunate than you. Buy a newspaper

from a homeless person who is selling them to make a living. A few afternoons or evenings helping out in a soup kitchen says more than a year of lectures about spending too much money on CDs or candy. Your house of worship may have an ongoing link to several charitable organizations in your town.

When your children were babies, did you give them candy every time they asked for it? Children want, and need to learn, boundaries and appropriate behavior. It won't make much difference what you tell your children about money if you spoil them silly. It's the old actions-speak-louder-than-words theory. Even if you have the means to give them everything they could possibly want, don't. Remember how—and why—you didn't give them all the sweets and treats they wanted way back when. Try not to focus major attention on material possessions. Fancy cars, expensive clothes, and huge homes don't mean anything to children. They'd much rather have you spend time with them. (And this never changes. As they get older, most children appreciate your time much more than they care about your money.)

QUESTION 50

HOW DOES DIVORCE AFFECT MY PERSONAL FINANCES?

Divorce can wreak havoc on your emotional and psychological state. It can also wipe you out financially, now and for years to come. Still, it's far better to be poor and happy than rich and unhappy. (If you can figure out a way to be rich *and* happy, more power to you.)

If you're getting divorced, there's a lot to think through, especially if you have kids. Even in the best of circumstances, where the divorce is as civil and amicable as it can be, funding two households will be a drain on your resources. You may find yourself with a reduced standard of living, particularly if you were formerly a stay-at-home spouse and you now have custody of the kids.

Here are some ways divorce might affect your financial future:

- *Two households.* Unless you're moving to another property you already own and pay for, divorce typically means setting up another household. In addition to rent and utilities, you may need to purchase furniture, drapes, dishes, silverware, glasses, sheets, towels, and the little stuff, like soap, shampoo, and razors. You may also need another car, and another set of toys and children's clothing, if your children will be spending time at both residences. And then there's the cost of two separate lives: money for entertainment, for insurance, for separate vacations.

- *Child support/spousal support.* If one spouse's income supported the entire family, that spouse may have to pay spousal support until the other spouse gets on his or her feet or for life. Traditionally, men paid support (also called alimony) to their ex-wives for life (or for a very long period of time). Today, more and more working women are paying support to their ex-husbands. If you're not receiving support and you have to live on what you earn—which may be only a fraction of your former joint household income—and you have the kids, you'll definitely feel the pinch. Depending on whom the children end up living with, the other spouse may pay something toward child support.

- *Marital assets.* If you came into the marriage with separate assets and kept those assets separate during the course of the marriage, you may end up with them when your marriage is over. But if you commingled assets, or mixed money, then those assets may be considered part of the marital estate.

- *Retirement funds.* These typically get divvied up, especially if one spouse has extremely high earnings and the other has put little or nothing away in his or her own name. The spouse who receives a portion of the other's retirement funds can flip those into his or her own IRA without paying taxes or penalties.

- *Litigation expenses.* Lawyers are expensive. And hiring two really, *really* good attorneys to battle it out in a nasty, drawn-out divorce will be expensive. If the divorce is amicable and you don't have much between you, try to work things out quickly, with your attorney's guidance or through mediation, rather than inviting protracted court proceedings.

- *Second families.* If you thought taking care of one family was expensive, wait until you get married again. And if you have children in that second marriage, you may find yourself spending even more on the children from your first marriage, to compensate them for not having you around more often.

If you want to protect your children from a prior marriage, you can do one of two things: (1) put some or all of your assets into a trust before you remarry, and name your children as the beneficiaries, or (2) have your soon-to-be spouse sign a prenuptial agreement that spells out what will happen if you get divorced. Experts say that your intended should have his or her attorney look over the agreement before signing it. Otherwise, if you divorce, you may hear attorneys arguing that you coerced your ex-spouse into signing. For more information, consult an estate or divorce attorney.

The Bottom Line

Divorce is complicated and is often nasty. I hear from many separated, divorced, and divorcing people whose ex-spouse has intentionally wrecked their credit; stolen money, belongings, or even children; and haunted them to this day. Each divorce, like each marriage, is completely unique. And each divorce will take its own toll on your financial life. Should your marriage fail, get the help you need, whether your concerns are emotional, financial, or legal.

Investments: In
the Beginning . . .

WHAT STEPS SHOULD I TAKE TO GET STARTED IN INVESTING?

What's the hardest part about investing? Taking the first step. But if you're ever going to move forward and turn your dreams into realities, you're going to have to put one foot in front of the other. For some people, socking money into mutual funds or individual stocks seems like an enormous leap of faith: Will the market continue to match its historical record? Will your money really grow over time?

Trust me: Investing your money is only tough the first few times you do it—and the first time you do it after an investment has failed. (But, to borrow a lyric, you've got to pick yourself up, dust yourself off, and start all over again.) Still, those first few times can be frightening. Investing may even feel like gambling. You may begin to question why you didn't just buy $25 worth of lottery tickets instead of putting your money where you can't see it, touch it, or smell it. But once you take responsibility for your investment decisions, and when your investments start to grow, you'll realize that investing your money is wise and satisfying and can even be fun.

Five Simple Steps Anyone Can Take

Okay, the first step *is* tough. But sometimes it's tough because you don't know what the second step will be. Here are five simple steps anyone can take toward a successful financial future.

1. *Determine your financial goals, and decide how quickly you want to achieve them.* What's on your wish list for your future? What kind of lifestyle do you want for yourself and your family? Do you want to pay for your children's education? Their weddings? Your retirement? How golden do you want your retirement parachute to be? Saving and investing money in a vacuum isn't much fun. Developing financial goals and setting a schedule for reaching them gives you signposts for your journey. If you've been reading this book from the beginning, you may have already done this bit of homework. If not, go back to Question 5 (p. 26) for some additional help.

2. *Gauge how much risk you want to take.* Risk is a defining factor of successful investing because the more risk you take, the more likely the returns on your investments will be superlative. The riskiest investments pay out the highest return. What is the risk you take? Your greatest risk is that your investment will drain away or implode overnight. If you're the kind of person who says about the stock market, "But it could go down," you'll probably want to take the more conservative road. You'll be able to sleep at night while earning a 7 or 8 percent average annual return on your investments. But if you're willing to invest in the stock market, your average annual return could be 10 percent or higher. What's the difference between a 7 percent return and a 10 percent return on your money? Over a lifetime of investing, the difference could amount to hundreds of thousands or even millions (you read that right!) of dollars. (See Appendix III.) Before you run out and put all your money into a speculative stock or an investment you may not understand, remember that risk isn't an all-or-nothing proposition. You can take none, some, or a lot, and, at any time, you can change the amount of risk you take in your investments. For a more complete discussion on risk, see Question 53, later in this chapter.

3. *Learn what types of investments will best meet your investment goals without exceeding the amount of risk you're willing to take.* This is the time to determine which combination of stocks, bonds, and mutual funds will stay within the limit of risk you're willing to take, while still providing you with the returns you'd like to have. For stocks and stock mutual funds, the basic choices are aggressive growth (riskiest investments, biggest return), growth (less risk), growth and income (some risk, but the investment gives off a regular stream of income), and income (conservative). The three basic types of bonds are: (1) corporate,

(2) government (typically, Treasuries and U.S. Savings Bonds), and (3) municipal. Treasury bonds and notes are generally the highest investment grade. Everything else runs the gamut from investment grade to the lowest category, junk bonds, and you can invest in bond funds that specialize in one kind or the other, and everything in between. Many advisers believe a well-balanced portfolio should also incorporate small-cap stocks (companies with a capitalization of less than $1 billion), plus a smattering of international companies. If you've decided that absolutely no risk is acceptable but you want sky-high returns, you'll probably find yourself out of investment choices before you even start selecting. If you want your returns to match those of the market, and you're willing to accept a modicum of risk, you will have many more investment options. If you're willing to accept quite a bit of risk, you may be able to reap above-market returns. Over the years, certain "rules of thumb" have been developed that will help you determine your investment mix. One of the most popular "rules" is to subtract your age from 100. What's left is the percentage of your investment that should go to stocks or other riskier investments. The rest, says the rule, should be invested more conservatively—in bonds or Treasury bills, for example. If you're more of a risk taker, or you believe you'll live to see your 100th birthday, subtract your age from 120 to 140, depending on how much risk you can endure and how old you think you'll live to be. For example, if I thought I'd live to be 100 and I like a lot of risk, I'd subtract my age from 130 or 140. (Hint: You can't put more than 100 percent of your holdings into any one investment, so, if you're age 25, your maximum number can only be 125.)

4. *Consider your investments carefully.* A key concept in investing is *diversification*—spreading out your risk by investing in a variety of companies, mutual funds, and bonds, while still earning the return you want. Overall, your goal should be to develop a *balanced portfolio*—one that will hold up in the bad times (and there will be bad times, I can assure you) while taking advantage of the good times. You'll want to include elements of real estate (owning your own home may suffice, or you may wish to add investment properties or to purchase shares of a REIT), mutual funds, individual stocks, and bonds. Depending on your faith in the company you work for, you may wish to hold a substantial amount of your 401(k) program in company stock. Just don't go overboard. Weighting down your portfolio with any one stock over a period of time raises your risk, perhaps to an unacceptable level, depending on your financial

253

goals and timetable. (I talk about this more in Question 54, later in this chapter.)

5. *Take responsibility for your investments.* I know a woman who puts responsibility for all of her investment decisions on her investment adviser. When her portfolio does well, it's because he's a genius. When her portfolio does badly, he's, well, not a genius. The problem with all this is that she hasn't taken responsibility for her investments. Like many other people, she hired an expert, and now completely relies on her adviser's expertise and guidance. While, this lady doesn't really know what kinds of investments she has, what she paid for them, or why she bought them, this isn't the way you should run *your* financial life. Even hiring the best and smartest advisers from among the legitimate folks waiting to help you doesn't absolve you of the responsibility of making basic decisions about

Sarah and Jacob's Story

Together, Sarah and Jacob earn a lot of money. They have no kids, and they live relatively cheaply. They are the ultimate "Dinks" (double income, no kids).

Every January, Sarah receives a large bonus from her company. The full amount goes right into the couple's joint money market account. Each year, they put the maximum allowable amount (under IRS rules for a tax deduction) into their retirement accounts, but a lot of their money is earning only about 2.5 percent interest.

When asked why they've been dillydallying around with their investments, Sarah says she and Jacob are looking for the right investment adviser. Over the past two years, they've met with five advisers. None of them has been right, Sarah explains. The truth is, Sarah and Jacob are afraid to jump in and start investing. "I don't know which mutual fund to buy," Sarah says. Even though she spends her workdays investing her company's employee pension funds, she has never linked what she does for a living and her personal finances. Jacob, who has little interest in investing, has left those decisions to Sarah.

They hope to start a family within the next couple of years, and, when children come, Sarah would like to leave her job and stay at home. But to do that without radically changing their lifestyle, they need to make their money work harder for them. And Sarah and Jacob can't seem to bring themselves to take that first step.

your investments. No matter how professional your adviser is, he or she isn't inside your head or living your life. Taking responsibility for your decisions means knowing the basics about the investments you make, keeping an eye on them as time goes by, and keeping track of where you are and whether you're meeting (or exceeding) your financial goals. No one absolutely needs to have a financial adviser. After you start paying attention to what you're doing, and educating yourself, you may find that by taking responsibility, you can do a perfectly wonderful job of managing your investments on your own.

If you have a Money Block, and it's preventing you from getting on with your financial life, take a step back and ask yourself: What's the *worst* thing that can happen if I invest this money? Easy answer: You might lose some, or all, of your investment. If losing it all is your deepest fear, explore where that fear comes from. Did your parents lose all their money in an ill-advised investment? Do you have friends who lost everything? Have you lost a significant sum of money on a "hot tip?" Even if all of these things happened to you, or to people you know, your fears won't go away by themselves, and you won't dispel them by *never* investing your money. Instead, work through your Money Block. Consider limiting your exposure in a way that will allow you to rebuild your financial self-esteem. Start small. Invest a small percentage of your money in a highly rated growth and income mutual fund. Invest another small percentage of your money in a safe place, like U.S. Treasury bills. They're backed by Uncle Sam, who has yet to default, ever. As these investments take hold and your confidence builds, you can diversify and purchase other kinds of investments. Your money will be there for you, growing faster than in your money market account, and certainly faster than in your checking account. (Do we even need to mention how the value of your money will shrink—or could be lost in a fire—if you leave it in your mattress?) While you're choosing your investments, spend some time dispelling your money fears. Then ask yourself: If I invest this money, what's the *best* thing that can happen? Another easy answer: It will grow, work harder for you, and allow you to do tomorrow some things you can only dream about today. And what happens if you wait to invest for another year? You'll be a year older, and your investments will have missed out on an additional year of compounding.

How often have you read about people who have been bilked out of vast sums by folks who seemed honest and brilliant but then absconded with all of their money? Unfortunately, there are a lot of scam artists who know that new investors spend more time researching their next microwave oven than evaluating the people they hire to manage their financial future. Taking responsibility for your money means spending time to understand your investments (and the costs of buying, selling, and managing them), as well as checking whether the person you hire to help you has a good agenda for your account. If all you care about is whether you have more money at the end of the month, you may be missing the big picture—how much money you could be earning if your funds were invested differently.

QUESTION
52

HOW DO TIME AND TIMING AFFECT MY INVESTMENT STRATEGY?

As the cliché goes, *timing is everything*. But there's the simple truth: No one can time the market. You won't be able to buy low and sell high every time you invest. And no one else will, either. If they could, they'd be off on a yacht somewhere, or selling you a newsletter that tells you, for $1,000 a year, how to time the market.

Some investment advisers appear to call a major market surge or correction. During 1987, one market analyst said, on television, that the stock market was due for a major correction. *Voila!* The market corrected. This same analyst correctly timed another major market climb, but then completely missed several other important turns. Repeat this as a mantra: *Market timing doesn't work.*

What does work? *Dollar-cost averaging*—a system of putting a little bit of money into the stock market, or a bond fund, or another investment, each week, month, or quarter, on a regular basis. Because the market is fluid—that is, it goes up and down—you'll buy some shares when they cost more and some shares when they cost less. If you don't change the amount you invest regularly, you'll end up paying an acceptable average cost for your shares and will probably own more shares (you'll be buying more shares, for the same money, when the market is down) than if you'd tried to time the market. Remember the mantra: *Market timing doesn't work.*

The best way to make dollar-cost averaging as painless as possible is to have the money automatically deducted from your paycheck or checking account. The theory goes like this: If you never see it in your monthly paycheck, you won't miss spending it. You're *paying yourself first*, a concept we discussed in Chapter 2. Either way, the money is deducted from your account and invested seamlessly in your mutual fund, or elsewhere, and all you'll see is a monthly report of your investment.

Dollar-cost averaging feels good, too. Along with your account balance, your self-esteem will rise as you recognize that you're taking responsibility for your financial future and that of your family. And never underestimate the power of self-esteem. Feeling good about yourself will give you the all-too-rare feeling that you can conquer the world.

How Time Affects Your Investments

Dollar-cost averaging is something you do regardless of what the market is doing week in or week out. But choosing the right investment vehicle is important, too.

Earlier, we discussed how to create and prioritize financial goals. Choosing the right investment has a lot to do with when you'll need the money. If you'll need the cash within two years, that's considered a *short-term* investment. (Three-month, six-month, or one-year bank certificates of deposit and Treasury bills are often considered temporary parking places for cash rather than individual investments.) Even if you purchase property, experts caution you to be especially careful if you're going to sell within three to five years. Instead of buying the most expensive house on the block, try to purchase a home in which you can build value.

If you'll need to cash out your investment anytime between three months and three or four years, don't put it into something risky unless you're willing to lose part of it. (Over the long haul, losing *everything* is a much smaller risk than you might imagine, especially if you choose good companies or highly rated mutual funds, and diversify.) Sure, you could triple your money in three months, but will you actually sell the investment at that point in time, pay your taxes, and be done with it? Probably not. It's not human nature. You'll become enthralled with your investment and addicted to the ego boost you'll get when you tell your friends about your big score. When the stock starts to decline, you'll hold onto it, sure that it will rise again. And, over time, if it's a solid, well-managed investment, it may. Or, it may not, and you'll end up back where you started, or perhaps even out some bucks. In the meantime, you'll be unable to fund one or more of your financial goals.

Short-term money should be put into a conservative or safe investment: a money market account, a money market stock fund, a short-term Treasury bill (T bill), or a short-term, highly rated municipal bond. You'll earn less on your investment, but it will be there when you need it.

Midterm money is cash you'll need in five to ten or fifteen years. You might be investing this money for your children's college tuition, or a wedding, or a big trip. Again, the type of investment vehicle you choose should reflect the amount of time you have until you'll need the money. If you're at the low end of the time horizon—say, five to seven years rather than ten to fifteen—you'll probably want to choose an investment that's considered conservative. A good investment might be a mutual fund that offers growth *and* income (a more conservative strategy).

Long-term investments are those that you don't plan to touch for fifteen to thirty or even forty years. For the best return over the long run, you'll want to plunk down your retirement cash in an investment that carries more risk but offers a better reward. But let's be clear here: I'm *not* suggesting that you find the riskiest stock around and plunk everything into it. That's speculation, not a calculated risk. You can leave your cash with some companies for 100 years and it still won't return a profit.

Pay attention to what your broker or financial adviser considers to be a short-, medium-, or long-term time frame. One Los Angeles-based financial adviser doesn't recognize a difference in any time horizon beyond five years. His idea of a short term is less than a year. An intermediate term is greater than a year but less than five years. Any span over five years is a long term. That may or may not jibe with your thinking. Again, make sure you're clear on the definitions from the get-go.

If you won't need to touch your cash for a long time, put it directly into a portfolio of stocks or an index fund (a mutual fund that holds the same stocks that make up a particular financial index, like the S&P 500, and tries to match the performance of the index). Why? Because you'll have the time to weather the stormy ups and downs of the market. In the end, you'll probably have a return that well outpaces inflation, but liquidating this investment ahead of schedule may mean you'll cash out when the market is down. Be aware that certain types of retirement accounts have a minimum age for withdrawal of funds. Fees, taxes, and penalties are attached to early withdrawal. (See Chapter 13 for more information on retirement accounts.)

Investing often requires strength of character. You have to stick to your principles and your own time horizons in order to earn the kinds of returns you want and have a nest egg available when you need it. It's tough to hold the line when your friends are boasting about three years' annual stock market returns of 30 percent or higher. Still, you have to have faith in your own vision. When we were getting the cash together to finance our home renovation, we refinanced when interest rates were, we thought, at a pretty low point. We took out a large sum in cash, and stuck it into a money market fund earning about 5.5 percent. We had an opportunity to put some money in an investment we had contemplated for a long time; we were assured that we could "double our money." (How many times have you heard that?) We ended up investing a small chunk of our house renovation fund—only the amount we felt we could lose and still proceed with the renovation. The minute the stock hit a certain dollar amount, we sold half, locking in profits and our initial investment. We sold the rest a week later because the stock, an initial public offering, was already coming down in value. Yes, we did really well. But then we played the "if only" game. If only we'd put all of our money in, we'd have completely paid for the renovation in cash. If only we'd put the cash in this stock or that stock, we'd have tripled our money and paid for the renovation and put away money for our kids' college education. If only we'd taken it all and bought lottery tickets for the $295 million Powerball lottery . . . . You can see where this line of thinking takes you. Meanwhile, we accepted our return, paid our capital gains tax, and put everything back in the money market fund. And by the time you read this book, our home renovation will be getting under way.

Don't feel like a failure if you've achieved a 10 percent or even a 15 percent return on your money and "everyone else" in the market achieved a 30 percent return. If inflation stays low, your 10 to 15 percent return, year in and year out, is fantastic and will produce terrific results. There's a sense, however, that you need to "beat the market" or your returns aren't worth anything. I think this is bunk. A 10 percent or 15 percent return over time is terrific, and few fund managers can boast about that kind of result over the long haul. It's nice to have the extra cash a higher return produces, but as long as you're meeting your goals and inflation doesn't go bananas (if it does, you can adjust your strategy), I think you should be satisfied. Emotionally, we always want the biggest bang for the buck, and we're extremely competitive by nature. Stick to the lesson in Aesop's fable of the tortoise and the hare. Slow and steady wins the race. As long as you achieve *your* financial goals, you win. No one ever carves this into their tombstone: "I wish I'd had a better return on my money."

QUESTION 53

HOW MUCH RISK SHOULD I TAKE?

When it comes to investing, the corollary to time is risk. As we just discussed, the longer your investment time horizon, the more risk you should take. Sounds easy—and to some extent, it is. But at least four other factors play into your decision about your investments and the risk you're willing to take:

1. *Age.* If you believe the ads on TV, you can beat the physical effects of time if you use a certain powder, skin cream, or makeup. But don't try to fight time when it comes to your investments. Let time work its magic for you. Your age should have an effect on your investment decisions, even if you need the money in the same number of years as someone half your age. A different age usually translates to a different stage of life. For example, if you're age 50 and need your cash for retirement in twenty years, you might treat that twenty-year horizon differently than if you were age 25 and were planning to pay for your children's education in twenty years. Twenty years is

twenty years, right? Maybe. Funding your retirement is a different need than your ability to fund your child's education. Your child can always get a loan, or maybe a scholarship, to pay for school if your savings plan hasn't worked out the way you thought. There are no loans for retirement (the reverse mortgages we talked about in Question 39 will help, but only in a very limited way). Your investing choices for your twenty years to retirement may be very different from the choices you make during the twenty years until your children are ready for college. (To some investment professionals, twenty years is twenty years. Others believe that any time line longer than five years is a long term. Again, if you're working with an investment professional, ask for definitions of these terms ahead of time, so you're speaking the same language.)

2. *Health.* If you have a serious illness, you may make different choices about your investments than you would if your health were good. If you need cash today, you may opt to liquidate your life insurance, sell investments, or take a more conservative investment stance.

3. *Wealth.* If you're already wealthy, short-term investing may take on a different meaning entirely. To you, a short-term investment may be a one-, two-, or three-month return. You may be moving money in and out of stocks rapidly, or investing through a *margin account* (short-term borrowing from your broker's account to pay for an investment, with the expectation that you will sell it before you have to repay the margin account). If you've already achieved many of your personal financial goals, your definition of a long term may have changed.

Personal finance is filled with all kinds of jargon that can make it difficult to understand. Shifting definitions make things even more difficult. That may be confusing when you talk about various investments. If you and your spouse or partner choose to work with a financial planner, make sure both of you, and the planner, see eye-to-eye and are working from the same page. This will go a long way toward eliminating complications in your working relationship, and helping you make sound investment decisions.

4. *Taxes.* If your goal is to defer taxes, or to pay as little tax as possible, you may: choose growth stocks over those that pay dividends; invest in tax-free municipal bonds rather than taxable bonds; create a trust to pass down a family asset, like a house, to family member; or set up a limited partnership to bequeath shares of a closely held business.

Not Every Risk Is the Same

As an investor, you'll face a wide variety of risks. The most common risks are associated with fluctuations in the stock market, rising inflation, a rise or fall in interest rates, and a change in your time horizon.

There are two ways to counterbalance these risks: (1) invest in less risky investments or (2) diversify into investments that offer a different type of risk and may move out-of-step with your other investments. For example, you can take down your stock market risk by investing in bonds. You can diversify your 100 percent holding in technology stocks by investing in other market sectors or in international stocks or funds that are capable of responding in different ways if the market experiences a "correction."

Increasing Your Risk

Instead of lowering their risk, many investors actually increase their risk by engaging in risky behavior. Here are some activities you should avoid:

- *Buying or selling without a good reason.* You can certainly buy or sell investments before your "scheduled time." But buying or selling on a whim, or trying to outtrade the market, is a risky behavior that should be left to the professionals. Until you become so wealthy that managing your money is your full-time job, you shouldn't buy or sell investments without a really good reason.

- *Failing to set goals.* If you invest without knowing why, or for what, or for how long, you're operating in a vacuum that may or may not produce results. The best strategy: Set goals, and stick to the investment strategy you've designed to reach them.

- *Having unrealistic expectations.* If you expect the market to deliver 30-percent-plus returns every year (as it did several years in a row during the 1990s), you're dreaming. If it happens, that's great. But the truth is, you'll be right on target historically if you aim for a 10 to 12 percent return. Invest in a promise of a "guaranteed" sky-high return, and you'll make investing mistakes from which you may never recover. *There are no guarantees in the stock market.*

- *Letting your emotions drive your investment strategy.* Getting emotionally involved with your investments is a bad idea. Becoming attached to an investment simply because you've owned it for a long time, or because your broker recommended it to you and you're worried that his or her feelings will be hurt if you sell it isn't a viable investment game plan. Voice these reasons and your friends and family will look at you strangely. In fact, you'll increase your risk by holding onto an investment whose time has come and gone. On the other side, if you get too emotionally charged by an investment, you may jump the gun and sell too early.

- *Putting all your eggs in one basket.* If you've decided to be completely invested in the stock market, that's risky enough. But investing a large amount in just one or two stocks is extremely risky behavior, especially if the companies in which you invest are start-up ventures. Yes, you might be rewarded with a 300 percent return in three months. You might also lose 100 percent of your investment overnight.

- *Confusing your perception of the market.* The stock market fluctuates—that is, it rises and falls, sometimes several times in a day. But just because your stock or bond mutual fund fluctuates in price doesn't mean you've made or lost money. You may think you've lost money, but to actually have a gain or loss, you must sell the investment. Acting in response to a temporary drop in price could increase your overall risk.

- *Getting greedy.* My grandfather often said that anyone who tries to always buy at the low and always sell at the high will never make any money in the stock market. He believed that plenty of reasonable gains could be made over the course of one's life. Chasing the biggest returns was a dangerous game he didn't want to play. It was sound advice then, and it's sound advice now. If you chase only the return, it will probably elude you.

Overheard in the street:

"How do you determine the right amount of risk for you?"

"It's the line between fear and greed."

Limiting Your Risk

Five things you can do to decrease your investment risk:

1. *Change your strategy to suit changes in your life.* If your retirement is forty years down the line, the stock market is a good bet for superior returns. According to Ibbotson, a Chicago research and consulting firm, the stock market hasn't lost money in a twenty-year period since 1926. But shorten the periods to ten years, and stocks have lost money 3 percent of the time. Shorten the time frame to five years, and stocks lost money 10 percent of the time. But nothing says you have to stay 100 percent invested in the stock market for your whole life. If you start at 100 or 120 (or up to 140, depending on your tolerance for risk and your expectation of seeing your 100th birthday) and subtract your age, you should be completely, or almost completely, invested in the stock market when you're young. In your thirties, that portion may fall to 85 to 90 percent. In your fifties, it may fall again to 70 to 75 percent; in your sixties, you'll be only 65 to 70 percent invested in the stock market, and so on. You can plan to switch strategies when you hit certain milestones, of age, wealth, or life-cycle events. For example, once your kids get through college, you may shift gears as you prepare to pay for their weddings, or your silver anniversary trip around the world.

2. *Stay the course.* Follow the path you've laid out for yourself, regardless of what the market has done or where it's going. If you contribute $100 per month to a mutual fund, continue doing so. If you set a portfolio mix of, say, 70 percent stocks, 20 percent bonds, and 10 percent real estate, readjust your portfolio periodically so that your investments continue in the appropriate mix.

3. *Reevaluate your investment returns.* On a regular basis, you and your spouse or partner need to sit down and evaluate where your investments are, what's working and what isn't, and whether your personal or emotional situation has changed enough to require a shift in your investment strategy. Keeping an eye on your monthly reports is one way to drastically reduce risk. The investments themselves aren't

less risky, but if an investment is failing, you'll be able to better judge when to get out.

4. *Don't invest money you can't afford to lose.* If you take out a home equity loan and invest the proceeds in a high-risk gamble when you can't really afford the monthly payments, you're a loser even if your high-risk gamble pays off. Investment situations like this keep people up at night.

5. *Do your homework, and be realistic.* When consumers complain to me that it takes a lot of work to buy a home, I remind them that buying a house will be the single largest investment of their lives. Why wouldn't they want to do everything they can to assure themselves that it's a good move? Why do some people spend more time and effort to buying a new dishwasher than they do to purchasing stock in a company? If your best friend told you No-Name Dishwasher Company makes the best dishwashers in the world, would you buy one sight unseen, without looking at competing models? I hope not. The best decisions—those you can live with—come from the knowledge that you know what you're getting into. You're not going to hit a home run every time. Even Warren Buffet can't do that. But if you really do your research, and purchase investments for solid reasons, you'll immediately eliminate a large category of risk.

How much risk should you take? Only as much as you can comfortably live with. How much risk do most Americans take? Not enough, given the amount of time they have available. If you don't feel comfortable taking as much risk as you should, start investing slowly— but get started! Remember that a child born in 1999 has a fair chance of seeing the year 2100. You should plan to have your money work for you for a long time and be able to live off of its returns. You'll never have enough if you don't take more risk.

HOW DO I DEVELOP A DIVERSIFIED PORTFOLIO THAT REFLECTS THE RISK I WANT TO TAKE?

QUESTION
54

Why is diversification the big buzzword in investing? Because if you don't diversify, you are taking an unnecessary risk to earn your reward. Over the long term, with diversification of your investments, you might earn slightly less on your investments, but you'll keep your exposure to risk at a minimum.

What is *diversification?* It is a strategy of investing in a wide array of investments, which ideally move slightly out-of-step with each other, to protect your portfolio. For example, if the U.S. stock market moves one way, an Asian market fund may move to the beat of a different drummer.

Experts will tell you that, to truly diversify, you should have a portion of your assets in stocks, a portion in bonds, and a portion in cash. To further diversify, the experts say, a portion of your stocks should be in small-cap stocks (companies with a market capitalization of $1 billion or less) and another portion should be in foreign stocks. That won't leave much room for large-cap American stocks, but it meets the definition of being *diversified.*

Another way to diversify is to buy mutual funds, which are composed of a variety of different stocks. Fidelity's Magellan Fund is perhaps the largest (around 500 stocks, give or take a couple dozen on any given day) under management. Buying that fund alone may be enough diversification, given that many experts feel investors are fully diversified if they own thirty different stocks.

Other investors diversify by having some of their portfolio in real estate—either rental properties or their own home—and the rest in cash (or a money market fund, or a short-term bond fund). Cash functions as the ultimate "safe haven" for your money. But by being the most conservative of investors (if you're lucky, your cash will beat the rate of inflation), you won't get much of a return.

Let's say you have risky investments and conservative ones. You have American investments and foreign ones. And you have real estate and cash to balance it all out. Now what?

Multiple Portfolios vs. the Family Portfolio

With all of the different investment goals we have (buying a home, paying for children's college education and/or weddings, and saving for retirement), it's tempting to consider having a portfolio of investments for each of our financial priorities.

But with multiple portfolios, we're dividing a pie into six pieces, and then taking one piece and dividing that up into six pieces. As messy as it would be to cut one pie into 36 pieces (6 × 6), that's about how messy it would be to own six separate portfolios, each designed to pay for a different financial goal. The real negatives are cost and time:

- *Cost.* Holding on to each investment costs money (management fees and up-front loads for mutual funds, transaction fees for stock purchases and sales, and annual fees). With so many portfolios, there's bound to be crossover in the types of investments purchased, so you're paying the same costs over and over again.

- *Time.* Managing your money takes time. If you're actively involved with your portfolio, you're probably spending ten hours a month (or more) analyzing what you have, how it's doing, and how you can improve its performance. (If you count time spent balancing your checkbook and paying bills, you might clock up to fifteen hours per month.) That's for *one* portfolio. Start creating miniportfolios, and your time spent will easily multiply. Your time is better spent elsewhere.

Instead, think of your money as family money, or the Family Portfolio. The same money is funding everything, from raising your children to paying for your retirement. This approach requires some discipline because the money isn't as compartmentalized. You don't want to raid your children's college fund to pay for your silver anniversary trip to Europe. Conversely, you don't want to cheat yourself out of your retirement by paying for junior's college or post-grad degree.

Think of the Family Portfolio as one large pot that needs to be diversified to meet your risk tolerance (see Question 53 for more details on how to define your risk tolerance). Your home represents one asset (the important piece is your home equity, which you build up each month when you send in your mortgage check, and which may escalate through price appreciation). Among your other assets are the stocks you own through your retirement and nonretirement accounts or in your children's college funds. Other assets include the bonds that you own and your cash on hand, excluding your emergency fund.

By cutting across all of the individual reasons why you have money saved, you can get to the heart of the question about diversification. You're now looking at everything you own for what it is and how it affects your overall family finances and family financial goals, as opposed to how it affects one particular goal. You're back to six pieces of pie, or however many you feel like cutting.

Cutting Up the Pie

The "classic" mix is a portfolio that contains 60 percent stocks, 30 percent bonds, and 10 percent cash. (This excludes the cushion of cash you have on hand for emergencies.) If you want more risk, experts say you can go to 70 percent stocks, 25 percent bonds, and 5 percent cash, or to 80 percent stocks, 20 percent bonds, and zero cash. For those who eat risk for breakfast: 95 percent or more in stocks, 5 percent or less in bonds, zero cash. If you look at your mix from the vantage point of time, some financial planners suggest if you won't touch the cash for more than ten years, you should be 100 percent invested in the stock market.

Go back to the concept of the Family Portfolio. Even if you have 100 percent of your retirement money (or more) in stocks (assuming your retirement is down the line), if you own a home that's worth $200,000 and you have 25 percent of that amount in equity, you have $50,000 available to tap if necessary.

If you have $200,000 salted away in stocks in your retirement account and $50,000 in cash in your home, your 100 percent stock market investment suddenly becomes only 75 percent of your Family Portfolio. What else do you have put away? The kids' college fund contains about $5,000 in U.S. Savings Bonds that they've received over the years plus $5,000 in long-term bonds you've purchased, plus $10,000 in stocks. So you really have $210,000 in stocks ($200,000 in tax-deferred accounts, plus $10,000 in taxable accounts), $10,000 in bonds, and $50,000 in equity. That means you have 78 percent in stocks, 4 percent in bonds, and 19 percent in cash.

Look at your own portfolio in this light: You're probably more diversified than you think.

Stock Diversification

Your stock holdings may be only 60 or 70 percent of your overall assets, but the types of stocks you own should be diversified also. The biggest mistake employees of large corporations make is that their own company's stock comprises too large a piece of their retirement. Longtime Microsoft or Intel employees may be secure (these two companies have made hundreds of millionaires over the years) and may even retire at the ripe old age of, say, forty, but a lopsided portfolio will not work out well if the company in which you have your largest stockholding goes belly-up down the line.

If you're at a level where your company requires you to own a large block of its stock, then shift some of your other Family Portfolio stock holdings into companies or areas that are not in the same industry and that move out of step with your company. For example, if you work in technology, shift your other stock holdings to another sector, such as manufacturing, or invest in index funds, blue-chip companies,

Some foreign stocks are considered fairly risky investments, which is why their rate of return, over the years, has remained high. Big global companies are considered less risky (on the same scale that says blue chips are less risky than start-ups). On the plus side, two-thirds of the world's economy is found outside of the United States. E-mail messages circle the globe in a fraction of an instant and are the hallmark of a truly global economy. With American cars assembled in Mexico and Japanese cars built in Ohio, it's clear that companies are integrated worldwide. By the same token, an investment in an American company typically has an international component. For example, McDonald's has restaurants all over the globe, and the company's biggest growth comes from its foreign restaurants. On the negative side, if you're buying the stocks of individual foreign companies, it's more difficult to get really good, timely information from them or about them. And if you do get information, it's not likely that it'll be in English or any language beyond the country's native tongue. Many foreign governments, currencies, and economies are unstable, particularly in the third world (where investment returns are often stratospheric to make up for the likely chance you'll lose one or more of your investments). Many folks who hand over the foreign stock picking to a mutual fund manager trust that his or her researchers have combed the globe and hand-picked the best investments. Maybe they have, but, either way, you need a long-term investment horizon for foreign stocks. I held a well-regarded foreign mutual fund for four years. The first year I lost 25 percent of my money (the previous year, the fund had returned 50 percent). Over four years, my average annual return was 4 percent. I finally withdrew the money and put it elsewhere. I knew the fund would do better, but I couldn't stomach it any more, knowing I could do so much more with the money. The year after I withdrew my money, the fund returned about 30 percent. Then it lost 40 percent. The bottom line: If you're going to invest in foreign stocks, make sure you have a ten- or fifteen-year horizon, so you can sleep at night.

or foreign stocks. If you work in the automotive industry, consider investing in technology, blue-chip, small-cap, or foreign stocks.

Many experts will tell you it's a good idea to spread out your stock holdings to as many as thirty or fifty companies. If one of them has a bad day (or year, or tanks completely), you're better insulated from any damaging effect on your overall return. Other experts point to billionaire Warren Buffett, whose company, Berkshire Hathaway, owns a small handful of stocks relative to its massive size. Some of Buffett's disciples and friends, who run various mutual funds, also invest in a relative handful of stocks. One of these fund managers says he can hope to have only eight or a dozen really good ideas at any point in time, so why invest in more? Compare this approach to Fidelity's Magellan Fund, which, as I noted earlier, invests in perhaps 500 stocks at any given time.

Some advisers may tell you to invest anywhere from 10 to 40 percent of your stock holdings overseas. Depending on where foreign markets are in relation to the U.S. market, your adviser might encourage you to invest as much as 50 to 75 percent in the international markets. Over time, foreign stocks have returned about 13 percent annually, compared to nearly 11 percent for U.S. stocks. But in the years when foreign stocks failed, as in the mid- to late 1990s, the crashes were stupefying. Some funds were down as much as 70 percent or more in a year. On the other hand, some foreign funds rose as much as 50 to 70 percent in a good year.

And then there are small stocks, like those listed on the Russell 2000 index. These stocks got hammered in the late 1990s. Will they come back in the next decade? Probably. If your investing horizon is twenty years or more, they will undoubtedly make a comeback. Almost everything does.

The One Best Investment

"If you had to choose the one investment that you think would be best to make right now, which would it be?" So goes a question in the investing poll that Louis Harris & Associates conducts for *Business Week* magazine. Since 1989, the number-one investment has been real estate; 25 to 40 percent of respondents have selected it as their top choice. Mutual funds came in second, but only in the latter half of the 1990s. Before that, money market funds and government bonds came in second. Common stock became the third most favorite investment in the latter half of the 1990s. Bank or savings and loan deposits, gold and other precious metals, money market funds, and corporate and government bonds trail even farther behind.

What do the numbers suggest? People invest in what they know, and one thing they think they understand is real estate. It's generally their single largest investment—though in the latter half of the 1990s, thanks to several years of unparalleled stock market returns, Americans' stock market portfolios began to exceed the value of their homes for the first time ever. And, every time homeowners (who make up about 68 percent of American households) write their mortgage check, they think about how their home is doing. Except for dips in the early 1980s and 1990s, real estate has been roaring along, increasing nicely in value since the 1970s, when the baby boomers started buying their first homes. Traditionally, real estate keeps pace with inflation. In the past thirty years or so, it has done at least that well, and, in some cases, far better.

Is it *the* best investment? If you're interested in the overall return, the answer is *no*. Stocks have historically returned more than 10 percent. Real estate has appreciated a mere 2 to 3 percent in value annually. If you're talking about an investment that also provides you with a warm bed at night, real estate outperforms just about everything else. After all, you can't exactly cozy up to your loved one at the end of a long day in the backyard of IBM's worldwide headquarters.

> The truth is, each investment should fill a need in your life, whether to build for retirement, provide stability once you're there, or help pay for your dreams. Homeownership remains the number-one American dream.

The Bottom Line

How diversified should you be? Not so much that you can't easily keep track of your investments. Computers do help, but if you've got forty or fifty stocks and funds to keep track of, you'll be spending a lot more than ten or fifteen hours per month keeping up. Some experts say if you can't recite your investments in rapid-fire fashion, you've got too many. Others say, look closely at which stocks your mutual funds hold in their portfolios, and try to purchase different types of assets.

No matter where you start, your portfolio's diversification will change as you age because your needs will change. In your twenties and thirties, you'll take the most risk, because your major investment goals (college, weddings, and retirement) are a long way away. In your forties and fifties, some of those goals (college tuition and, perhaps, weddings) will have come and gone, and you'll want to use diversification to lower your risk, while still achieving decent returns for your retirement. In your sixties and seventies, you'll want to protect what you have for your retirement years, and start living off your investment interest.

Just remember: If you diversify too much, you'll spend too much time and money keeping up with your portfolio. Make it manageable and keep your eye on the costs; you may be able to boost your returns by a couple of percentage points. Over the years, those few points can add up to more money than you ever dreamed you'd have.

QUESTION 55

HOW DO I FIGURE OUT HOW MUCH MONEY I'LL NEED TO PAY FOR MY CHILDREN'S COLLEGE EDUCATION?

Most people think they should *save* for their children's college education. I think that's the wrong approach. Instead of simply saving, you should also *invest* in order to pay those forseeably hefty bills. And how should you invest for your children's college education? Prodigiously.

How else are you going to accumulate the vast sums needed to send your child geniuses to Harvard and MIT, where the annual tuition, in eighteen years, will likely exceed $60,000 per year?

Brad and his wife are expecting triplets who, if all goes well, will be born just after this book is published. Brad attended Northwestern University, in Evanston, Illinois (just outside of Chicago). He estimates, not unreasonably, that the tuition bill to send three kids through Northwestern will approach $750,000. And that's just for undergraduate degrees. Add an MBA, JD, and MD to the mix (why not?) and he'll be shelling out another few hundred thousand dollars.

That's a cool $1 million for three undergraduate and graduate school tuitions. All at the same time.

Perhaps Brad can get a multiples discount or some financial aid. Or, perhaps his three geniuses will be worthy of merit scholarships or will be physically gifted and earn sport scholarships.

Most likely, however, he and his wife will be in the same boat as most other parents—saving as much as they can for the college education (whether private or public) they want their children to have.

Bad News First

Let's get it over with. During the latter half of the 1980s and into the 1990s, college tuition and housing costs rose between 7 and 9 percent *per year* (although this rate was expected to taper off). As we go to press, the famed Ivy League (Harvard, Princeton, Yale, Brown, and so on) has the most expensive schools in the nation. Send your child there today and you'll pay a list price approaching $30,000 per year. State schools have long been a bargain, particularly if you live in a state where the primary state school offers an education (if not a name) that competes handily with the top schools in the nation. The cost of tuition at state schools has also been rising rapidly. Today, you'd pay about $11,000 for a year at a state university. Private colleges and universities fall somewhere in between: you might pay $17,000 to $25,000 for a year at one of these schools. Community colleges are a relative bargain: $1,500 to $2,000 per year, and your child can live at home with you for another year or two.

That's fine, you say. But I've got a toddler and a newborn. What's it going to cost in eighteen years, when they're ready to go? The charts on page 274 should give you an idea of what you're facing.

Okay, Now What?

A university that costs approximately $30,000 per year today will cost you a minimum of $60,000 per year (excluding financial aid) when your newborn is ready for school. That's quite a load. The key is to *start early*. As with your retirement planning, the longer your dollars have to compound, the harder they'll work for you. In other words, time is your friend, so the sooner you start saving for the college tuition you'll be paying, the better off you are.

Let's say you have nothing saved today. (According to a 1997 *Money* magazine poll, half of all parents ages 35 to 44 haven't saved anything for their children's education. Only 4 percent had saved more than $5,000. So you're not alone if you don't have a dime in the college fund.) Let's also assume that every dollar you save will earn a modest 8 percent return. If your kid wants to go to Harvard, you'll

273

Calculating the Cost of College

Cost of the Ivies. If you want your child to live, work, and (hopefully) study the preppy way, it'll cost you $30,000 per year today. This is what you can expect to pay over the next 30 years.

				Rate of Inflation				
Years	3.00%	4.00%	5.00%	6.00%	7.00%	8.00%	9.00%	10.00%
1	$30,900.00	$31,200.00	$ 31,500.00	$ 31,800.00	$ 32,100.00	$ 32,400.00	$ 32,700.00	$ 33,000.00
2	31,827.00	32,448.00	33,075.00	33,708.00	34,347.00	34,992.00	35,643.00	36,300.00
3	32,781.81	33,745.92	34,728.75	35,730.48	36,751.29	37,791.36	38,850.87	39,930.00
4	33,765.26	35,095.76	36,465.19	37,874.31	39,323.88	40,814.67	42,347.45	43,923.00
5	34,778.22	36,499.59	38,288.45	40,146.77	42,076.55	44,079.84	46,158.72	48,315.30
10	40,317.49	44,407.33	48,866.84	53,725.43	59,014.54	64,767.75	71,020.91	77,812.27
15	46,739.02	54,028.31	62,367.85	71,896.75	82,770.95	95,165.07	109,274.47	125,317.45
20	54,183.34	65,733.69	79,598.93	96,214.06	116,090.53	139,828.71	168,132.32	201,825.00
25	62,813.34	79,975.09	101,590.65	128,756.12	162,822.98	205,454.26	258,692.42	325,041.18
30	72,817.87	97,301.93	129,658.27	172,304.74	228,367.65	301,879.71	398,030.35	523,482.07

State U. It costs about $11,000 per year today, a heck of a lot less than the Ivies. Here's what you can expect to pay over the next 30 years.

				Rate of Inflation				
Years	3.00%	4.00%	5.00%	6.00%	7.00%	8.00%	9.00%	10.00%
1	$11,330.00	$11,440.00	$11,550.00	$11,660.00	$11,770.00	$ 11,880.00	$ 11,990.00	$ 12,100.00
2	11,669.90	11,897.60	12,127.50	12,359.60	12,593.90	12,830.40	13,069.10	13,310.00
3	12,020.00	12,373.50	12,733.88	13,101.18	13,475.47	13,856.83	14,245.32	14,641.00
4	12,380.60	12,868.44	13,370.57	13,887.25	14,418.76	14,965.38	15,527.40	16,105.10
5	12,752.01	13,383.18	14,039.10	14,720.48	15,428.07	16,162.61	16,924.86	17,715.61
10	14,783.08	16,282.69	17,917.84	19,699.32	21,638.66	23,748.17	26,041.00	28,531.17
15	17,137.64	19,810.38	22,868.21	26,362.14	30,349.35	34,893.86	40,067.31	45,949.73
20	19,867.22	24,102.35	29,186.27	35,278.49	42,566.53	51,270.53	61,648.52	74,002.50
25	23,031.56	29,324.20	37,249.90	47,210.58	59,701.76	75,333.23	94,853.89	119,181.77
30	26,699.89	35,677.37	47,541.37	63,178.40	83,734.81	110,689.23	145,944.46	191,943.42

Community College. For kids who aren't quite ready to live away from home, attending a community college for two years, and then transferring to the best university they can get into, will essentially cut the cost of college in half. Figure it costs $2,000 per year today.

				Rate of Inflation				
Years	3.00%	4.00%	5.00%	6.00%	7.00%	8.00%	9.00%	10.00%
1	$2,060.00	$2,080.00	$2,100.00	$ 2,120.00	$ 2,140.00	$ 2,160.00	$ 2,180.00	$ 2,200.00
2	2,121.80	2,163.20	2,205.00	2,247.20	2,289.80	2,332.80	2,376.20	2,420.00
3	2,185.45	2,249.73	2,315.25	2,382.03	2,450.09	2,519.42	2,590.06	2,662.00
4	2,251.02	2,339.72	2,431.01	2,524.95	2,621.59	2,720.98	2,823.16	2,928.20
5	2,318.55	2,433.31	2,552.56	2,676.45	2,805.10	2,938.66	3,077.25	3,221.02
10	2,687.83	2,960.49	3,257.79	3,581.70	3,934.30	4,317.85	4,734.73	5,187.48
15	3,115.93	3,601.89	4,157.86	4,793.12	5,518.06	6,344.34	7,284.96	8,354.50
20	3,612.22	4,382.25	5,306.60	6,414.27	7,739.37	9,321.91	11,208.82	13,455.00
25	4,187.56	5,331.67	6,772.71	8,583.74	10,854.87	13,696.95	17,246.16	21,669.41
30	4,854.52	6,486.80	8,643.88	11,486.98	15,224.51	20,125.31	26,535.36	34,898.80

need to save approximately $4,700 per year to pay the tuition in cash. If you have three children, you'll need to put away $14,100 each year—in addition to saving for your own retirement.

Let's change the assumptions a bit. Say you have $1,000 currently saved, and you have it stashed in a stock mutual fund, where it's likely to earn 10 percent a year. If Harvard is still the goal, you'll need to put away only $3,712 (and change) each year. The difference is in the compounding. The higher annual yield from the stock market makes your dollars work a lot harder.

Here's how the numbers look (I did this in about two seconds on my Quicken Deluxe 98 College Planner, but any decent financial software will allow you to create the same numbers and fiddle around with them. See the Resources section, on pages 282–283 for other ideas on where to find help).

College Costs: Take 1

I've assumed that today's annual college tuition, room, and board totals $25,000. You've got eighteen years to prepare until your eldest is ready. He'll attend for four years, you'll get 10 percent on your money, and we'll suppose that college costs will inflate a mere 4 percent (actual inflation is about 1.5 percent as I write this, though college costs have been inflating an average of 7 percent a year).

Year	Deposit	Tuition	Balance
1998	$3,826.22	$ 0.00	$ 3,826.22
1999	3,826.22	0.00	8,035.06
2000	3,826.22	0.00	12,664.79
⋮			
2015	3,826.22	0.00	174,472.47
2016	3,826.22	50,645.41	140,035.98
2017	3,826.22	52,671.23	99,927.45
2018	3,826.22	54,778.08	53,490.52
2019	3,478.68	56,969.20	0.00

College Costs: Take 2

A state school, at a mere $11,000 per year (in 1998) is looking pretty good. Here's how the numbers shake out.

Year	Deposit	Tuition	Balance
1998	$1,683.54	$ 0.00	$ 1,683.54
1999	1,683.54	0.00	3,535.43
2000	1,683.54	0.00	5,572.52
⋮			
2015	1,683.54	0.00	76,768.03
2016	1,683.54	22,283.98	61,616.00
2017	1,683.54	23,175.34	43,968.26
2018	1,683.54	24,102.35	23,536.04
2019	1,530.41	25,066.45	0.00

That seems more reasonable. But what if your eldest child is now age 10? That gives you only eight years. How do those numbers look? You'll have to step up your savings, even though, in eight years, college won't cost twice as much as it does today.

College Costs: Take 3

Okay, you've got eight years to go, and then perhaps Yale. Here's the worst case scenario timewise.

Year	Deposit	Tuition	Balance
1998	$8,630.92	$ 0.00	$ 8,630.92
1999	8,630.92	0.00	18,124.93
2000	8,630.92	0.00	28,568.35
⋮			
2005	8,630.92	0.00	98,702.24
2006	8,630.92	34,214.23	79,567.73
2006	8,630.92	35,582.80	57,014.35
2008	8,630.92	37,006.11	30,639.99
2009	7,846.37	38,486.35	0.00

How You Should Save

I began answering this question by telling you to invest prodigiously. Now you can see why. But where you stash your cash is at least as important as the stashing itself. Put your money in a money market account, or even a CD, and you'll never earn enough on it to get you where your kids want to go. You need the rate of average annual appreciation you'll find in the stock market.

According to PIMCO Advisors Fund, from 1985 to 1995, if you had invested $10,000 annually in stocks at the worst possible moment (the day the stock market hit the high note for the year), your $100,000 would've grown to $195,893 (a 13.7 percent annualized return). If you'd invested on the best day of each year (the day the stock market tanked), you'd end up with $237,791 (a 16 percent annualized return). If you'd put the $100,000 into a bank certificate of deposit (CD), you'd have only $134,873 (a 5.4 percent annualized return).

Putting 100 percent (or nearly that) of your children's college fund in the stock market is risky. But if you have ten or twenty years to ride out any market ups and downs, you have a much better chance of meeting your financial goal than if you put these funds in more conservative investments. You can choose to invest in either individual stocks or stock mutual funds. (I discuss both options later in this chapter, and again in Chapter 10.) If you choose a stock fund, go with a strong fund family that has a good short- and long-term record. And, choose a no-load fund. (Why pay extra when your dollars need to work so hard for you?)

When you're four years away from paying tuition, take a look at where you are. If you seem to be in good shape, you can either lock in some of your profits and move a bit into bonds, or keep rolling ahead. When it comes time to pay the bills, think about which investment it pays to liquidate first. You'll want to consider long-term capital gains, dividends (if any), and any weak spots in your portfolio.

Don't make the mistake of plunking in your money each year and forgetting about it. Too often, people assume that a fund is performing the way it has in the past. If your fund isn't performing well compared to its peers, you may want to make a change.

Other Ideas

Salting away money on a regular basis should be the cornerstone of your college savings plan. (It's that theme of spending less than you earn.) Here are some places to put it:

- *The Education IRA allows you to put away up to $500 per year for your children's education.* Over eighteen years, with a 10 percent growth rate, your tax-deferred money (you're not taxed on the

277

gain) will grow to $22,800. That's not much, considering a private college might cost twice that per year when your infant is ready to go. Other issues should be considered with an Education IRA. If you cash in your Education IRA in the same year you take the new Hope Credit (see page 280 for more details), you'll have to choose between taking the IRA dividends tax-free, or not using the Hope Credit. Also, you can't contribute to your Education IRA and your prepaid tuition plan in the same year. Finally, Education IRA money must be used by the time your child is age thirty (for undergraduate or graduate school). If there's some money left, it can be transferred to a younger sibling or another qualified family member. If you take cash out of the account for noneducational purposes, you'll pay income taxes and a 10 percent penalty. Finally, the full benefits of Education IRAs are limited to those with adjusted gross incomes of less than $150,000 (couples; 1998 limits) and $95,000 (singles; 1998 limits). Benefits phase out completely, just above these income levels.

• *Make use of a Roth IRA.* Some financial planners recommend using a tax-deferred Roth IRA account to boost your college savings. You can put up to $2,000 per person ($4,000, if you're married) into a Roth IRA, which, over the same period of time and with the same 10 percent growth rate, should yield $91,198 (or close to $200,000 if you put away $4,000). You must keep the funds in savings for at least five years. When you reach age 59, you may withdraw your contributions and earnings tax-free. (If you're an older parent, or a grandparent hoping to help out your grandchildren, this might be a really good idea.) If you tap the account sooner, you pay tax on your earnings, but not on your contributions (on which you paid taxes before you put the money into your account). There's no penalty if you tap a Roth IRA early to pay tuition bills. Another good thing about a Roth IRA is: the money stays in your name until it is needed. And, because retirement funds are typically excluded from college financial aid formulas, your aid package may be larger because the funds aren't in an Education IRA. (For more information about Roth IRAs, see Question 83.)

• *529 plans.* Named for the section of the Internal Revenue Code under which they fall, 529 Plans are tax-deferred state college savings programs that have grown out of enhancements made to qualified state tuition plans under the 1997 Taxpayer Relief Act. These programs vary from state to state, but the money you invest is tax-deferred until you withdraw it. If you use it for educational expenses—including tuition, room, board, or fees—the gains are taxed at the student's rate, not yours. You may even avoid state taxes on the gains. You may also use the funds to pay for any college or university anywhere in the country. There are no annual income limitations, as there are with Education or Roth IRAs, and you may be able to contribute up to $50,000 per person in a single year (though that precludes additional gifts for five years) without triggering the federal gift tax. Another terrific feature is that the contributions and earnings may be withdrawn for any financial emergency (though you'll pay income taxes and a penalty on the withdrawal). The only drawback is that you can't directly manage these funds. Some states are planning to invest in a conservative portfolio; others will hire brokerage firms, like Fidelity, to actively manage the plans and put funds into portfolios that are a mix of stocks and bonds.

- *Pay now, go later.* Your state may allow you to pay college tuition at today's prices and send your child eighteen years from now. The big catch? Your state may not guarantee admission to the state university of your choice, but to one of the other universities in the state system. A similar arrangement is developing within the Ivy League. Several Ivy schools have joined a consortium that allows you to pay tuition to any of the participating schools. If your child attends a different school but is still within the consortium, your tuition and fees will be considered covered. If your child attends a school outside the list, you'll get your money back, plus a small amount of interest. (The details of the Ivy League's plan were still being worked out as we went to press.)

In addition to saving any amount you can, you might want to tap into a few of these ideas.

- *Get grandparents involved.* Under current tax law, you can give up to $10,000 per year, tax-free, to anyone. If the money is earmarked for tuition, there's no limit, but you must pay the money directly to a school. If your parents or in-laws can afford it and want to do it, this is a helpful way to defray all or part of a tuition bill.

- *Put assets in your children's names.* The Uniform Gift Act for Minors used to be a popular way of giving gifts to children, and sheltering income along the way. But the new Kiddie Tax provisions require children to pay income tax at their parents' rate if their income exceeds $1,300 per year (1998 figure). The tax provision goes away once your child is age 14. The Uniform Gift Act for Minors does not apply when your child is age 18 or 21, depending on the state in which you live. If you wait to sell your assets until your child is on the way to college, you may save capital gains taxes by paying at your child's reduced rate (10 percent tax if you're in the 15 percent bracket, versus 20 percent if you're in the 28 percent bracket).

- *Try a trust.* Consider setting up an irrevocable trust in your child's name. You can give your child up to $10,000 per year and put it into the trust. (See Questions 92 and 93 for more information about trusts.) Ask your tax adviser or an estate planner to figure out which strategy might be right for you.

- *The Hope Credit.* Geared toward first-time college students, a Hope Credit of up to $1,500 (remember, a tax credit is a dollar-for-dollar reduction in the amount of money you pay to the government) is available for the first two years of college cost. There are income limitations here, and if you use proceeds from an Education IRA, you may wipe out any Hope Credit benefit.

- *The Lifetime Learning credit.* A tax credit is allowed for up to 20 percent of the cost of taking college courses. The maximum credit is $1,000 per year.

- *Regular IRAs can be tapped, too.* If you use proceeds from your traditional IRA to pay for college or graduate school expenses, the government waives the 10 percent withdrawal penalty.

Some Tips on Borrowing

Some folks simply can't save enough to pay the full bill for their kids. There's nothing wrong with that. Most parents need some form of financial aid: a scholarship (or two), a package of loans and a job from the school, or student loans.

To qualify for financial aid, children must put up 35 percent of their savings. Parents must contribute 5.6 percent of their assets, but retirement money is not counted with those assets. (That's why putting your children's tuition money into a Roth IRA might make

One thing you *shouldn't* do is lie about what you earn, in order to boost your child's financial aid package. For one thing, it sends the wrong message to your kids. It also reduces the amount of aid available to people who really need it. And finally, you shouldn't lie because it's illegal and it's getting easier and easier to get caught. *Smart Money* magazine reported that of the 2.3 million recipients of 1995–1996 Pell Grants, 300 students "overlooked" $100,000 or more in income. One recipient, the magazine reported, filed an IRS return showing an adjusted gross income of $1.2 million, but claimed no income on the Free Application for Federal Student Aid. When you file financial aid forms, you typically give permission for the university to look up your IRS tax form. With more detailed information coming online, many more colleges and universities will be cross-checking the data you file.

some sense.) The best news of all affects student loans. Beginning in 1998, the first five years of interest on repayments are deductible, even if you don't itemize. The deduction is limited to $1,000 per year.

If you're going to borrow money for your children's education, here are some ways to do it.

- *Retirement accounts.* If you've got money stashed away in your retirement accounts, you could borrow from them to finance your children's college education. But because one of the big mistakes parents make is to pay for their children's college education by mortgaging their future retirement (see below), this should be only your last, no-other-choice step.

- *Home equity loan.* If you've got enough equity in your home, you can take out a tax-deductible home equity line of credit (up to $100,000), and fully deduct the cost of paying for your child's education.

- *Refinancing your loan.* Because home equity loans are deductible only to the first $100,000 borrowed, consider refinancing your entire home and using your equity to pay for college attendance.

- *Borrowing against your life insurance.* If you have a whole life policy, you may unknowingly have built up a cash value reserve that you can tap for college or graduate school expenses.

- *Government loans.* Sallie Mae (Student Loan Marketing Association) loans from the U.S. government are now tax-deductible up to $1,000 per year (for the first five years), even if you don't itemize your deductions on your annual income tax form.

Mistakes Parents Often Make When Planning for Their Children's Education

Here are three mistakes that parents make when they are saving and investing for their children's college education:

1. *Choosing to fund college over retirement.* Why is this a mistake? You can borrow money to pay for your children's education, but you won't find anyone who'll lend you money to pay for your retirement. The notable exception, of course, is a reverse mortgage, but if you get one of those, you may end up paying a lot more for a lot less. (See Question 39 for information on reverse mortgages.)

2. *Doing before thinking.* You may have the best of intentions when you transfer assets into your child's name. But if you increase your taxes as a result, the transfer won't help much. Think through all the possible scenarios before you move your money from one place to another. If you can't reason them all out, or they get overwhelming, talk to a fee-only professional financial planner. The fee you pay for a few hours of advice will be well spent.

3. *Being too conservative.* You want the money to be there when it comes time to pay for college. But if you invest too conservatively, you'll never keep up with today's spiraling college costs. Experts say that, in the early years, most or all of your college fund should be in stocks. Later on, you should have a mix of stocks and bonds, lowering your risk that a market swing could go against you at the time you most need your cash.

RESOURCES

Even if you think you make too much money to qualify, you should still apply for financial aid. You may be surprised at what you'll be offered. To receive your Free Application for Federal Student Aid (FAFSA) packet, call 800-433-3243. That's also the number for the

Federal Student Aid Hotline (part of the U.S. Department of Education). Also contact the College Board (212-713-8000), the College Scholarship Service (CSS) (609-771-7725), and the Student Loan Marketing Association, better known as Sallie Mae (800-831-LOAN).

The Internet has made searching for a scholarship incredibly easy. Try the Financial Aid Information Page (www.finaid.org), which is funded by the National Association of Student Financial Aid Administrators. The College Board (www.collegeboard.org) is online, too. The Scholarship Resource Network (www.srnexpress.com) focuses on private "portable" scholarships. FastWEB (www.fastweb.com) offers information on nearly 275,000 scholarships. New financial aid and scholarship sites are being started all the time, so keep an eye out for them.

> Don't forget to check out some of the major personal finance sites on the Web, including major brokerage firms like Schwab (www.schwab.com) and Fidelity (www.fidelity.com), as well as Quicken (www.quicken.com). These sites often have excellent college planners that will help you run your own numbers.

SHOULD I PREPAY MY MORTGAGE?

QUESTION
56

As we discussed earlier, prepaying your debt is a kind of foolproof investment. Every dollar you prepay "earns" you interest equal to the rate on your mortgage loan. (It doesn't really *earn* you the interest; it keeps you from having to pay it, which keeps more pennies in your pocket.)

For most homeowners, their mortgage is their biggest debt. And although the interest rate on that debt is low (in 1998 you could've refinanced your loan with a thirty-year, $100,000 loan, carrying an interest rate of less than 6.75 percent paying zero points, a thirty-five-year low), it's still cash out of pocket.

Because of the way debt is compounded, a dollar prepaid on your mortgage effectively earns an interest rate equal to the net interest rate you're paying on the debt. Because mortgages are tax-deductible, the amount you earn would be roughly your interest rate minus your tax bracket. On credit card debt, which is no longer tax-deductible, every dollar you prepay earns you the interest you're paying on your debt. If your card charges you 24 percent interest, you'll effectively earn 24 percent on every dollar you prepay.

The reason you earn the interest rate is that, by prepaying your mortgage (or any other debt) you pay off your loan early. Because you're paying off a thirty-year loan in, say, fifteen years, you're actually saving fifteen years' worth of interest payments. How much is that? On a $100,000, thirty-year loan at 8 percent interest, you'll pay approximately $150,000 in debt. Cut that loan to fifteen years, and you'll pay about $75,000 in debt. Now you're talking real money.

How Does It Work?

If you have a thirty-year loan, prepaying works neatly. If you make one extra payment per year (a thirteenth payment), you can effectively cut your thirty-year loan to about twenty-one years. If you make that single extra payment on January 1 rather than December 31 of the same year, you can shave more years off your loan term. If you spread out the payment into 12 equal installments, adding to your regular monthly mortgage check, your loan term will be somewhere in the middle. Make two extra payments a year, and you'll pay off your loan in less than fifteen years.

So why not get a fifteen-year loan? If you take out a loan with a fifteen-year amortization, you'll achieve even more savings than if you make that thirteenth payment every year. Why? Typically, a fifteen-year loan will have an interest rate that is .25 to .50 percent less than the thirty-year loan rate. Because that interest rate is spread over the entire loan amount, you're saving quite a bit, from day one.

You can prepay a fifteen-year loan, but one extra payment a year won't cut it down to eight years (less of your monthly payment goes toward the interest with a fifteen-year loan). Depending on the month when you pay it, one extra payment a year (the thirteenth payment) will cut your loan from fifteen years to twelve or thirteen years. Two extra payments per year will cut your loan to ten or eleven years. (Imagine paying off your mortgage in 10 years!)

Figuring the Numbers

If you want more precise calculations, loads of calculators on the Internet will tell you how much you need to prepay if your goal is to pay off your loan in a particular number of years. One of the easiest to use? San Francisco-based mortgage broker Dick LePre's Home-owners Finance Center (www.homeowners.com) offers an easy-to-use calculator and, like most of the best stuff on the Web, it's free.

On the better financial software programs, you can create your own amortization tables. They'll tell you how much you have to pay each month in order to pay off your loan in a specific number of years. You can change the number of years and, in some cases, the amount you're going to pay, so you can work with them to figure out the right payoff schedule for you. If you have Microsoft's Excel, you can create your own amortization schedule.

Prepayment Penalties

When no-cost loans were introduced, some folks started refinancing their mortgages frequently—sometimes, as often as every six months. These *refi junkies* played havoc with what had previously been a quite dependable investment for secondary market investors (the folks who buy loans, package them, and resell them to other investors, such as pension funds). Because of the refi junkies, instead of getting a solid return for five or seven years, the returns (or yields) on the securitized loans were falling. To keep them in place, lenders started imposing *prepayment penalties* (fees you have to pay if you refinance or pay off your loan within a certain number of years). To make borrowers feel a little better about sticking with the loan for a certain number of years, lenders will offer their very best rates on loans with prepayment penalties.

The good news is: prepayment penalties usually kick in only if the loan is refinanced within the first three or four years. Also, you may *pay down* your loan as much as you like without triggering a

If you think you may want to refinance your loan (or sell your home and pay off your loan) within the first three or four years (or within the penalty period), don't get a loan with a prepayment penalty. The penalty will more than wipe out any savings you'll get in interest rate. To be sure that your loan doesn't have a prepayment penalty, ask your lender. If there is a prepayment penalty, the lender will require you to sign a disclosure form at your closing.

285

prepayment penalty, as long as you don't *pay off* your loan within the penalty period.

How steep are the penalties? They can range from a flat fee to as much as 2 or 3 percent of the loan amount, or $2,000 to $3,000 for every $100,000 you borrow. That's a pretty hefty penalty.

Prepaying your loan is an easy, hassle-free, no-muss, no-fuss way to earn a pretty decent rate of return on your money. You should think of yourself as earning your net interest rate on every dollar you pre-pay, but one finance professor thinks you actually may be earning a much higher rate of return. If your interest rate is 7.5 percent, and your net rate (if you're in the 28 percent bracket) is about 5.5 per-cent, you'd actually have to earn 8 percent or better on your money if you were trying to achieve that rate of return in a taxable account. And you won't get that kind of return without taking a lot more risk than prepaying your mortgage.

The financial return on prepaying your mortgage is quite staggering. You'll save a huge amount of interest, and a significant monthly cash outlay will be available to invest for your retirement or for your chil-dren's college tuition. In addition, you're earning each dollar back at your net rate of interest. For many homeowners, the emotional re-turns sweeten the moment that much more. Their happiest day is the day they pay off their loan and can tear up their loan papers. It rep-resents a tremendous financial achievement, and removes an enor-mous financial burden. Prepaying a loan even $25 per month will bring that happy day years closer.

Should You Prepay Your Loan?

Are you one of those folks who have taken out the biggest mortgage they can afford and who keep refinancing to take out ever larger sums of money? Do you know of a better place to put your cash, a place that will earn you better guaranteed returns (including taxes paid, if any are owed on the investment) than prepaying your mortgage? Then by all means go ahead and do it. If you can get 15 percent on your money (about a 10 percent return after taxes) and your mortgage interest rate is only 7 percent, you should make that investment.

Interest rates hit a new thirty-five-year low in the late 1990s, so the argument for taking out the largest affordable mortgage and investing the cash in other places became that much more compelling. If you get a thirty-year loan at 6.5 percent, and you're in the 28 percent tax bracket, you're really paying only about 4.7 percent for that money. With that interest rate, it's a good bet you'll find plenty of other places to invest and reap a substantial windfall. If your interest rate is 10 percent, it's harder to make that argument.

No returns are guaranteed. Even T-bills can lose some of their value if interest rates go up (although your interest payments remain the same). A larger mortgage also means you have higher monthly expenses, which many folks would rather avoid. Cash out of pocket is still cash out of pocket, particularly if you can't deduct the mortgage interest you pay because you don't itemize your deductions on your federal income tax forms.

Another common argument is that your money is just sitting there, not doing anything. By prepaying your loan, you're earning (saving) an interest rate equal to your net interest rate. If you want your money, you can either refinance your loan to get cash out, or get a home equity loan or line of credit.

Some financial planners argue that you should always have the largest loan balance possible because home equity money isn't available when you need it most. When's that? When you lose your job or become disabled. You *will* have greater difficulty borrowing against your home's equity if you're not bringing in enough income, but there's a way to circumvent the problem. When you refinance your home the next time, consider getting a home equity line of credit. Your lender will give you a booklet with checks. When you need money (for emergencies, not a trip to Hawaii), you can write a check against your home equity no matter what your financial situation is at that time.

For most people, prepaying their mortgage is a pretty good way to go. I try to do it myself.

SHOULD I BUY OR SELL INVESTMENTS BASED ON A TIP?

"Have I got a tip for you . . . ! "

How many times have you heard that, particularly from a stockbroker who cold-calls you in the middle of dinner?

Taking stock tips from *anyone* (brokers, relatives, your doctor, or your best friend) is generally a really bad idea. Unless people are intimately involved with the company they're recommending, chances are that they don't really know what's going on.

If you take and act on a stock tip from someone who works in high management echelons in a company, and who reveals classified or nonpublic information, you may be guilty of insider trading. (It's the old "Damned if you do . . . " syndrome.)

Insider trading refers to making stock trading decisions based on important (also known as "material") information that comes from inside the company and has not yet been made public. For example, let's say you own a shipbuilding stock, and the executive vice president of the company is your brother-in-law. One Sunday, at a family barbecue, he tells you that the company is about to land a huge contract to build warships for the government. The contract will triple its revenues and quadruple its profits inside a year. Your brother-in-law tells you to buy as much of the stock as you can, and wait for the price to jump. But you have to buy first thing Monday morning, because the contract is going to be announced at noon. The next day, as soon as you wake up, you place, via your computer, an order to buy 100,000 shares of the shipbuilding company. When the market opens, the buy order is executed, and you now own all those shares. At noon, when the contract is announced, the shares start climbing, and the price doubles by the end of the day. The next day, your brother-in-law calls to tell you that it looks like the contract will fall through because someone found out that the government had already placed an order with a different company. You immediately go online and dump all of your shares, reaping a tidy profit of $500,000 in a single day.

Your profit was entirely derived from insider information. You traded based on knowledge illegally passed to you by your brother-in-law, who probably did it with the best of intentions. But he broke a law, and so did you. And if you'd told a friend, who told a friend, who told two friends, and all of them traded on your knowledge, they'd all be guilty of insider trading.

What *doesn't* constitute insider trading? You ask your brother-in-law how his company is doing, and he tells you he thinks the company could grow by as much as 15 percent a year. But he's not sure, and he doesn't reveal anything that hasn't already been made public. If you buy shares in his shipbuilding company based on his feeling that the company will grow, it's perfectly legal. You have access, but not unfair access.

An open and fair marketplace operates on the idea that everyone is entitled to equal information. Everyone then trades on the same knowledge—or lack of knowledge. The Securities and Exchange Commission (SEC), which regulates the stock market and all market activity, limits the times during the year when company executives can sell their own stock. That's why companies will often send out a press release detailing, for example, a highly placed executive's sale of shares. "Alex Goldblatt, president and CEO, sold shares for estate-planning purposes and to meet certain tax obligations," is a typical explanation. Investors are informed that the chief executive officer of the company sold some of his holdings for reasons outside of the business.

Never purchase any stock without first doing all your own research. Go online to the company's Web site (if it has one). Read past releases and check out past issues of the annual report. Did the president's forecast of earnings and profitability actually come true? Look up recent news articles about the company, and see what its competitors are doing that could eat into future profits. You can get most of this information by calling the company directly (ask for investor relations) and asking to have it sent to you. Look at sales revenue and profits, debts and liabilities. Compare the projections for future growth with those of other companies that make similar products. In this way, you'll find out whether a company's stock is worth purchasing, and you'll surely do better on your investments than if you buy on someone else's stock tip. For more recommendations on research before purchasing a stock, see Question 58.

Avoiding Insider Trading

How do you avoid insider trading? Easy. Avoid taking anyone's advice on buying or selling the stock of the company for which that person works.

In fact, it's a bad idea to trade on any stock tips you receive. If you think someone has a great idea, take the time to independently evaluate the company, and think through whether it is right for your portfolio.

Investments: Stocks and Mutual Funds

WHAT DO I NEED TO KNOW ABOUT STOCKS AND THE STOCK MARKET TO START INVESTING?

The first thing to know about the stock market is this: If you stacked up all the advice, timing tricks, trading theories, and stock tips that so-called experts dispense for free or for a fee, and the stack toppled over, it would probably reach from wherever you are to Wall Street.

Folks *have* become wea lthy by investing in the stock market. Thanks to an unbelievable bull run, many Americans now have stock portfolios worth more than their homes. If you were lucky enough to invest $1,000 with Warren Buffett when he started investing back in the 1950s, your holdings would have been worth more than $8 million by the summer of 1998.

If you've never bought or traded a single share of stock, all of this awaits you. But be aware that plenty of folks lose money in the stock market. They take risks they shouldn't take, invest in companies they don't know, trust products they don't understand, and hold when they should sell.

The bottom line: If you take the time to understand a little bit about the stock market, and research companies before you buy shares in them, you'll do better in the long run than someone who just jumps in.

This chapter covers some basic things you should know about stocks and the stock market before you start investing.

Stock Exchange Basics

A stock exchange is a place where people buy and sell shares of stock in various companies. You'll hear people refer to three primary stock exchanges: The New York Stock Exchange (NYSE), the American Stock Exchange (AMEX), and the exchange of the National Association of Securities Dealers (NASD), which is more commonly called NASDAQ (National Association of Securities Dealers Automated Quotation). You may trade stocks on any of the exchanges. Regional stock exchanges—in Boston, Phoenix, Philadelphia, Cincinnati, and Chicago (called the Midwest Stock Exchange)—generally trade national stocks on a smaller scale, "penny stocks" that generally sell for a few dollars a share, and other shares of the NYSE and AMEX.

In the Over-The-Counter Market (OTC), traders create their own market for a particular company's stock by purchasing the stock and then reselling it for whatever price they can get. Stocks traded this way are said to be *unlisted* because they don't trade on a formal exchange; typically, the companies are smaller, with newer issues. (Actually, they're now mostly traded via computer through NAS-DAQ.) *The Pink Sheets* (which provide quotes for OTC stocks) are published daily, giving the prices for more than 11,000 OTC stocks that don't appear on the NASDAQ list. The fact that the prices are published doesn't mean they're firm. They change frequently.

In addition to shares on the stock exchanges, people trade all sorts of other financial products, such as options, futures, and currencies. These products are typically more complicated and risky, although the rewards can be worth the risk. (For more information, check out Chapter 12.)

An Exchange Is Different from an Index

An *index* is a specific group of stocks that experts use to judge the health of a particular industry sector or group of stocks. Some of the most common indexes are the Dow Jones Industrial Average (the first index, created by Charles Dow in 1896, it tracks just 30 stocks, called "major propellants of the economy"); the Standard & Poor's 500 Stock Index (commonly called the S&P 500), which primarily tracks large companies; the NASDAQ Composite (primarily a technology index); and the Russell 3000, which is made up of the Russell 1000 (the 1,000 largest companies) and the Russell 2000 (the next 2,000 companies in size—typically, those with a market capitalization of

$150 million to $1 billion). The Wilshire 5000 Stock Index actually tracks the movements of 6,500 companies, which is a large percentage of all companies that are traded in the stock market.

Price changes in individual stocks during a trading day cause either a rise or a fall in the index, in proportion to its market value. If Microsoft or Intel rises or falls dramatically, it can sway the NASDAQ Composite Index, even if the rest of the stocks that compose the index don't change much that day.

If you want to mirror the performance of an index, you can: (1) purchase stock in all of the companies that make up a particular index, or (2) buy an index fund—a mutual fund composed of companies in the index. (Hint: Buying an index fund will be by far the cheaper and easier choice.)

Buying and Selling Stocks

How can you purchase or sell stocks? Use a *full-service broker*, a *discount broker*, a *deep discount broker*, or purchase shares directly from the company through a *dividend reinvestment program* (DRIP). You can also go online with a full-service, discount, or deep discount broker, and purchase or sell stocks or mutual funds through the Internet.

A full-service broker is someone who handles trades for you, usually as an employee of a brokerage firm. He or she provides you with market, stock, and economic information created by the researchers and analysts the brokerage firm hires; recommends specific stocks and mutual funds; and executes trades. Some folks hire full-service brokers simply to have them pick up the telephone to answer a question or take a trade order. Such service comes at a steep price, however. A full-service broker may charge you a flat fee or, more commonly, a percentage of your trade. The bigger your trade, the more you pay the broker.

There is a wide range of discount brokers out there, and they offer a variety of services, usually for a fee. But when you trade, typically via an automated telephone system, you pay only a fraction of what a full-service broker charges. The difference is that you typically do your own research and make your own investment decisions.

Deep discount brokers offer only a trading service. Online, a deep discount broker's Web site might also offer research tools you can use to glean information about a particular company or mutual fund. You may use an automated service through a telephone, or an electronic service through the Internet. For this access, companies charge almost nothing. As of this writing, the lowest price online was about $5.00 per trade, no matter how much the trade is worth. A full-service broker might charge $150 for a medium-size trade, so this route puts an additional $142.05 into your pocket. There's not much room for this trading fee to fall further, but as the technology improves, you may soon see trading fees fall below $5.00 per trade.

Is it safe to trade stocks online? You can bet your bottom dollar that brokerage firms have spent millions to ensure the security of their customers' accounts. That isn't to say everything will go swimmingly every time, but the error rate is small. Experts say your broker is more likely to make a mistake than an electronic trading system.

Executing a Trade

When you purchase stock, you have three days to get enough money into your account to cover the trade. If you have enough cash in your account to cover the cost of the purchase, the broker will simply deduct the amount from your account. In industry jargon, this three-day period is referred to as *T-3*. If you trade online, you will not be allowed to complete a purchase unless you already have enough cash in your account.

There is no *T-3* on the Internet. If you don't have enough cash in your brokerage account, you will not be allowed to complete your transaction.

If you don't have enough money in your account to cover the trade after three days, the broker may elect to rescind the trade, take over the trade, or charge you a fee. (You can just about count on the fee.) If you sell stock, you have three days to get your stock certificates to the broker so that he or she can complete the sale. Because the mail is slow, and it's expensive to send shares of stock overnight, many folks have the broker hold their shares in *street name*—the name of the brokerage firm. Some brokers charge a fee of perhaps $25 to $50 per year for having the firm hold shares. Other brokers charge for the brokerage account, but will hold the stocks for free. Other firms do not charge for these services. Many people feel it's well worth the annual fee to have the firm hold their stocks in street name.

When you purchase stock, you'll be asked what kind of purchase you want to make. With a *market order*, you purchase your shares at whatever price the market is at when your trade goes through. A *limit order* indicates the price (high or low) at which you will purchase the stock. If the stock gets to that price, your order will be processed. If you're holding stock and worrying about locking in profits, you can put in a *stop-loss order*; the shares will then be sold automatically if the stock falls below a certain price. (There is no guarantee that the trade will take place at the price you request.) There are other variations of these orders, and you should become familiar with them before you make your first trade.

A *round lot* is an order of 100 shares or a multiple of 100. Anything bought or sold in anything but 100-share increments is called an *odd lot*. Full-service brokers typically charge a minimum order fee, so the per-share fee on a round lot is cheaper (sometimes a lot cheaper) than the per-share fee on an odd lot. However, the fees that discount brokers charge are typically fixed, no matter how many shares you order. The same is true for Internet trading. If you don't have the cash to purchase 100 shares, you should really consider purchasing your stock the cheapest way possible.

When you're purchasing stock through an automated system, it will explain all of your options to you again and again, in case you forget. Be sure you know the stock symbol for the company you're trading; you'll need that information to put in your purchase or sale order. You can find companies' stock symbols in the business section (look at the stock tables) of your local newspaper, online at any brokerage firm or personal finance Web site, in literature that the company sends you, or by calling the company directly.

After-Hours Trading

The New York Stock Exchange, NASDAQ, and the American Stock Exchange are open from 9:30 A.M. to 4:00 P.M., Eastern Standard Time (EST), Monday through Friday, excluding federal holidays. If you're trading from California, the market is open from 6:30 A.M. to 1:00 P.M., Pacific Standard Time (PST). (You'll be up very early if you're trading from Hawaii.)

Though most of the trading activity goes on while the market is open, you can trade twenty-four hours a day through trading networks like Instinet (run by Reuters). This makes some sense: stock markets all over the world are open at different times of the day and night. Morning in New York is night in Toyko, so why shouldn't New York traders stay up all night to trade in that market? Some do.

Today, after-hours trading doesn't hold a lot of promise for the average investor. It's volatile, there is very little volume, and traders have to work through an institutional firm.

Researching Stocks and Mutual Funds

When you're researching stocks and mutual funds, you definitely need to do your homework to avoid making a bad investment. But what kind of information do you need to make a good investment decision?

For stocks, you should know what the company is, what it does, and how much it makes doing it. Does the company have debt? What does the industry in which this company operates look like? Is it healthy or not? What is the company's and the industry's growth rate? Find out the history of the stock over the past few years, and what its highest and lowest trading prices were during the previous year. This information will tell you what investors think of the stock and its prospects. Again, make sure you know the stock symbol before you make a trade, and enter it correctly (if you're trading through the Web or over the telephone). More than one investor has incorrectly entered a stock symbol and bought or sold the wrong stock.

Where should you look for all this (and much more) information? The Value Line Investment Survey provides an excellent analysis of the stocks it covers. Standard & Poor's Stock Reports publish the historical and current performance of many stocks. Moody's offers company data that can help you determine whether a company is healthy economically. Most libraries have at least some of these tools. Increasingly, you can find them on the Internet, for free.

If you want the legwork done for you, you can either use a full-service broker or purchase a report about a particular company. A report from Standard & Poor's Research Service (800-642-2858) will run you $10 (plus $2 to fax it), but will give you an eight-page report covering a business summary, recent news, a fifty-two-week price and earnings history, balance-sheet statistics, and a page that compares the company to others in the industry. You'll get a break on the price if you have an account with Fidelity Investments or Quick & Riley. Schwab Investment Reports (800-752-9295) cost $5.50 (plus $2.50 to fax) and provide just about as much information as the S&P service. However, you must have a Schwab account to purchase a report. Other brokerage firms may have similar offerings.

Most major companies have a Web site featuring basic information about the company's management, products, and services, plus an online copy of its annual report, and a list of places to go for more information. You should definitely check the site. If you're not online, call the company directly (there may be a toll-free number) and ask for shareholder services. If you're calling to have the annual report sent, be sure to ask for the last three years' data, so you can see whether past predictions came true.

A lot of wonderful information is published continually for investors. Some mutual fund managers say they find their best ideas while reading the daily paper, or, more particularly, *The New York Times* or *The Wall Street Journal*. *Investors Business Daily* carries business news of the day as well as good articles that help you understand different types of investments. An average airport magazine rack contains enough personal financial advice to keep you busy on several 'round-the-world trips. *Worth* magazine, *Smart Money*, *Forbes*, *Fortune*, *Money*, *Kiplinger's*, and others, offer longer stories that help explain various investing concepts.

On the Internet, you'll run into hundreds of "advice sites." Some are great, some are pretty iffy. Make sure you know the authors of what you're reading, what their credentials are, and whether they have a bias (for instance, if they're funded entirely by insurance companies, the site might not be giving you objective advice). Be leery of sites that charge for access.

With so many options, it's easy to get overwhelmed with information. Many investors look at each investment as a company, not as stock. Is the business solid? Is it managed well? Does the industry have a good growth rate? These are the kinds of issues you should be focusing on when compiling your research. Then you can make an informed decision.

When you're researching mutual funds, you're looking for a few different things. You're paying a fee to a mutual fund manager for his or her expertise in picking stocks. Investigate the *expense ratio*—that is, the fees that are associated with the fund. Look at the fund's investment philosophy and strategy, and the background of the fund manager. Make sure you know how the fund compares to its peer group over the past three, five, and ten years.

In many ways, it's a lot easier to pick a mutual fund than a stock, which may be part of the reason mutual funds are so popular with typical investors. Start with a rating company like Morningstar (www.morningstar.net). Morningstar rates companies on a bell curve; the top 10 percent receive five stars, and the bottom 10 percent receive one star. Companies with four- or five-star ratings typically have the lowest costs and the best returns. Many mutual fund Internet sites offer fund and fund manager information. Funds are much more open about their managers today than they were even five years ago. Once you look at the three-, five-, and ten-year performance of the fund, read about the fund strategy, and analyze the expense ratio, you'll just need to sift through the more than 10,000 funds available. (For more information about mutual funds, see Questions 64 and 65.)

Investment Theories and Clichés

Sometimes it seems that everyone has a scheme to get rich in the stock market. Does your Uncle Rich buy a company's stocks because of the color of the chairman's tie? Don't laugh. Some folks actually throw darts at a wall covered with company names (because they've read over and over again that the "dart method" typically beats Wall Street professionals).

What are the rules of investing? There are no rules. You can buy and sell frequently and make a lot of money, or you can buy something and hold onto it forever and make a lot of money.

Here are some of the rules investors use when they trade equities:

- *Buy and hold.* One of the most solid investment theories is the buy-and-hold strategy. It works just like it sounds. You buy quality stocks and then you hold them, sometimes for decades, until the company, your personal finances, or the general economy dictates a change of action. The only people who might not recommend the buy-and-hold theory are those who make money when people trade stocks. If you buy and hold, that's only two commissions, far apart, for the broker—one when you buy and one when you eventually sell.

- *Sell half when it doubles.* This was the rule my grandfather swore by. When a stock doubled in value, he sold half of his holdings to lock in his costs and some profit. He let the rest ride until it doubled again. He'd sell if the company changed hands, changed its dividends, or fell upon hard times. When he died many years ago, he'd accumulated a portfolio worth more than a half million dollars.

- *Buy low, sell high.* Isn't this every investor's goal? Sure, but some folks simply have atrocious timing. After the market crashes, they feel bad and sell. Once it has returned to its former high, they feel better and buy. Go figure.

- *Buy on market dips.* The stock market crash of 1987 more than corrected itself within a year. Those who hung on made great money, those who sold learned a valuable lesson that has carried through other market dips: When you're in a bull market, dips are like stock sales; 5 percent, 10 percent, or even 20 percent goes off the retail price. Many investors identify stocks they'd like to acquire, and then buy them during a market swing, or when earnings don't meet market expectations.

- *Order a stop-loss sale.* Many investors set predetermined floors for individual stocks. If the price drops below that floor, they automatically sell the stock. Fund managers who use the stop-loss rule say it helps them keep their perspective and not become too attached to a particular investment.

My personal favorite saying is: "Pigs get fat. Hogs get slaughtered." I'm not sure where this first appeared—perhaps it's an old slaughterhouse phrase—or even whether it applied to investors. But the truth is, if you really buy at the bottom and sell at the top, you'll do it once in a lifetime. The good news is, you don't need to buy at the bottom and sell at the top to make money. You have to have a strategy and pursue it, regardless of what happens. I happen to favor the buy-and-hold strategy. When I haven't followed it, I've been sorry.

That's Why They Call 'em Market Waves

The only thing you can predict about the stock market is that it's utterly unpredictable. It's going to go up and it's going to go down.

Historically, the market has gone up more than it has gone down, and that's what you're counting on.

But you have to make sure you're prepared to ride out the storm. Take a look at your investments. What would you do if the stock market dropped 10 percent tomorrow? What if it dropped 20 percent? or 30 percent? Would your portfolio drop that much in value? Would your lifestyle be affected? Would you hang tight or sell quickly?

Prepare a plan in case your worst investing fears come true. Diversify enough to protect yourself and those who depend on you.

QUESTION
59

HOW SHOULD I DECIDE WHICH STOCKS TO INVEST IN?

If you're going to do your own stock picking, you should know what you're talking about. Here are some basic definitions.

Bear Market. When the stock market drops at least 20 percent from its high.

Blue chips. Large, well-established companies that offers investors some growth with a solid dividend. They're typically the most prominent 100 to 200 companies. The label refers to their capability of weathering even the worst market fluctuations.

Calls. A company's orders to preferred stock or bond holders to turn in their stock or bonds for money. Don't confuse this term with a call option. (See page 354 for more information on puts and calls.)

Common stock. A share of ownership in a company.

Convertibles. Preferred stocks or bonds that may be converted into common stocks at a fixed price.

Dividends. Your share of a company's profits, typically paid out in quarterly installments. To find out how much you'll receive, multiply the per-share dividend (published in your local paper) by the number of shares you own.

Equity. Your share of ownership in a company. Stockholders are often referred to as equity investors because they own a piece of the company.

Growth stock. A company that is focusing on growing, above all else. Because all profits are typically reinvested into the company to keep it growing quickly, little if any dividends are paid.

Hostile takeover. A company's purchase of another, against the will of the purchased company's management.

Income stock. A company that tends to pay out more of its profits to shareholders (in the form of dividends) and put less toward growth.

Initial public offering (IPO). A young company hoping to finance future growth will often "go public"—that is, issue stock in the company and sell it to the public—to raise additional funds. Many IPOs rise dramatically on the first day of the offering, then settle back down to a more reasonable share price. Some investors try to get in on the ground floor of an IPO and then sell their shares the first day or week the company goes public.

Management buyout. When the individuals who run a company get together, borrow money, and buy most or all of its common shares.

Market correction. When the stock market drops at least 10 percent from its high.

Market sector. The categorizing of companies based on the industry in which they operate. Examples of market sectors include technology and transportation.

Merger. When two companies voluntarily join together. Some mergers are really takeovers; one company becomes the dominant presence. In this situation, the joining is more accurately called an acquisition.

Preferred stock. A special class of stock that may have certain voting privileges. Companies typically pay a fixed, high dividend that yields a return similar to the amount you'd get on a bond. The price of preferred stock can rise, but common stock prices typically rise faster than preferred stock.

Price-to-earnings (P/E) ratio. The price of the stock divided by a company's prior-year earnings per share. Typically, newspapers publish a company's P/E ratio in the stock market tables. When a company's stock has a high P/E ratio, its earnings have risen rapidly and investors have bid up the price of the stock even higher, guessing that continued high growth is in the company's future. If the P/E ratio is low, investors have bid down the stock because they expect that growth won't match previous years' growth or the company's estimate. But stocks tend to trade in a certain P/E range, based on the market sector they're in. Because the Internet is such a new industry, Internet companies' stocks normally trade in a P/E range that's far higher than, say, a banking sector stock or a blue-chip stock. If a stock has a super-high P/E ratio, it could be a warning sign.

Spin-off. A company may divide itself into several units and give new shares in the company to current shareholders. Your 100 shares of stock in one company may turn into 100 shares of three different companies if the company divides itself into three units, and rewards stockholders with one share in each new unit, for each share currently held.

Stock rights. Your right as a shareholder to purchase new shares, often at a discount. Sometimes you'll see this opportunity if you have an account at a savings & loan institution that intends to go public. Account holders are offered the right to purchase shares of stock in the company before the initial public offering.

Takeover. When one company purchases another. Takeovers are considered to be "friendly," but there is often a lot of ill will as the company that was taken over adjusts to the new corporate culture.

Tender offer. When a company wants to take over another company, it will offer a price per share that is typically above the market price. As a shareholder, you will be asked to tender, or surrender, your shares for the higher price. In reality, after the tender offer is made, the market price for your stock will go up and match the offer. (If it doesn't match the offer, there is some concern in the market that the deal may not go through.)

Total return. Your total return is your dividends plus the gain or loss in the price of the company's stock. If the stock rises 5 percent and your dividends are 2 percent, your total return is 7 percent.

Warrants. When you buy preferred stock or bonds of speculative companies, you sometimes receive warrants, or the right to buy additional shares of stock at a predetermined price. This sounds great, but the company usually has the right to call in the warrants, forcing you to exercise them (i.e., buy stock at the current price) or receive only a few cents for each warrant you hold.

What Are You Looking For?

Before you decide to purchase individual stocks, you should figure out what you're looking for. As an investor, there are typically three reasons why you might buy a particular stock:

1. *Income.* If you're looking for a steady stream of income, you'll want to purchase the stock of companies that are growing but pay dividends on a regular schedule. Find out how steady the dividends are for a particular company; some companies

increase their dividends each year without fail. One thing to research is when the dividends are paid. To capture a steady stream of income, you'll want to own stocks that pay dividends at different times of each quarter. It's easier to pay your bills if you know when the checks will arrive. For example, some companies pay dividends on the thirtieth day of the payment month, others on the fifteenth day. Quarterly payments may be made in December, March, June, and September; or February, May, August, and November; or January, April, July, and October.

2. *Growth.* Companies experiencing what experts call "moderate growth" typically see their revenues growing 12 to 18 percent per year. Fast-growing companies grow at 20 percent (or higher) each year. Superstars may double their growth each year. But don't confuse growth with profitability. Stocks rise and fall based on real growth and a company's projected growth. Some companies, like Microsoft, are amazingly profitable and enjoy huge growth. But a company can double its business every year and still lose money. Some Internet companies have had this problem, although their stocks continue to rise to incredible prices. Investors typically purchase growth companies to add a bit of zing to the return on their portfolio. The key thing about companies focused on growth is this: They typically don't pay much, if anything, in dividends. All of their profit is funneled back into the company. As an investor, you only realize the benefit of investing in a growth company when you sell your stock. And because growth companies pay no dividends, your investment is an all-or-nothing proposition. If you choose a company that pays dividends, even if the stock price goes nowhere, you still have something to show for your investment.

3. *Diversification.* If you're purchasing stock to round out your portfolio, you'll want to carefully identify what holes need filling. Do you need foreign stocks? Small- or midcap stocks? If you need income, look for stocks with a dividend, or perhaps a bond that pays out income when you need it.

How Do I Find the Next Intel?

Choosing the right stocks means more than simply relying on luck. You need to find companies with good fundamentals, good leadership, and good products in a fast-growing industry that rewards innovation. And, you have to be lucky. As my friend Ralph says, "You can have a million good ideas. But the one that will succeed is the one in the right place, at the right time, with enough money to get it going."

Here are some topics you should think about before you make your first trade.

- *Lasting trends.* Avoid falling into a "flavor of the month" trap: hot today, not tomorrow. Any change in the way we live, the way we purchase and consume products, or the way we think, could help fuel the growth of companies that are riding the crest of that change. WalMart's stock has done well because the company capitalized on customers' need to purchase goods in a cheaper, faster way. Internet stocks have done well because investors believe these companies will fuel a lasting change in how we use technology.

- *Promising industries.* Technology is hot today, and perhaps it will be in the future. But you need to think more broadly. What will the baby boom generation (Americans born between 1946 and 1964) need as it ages? Some investors, believing that as Americans live longer, they will have more medical needs, are buying health care stocks. When you spot a promising industry, find the companies that lead that industry.

- *A contrarian view.* Financial writer Andrew Tobias writes that he bought his home in New York just after the city was proclaimed dead and gone in a major news magazine. Like many other folks, he made a lot of money by going against the grain. The theory behind this approach is that everything (or nearly everything) comes back. During the Asian Crisis of 1998 and 1999, contrarian investors picked up super-deflated Asian stocks. They were betting that the global economy wouldn't let an entire region fail economically or financially.

- *Political or economic gyrations.* A political or economic shift in a foreign country can provide a window of opportunity for buying and selling stocks, but study a country's stability (or lack thereof) before you purchase foreign stocks. A foreign government can change the rules overnight, or take over a company, in the interests of "national security," with no warning to the company's investors.

- *A company's popularity with investors.* If a stock is trading at a very high P/E ratio and doesn't live up to future earnings projections, you may buy at the top and ride it all the way down. On the other hand, if earnings keep up with projections, a high-priced stock may get higher still.

- *Company insiders' percentage of shares.* A company's annual report will divulge this information. Company insiders who own shares, and whose pay is based on share performance, are supremely motivated to boost the share price. That can be great for investors.
- *Mergers and acquisitions.* Plenty of wealthy investors do nothing but bet on whether certain companies will be taken over by other companies. If they're right, their shares could double or triple in value. If you plan to speculate in this market, keep close tabs on the news and pick a group of companies to follow. Be aware that mergers can come from out of nowhere, creating the unlikeliest of bedfellows.

The Bottom Line

It's extremely important that you keep up with all of your investments. Read all the mail the company sends you, and follow your company in the news. If you don't, you may miss a lot of opportunities to keep your money growing. For example, if you own warrants and the company calls the warrants, you must turn them in or risk losing them. If a company calls your preferred stock and you ignore the call, you may receive less in dividends because you delayed turning in your stock.

If you don't feel you have the time it takes to really manage your stock portfolio, there is a simpler solution: Buy a quality mutual fund that invests in the same stocks you want to own. You may not achieve quite the same level of return or price appreciation on a particular individual stock, but you'll know that someone with experience is working to make your entire investment grow.

WHAT IS A STOCK SPLIT?

A stock split often occurs when a company feels its per-share price has gone beyond the reach of average stockholders. When the share price goes over $100, it costs $10,000 or more to buy a round lot of 100 shares. Ten thousand dollars is a big chunk to spend at any one time, which is why individual investors feel more comfortable buying a stock when its per-share price is less than $100. (Don't forget: brokers often charge more for an odd lot, a stock purchase of less than 100 shares.) A split in shares doesn't mean the company is suddenly on sale, though many investors treat it that way.

A company may split its stock 2-for-1 (you'll get two shares for every share you own), 3-for-1 (you'll get three shares for every one you own), 3-for-2 (you'll get three shares for every two you own), or some other configuration. Another possibility is a *reverse split*. In a ten-for-1 reverse split, you'll get one share for every ten shares you own.

When a stock splits, the price at which it's listed will reflect the split. If your stock is worth $1 per share and there is a 10-for-1 reverse split, each new share will be worth $10. If the stock is trading at $150 and there is a 3-for-1 split, each new share will be worth $50.

Share prices sometimes jump when a company announces that it is splitting its shares. The new stock price will be more attractive to prospective shareholders, and the market is betting that demand for the stock will rise.

Why doesn't every stock split? Some companies simply don't buy into the notion. Perhaps the most famous opponent of stock splits is Warren Buffett, who has never split the shares of his company, Berkshire Hathaway, even though the per-share price of the stock surpassed $60,000 per share in 1998. Recently, a mutual fund company announced a fund that would hold only Berkshire Hathaway stock, at a share price that would be accessible to the average investor. In response, Buffett created a second class of Berkshire Hathaway stock priced around $1,000. That stock has since climbed.

Should you buy the shares of a company that has just split? Only if you like the company and would have bought it at the presplit price.

Stock splits don't create a "sale" price for a company. If you buy just after a company's shares split, because you think you're getting a great deal, you may be in for a big surprise. Share prices traditionally *rise* on news, or even rumors, of a split. By the time the shares split, the stock may have already appreciated. If you buy then, you'll buy at the new high. That's why it's helpful to look at a company's fifty-two-week high and low before you purchase shares. If a company's stock has split 2-for-1, the fifty-two-week high and low will be adjusted to reflect the new share price.

Watch out when a company that is already priced well under $100 splits its stock. Ask why that stock is splitting. Is it an effort to raise interest in the company and artificially inflate the stock price?

Here's how to update your record-keeping system to reflect a split. If you own 100 shares that you purchased for $10, and the stock rises to $100 and then splits 3-for-1, you now own 300 shares that you purchased for an effective price of $3.33 (divide your purchase price by the ratio of the split). If a stock splits 2-for-1, your effective purchase price is half of what you originally paid.

SHOULD I BUY PREFERRED STOCK OR COMMON STOCK?

QUESTION
61

Let's go over the definitions again. Common stock is your basic form of ownership in a company. As a common shareholder, you have the right to monitor the performance of the company and to vote on major issues that are presented to the shareholders at the annual meeting. If you can't attend the annual meeting, you will be issued a proxy statement that allows you to vote your shares ahead of time, or to give your vote to someone else or to the board of directors.

When you own preferred stock in a corporation, in addition to owning shares (which may or may not carry voting rights), you are paid a fixed, usually high, dividend. That's the good news. Unfortunately, the price of common stock tends to rise higher and faster than preferred shares. A company has the right to cancel dividends if it isn't doing well, or to call its preferred stock at any time. If your preferred stock is convertible, you may convert it (the company will give you a ratio) into common shares of the company (something you may or may not want to do). You may get excellent income from a preferred stock, but the risk of having it called makes bonds generally safer.

WHAT IS A DIVIDEND REINVESTMENT PLAN?

QUESTION
62

When I was a little girl, my grandfather bought each of his five grandchildren ten shares of stock in a company called Comsat, a maker of satellites. The idea was to invest in a technology of the future. The company paid a tiny dividend of about 20 cents a share, so, every quarter, I'd receive a check for roughly $2.00. The checks would come in, my father would sign his name, and supposedly would deposit our checks (mine and my sisters') into our respective checking accounts. (Did he? Probably.) As the years went on, I moved a dozen times back and forth to college and apartments. Some of those checks disappeared and were never found.

One day, I realized that Comsat would allow me to reinvest my dividends in the company for free, under a *dividend reinvestment plan*, commonly called a DRIP. By this time, the stock had split and I now had 40 shares. Having the cash dividends when I was a kid meant nothing to me because my parents were providing for me. I didn't think the $6 or so per quarter was going to make much of a difference in my lifestyle, so I began reinvesting my dividends in Comsat stock.

Over the years, these extra shares of Comsat, purchased with my dividends, have done just okay. I wish the shares had been in a different company, like Microsoft. But at least I know exactly what I've done with my dividends.

Millions of other shareholders across the country are also taking advantage of DRIPs, thanks to the Securities and Exchange Commission (SEC), which relaxed the rules and regulations governing these accounts. More than 1,000 companies now offer DRIPs, including blue chips such as Exxon, Motorola, McDonald's, and Procter & Gamble.

The nice part about DRIPs is that you can automatically purchase additional company stock with your dividends without paying a commission (you may, however, be charged a small fee for buying or selling your shares). That means almost every dollar of your investment goes to work for you instead of lining someone else's pocket. Some companies might ask you to purchase your initial shares through a broker, but you may do that cheaply online or through a discount brokerage firm; you don't have to use a full-service broker. Many companies will even let you purchase your first shares through the DRIP, as long as you meet the minimum purchase, perhaps $250. (You may see these plans referred to as "no-load" DRIPs, because there is no fee attached to them.) Subsequent purchase minimums might be as low as $50 each, with a maximum purchase of perhaps $100,000 per year.

Companies looking to draw in new funds from existing shareholders will offer a discount on the purchase of additional shares through a DRIP. Remember, it's only a good idea if you believe in the company and its future (which, I hope, is why you own shares in the corporation in the first place).

The Bottom Line

If you're receiving dividends in a company and don't need the money to live on, and the company offers a DRIP, it's probably a good idea to simply roll over your dividends into additional shares of stock in the company. You'll have to pay taxes on your dividends, but you'll be putting your cash to good use by building up additional shares (and there's no danger of losing the check). The DRIP may even allow you to purchase additional shares without charging a broker's commission. (Be careful; some DRIPs do charge a small initial purchase fee and/or a maintenance fee.)

If you purchase your initial shares through a full-service or discount broker that is holding your shares, the firm may allow you to reinvest your dividends for free, but may charge you its regular fee to purchase additional shares. You may be able to circumvent the broker by going directly to the company and purchasing additional shares. (Check with the stockholder relations department of the company in which you own shares.)

Regularly adding to your DRIPs is another way to dollar-cost average your stock purchases. And because you're buying through the DRIP program, almost every dollar is working for you.

There are two primary disadvantages to DRIPs. First, if you want to sell some of your shares, you'll have to request the sale in writing, send it through the mail, and wait for the order to be executed. You may or may not get the price you want. The second disadvantage is that you're purchasing your stock on different days of the year, and the price will undoubtedly fluctuate. Depending on the price of the stock, you may purchase only a fraction of one share over the course of the year, and each share may cost a different price. Figuring your capital gains or losses may be a little tough when you're purchasing pieces of shares over a number of years.

RESOURCES

For a list of companies that offer DRIPs, plus details on their plans, contact Evergreen Enterprises, P.O. Box 276, Laurel, MD 20725 (301-549-3939). Its *Directory of Companies Offering Dividend Reinvestment*

Plans costs around $30. Or, you can purchase the DRIP Investor, www.dripinvestor.com, or write to 7412 Calumet Avenue, Hammond, IN 46324. For a list of DRIPs with no details, send $2 to Standard & Poor's, Direct Marketing, 25 Broadway, New York, NY 10004.

WHAT IS A MUTUAL FUND?

A mutual fund is a pool of cash that is invested in either stocks or bonds, or a combination of the two. Mutual funds are popular because investors can easily acquire a diversified portfolio of stocks and bonds for far less money than if they had to purchase a portfolio of different stocks and bonds on their own. For very little money, perhaps $1,000 (or less if you're going to electronically transfer money into the fund each month), you're basically buying a diversified portfolio.

You're also buying talent, which is the second reason mutual funds are popular. Mutual funds are run by a fund manager whose job is to pick stocks. In a successful fund, the fund manager has had years of experience in picking companies that have done well during good times and bad. The fund manager is backed up by analysts and researchers, whose job is to stay on top of companies in the particular sector in which the fund is investing.

What a good idea, you think. I'll leave the stock picking to a professional and just keep investing in a solid mutual fund. Actually, that's a fine strategy; it is recommended by many personal finance experts and advisers. If you find a good fund with a decent return, and you continually pump money into it, you should be able to meet your financial goals.

The question is: With more than 10,000 mutual funds out there (as of this printing), and with that number growing by the hundreds every year, how are you going to find a good mutual fund?

Carefully. Let's start with some terms you're likely to encounter when you start investigating mutual funds.

Load. A load is the fee you're charged to participate in certain mutual funds. If the fee is charged when you buy into a fund, it's called a *front load*. If the fee is charged when you cash out of the fund, it's called a *back load*. Why would you pay a load? The idea behind a load is that you're paying for a professional who works for a mutual fund company, or an investment company, to sit down with you and find the mutual fund that's right for you.

When you're paying a load, you have to wonder whether the broker who works for the brokerage firm really has your best interests at heart. Some do, but a lot don't, particularly near the end of the month, when there are quotas to make and free trips to be won. When I had just started working, I put $2,000 into my first IRA. I didn't know where to put it, so my uncle, who has done well in the market, suggested I make an appointment to see his longtime friend—a top broker with a large investment house, who has managed some of my uncle's and cousin's money for thirty years. My uncle thought I should get some professional advice about where I should put my money. I sat down with his friend, and, within two minutes, he put my $2,000 into a mutual fund with a 6 percent load, which dropped down to 3 percent if I held it for four years. He didn't explain that there would be this charge; in fact, when I told him I just wanted to place the money temporarily while I figured out my options, he said this would be a good place. To add insult to injury, the market performed during those years at 14 to 18 percent annually, while this fund barely moved 6 percent. I filed a complaint with the company, but because this was one of its top brokers, nothing ever happened. This broker represented my uncle and, I found out later, my mother. He could've had me too. If the load hadn't been so horrific, I'd have never even realized what had happened.

No-load funds. Mutual funds that charge no fees to buy in or cash out. There are other charges. (There are with load funds, too. See Question 64 for details on how to figure out how much a mutual fund really charges.)

Open-ended fund. A mutual fund that continues to welcome new investors.

Closed-ended fund. A mutual fund that has closed its doors to new investors and their cash in order to maintain its size and position in the market. If shares in the fund are traded on various exchanges, like stock, you may be able to purchase them.

Fund supermarket. A relatively new concept. An investment firm (often called a "family") offers not only its own mutual funds, but the ability to invest in the mutual funds of other families. The nice thing is that all of your investments in these funds would be displayed on one statement from your primary family. On the down side, supermarkets sometimes tack on additional charges for investing in a fund outside the family if that fund doesn't separately pay a commission.

Specialty funds or sector funds. A mutual fund that specializes in one particular market sector or industry, or even a specific piece of an industry.

Fund of funds. A mutual fund that is made up of other mutual funds. The idea here is that you're not diversified enough when you choose a diversified mutual fund, so you buy one fund that diversifies by purchasing several different funds. Be careful that you're not paying double expenses (a fee for the fund of funds, plus fees for all the other funds it buys).

Asset allocation. A term used to express your choice among different types of asset classes and styles. You might have *growth or value funds*—mutual funds typically focused on companies that are growing quickly, or on companies that are perhaps out of favor temporarily, and are typically priced cheaply relative to their assets, profits, and potential. Value funds are betting that these stocks have a lot of room to grow. Your fund may be *international* (holding shares of international companies or indexes) or *domestic* (holding shares of U.S. companies only). It might be *large-cap* (focused on huge corporations), *midcap* (medium companies), or *small-cap* (small companies).

Hard asset funds. Mutual funds that hold a portion of their assets in gold or silver, or similar commodities, or in indexes that are based on hard assets. Hard asset funds may also be invested in real estate.

Contrarian funds. Funds that are positioned against conventional wisdom. When Asia was headed into a recession during the late 1990s, contrarian international funds swooped in and began buying up the stocks of companies, betting that they'd come back.

Diversified funds. According to the Diversified Mutual Fund Investment Act of 1940, a mutual fund calling itself diversified must spread its assets around. Seventy-five percent of its assets must be divvied up so that no more than 5 percent of the fund's assets are invested in a single stock. Funds that do not call themselves "diversified" may invest a larger percentage of their holdings in a single stock.

Index funds. Mutual funds designed to mimic the movements of a particular index. For example, a fund trying to mimic the movements of the S&P 500 will either purchase every stock on the S&P 500 (in the same ratio that those stocks appear on the index), or will purchase a representative sample of companies that closely approximate the index. Because index funds rarely change their holdings, they are typically cheap to hold and may do better for investors over the long haul.

Life-cycle funds. Mutual funds specifically designed to mirror what many experts feel are optimum ratios of stocks and bonds throughout the different stages in your life. You may be able to choose from three or four funds, one designed for 20–30-year-olds, one for 40–50-year-olds, and so on.

Net asset value (NAV). The value per share of a mutual fund. This is similar to a stock price.

Classified shares. Mutual fund shares grouped alphabetically. "A" shares are like those of a traditional load fund; you pay the broker right off the top of your investment. "B" shares still pay a commission, but the mutual fund puts up the money and then gradually withdraws it from your account. "C" and "D" shares are sometimes called *level-load* funds. The broker gets no commission up front, but instead gets an annual fee (called a *trail commission*) from the investor's account. *Wrap accounts* are mutual funds that have no up-front load, but charge a fixed percentage of assets each year to cover the cost of the commission and management expenses.

Mutual Funds vs. Individual Stocks

Now that you know what the jargon means, let's get back to the idea that mutual funds are an easy and cheap way to purchase market diversification. They are, but before you run out, checkbook in hand, let's talk about some of the problems with mutual funds.

- *Overdiversification.* Sometimes, fund managers go too far down the path of diversification, purchasing too many stocks. Fidelity's Magellan Fund (in which, I should point out, I had some retirement funds invested when we went to press) has investments in more than 500 stocks. Part of the reason for buying so many stocks is that Magellan is a huge fund with many billions of dollars to invest. Some investors argue that the fund is too diversified. Perhaps yes, perhaps no. If a fund is overdiversified, returns may be watered down. Remember, unless you have millions of dollars to invest, experts say the average family can usually be properly diversified by holding the stocks of around thirty different companies, or between three and five mutual funds.

- *Taxes.* If you don't pay attention to taxes, you might inadvertently slice off a few percentage points of your total return. When a fund sells a stock and reports a gain or capital gain, you must pay your pro rata share of that profit to the IRS, even if you've reinvested the distribution paid by the fund. If you hold the fund in a tax-deferred retirement account, you will not owe any taxes. But the mutual fund tax situation can pose a quandary, especially when you're considering when to buy or sell.

- *Buying shares.* Mutual funds typically distribute gains to fund holders at the end of the calendar year. If you purchase a mutual fund just *before* the distribution, you'll get the fund when the price is at its highest point. The fund will then distribute, and you'll pay income tax on the gains at your marginal rate (the highest rate you pay on any of your income), or capital gains tax if there are capital gains. If you purchase just *after* the distribution, you'll have a higher capital gains cost when you sell the fund (because you're buying at the lower share price), but the maximum capital gains rate for an investment held at least a year is now only 20 percent. If you're in the 15 percent bracket, you'll pay only 10 percent. You'll save money if you focus on long-term capital gains and buy after the distribution.

- *Selling shares.* When it comes time to sell, you might be better off selling *before* the distribution, for the same reason. You'll pay more capital gains tax, but that's preferable to paying more income tax. If you've held onto your shares for less than twelve months, it may pay to wait and sell after the distribution because some portion of the distribution is usually treated as a long-term capital gain.

- *Buying the flavor of the month.* Hot mutual fund managers don't tend to stick around long. As soon as they post that 30-percent-plus gain, they're off to a different fund, pocketing signing bonuses that are sometimes in the millions of dollars (of your money). Following someone who's hot can be a real crapshoot. He or she could follow the same philosophy or change directions completely. It's not the smartest way to invest in funds.

- *Short-term management.* Be wary of trusting fund results if the current manager hasn't been there for at least two years. If the manager has been there only six months, it's tough to argue that the current results are based on his or her decisions, unless the fund has an unusually high turnover rate.

If you're buying and selling mutual funds in a tax-deferred account, your decision needn't take taxes into consideration; you won't be paying any until you start withdrawing from the account. Another thing to think about is what kind of mutual funds you're investing in with your tax-deferred money. Tax-free municipal bonds may seem sensible, but they're not a good idea for a tax-deferred account. Instead, you'll want the higher gains that come with taxable investments.

Now that you know some of the good and bad points of mutual funds, the question is: How do they stack up against buying individual stocks?

Here are three reasons why stocks might be considered a better investment than mutual funds:

1. *Over the long run, stocks are cheaper.* You'll pay less to buy and sell stocks than to purchase most mutual funds (except, perhaps, an extremely inexpensive no-load index fund).

2. *Control.* You decide when you want to buy or sell, and how much of a particular company you want to hold. And, you decide the strategy. If you decide to buy and hold a particular company, you can.

3. *No tax worries.* You'll pay income tax on any dividends you receive, but if you hold your stock and pass it down to your heirs, you'll pay no capital gains tax on it (though *you* may owe estate tax).

An obvious problem remains. With stocks, you'll still have to diversify to protect your investment—something that's difficult to do (even when spending only $7.95 for each trade online) when you have a small amount of money. And, you have to be pretty good at picking stocks. One expert has noted that some of the brightest minds in investing are running big mutual funds. You might stumble on an idea most of them missed, but if you go with one of these funds, you should get average or above-average returns.

Choosing a Quality Mutual Fund

Currently, about 10,000 mutual funds are waiting for you to invest in them. In a given year, anywhere from 70 to 95 percent don't beat the index they're tracking. Why such a dismal performance? It could be that the fund manager has either made poor choices or has overdiversified to the point of eliminating higher gains. Another possibility is that the fund is spending too much money on commissions (turning over the portfolio perhaps 150 percent in a year), on 12(b)-1 fees (the marketing expenses a fund incurs, including all the courtside, ringside, and corporate box seats that mutual funds give away to brokers in the hope that they'll remember the fund fondly when they're giving their clients some impartial advice), and on inflated salaries (mutual fund managers routinely make hundreds of thousands of dollars a year, if not millions). If you are a fund investor and the fund does really well, you might not mind all of these expenses. If Bill Gates wanted a $20 million salary every year, would you, a Microsoft shareholder whose share value has surged, begrudge him? Probably not. On the other hand, if your shares lost 50 percent of their value, you might not be so benevolent.

How can you recognize a good fund? Here are some issues to think about.

1. *Choose a good fund family.* Some of the biggest fund families (and those that consistently rate high in independent evaluations) include Fidelity, Vanguard, Charles Schwab, and T. Rowe Price. (These aren't the only ones out there, but they're among the biggest and best known.) Each of these families offers dozens, if not hundreds, of their own mutual funds, and they're developing (or currently have in place) fund supermarkets that allow investors to own mutual funds managed by companies outside the family. Pick a fund family that offers plenty of no-load mutual funds, limited expenses, and a good track record. Your entire account list should come on one statement each month, and you should be able to trade via telephone and Internet, and to have access to your accounts, via telephone or home computer, twenty-four hours a day. If it's important to have an

office nearby, choose a fund family with convenient locations. If you want other services, make sure they're offered and at what price.

2. *Decide how you want to allocate your assets.* Do you want blue-chip stocks, an income and growth fund, something in the technology sector, and a gold fund to balance things out? Look at the different types of funds that are available, and talk to someone at the investment house who can explain what each fund does, if you're not sure after reading the prospectuses.

3. *Check out the fund's performance.* Research how the fund has performed during the past three, five, and ten years. Remember that the ten-year performance numbers no longer include the 1987 stock market crash, though they will include the volatility in 1998. That fact alone may make the results of most funds seem rosy. Morningstar, the Chicago-based mutual fund ratings publisher that gives a one- to five-star rating to mutual funds, rates funds on a bell curve. The funds performing in the top 10 percent get five stars, and the bottom 10 percent of performers get a single star. You should get at least two independent ratings for each fund. The good news is you can now get this information online; most of the fund families offer links to independent ratings agencies. You should also check out how often a fund turns over its portfolio. In addition to higher expenses, a fund that turns over its stocks frequently may also have higher taxes for you to pay. The Beta factor indicates how much risk the fund manager is taking to achieve his or her returns.

4. *Check out the expenses.* You can pay big bucks or just a few dollars for a quality mutual fund. As we'll discuss later, plenty of studies show that no-load funds do as well as or better than load funds. Whichever way you go, remember this: Whenever you cut down on your investment expenses, you boost your returns.

5. *Investigate the fund manager.* Who is he or she? How long has the manager been there? What is his or her background? It used to be tougher to get these data, but more fund companies are now putting this information online, where it is accessible to everyone. If you want additional facts, call the fund and ask for them.

6. *Are there any odd or inconvenient items?* Does the fund allow you to cash out only by mail, or can you call in your redemption? Is there a minimum investment amount? Are there consolidated

statements? Does the fund have any redemption fees if you change your mind within, say, the first ninety days? Are there any redemption fees at all when you sell, no matter how long you've held the fund? Are there fees if you cash in because the stock market has nose-dived in the previous five days? If any of these or other conditions exist, you'll want to know ahead of time.

7. *Avoid redundancies.* If you buy six different funds that all specialize in the technology sector, you'll probably have funds that own pieces of the same companies. This may give you an illusion of being diversified ("I have six funds," you might think) but the truth is, you're only as diversified as the holdings of each mutual fund. Carefully look at the companies the fund invests in, and make sure they fill holes in your portfolio rather than duplicate what you already have. Be sure to read your statement and any information sent to you by the fund's management.

8. *Make sure the fund is as risky or as conservative as you want it to be.* Don't get suckered in by a speculative international fund's one-year return if you're looking for a bond fund. Remember that a mutual fund doesn't ameliorate risk, nor is it insured. Take only the amount of risk you can really live with.

Are you investing through a brokerage firm (but perhaps not with a broker)? The bigger firms all offer copious amounts of information, and much of it is free to investors. Stop by a local office, or head to your brokerage firm's Web site for more information than you'll be able to digest at one sitting.

Knowing When to Sell

Knowing when to sell is the key to cementing your return. Mutual fund experts suggest you should sell for one of the following reasons:

1. *Your needs have changed.* You've fulfilled a financial goal or set a new one. You're older and decide to take less risk. You've reevaluated your returns and decide you need more risk.

2. *The fund has changed fundamentally.* If the fund is no longer doing what you want it to do, it may be time to move your money elsewhere. A fund that specializes in small-cap companies that are successful and grow may turn into a midcap fund. That may be a great choice for you, but you need to reevaluate that new midcap fund against others in the midcap group. It is no longer a small-cap fund. If you have a need for a small-cap fund, you'll have to go elsewhere.

3. *There's a change of management.* Your fund manager leaves and a new one takes his or her place. If you're not comfortable with the change, it could be a reason to sell.

4. *The fund hasn't kept pace.* If the fund hasn't kept pace with other funds it has competed with over the past three to five years, it may be time for a change. If you understand the strategy and buy into the long-term vision of the manager, it may not be a problem. But if, for example, other S&P 500 index funds all meet the index and yours gains less than all the others, there could be a larger problem. Still, don't be too hasty to judge. If you criticize your fund manager for a three-month performance, for example, you may ultimately shoot yourself in the foot.

5. *Tax issues have developed.* If you have a loss in one fund, you may want to sell it to offset a gain from another investment.

Mutual Fund Myths

There's great advice everywhere, regarding mutual funds. Still, some folks harbor notions that are only going to get them into trouble:

1. *"All that matters is what happened last year."* Right. And the moon is made of green cheese. To properly evaluate a fund, you need to look at its performance over the past three, five, and ten years. If you can go back fifteen years, or since its inception, you'll see what happened to the fund during the 1987 crash.

2. *"Great family, good fund."* Although I said earlier that Fidelity, T. Rowe Price, and Vanguard were good fund families, each of them has had big-time problems with a few funds over the years. They've allowed poor-performing funds to disappear or be swallowed up, and they've had management problems as

well. Don't think you're safe just because you're within a well-respected family. Even the best families have skeletons in their closets.

3. *"I can buy in and forget about it."* Mutual funds may not be as time-intensive as stock investments, but you'll still need to properly research them, and then make sure they're performing to the level you want. If they're not, its time to switch to another fund.

4. *"I need to pay someone to choose my mutual funds for me."* If you take the time to learn about funds and how companies rate them, as well as your needs and your risk for tolerance, there's no reason why you can't do as well, or better, on your own.

5. *"Load funds have higher returns than no-load funds."* No studies that I'm aware of support this position. Sheldon Jacobs, editor and publisher of the "No-Load Fund Investor" (800-252-2042) and author of *Sheldon Jacobs' Guide to Successful No-Load Fund Investing*, believes there is no correlation between loads and success. *Consumer Reports* studied the performance of more than 1,000 stock funds from 1988 to 1992 and found that no-load funds had a slightly higher rate of return. Other studies have concluded that there is basically no difference in the rate of return.

6. *"I should buy as many funds as possible to be truly diversified."* If you buy into ten funds doing exactly the same thing, you have as much exposure as if you bought one fund. If you have 60, 40, or even 20 separate mutual fund holdings, you may well be classified as a mutual fund addict. There's no way you can keep track of all of them, so, undoubtedly, you're holding some dogs.

7. *"I need to beat other funds, or my investment is a failure."* Investing isn't a horse race, though it can sometimes feel like one. The real issue isn't whether you beat your neighbor's return, or the index you're tracking, or the general market's performance (although these last two may be good ways of telling whether a fund is doing its job). The real issue is: Are your funds getting you where you need to go? Are they successful enough to pay for your financial goals? If the index your fund is tracking returns 25 percent annually and your investment returns only 20 percent, but inflation is 2 percent, you're doing really well. Could you do better? Sure. Will you get where you want to go? Yes.

RESOURCES

Morningstar (www.morningstar.net; 800-876-5005) and Lipper Analytical (XXX) rate funds, as do several other companies. You can also get to either of these companies through a fund family's Web site. Value Line Survey (800-284-7607) is another terrific source of information.

The Mutual Fund Education Alliance (www.mfea.com), a nonprofit trade association, has literature that explains some of the details of the mutual fund industry. You can download, from the Mutual Fund Channel (www.mutualfundchannel.com), free software that will help you organize your mutual fund holdings and will update your portfolio daily or weekly. For great information about investing, try S&P Personal Wealth ($9.95 per month; www.personalwealth.com).

HOW DO I ANALYZE HOW EXPENSIVE A MUTUAL FUND IS?

QUESTION 64

No matter what mutual fund you invest in, it's going to cost you something. The smallest fee may be a fraction of 1 percent, but it's still there. With that in mind, let's look at the different fees you might run across when you start investing in mutual funds.

- *Load.* A sales charge that can range from 1 to 7 percent. It might be a front-load fee (payable when you buy into the fund) or a back-load fee (payable when you cash out). You typically pay it because you want the service of a financial professional in selecting and building your portfolio. Your load may decrease, the longer you hold the fund. If you cashed out in the first year, you'd pay 6 percent. Cash out three years later and the load may be only 3 percent.

- *Redemption fee.* Typically, a charge that's imposed on people who redeem their shares within a short period of time, which might be ninety days or three years. Some funds impose a .25 percent redemption fee no matter when you cash out. Why? This is another way for funds to be profitable. There may be some additional costs if too many people take their money out at exactly the same moment. Funds have to keep some cash in reserve, in case investors want to redeem their shares. If too many people want to redeem their shares all at once, the fund has to sell some stock, perhaps at an inopportune time.

- *Wrap accounts.* Your broker might offer to wrap your mutual funds in with other investments you own, and keep an eye on all your holdings, for a 1 to 3 percent wrap account fee.

- *12(b)-1 fees.* These are marketing expenses the fund must meet. They could cover anything from printing brochures to picking up the cost of entertaining or compensating brokers who put their clients into the fund.

- *Transaction fees.* The costs mutual funds incur when they buy and sell shares of stock on the open market.

- *Operating expenses.* The costs of administration and management, including salaries and bonuses. The charge can be .05 to 2 percent per year.

- *Classified shares.* As we discussed earlier, mutual funds now assign "A," "B," "C," and "D" designations to distinguish the different types of payments made to brokers as commissions. (See page 473 (in Glossary) for more information.)

Mutual funds are required by law to tell their investors how much they spend each year. When you look at a prospectus, look for the *expense ratio.* This number, expressed as a percentage, is the amount the mutual fund spent the previous year, and it is a good indication of what the fund spends on average. If the expense ratio is 2 percent and the fund has $500 million in assets, the fund spent $10 million on expenses.

If you're wondering why your personal return doesn't look quite as good as the fund's return, you need to ask some basic questions. The fund's reported performance should include its expense ratio. If you

Two funds have approximately the same return and offer about the same (or perhaps the same) stock holdings. One fund has an expense ratio of 3 percent, and one has expenses of .05 percent. Which fund would you choose? The one with the least amount of expenses, because they come right off the top of your return. That's how many folks view the choice between load and no-load funds. If the return is the same, and the expenses are the same, and the funds hold approximately the same stocks, why would you pay a 3 percent load?

don't understand the number, ask your broker or financial planner for assistance.

The least expensive type of fund to own is a no-load index fund. Vanguard has some of the least expensive index funds. They're cheap to run because a company normally stays in an index for a long time, so the fund doesn't do a lot of buying and selling. After the fund is set up, management or overhead expenses, other than those for administering the fund, are minimal.

WHAT IS A REAL ESTATE INVESTMENT TRUST (REIT)?

QUESTION
65

A *real estate investment trust* (which I'll now refer to as a REIT) is basically a pool of investor cash that is used to purchase real estate rather than the stocks of individual companies. I like to think of it as a mutual fund made up of apartment buildings, shopping centers, and office buildings.

Congress created REITs in 1960 to help individual investors tap into the world of large-scale, significant-income-producing real estate. Congress reasoned that because few individual investors have $2 million to toss into a strip mall, pooling money would enable the rest of us to participate in the marvelous returns that are available to savvy commercial and industrial real estate developers. REITs would also pump a huge amount of money into the real estate world, making cash available to finance commercial, industrial, and large-scale rental development.

Until the mid-1970s, REITs weren't great for the average investor. Since then, equity REITs have produced fairly good returns. (Earlier, Congress had a couple of other really good real estate ideas, chief of which were: the creation, in the 1930s, of the government-backed FHA mortgage, and, in the aftermath of World War II, the introduction of the VA loan to help returning GIs pay for a home.) Some fundamental changes in the way REITs operate since their creation that have allowed them to function more efficiently.

In the beginning, for example, REITs could only own property, not operate or manage it. That arrangement didn't work out well. Also, the federal tax code, which distorted the real estate market with tax shelters, created an economic hurdle. Because they are specifically designed to create taxable income (REITs must pay out 95 percent of their taxable income to investors, in order to qualify for corporate tax exemptions), and they may not pass losses along to shareholders, REITs couldn't compete with other tax-sheltered investments.

The Tax Reform Act of 1986 basically did away with real estate tax shelters (and eliminated deductions for consumer debt, such as credit card debt) and began permitting REITs to own, operate, and manage most types of commercial properties.

The recession of the early 1990s had an important effect. Capital and credit for real estate developers basically dried up, and commercial property values dropped 30 to 50 percent (or more) in various parts of the country. Developers approached consumers, who started pumping money into REITs. Since the early 1990s, real estate has been on a upswing. Lower interest rates (we've hit thirty-year lows at various points in the 1990s) have sparked incredible development. A solid, growing economy and the lowest levels of unemployment in years have sparked tremendous consumer confidence. When consumers are spending more, they need more places to shop. When they buy more homes, they need products to furnish, improve, and keep up those homes. The meteoric rise of the stock market during the 1990s has helped fuel this growth.

Modern REITs have a lot to offer the average investor. Owning real estate has always been a good way to diversify a portfolio. For many folks, owning a house is about all that comes to mind when real estate is mentioned. But others purchase rental properties. If you're not up to the 2:00 A.M. calls about leaking toilets, REITs are a way to tap the rental real estate market. Also, because REITs are traded publicly, they have made real estate more liquid than it has ever been. You can generally buy and sell shares of many REITs the way you'd buy and sell shares of General Electric.

According to the National Association of Real Estate Investment Trusts (NAREIT), REITs have proven to be a competitive investment, though there have been a few scary years. NAREIT's Web site (www.nareit.com) offers a year-by-year return for REITs, starting with 1972. Since then, an investment in a REIT ranged from a one-year low of – 42.23 percent in 1974 (that's right, it lost more than 42 percent of its value, or a total of 69 percent if you tack on the loss in 1973) to a one-year high of nearly 49 percent in 1976. In fact, by 1976, REITs had more than made up for losses during the 1973–1974 period (a time when the stock markets didn't perform particularly well either). More recently, REITs have fared better, though 1998 will prove to be another down year. By midyear, REITs had taken a 20 percent hit in share price.

Note: Equity REITs buy property such as apartment rental complexes, shopping centers, and hospitals. Mortgage REITs buy mortgages or mortgage-backed securities. Hybrid REITs do a little of each.

REIT Return, 1991–1996

Year	All REITs	Equity	Mortgage	Hybrid
1991	35.68%	35.70%	31.83%	39.16%
1992	12.18	14.59	1.92	16.59
1993	18.55	19.65	14.55	21.18
1994	0.81	3.17	−24.30	4.00
1995	18.31	15.27	63.42	22.99
1996	35.75	35.27	50.86	29.35

All data are courtesy of the National Association of Real Estate Investment Trusts, 1875 Eye Street, NW, Suite 600, Washington, DC 20006. For more information, call 800-3NAREIT. As we went to press, the 1998 data were not available.

In 1997, REITs returned approximately 20 percent, but by the third quarter of 1998, they had fallen about 20 percent. Their average annual historical return has been about 16 percent. The S&P 500 has done better—in some years, much better—but real estate (whether your home, an investment property, a limited partnership, or shares of a REIT) has always been used to diversify a portfolio. REITs tend to move either in opposite directions or slightly out of step with stock and bond investments, which is the reason you diversify your portfolio in the first place.

Things You Should Know about REITs

As you can see in the above chart, there are three types of REITs. An *equity* REIT makes purchases, a *mortgage* REIT makes loans, and a *hybrid* REIT does both.

I noted earlier that a REIT is required to pay out at least 95 percent of its income to investors each year. As a result, much of the return of a REIT comes in the form of a large cash dividend. REIT growth is typically secondary, although a good year will yield a lot of income *and* significant growth. Investors may earn a cash dividend (also known as the yield) of 6 or 7 percent, plus share price growth of perhaps 2 to 3 percent, for a total return of 8 to 10 percent. Statistically, approximately 70 percent of a REIT's return comes from the dividend, versus 20 percent from an S&P 500 stock.

Most REITs specialize in a particular type of building or in one region of the country. REITs are specialists in industrial parks, shopping malls, offices, hotels, retail stores, or apartment buildings. Although there are fewer than 250 REITs as this book goes to press (as opposed to 10,000 mutual funds), more are being created every day, and they are trying to find niche areas that haven't yet been tapped. If you're serious about investing in a REIT, here are some issues to consider:

- *Type of property.* Think about which type of property you want to invest in. Your choices are: industrial buildings and office parks, rental apartments, shopping malls or other retail developments, hotels, and health care buildings.

- *Good management.* Some of the best real estate companies in the country have created or are managing REITs. For example, billionaire Sam Zell has swooped in, spending more than $2 billion to purchase property all over the country and form a REIT. It's important that you invest in a REIT that has superb management. Without it, costs can spiral out of control, and the REIT (and your investment) may lose money. Unfortunately, you'll have to do whatever legwork you can to check out the fund management. Look at the REITs track record, the types of properties it has owned and managed, and any articles about the REIT in newspapers and magazines.

- *Location, location, location.* These are the three most important words in real estate, whether you're buying your own home, an investment property, or a REIT. Where are the properties located in your REIT? Are they immune or susceptible to future downturns?

- *Rising interest rates.* As long as interest rates are low, the real estate market will be strong. When interest rates start to rise, demand for real estate could slow down, and REITs could be in trouble.

- *Economic downturn.* When the economy falters and people don't have jobs, they don't spend money and they don't need more places to invest money. REITs will be hard hit in an economic recession, though their downturn will lag the fall in the general economy.

- *Overbuilding.* Real estate is cyclical. Developers build to meet a current need, but because it takes so long to get a project up and running, the need has already been met or has abated by the time a project is finished. That's how areas end up being over-built. The economy struggles to catch up with and absorb what has already been built. During that period, there isn't too much commercial development. Once there is a shortage, developers will once again start building.

• *FFOs and other important numbers.* Carefully examine a REIT's numbers before you invest. One of the more important numbers is the *Funds From Operations* (FFO), which is like a company's earnings. This number is important because it factors in real estate depreciation, which is a complicated calculation. Also look at the REIT's past growth and its growth projections, as well as the share price divided by the FFO (similar to the P/E ratio of stocks).

People who invest in REITs for the long term really like them. They don't always do well, but they can throw off a lot of cash, which makes them an excellent investment for people who like to receive income and some growth. But they're quite a bit riskier than bonds, so if this income is needed to purchase food and clothing and pay the rent, consider purchasing something a bit more stable.

WHAT ARE THE BIGGEST MISTAKES INVESTORS MAKE?

QUESTION
66

It would be nice if we were all perfect. We'd always buy when prices are low and sell when they're high. We'd be rich and carefree, and the Caribbean would be littered with our yachts.

Unfortunately, life isn't some movie set. We work hard for the money we invest, and because investing is complicated and much of it is beyond our control, we all make some classic mistakes when we're deciding how to invest our money. Perhaps if we knew where all the potholes were, we would have a smoother journey.

Top Ten Financial Mistakes Investors Often Make

1. *Losing track of investments.* If you have more stocks, bonds, and mutual funds than you can remember, something's probably

slipping through the cracks. Consider paring down your investments to a manageable handful, preferably placed within one or two brokerage firms. When your monthly statements come in, you'll only have to look at one or two instead of a deskful. Organize your investments so that you know where they are and what they're doing for you. It will then be much easier for you to make prudent financial decisions.

2. *Owning redundant investments.* Too often, we end up with a fistful of mutual funds, each of which may own some of the same investments. When that happens, we fool ourselves into thinking we're diversified, when in fact we've ratcheted up the risk by buying the same investment over and over again. Take a look at your investments, particularly your mutual funds, and try to identify the reasons why you bought them. Then look at the kinds of investments the fund is holding today. Do they still meet your needs and your goals?

3. *Losing control of investment costs.* Every dollar spent purchasing, managing or paying taxes on your investments comes right off the top of your return. Afraid to trade on the Internet? Get over it. For the money you save by not paying a broker to complete a trade for you, you can buy more shares of your actual investment. If you're going to trade investments frequently, do it in your retirement account. You won't have to pay taxes on your gains until later, and the paperwork is almost nonexistent. By focusing on costs and shaving them where you can, you'll dramatically improve your return, no matter what the market does.

4. *Buying without researching.* If you buy a company because you like how the CEO sounds in a television sound bite, good luck! You'll need it. If you tend to make impulsive decisions, buy clothing instead; at least clothes are usually returnable. Before deciding on an investment, take the time to find out at least the bare minimum about the company. You'll exponentially increase your odds of making a good choice.

5. *Taking a hot stock tip from a cold call.* If a stockbroker you've never heard of calls you in the middle of dinner and gives you a hot stock tip, what should you do? Hang up. Unfortunately, too many folks are suckered into buying stocks over the phone and sending in their money. If your own broker calls you repeatedly toward the end of a month, urging you to buy "the greatest investment ever," find out everything you can about

the recommended company, and carefully assess how it fits into your portfolio, *before* you say yes. And if your careful approach makes you miss an "opportunity of a lifetime," think about all the other horrible investments you avoided because you didn't blindly follow the leader.

6. *Failing to follow an investment strategy.* Once you decide on a strategy, be it buy and hold, or sell half when it doubles, make sure you stick to it unless you have a darned good reason. Remember Aesop's fable of the tortoise and the hare. Slow and steady wins the race.

7. *Failing to diversify investments.* Only you know how much risk you can take and still sleep at night. Once you figure out your risk limit, diversify your investments without exceeding your tolerance. The alternatives are a lot of sleepless nights and a nervous stomach.

8. *Ignoring an investment.* If you own many different investments, a few may end up slipping through the cracks. Maybe you're too busy to read the literature that comes from the company, or you forget about the stock for a while, only to wake up one morning and hear that the company declared bankruptcy. Or, you become bored with an old investment and prefer to concentrate on new ones. If you find that you've spread yourself too thin and your investments aren't getting the attention they deserve, consider pruning your portfolio down to a manageable size. Focus on the areas you really know and enjoy. If you enjoy buying, fixing up, and managing rental properties, and you do well with them as an investment, concentrate on that activity. No one says you have to buy pork belly futures just because you don't own any yet.

9. *Not reacting when new management comes in.* If a company in which you've invested suddenly announces a change of leadership, or if one of your mutual fund managers leaves, reassess where the company or fund is going and whether that investment will get you where you want to go.

10. *Losing sight of the forest.* It's common to get caught up in a market moment and forget that investing is something we're going to do for the rest of our lives. We can easily lose sight of our larger investment goals when we're concentrating on whether we outperformed the market or beat the returns enjoyed by our neighbors. Instead, it's important to stay the course and end up with enough money to fund our plans and dreams.

Ten Emotional Mistakes Investors Make

1. *Buying or selling based on feelings, not numbers.* The market goes down, so you sell because you feel bad that you're losing money. You then wait for the market to recover. Once it does, and you start feeling better about the future, you buy. But by then, you've missed out on a lot of the recovery.

2. *Sabotaging a sound financial future.* You know you *should* research your investments before buying them. You know you should buy quality companies and then keep them in your portfolio for a long time. You know that rapid trading rarely produces great results. But you just can't help yourself. For whatever reason, you can't seem to keep yourself from buying into that hot tip your friend just gave you. When you know what you should do with your investments and then do the opposite, you're sabotaging yourself and your financial future.

3. *Putting it off until tomorrow.* When it comes to investing, procrastination doesn't cut it. What happens if you wait until next year to start contributing to your 401(k) program at work? You'll be a year older and many thousands of dollars poorer at retirement. The benefits of compounding work their magic as long as you have time on your side. Start today. Every day you delay puts your financial goals in jeopardy.

4. *Getting paralyzed by information overload.* The information available to investors today seems infinite. Newspapers, magazines, newsletters, pamphlets, television and radio programs, and the Internet all disseminate personal finance information and advice twenty-four hours a day. If you're savvy, you'll screen out the noise and take only what you need to keep moving ahead with your investment strategy. Some people take everything in and become financially paralyzed. Money Blocks are hard to dispel once they settle in.

5. *Adopting our parents' money attitudes.* How did your parents feel about money? Many people seem to either adopt their parents' attitude about money, or go in a polar opposite direction. Your money worries may be real or, for your actual financial situation, they may be overblown. Recognize the role money plays in your life. Accept it, and then find a way to make it work.

6. *Ignoring the need for discipline.* You resolve to make regular contributions to a mutual fund or dividend reinvestment plan. And in some months you actually make them. But only in some months. Why? Expenses have a way of creeping up on us. Charge cards are easy to use; checks are harder to write. As an investor, there's nothing better than paying yourself first. If you're not disciplined enough to write an investment check every month, authorize your mutual fund or retirement account to automatically withdraw an amount on the same day of every month.

7. *Waiting for the perfect investment.* Waiting for the perfect investment is like waiting for the perfect man or woman to walk into your life. He or she doesn't exist. Everyone is flawed. Everyone has baggage. And the older you get, the more flawed you are and the more baggage you have. There is no perfect investment. If you recognize that, you'll find plenty of good options that, despite their flaws, fit perfectly into your investment strategy.

8. *Being impatient about results.* Patience is generally rewarded in investing. I'm not saying that you can postpone doing something and still end up with more money in retirement. But if you jump the gun and sell on impulse, you'll almost certainly end up with less than if you wait for your strategy to work and for your investments to mature.

9. *Gambling instead of investing.* If you want to gamble, withdraw $100 or $1,000 and head to Las Vegas, Reno, Tahoe, Atlantic City, any of the Native American reservations that have casinos, or a local race track, or buy lottery tickets. Investing for your future should be done deliberately—not wantonly, not lustfully, and certainly not with a gambler's instinct. Casinos stack the odds in their favor. When you invest, if you spend time carefully planning and researching your investments, you can have the odds in your favor.

10. *Operating under misguided assumptions.* Just because everyone else is doing something doesn't mean it's right for you. Everyone has different goals, attitudes, and dreams when it comes to money. No investment is uniformly perfect. That's a good thing, but it means you have to take responsibility for your actions and for your financial future. You have to figure out what will get you where you want to go.

Investments: Annuities, Bonds, and Certificates of Deposit (CDs)

QUESTION 67

WHAT IS AN ANNUITY?

A tax-deferred annuity is an investment product dreamed up by the insurance industry. It offers a limited amount of benefit to some people.

Here's the basic concept: Annuities are tax-deferred accounts with an insurance wrapper. You either pay a lump sum of cash to an insurance company (or a bank that's working with an insurance company), or you pay into an account in dribs and drabs—usually, a minimum of $100 per month. (There is no limit on how much money you can put into an annuity, which is one reason people like them.) The after-tax cash you put in then grows *tax-deferred*. When it comes time to withdraw your money, you'll pay tax on it at your current marginal tax rate (the highest rate you qualify for). If your marginal rate is 31.5 percent, that's the income tax you'll pay on the portion of your annuity payment that represents growth. (You pay no tax on the principal.) Like a Roth IRA, your contributions have already been taxed.

Another lure of an annuity is the life insurance component (which is where the insurance company comes in). If you die while the annuity is in force, the company promises to pay at least what you paid in, or the current market value (whichever is higher), to your heirs.

When you sign up for an annuity, *you* decide how it's going to pay out. You can choose to receive payments for life, for a set term with a lump sum coming at the end, or not at all. More on this later.

In the Beginning . . .

There are two types of annuities: *fixed annuities* and *variable annuities*. Fixed annuities give you a fixed rate of return on your investment. Variable annuities put your investment into a pool of stock mutual funds (called *subaccounts*) that yield varying rates of return. Typically, a minimum return is guaranteed, but don't stake your life on it.

Here are some of the key issues you should think about before you sign an annuity agreement:

- *Can you handle the expense?* You'll pay a yearly contract fee ($25 to $50, or more), an annual insurance premium (.15 to 1.75 percent of assets), plus annual mutual fund fees. I'm not aware of any studies proving that higher-priced annuities offer better returns, so go with a no-load or low-load (as in cheap) annuity. Aim to keep costs to less than 2 percent. Remember: the more you pay, the longer you must hold an annuity, if your investment is to make sense; and, several studies have shown that annuities underperform as an investment.

- *Is the timing right for you?* You can't withdraw money from an annuity before you're age 59. If you do, you'll pay a 10 percent penalty plus income tax. (The penalty is waived for medical emergencies.) Most annuities have a surrender fee (a fee you'll pay to terminate the annuity and get your money back). The fee can be as high as 7 or 8 percent of the annuity's value, though it typically dwindles down to nothing, or a flat fee, within seven to ten years. Some companies try to keep the surrender fee for as long as twenty years.

- *Have you selected a good company?* The insurance company you select should be rated among the top 20 percent by a ratings company such as Lipper Analytical Service. (Try the Lipper Variable Insurance Product Performance Analysis Service, which may be available online or at your local library, or call 212-312-0300.) The company should offer a good pool of funds from which to choose, and you should be able to switch back and forth between funds without penalty. The company should have annuity assets of over $100 million, and a good track record for returns over the past five years. Beating the average is recommended, and it's even better if you can get returns in the top 20 percent of the annuity's peer group. Remember, if your insurance company fails, you're probably out of luck (and might not see a dime of your annuity).

- *Are you buying tax-free investments for your annuity?* Annuities, like 401(k) plans, grow tax-deferred. That means you pay income taxes on the money when you withdraw it during retirement. By purchasing tax-free investments for a tax-deferred account, you're losing some of the tax-deferred status. Also, taxable investments tend to have higher returns than tax-free investments, so more of your money is working for you through the magic of compounding. One statistic says 70 percent of all annuities are held in tax-deferred retirement accounts. Clearly, these annuity holders don't recognize that they're paying two sets of fees (one for the annuity and one for the retirement account) to do the same thing.

- *Do you know how and when to get your money out?* You'll have several options to choose from. Remember, when you receive any payments, you'll have to pay income taxes on the portion that constitutes earnings. Choose a *lump-sum distribution* and you'll get your cash all at once, along with a hefty tax bill. *Periodic* or *systematic withdrawals* allow you to take money out when you need it, while the balance continues to grow. *Annuitization* means you get monthly payments either for life (called *life-only*), or for a certain period of time (five, ten, fifteen, or twenty years). *Joint life* and *survivor* provides income for two people: the annuity owner and a beneficiary (spouse or partner). Payments stop after the second person's death. You may also choose *term certain*, which guarantees payments for a certain number of years, with any remainder going to a beneficiary, or a *commutable contract*, which gives you today's cash value for your future payments.

- *Will you use it or lose it?* If you choose to *annuitize*—that is, get equal payments throughout the rest of your life or for a fixed period of time—and if you die halfway through, you may forfeit the rest of your cash to the insurance company.

- *Have you maximized all of your other tax-deferred options?* You should fund your 401(k), IRA, Keogh, and other tax-deductible retirement plans *before* you even think about buying into an annuity. All of these plans allow you to fund these plans with pretax dollars, which means you don't pay tax on the money today. Annuities and Roth IRAs are funded with after-tax dollars, but your Roth IRA earnings are tax-free.

- *Is an annuity your last choice for an investment?* After you've funded your tax-deductible retirement accounts, consider funding a Roth IRA. If you still have cash left over, consider tax-free municipal bonds. Then, finally, think about an annuity.

Gift Annuities

This is a way to give a donation and still benefit from it. A *gift annuity* allows you to purchase an annuity, give it as a gift to a charity, and

Two of the best things about annuities are: (1) the contributions aren't capped, and (2) there is no specific age at which you have to start withdrawing money. (You have to tap into regular IRAs by age 70.) Choosing an annuity is a complicated, long-term decision. Before you make that choice, talk to a fee-only financial planner about your current needs, your future needs, and how annuities might help you with your estate planning. You'll also want to examine several different annuity products. Look for the cheapest one that's offered by one of the best companies, make sure you won't need the cash for at least ten to fifteen years, and go with the most aggressive investing options available to you. Insurance agents reap a huge commission from any annuity, so it's in their best interest to sell you an expensive one (where the commissions can be staggering). Make sure you ask to see the *past* interest rate performance, not what they think will happen. Their forecast charts will show your investment multiplying faster than jackrabbits in summer. Look to past annuities' performance as a guide. (If no "apples-to-apples" annuity comparisons are available, make sure you ask to see "comparable" programs' results.)

If the agent with whom you're dealing refuses to provide you with the data you want, and doesn't seem to be answering your questions honestly, find another agent. This is an expensive, long-term purchase. You should be absolutely sure you're getting what you set out to get. Read the prospectus. More than one consumer has been talked through one type of investment and then shunted into another. If you don't *read your prospectus and the contract* before you sign up for an annuity, you'll get what you deserve.

receive a monthly payment for life (at a rate based on your age). You can even give a gift annuity when you're young and receive payments when you retire.

Because the charity gets only a portion of the gift annuity, you get to deduct only that portion.

RESOURCES

The National Association for Variable Annuities, based in Reston, Virginia, offers free information. Call 703-602-0674, extension 17. Lipper Analytical Services (212-312-0300; www.lipperweb.com) provides information on annuities to newspapers *(The Wall Street Journal)* and magazines *(Smart Money)*. Check out Morningstar's Web site (www.morningstar.net) for its variable annuity report. *The Annuity Shopper* (800-872-6684) is a quarterly magazine that lists the annuity products available from several hundred insurance companies, the companies' ratings, and the percentages they are paying on individual accounts. The cost is normally $29 per year, but the publisher often runs special offers for less.

QUESTION 68

WHAT IS A BOND AND WHAT KINDS OF BONDS CAN I BUY?

You basically have two ways to invest your money. First, you can buy a piece of the action. That's called *investing in equities*, and we most commonly think of it in terms of buying shares of stock of a company. As a stockholder, you actually own part of the company.

The other way you can invest your money is to loan it to someone else and be paid back with interest. If you give someone money to purchase a house, that loan is called a mortgage. But if you loan money to the U.S. Government, utility companies, or even your local village, that loan typically takes the form of a *bond issue*.

Bonds have become a mainstay in the average American portfolio, for good reasons. They are steady and fairly predictable, and they help balance out your portfolio in terms of risk and bringing in income. But, as we'll discuss shortly, invest too heavily in bonds and you may rob yourself of the opportunity to grow your money above and beyond the rate of inflation.

There's no question that bonds can figure into a healthy portfolio. In 1998, Federal Reserve Chairman Alan Greenspan disclosed that a large portion of his wealth was invested in bonds whose value depends greatly on interest rates.

In the Beginning . . .

Bonds are perhaps less complicated than some other kinds of investments. But the bond market has a language all its own. I'll be using the following words and phrases to describe what you need to know, so keep this list of bond jargon handy.

Bond. Essentially, a bond is a loan to a government (federal or municipal) or a corporation. You earn interest on your money as well as a promise to get your principal back at a predetermined date (also known as the date of maturity).

Bond fund. A bond fund is a quick-read term for a mutual fund made up of bond issues.

Callability. A bond may be *called in* before it is due. This usually means that the issuer of the bond has decided to refinance its debt and pay back all of the bondholders early. If interest rates fall, the chances of a bond's being called increase because the bondholder can refinance the debt for less money (just as you'd refinance your mortgage if rates dropped).

Convertibles. Nope, it's not something you drive. A convertible bond is one that can be converted into shares of stock.

Corporate bond. A bond issued by a corporation.

Coupon. The actual interest payment made on each bond. If you have a $5,000 bond paying 7 percent interest, you will receive $350 each year, perhaps in two $175 payments. The $350 is the coupon. The interest rate of the bond is referred to as the coupon rate. The name originates from how people used to collect bond interest (and some still do). They would actually clip a coupon (similar to a newspaper coupon for a discount on groceries) and bring it to the bondholder to receive their interest. More and more, this is done electronically. The interest is simply deposited in your bank account.

Current yield. The interest payment divided by the bond's price. The amount will fluctuate, based on where interest rates are and what you could currently sell your bond for in the marketplace.

Discount. Newly issued bonds are typically sold at a discounted price. A bond that has a face value of $1,000 and sells for $925 has a $75 discount. When interest rates rise, bonds are discounted more because a less expensive bond is needed to achieve the desired interest.

Market price. On any given day, your bond will be worth more, or less, than the face value because the bond market is continually active. Traders bid the value of bonds up and down, based on the current interest rate of the day. When interest rates rise, bonds are worth less (it takes a smaller amount of capital to earn the same amount of interest). When interest rates fall, bonds are worth more (a greater amount of money is needed to earn the same amount of interest).

Matured bond. A bond that has been paid off. The bondholders have received all of their principal, plus the interest due as of the date of maturity.

Municipal bond. A bond offered by a local municipality. Munis, as they are commonly known, are not taxed by the federal government.

Par. A bond's face value. A $1,000 bond will have a par value of $1,000. The term *par* may be a bit confusing because even if your bond is worth $10,000, par also refers to 100, as in 100 percent of a bond's value. So you may hear that your bond cost 95, another way of saying 95 percent of par. That means you'll get a 5 percent discount, or pay $950 for every bond with a $1,000 face value. If a bond costs 116, its price is 116 percent of par. You'll pay $1,160 for a bond with a face value of $1,000.

Principal. This is the amount you're lending. Typically, you'll buy bonds with a face value of $1,000. If you buy at a discount—an example is a zero-coupon bond—the discounted amount is your principal. If you buy a $1,000 bond and pay $1,000, your principal is $1,000.

Real rate of return. Your rate of return with a bond consists of two elements: (1) the interest you've earned on the bond and (2) the actual market value of the bond (it could be above or below face value) when you sell it. If the market value of the bond has appreciated, you will owe capital gains tax on its rise in value. The interest you earn on a bond is taxed like income.

Term. Short-term bonds run up to three years in length. Intermediate bonds are from three to ten years in length. Long-term bonds run up to thirty years in length. Generally, long-term bonds pay the best. Depending on market conditions, however, you'll earn only an extra percentage point or so on money that's tied up for a really long time.

Some financial planners say a better bet is to purchase intermediate-term bonds, which are more flexible.

Treasuries. The federal government offers three types of products to raise money: (1) Treasury bills (also known as T bills), (2) Treasury notes, and (3) Treasury bonds. Uncle Sam uses the money raised from the sale of these three products to pay for social and spending programs. Collectively, this debt is our national debt. Treasuries are considered fail-proof because they are backed by the U.S. Government.

Yield to call. If interest rates go down, your bond issuer will want to refinance the debt by calling in the bond as soon as possible. If your bond has five years until the call date, the important yield will be the yield until the bond is called. The yield to maturity will become immaterial because the bond issuer will never let the bond mature. (Why pay interest that doesn't have to be paid? If interest rates were to go down, you would refinance your home loan.)

Yield to maturity. If you were to hold your bond until it matures and reinvest every interest payment at the interest rate on your bond, you would end up with your yield to maturity. If you spend your interest payments, or reinvest them at a lower rate (in a passbook savings account, for example), your yield to maturity will be less. If you invest them at a higher rate, your yield to maturity will be higher.

If you're buying an older bond (other than newly issued bonds) from a broker, the three important things to know are: (1) the current yield, (2) the yield to maturity, and (3) the yield to call. But be aware that the price is subject to competition and the market, and brokers can pretty much price older bonds where they want to. If you're looking to buy an older bond, get at least two or three price quotes, and let both brokers know you're shopping around.

Types of Bonds

Bonds come in all shapes and sizes. Generally speaking, you can choose from Treasuries, mortgage-backed securities, tax-exempt municipal bonds, corporate bonds (which include bonds from utility companies), junk bonds (remember Michael Milken?), convertible bonds, and unit investment trusts. Here's a quick look at each category.

U.S. Government Securities

Backed by the "full faith and credit" of the United States government, these bonds are considered to be the safest investments you can make. For Uncle Sam to default, the country would have to just about completely dissolve, which is pretty unlikely.

This lack of risk carries a price tag. You'll receive less interest on your loan than if you had bought a corporate bond, and far less than if you had bought a very risky junk bond. Like the prices of other bonds, the price of a Treasury bill, note, or bond will fluctuate, depending on whether interest rates rise or fall.

- *Treasury bills (T bills).* Treasury bills now have a minimum purchase price of $1,000 and are offered in three-month, six-month, and twelve-month lengths. You buy a T bill at a discount which, when divided by the effective cost, equals your rate of interest. (If you purchase a $10,000 T bill for $9,300, your interest rate is $700 ÷ $9,300 = .08 or 8 percent.) The discounted principal is deposited immediately into your account, and the rest of the face value (the interest) arrives on the day the T bill matures. At that time, you have the option of rolling over your T bill for another period. Because T bills, like all offerings from the Treasury Department, are backed by the U.S. Government, they're considered just about the safest investments around.

- *Treasury notes.* These function just like T bills, but they last two to ten years (they're considered equal to intermediate-length bonds). Like T bills and long-term government bonds, they're exempt from state and local taxes. The minimum investment is $5,000 for bonds of two and three years in length. Buy anything longer and the initial investment drops to $1,000.

- *Treasury bonds.* These are the long-term offerings from the Treasury Department. The minimum investment is $1,000. Because they're long-term, they typically pay the highest interest.

- *Zero-coupon bonds.* Zero-coupon bonds pay zero interest throughout the bond term. However, you buy the bond at a steep discount that includes the implied interest rate. For example, a $1,000 bond paying 8 percent might be purchased for $456. The Treasury Department offers zeros (as they're commonly called), as do municipalities and some corporations. Folks like zeros because all of the interest compounds internally at the same rate; you don't have to reinvest your interest to get the total yield. Zeros from the Treasury can be bought directly (through a program called Treasury Direct) and are sold by stockbrokers through the STRIPS (Separate Trading of Registered Interest and Principal of Securities) program and also under the acronyms of LIONs, TIGRs, and CATS (although less frequently than STRIPS). If you buy a zero (or any Treasury bill, note, or bond) through a broker, you'll pay a commission, which will decrease your return. Although you'll receive no income during the bond term, you'll still owe taxes on the imputed yield. Many folks put zeros into tax-deferred accounts, or in the name of their children who earn less than the minimum tax threshold. You should also know that some zeros are callable. If a zero is callable, the holder is typically offered a higher interest rate. Still, because your money compounds internally, your biggest years of earning would come at the end of the bond's life. (Think of a savings account. You'll earn more in the last six years of the account than in the first twenty-five, because of compounding.) You'll earn far less money if the bond is called early.

- *Savings bonds.* At some point, you probably received a savings bond from a relative or family member in celebration of a special event in your life, like a birthday or a graduation. Savings bonds (which come in different series, such as EE and HH) are zeros but you can purchase them in much smaller amounts directly from a bank or from the Treasury Department, or through a broker. They're also nontransferable; they aren't traded. (Other government offerings are.) In September 1998, the federal government began selling inflation-indexed ("I") savings bonds. The newcomer guarantees that your return will outpace inflation, and is actually based on the rate of inflation plus a fixed rate of return, perhaps 3 to 3.5 percent.

Mortgage-Backed Securities

You may have heard of the secondary mortgage market, where companies like Fannie Mae (Federal National Mortgage Association) and Freddie Mac (Federal Home Loan Mortgage Corporation) are major players. These companies purchase mortgages (paying cash for the loan note plus the servicing rights) from lenders, who then turn around and relend the money to new home buyers and homeowners looking to refinance their existing mortgages. Fannie and Freddie repackage mortgages as securities and sell them to investors (large pension plans, for example, as they're commonly called). If you think mortgages are good, long-term investments, you could lend money to an individual and receive interest payments over thirty years (like a lender would). Or, you can purchase a security from Ginnie Mae (Government National Mortgage Association). Loans backing securities are insured by the Federal Housing Authority (FHA loans) or guaranteed by the Department of Veterans Affairs (VA loans).

Unfortunately, if you're going to buy in, the minimum investment is $25,000. But there are bond funds that hold Ginnie Mae securities, and this is typically a good way to go. The most important reason is that each payment you receive from a Ginnie Mae investment is part interest, part principal, which is the way you pay off *your* mortgage. Each month, you have to think about where to reinvest those dollars. In a bond fund, all of that interest and capital can be reinvested.

Municipal Bonds

Municipal bonds ("munis") are loans you make to a local government body—your home town, a neighboring city, your state, or a different state. Munis are not only typically free from state and local taxes, they're exempt from federal income tax as well. That feature and their high degree of safety make them extremely popular, especially with taxpayers in the highest income brackets, even though they pay less interest than other types of bonds. They're also easily salable if you need to unload them before they mature.

The most important thing to remember about municipal bonds is that the higher your tax bracket, the more valuable they are to you. A $10,000 municipal bond that pays 6 percent will put $600 per year in your pocket. A $10,000 taxable bond that pays 6 percent interest a year will put anywhere from $366 (39.6 percent tax bracket) to $510 (15 percent tax bracket) in your pocket.

When comparing taxable and tax-free bonds, remember that you'll get a lower interest rate on tax-free bonds. You'll need to compare your after-tax returns to see which makes the most sense for your portfolio. (See Appendix III for a useful chart.)

How safe are municipal bonds? They're considered to be slightly riskier than Treasuries, but have proved to be pretty safe. Check the ratings of *all* bonds before you purchase them. (See Question 69 for information on bond ratings.)

Some municipal bonds may be called. Others cannot be called. You'll get a bit more interest for bonds that are callable, but they're riskier. If you buy a callable muni, make sure you know the date of the call (it could be five or ten years later).

Corporate Bonds

Corporate bonds are issued by companies that need to raise capital. Companies that issue bonds tend to be in five main sectors: (1) public utilities, (2) transportation companies, (3) industrial corporations, (4) financial service companies, and (5) conglomerates. The companies may be domestic or foreign-owned.

Typically, the minimum buy for a corporate bond is $5,000 (or five $1,000 bonds). You can purchase either newly issued bonds (you'll know exactly what you're getting and how much you're paying) or older bonds through brokers. Corporate bonds are taxed by the federal government, as well as state and local governments, so if you're going to buy them, you might want to hold them in a tax-deferred account.

Corporate bonds can be risky. A company can get into deep financial trouble, and the gurus in the executive suite might decide to use any available cash to prop up the stock price. If the bond issue is subordinated, bondholders may get paid last and will receive only cents on the dollar if the company goes belly up. If the bond's rating is cut, it may be harder to sell before the maturity date. If you can sell it, you'll probably get less than you'd have otherwise received.

Financial planners often recommend getting exposure to corporate bonds through mutual funds. There are load funds and no-load

When you buy corporate bonds, they're backed by the company that issues them. The risk you take is the reason corporate bonds tend to pay better—sometimes a lot better—than T bills.

343

Bonds may be registered in the name of the individual who owns them. If they're registered, the interest is paid automatically to a specified account, and the bondholder is protected against the loss or theft of the bonds. Bearer bonds belong to whoever is holding them. The bearer clips coupons from the certificate and presents them to receive the interest payment. When thieves crack open a safe and steal stacks and stacks of bonds, they're after bearer bonds, which can be cashed slowly over time.

funds that specialize in corporate bonds. Remember, many studies show you'll generate the same return (or better) with a no-load fund, so save yourself the commission.

Junk Bonds

Junk bonds are high-yield bonds. They're often issued by companies in trouble or by companies looking to raise cash without selling more shares. Consequently, they receive a low rating and can be an extremely risky investment. Michael Milken made them famous in the 1980s, and his name will forever be associated with them.

Many financial planners recommend that even conservative portfolios should take on more risk by investing in junk bonds or junk bond mutual funds. Before you start down this path, make sure you fully understand the issuing company or municipality and why its bonds are rated as junk.

Here are two other possibilities:

1. If you find a company in trouble, you may want to purchase its stock rather than its junk bonds. If the company is in real trouble, the stock price is probably depressed. At the first signs of life, the stock may recover nicely (and over a shorter period of time).

2. Some savvy investors speculate on companies by buying junk bonds whose prices have become severely depressed because of deepening company financial woes or because interest payments have stopped, or both. If you buy a bond for a few cents on a dollar, you're essentially betting that the company will come back. If it does (few that are priced a few cents on a dollar

do, but those priced at around 20 cents on a dollar stand a better chance), and it resumes interest rate payments, you might earn 1,000 percent on your investment.

The Bottom Line

Junk bonds, even in a mutual fund, aren't for rookies. After you've mastered the basics of investing, junk bonds may be an area you'll want to explore further. Meanwhile, you can earn a fine return with other investments.

Convertible Bonds

Some companies offer bonds at slightly lower than market rates but with an option of being able to convert the bond into a specific number of shares at a certain price point. This sounds great, but most convertible bonds are callable, and the company will probably call the bond before the stock rises too much above the convertible price.

You'll get a lower interest rate plus the iffy prospect that you might be able to convert your bond if the stock rises in price. This is a complex hybrid bond product that requires fairly high maintenance. I think it's easier to simply buy bonds with the highest rate you can get for the amount of risk you want to take, and buy separately the stocks of companies you like.

Unit Investment Trusts

Unit investment trusts are bond funds that are not actively managed, so only a small management fee is assessed each year. However, you'll almost always pay a load (sales commission).

What do you get for your money? A portfolio of bonds—some good, some bad; some with high yields or low yields. Typically, these bonds are held until they mature or are called. The income isn't particularly dependable. It can be a lot more in some months, if a bond is sold and your principal is returned to you. You might get less in other months because once a bond is sold or expires, your share in the trust goes down.

Unit investment trusts (also known as unit trusts) are listed in *The Wall Street Journal.* There may be a market for your shares if you decide to cash out early. Or, the trustee may elect to buy back your shares. Apparently, a lot goes on behind the scenes, and you may never really know what is driving your return. This is a complicated investment. You *can* have a well-diversified investment portfolio without it.

You're fooling yourself if you think you're going to outsmart the market. There are plenty of full-time investors out there who have become expert in the ways of Wall Street through years of trial and error. I'm not saying that you can't find a good investment. But the time you have to spend on your investments is probably limited and, as the saying goes, you can't buy time even if you buy futures. If you're working your way through this book, you're already planning to spend plenty of time on your personal finances. Add a full-time job, perhaps a second job, and a personal life, and the last things you need are investments that require intense concentration. You might want to save unit trusts, convertible bonds, options, and futures (which I'll talk about in the next chapter) for a few years from now, after you've had a chance to make hay with the more straightforward types of investments.

QUESTION 69

HOW CAN I PURCHASE A BOND?

Before you purchase a bond, you'll want to see how the experts have rated it. Rating bonds is now an industry of its own, and there are companies that do only this, and make a nice living at it. The good news is, rating companies are going to save you a ton of time. (There is no bad news.)

The top bond-rating companies are Moody's Investors Service, Standard & Poor's, Fitch Investors Service, Inc., and Duff & Phelps Credit Rating. Checking a bond's rating before buying couldn't be easier. Ask your broker, look in your local library, or go online. Many of the big brokerage firms have links to one or more of the rating companies' sites.

Investment grade is the term used to describe bonds that are safe enough for most investors. Bonds that are below investment grade are often called *speculative*. Treasuries are investment grade, junk bonds are speculative. Some brokers will try to confuse you on the phone. As this book was going to press, Carie, my editor, told me a broker had offered her "investment-grade junk bonds." She was never quite clear about what he was offering her.

Here are the credit ratings that the four rating companies give to bonds.

Credit Ratings Designations for Bonds

Credit Risk	Moody's	Standard & Poor's	Fitch	Duff & Phelps
Investment Grade				
Highest quality	Aaa	AAA	AAA	AAA
High quality	Aa	AA	AA	AA
Upper medium grade	A	A	A	A
Medium grade	Baa	BBB	BBB	BBB
Below Investment Grade				
Lower medium grade (somewhat speculative)	Ba	BB	BB	BB
Low grade (speculative)	B	B	B	B
Poor quality (default possible)	Caa	CCC	CCC	CCC
Extremely speculative	Ca	CC	CC	CC
No interest being paid or bankruptcy petition	C	C	C	C
In default	C	D	D	D

There are bonds that are not rated at all. That may mean they are an extreme risk or are fine but have not been rated for one reason or another. Ask your broker for evidence of a bond's quality before you purchase it.

High-yield or junk bonds are considered below investment grade. They offer terrific yields, but purchasers take a large measure of risk. One of the best ways for the average investor to test these waters is through a junk bond mutual fund. Because the fund will invest in a number of high-yield bonds, the risk will be somewhat spread out among many different issues. (They could all fail, but that's part of the risk you take.)

Buying Through Bond Funds

As we discussed earlier, buying bonds through mutual funds can be an excellent way to spread out your risk and perhaps take on additional risk that you wouldn't otherwise consider. As with all good mutual funds, the best bond funds will offer:

- *Diversification.* Lots of different bonds within a similar grouping.
- *Professional management.* Leave the bond picking to them.
- *A small minimum investment.* Some bonds require a high minimum, as much as $25,000. With a bond fund, you can buy in for as little as $1,000, and then continue to add to the fund in dribs and drabs.
- *Automatic dividend reinvestment.* You don't have to worry about what to do with a $170 interest check twice a year.
- *Liquid market.* You can basically cash out whenever you want.

You'll pay for all these privileges. Like regular mutual funds, bond funds come in load (sales commission) and no-load (no sales commission) varieties. Studies have shown that load funds don't have a higher rate of return than no-load funds, so check out the no-loads. Other items to check: the expense ratio for the fund, and the three-year, five-year, and ten-year performance history of the fund.

Buying Individual Bonds

Before you run out and purchase a bond fund, consider purchasing individual bonds, particularly if you're going to buy Treasuries or municipal bonds.

If you're buying Treasuries or zeros, you can purchase bonds with maturation dates timed for when you'll need the cash. You can also purchase bonds so that they expire each year (a process called "laddering"). When one bond expires, you purchase another to take its place.

If you've decided to simply buy Treasuries (bills, notes, or bonds), I encourage you to save the commission and purchase them through a program called Treasury Direct. You won't pay a dime in sales commissions or other fees, so all of your capital is going to work for you. Simply call the nearest Federal Reserve Bank or go online. (See the Resources section at the end of this chapter for the phone number and Web site address.) You can mail in your payment or walk in and purchase what you want.

If you think you might not hold your Treasuries through maturity, consider paying the commission and buying through a broker. Selling your bond down the line will be a little easier.

You'll probably end up buying older bonds through a broker. Try to get at least two quotes for the same bond. Because brokers can pretty much price older bonds where they want, make sure each broker knows you're getting a "second opinion." They're bound to wake up and give you a better price.

If you're buying municipal bonds, you can purchase them individually as well. Munis come in a few flavors, but you should only consider investing in *general obligation bonds* (backed by local taxes and used typically to build schools), *revenue bonds* (backed by the revenues a project will create, like a toll road), and *industrial development and pollution-control bonds* (finances buildings and equipment leased to private companies). General obligation bonds are the least risky; industrial development and pollution-control bonds can be very risky.

Here are a few things to keep in mind before you buy. Municipal bonds can be difficult to resell in a pinch. They're exempt from state and local taxes when you buy issues floated in your state or municipality. But that may not spread your risk around. Consider purchasing munis from other places; they're best for folks in the highest tax brackets. If you're in the 15 percent bracket, consider Treasuries instead. Be aware that municipal bonds don't have to show you the same kinds of financial statements a corporation does. Stick with munis that are highly rated.

Before You Buy

If you're trying to decide whether to purchase a taxable bond or one that's tax-free, do this simple calculation. Multiply the interest rate on the taxable bond by your marginal tax rate (the highest one you qualify for). Then subtract that number from the original interest rate. For example:

$$8 \text{ (percent)} \times .31 \text{ (31 percent tax bracket)} = 2.48$$

$$8 - 2.48 = 5.52$$

$$8 \text{ percent taxable bond} = 5.52 \text{ percent tax-free bond if you're in the 31 percent tax bracket}$$

If you're in the 28 percent tax bracket, multiply $8 \times .28$ (28 percent). If you're in the 15 percent tax bracket, multiply by .15 (15 percent).

RESOURCES

Treasury Direct, the program from the U.S. Treasury Department, is now online and even more accessible, especially if you don't live near a Federal Reserve Bank. The three branches of the program are Pay Direct, Reinvest Direct, and Sell Direct. Sell Direct allows you to sell your Treasuries for only $34 per security, which is quite reasonable compared to what a broker might charge. The toll-free phone number is 800-943-6864. If you go online (www.publicdebt.treas.gov/sec /secdirec.htm), you'll find loads of information as well as help with the Treasury Direct program. You can even find out how much the national debt is today.

For corporate bond ratings, check out at least two independent ratings companies. You can find Standard & Poor's (www.standardpoor .com) and Moody's (www.moodys.com) on the Web.

Bonds are supposed to be the part of your portfolio that you can count on. If you buy speculative bonds, or even the lowest investment grade bonds, you may have a few bad nights' sleep (best case) or lose your money (worst case). Before you buy bonds, think about their intended role in your portfolio, and then buy what makes sense. There's no problem speculating here and there with throwaway money. But if you're investing money you need, go with something that lets you sleep at night.

WHAT DOES THE BOND MARKET TELL ME?

QUESTION
70

Like all things financial, bonds get traded by brokers who either are sitting in front of their computer screens or are screaming and throwing hand signals at each other in the pit of an exchange.

People get confused about which way the bond and stock markets travel in relation to each other. The truth is, they might move in the same direction, though perhaps at different speeds.

For bonds, the key thing to keep in mind is what's happening with interest rates. Bond prices and interest rates move in opposite directions. *If interest rates go up, bond prices fall. If interest rates go down, bond prices go up.*

If, while listening to the evening news, you hear the phrase "The bond market rallied," that means interest rates have come down. If the bond market crashes, interest rates are rising. By the way, pay close attention if the bond market really does crash. In the spring of 1987, the bond market crashed. In October 1987, the stock market crashed.

One final note. Many newspapers will detail the daily happenings of the bond market next to stock market listings (typically, in the business section). *Barron's, The Wall Street Journal, Investor's Business Daily,* and *The New York Times* do a particularly thorough job. Part of keeping up-to-date on your investments is becoming knowledgeable about the working world, particularly about business. These four publications may be a little difficult to get through at first, but you'll get a lot for your money. (They're usually available in your local library.)

WHAT ARE CERTIFICATES OF DEPOSIT (CDs)?

QUESTION
71

Certificates of deposit are typically offered by banking institutions. You put up a certain amount of money for a fixed amount of time (say, six months or a year) and the bank will pay you a fixed rate of interest. They are extremely safe and simple, and you'll avoid paying commissions and fees.

They're also extremely easy to purchase, which, unless you have a Federal Reserve Bank in your hometown, makes them easier than Treasuries (which can be purchased fairly easily through the mail or on the Web). CDs are a good place to park short-term money while you're figuring out what else to do with it. (Money market accounts now offer almost the same yield but are totally liquid.)

CDs can also provide a good way of deferring income into the next year—a useful tactic if you're trying to keep your income at a certain level for tax purposes. Finally, many CDs are insured up to $100,000, as long as the institution from which you're buying them is insured by the Federal Deposit Insurance Corporation (FDIC) or Federal Savings & Loan Insurance Corporation (FSLIC).

On the negative side, CDs are taxable, and you can't buy or sell them on the open market. Once you have them, you're stuck with them. If you suddenly and urgently need your money the day after you open a six-month CD, expect to be hit with a penalty for withdrawal.

Investments: Taking a Walk on the Wild Side

As you become more sophisticated in your investing, you're going to hear about people who made "fortunes" investing in options, buying on margin, shorting gold—whatever. Maybe they did and maybe they didn't. If they did, you have to wonder about all the investments they made that didn't go so well.

This is really a chapter for armchair investors. (It'll make you sound smart at parties, too.) You don't have to do any of these things to make a lot of money with your investments. But you'll be tempted. And before you say "Yes," you should know what you're getting into.

WHAT ARE OPTIONS?

Purchasing an option gives you the right to control a large investment with a relatively small amount of money. If you're right about the direction in which an investment is headed, you'll be richly rewarded. If you're wrong—well, let's just say losing everything could be an understatement.

Does this sound like gambling? Consider this: Of everyone who invests in options, most studies conclude that between 70 and 80 percent lose money. That's right: 70 to 80 percent of those who invest in options lose money. What the studies don't show is how folks like us (who aren't trading options for a living) tend to do in the option market. My guess is that close to 99 percent of all amateurs lose money. It's highly speculative stuff, not for the faint of heart. Your odds, frankly, are better in Las Vegas.

If churning $1,000 into $100,000 on cattle futures (as First Lady Hillary Rodham Clinton did) still sounds appealing, despite the odds, here's some basic information on how options work.

There are two kinds of options: *calls* and *puts*. You can buy or sell a call, and you can buy or sell a put.

When you buy a *call option*, you gain the right to purchase a particular stock at a certain price (known as the *strike price*), no matter how high the stock price goes, until the option expires. So let's say you purchase an option on IBM. The day you buy your option, IBM is trading at $100 per share. Your strike price is $105. If during the next three months, or however long the option runs, IBM's stock price rises above $105—let's say it hits $120—you can exercise your option and purchase the stock at $105. Or, you can sell the option for a healthy profit. If the stock never gets above $105, you can simply let your option expire. You then lose all of the money you spent to buy the call option.

How do the numbers work? Typically, you buy an option on 100 shares. For this option, you might pay $100 (the price varies, but is less than the cost of a share of stock). If you have an option on 100 shares and the stock rises from $100 to $120 per share, and your strike price is $105, you'll earn a profit of 15 per share, minus the $100 you spent to purchase the option for a net profit of $1,400 on your option. You'll have some commissions to pay, but that's not a bad gain on your investment! If your option expires, you've lost your $100 investment.

If you buy *put options*, you gain the right to sell stock at a certain price until the option expires. Let's go back to our IBM example. If you have a put option to sell IBM at $105, and the stock price drops dramatically, you now have the right to sell your shares at $105, even if the stock goes to $80. If you already own IBM, you will be selling at a profit (that's known as a covered put). If you don't own the stock, you can buy IBM at $80 and the put option gives you the right to turn around and sell those shares for $105. So if you purchase 100 shares at $80 per share ($8,000), your profit is the difference between your $8,000 purchase price and the $10,500 you get when you sell, minus the cost of the put and sales commissions.

You can also sell a call option or a put option and make a killing. But you take a huge risk if the market moves in the wrong direction. When you sell an option, your risk is unlimited, unless you already own the underlying stock. When you sell a put, you're committed to buying back the stock at the put price, no matter how low it goes.

Remember one thing about options: If you think the market is going to go down (or the price of the investment will decline), buy a put option. If you think the market or the price is going to go up, buy a call option.

If you want to cover your back, sell only options on stock you currently hold. With that strategy, if the market moves in the opposite direction, you'll be able to deliver without incurring large losses.

You can purchase or sell options on just about anything: individual stocks, a stock market index, commodities, and futures. (I'll talk about futures in Question 73.)

RESOURCES

For more information on options, you might as well go to the place that invented them. The Chicago Board Options Exchange (CBOE) offers free information to consumers. You can visit the CBOE Web site (www.cboe.com) and learn about buying and selling options on the Dow Jones Industrial Average, Dow Jones Transportation Average, and Dow Jones Utility Average. Or, call your broker. (If you seriously get into options, he or she is going to become your best friend.)

WHAT ARE FUTURES?

QUESTION
73

When you buy a futures contract, you're betting on whether the price of gold, commodities (orange juice, wheat, coffee, or pork bellies), or foreign currencies will rise or fall before the contract expires. You put up a fraction of the contract price to control a much larger piece of the action.

The problem is, everything moves each market in a different direction. If there is too much rain early in the growing season, the wheat farmers are unhappy. The price of wheat futures skyrockets because of speculators' reasoning: wheat is being planted late, so there won't be as big a harvest. A shortfall will follow, which means prices will go up. Later in the summer, there isn't enough rain, so wheat futures rise higher. Farmers are delighted because they'll get at least a few pennies more for their bushels of wheat. But, by

August, the rains have come back in regular amounts, and it looks like this will be the biggest bumper crop of wheat ever. The price of wheat drops through the floor. If you bet that the price of wheat would go up, and you sold on July 31, you're rolling in dough. But if you hung on until it appeared that things would be all right, you're losing money. If you close out your futures contract, you have to purchase the actual commodity and could end up with a living room full of wheat—or pork bellies.

Here's a key difference between options and futures. Options deal primarily with stock or stock indexes (although you can purchase and sell options on futures, a really confusing transaction that we'll get to in a moment). With futures, you're contracting to buy or sell the commodity itself. If you don't sell your contract or close it out, you'll end up with all the pork you can eat or all the coffee you can drink. (And you'll know what you're giving the family for their birthdays.)

Here's a similarity: With futures, as with selling puts, you can really lose big. Most people, even the experts, lose money when they trade futures. What you're hoping for is one really big win. But even if you get that huge win, you won't be satisfied. You'll think you're really smart and will try to duplicate your success. And, of course, you won't. (Doesn't this sound a little like gambling?)

If you buy or sell financial futures, you're betting that the ruble, the peso, or the pound will go up or down. If you're wrong, you'll lose money—sometimes, a lot of money.

You can also purchase stock futures. In this case, stocks (or a stock market index) are the commodity. You are betting that the

I don't really need to say it again, but I will. You can live your entire life without betting on options or futures contracts. Lots of folks lose money. Professional traders who have made hundreds of thousands of dollars in a year lose their focus for one instant and go *belly up*—bankrupt, out of business. If anyone is going to win at this game in the long term, it's someone who has nerves of steel, is extremely good with numbers, and can work those numbers like lightning, day in and day out. Or, it's an investor who uses options to cover gains already earned (another complicated investment strategy). Options and futures are not for the average investor. And you can make plenty of money without them.

market will go up or down. If you're right, it's a bonanza. If you're wrong . . . , well, mostly you will be wrong, and we've already covered what happens.

A final thought: You can purchase options on futures contracts. When you have an option on a future, you're betting that the price of the contract will go up or down. See the discussion of options (Question 72) for more details.

WHAT IS BUYING ON MARGIN, AND WHAT IS SELLING SHORT?

QUESTION 74

Buying stocks on margin is another risky investment tactic that you can very well live without. Some brokers say, correctly, that it allows you to tap your capital without having to incur capital gains tax.

When you *borrow on margin*, you're essentially borrowing against the value of your portfolio—typically, the portion of the portfolio that is held in street name at a brokerage firm. If you want to buy an option but don't want to sell stock (and pay capital gains tax) to pay for it, your broker may allow you to borrow against your portfolio. (You will pay interest and perhaps fees on the loan.) Your broker will put up the cash, and you'll execute the trade.

Selling short is taking a bet that the stock market will decline in value. You're selling your stock at what you hope will be the high, and you will buy it back when the price drops lower. The difference between your intake when you sell and your expense when you buy the stock back is your profit.

Many folks wonder how you can sell something you don't own. Essentially, you sell shares you don't own and then have three days (T-3 that we talked about earlier) in which to come up with the shares. Your broker may allow you to borrow shares from the firm's account to meet your T-3 deadline and then replace the shares later.

The big risk of selling short comes if the stock appreciates in value. Let's say Coca-Cola costs $60 a share. You think the price is going down because Coke can't sell any more soda than it's selling today, so Coke's profit margins are going to erode. You sell 100 shares of Coca-Cola short, and receive $6,000 in the short sale. If the stock rises to $100, you'll have to pay $10,000 to buy it back and close out your position. You'll lose $4,000 plus commissions.

Shorting has actually been called one of the most hazardous investment strategies for folks like us. From the above example, it's easy to see why. If you'd shorted America Online and it quadrupled in value, you'd be out the cost of a Harvard education.

Experts say that if you want to get into borrowing on margin and shorting stocks, go slowly. Invest no more than 5 or 10 percent of your holdings. Start small, and get the hang of it. Diversify among several stocks. Watch the market closely, to limit your losses. And

There's another side to the borrowing-on-margin coin, and it makes much more sense. A mortgage lender may allow investors who have brokerage accounts with the firm to borrow against the value of their portfolio to purchase a home. (Merrill Lynch has a program where it not only permits you to borrow against your own brokerage account in lieu of a cash payment, but also will lend you the money as well.) That's right. They'll give you a traditional mortgage, with a loan-to-value ratio of, say, 80 percent, and instead of coming up with the remaining 20 percent in cash, you can borrow against the value of your portfolio to a certain limit and pay interest on this secondary loan. This allows you to keep your investments in stocks, where they'll be appreciating (hopefully), instead of paying taxes on the money and then parking it in your home equity. Be aware, however, that this is a risky strategy. If the market crashes and your portfolio falls in value, you may have to come up with the cash anyway.

Dennis and Karen's Story

When his margin account was called for insufficient funds, Dennis and Karen were in an airplane hangar in Africa. They were about to get into a six-seater plane for a ride into a remote region for a safari. As they were getting ready to board the plane, Dennis heard his cell phone ring.

Back home, the market had crashed. Dennis had borrowed on margin to buy a fair amount of stock in the company he was running. But the value of the account had fallen below the limit. The broker wanted to start selling Dennis' shares to replenish the account. Dennis' secretary didn't know what to do, so she kept stalling; when Dennis heard the phone ring, he knew his secretary was in trouble.

"Should I answer it?" he asked Karen. "We could lose everything."

"Richer or poorer," Karen said. They got on the plane without answering the phone. When they returned home two weeks later, they found out that Dennis' secretary had been able to hold off the broker long enough for the market to rise—and Dennis's account balance with it.

don't listen to your broker. Analysts at brokerage firms who spread bad news about stocks are generally fired. If they're not fired, they're sent to the investing equivalent of Siberia, even if they're right. So if you're looking for a stock that's going to fall in value, you're on your own.

You can make a great amount of money without entertaining this much risk.

WHAT IS A LIMITED PARTNERSHIP?

QUESTION
75

From time to time, your broker (or perhaps a broker you don't even know) may offer you an "opportunity of a lifetime"— purchase of a limited partnership in some sort of venture. Or, you might get, in the mail, an invitation to a free lunch or dinner in a fancy hotel in your hometown. (What have you always heard about free lunches?)

You go, and while you're munching on crustless turkey sandwiches (or perhaps smoked salmon, if it's a particularly expensive proposition), you flip through a 100-page prospectus that basically promises to repay all of your investment with a *minimum* of an 8 percent return (and that's on the downside) but *real* expected returns of, say, 14 percent or more. What's the investment? Perhaps it's airplanes or contracting equipment that will be bought and leased to airlines or contractors; or a load of paper that's going to be resold; or a planned strip shopping center.

You're being offered a piece of the action, and all it may cost you is everything you invest.

As a limited partner, you are a small passive investor in a large venture. A general partner will control the investment, make all the decisions, take a general partner managing fee, and perhaps other fees, and then share whatever is left with you and the other limited partners.

Susanne's Story

My mother used to invest in real estate limited partnerships (she went into about a half-dozen deals over a ten-year period). The general partner of these deals was a longtime friend who actually hired my mom when she was first starting off in the real estate business seventeen years ago.

In the early 1980s, passive investors in limited partnerships were allowed to deduct on their tax return their pro-rata share of a loss within the partnership. This tax loss was the reason many folks sought out limited partnerships in the 1970s and early 1980s. They were actually hoping to lose money each year, and then make a killing when the property was sold. My late father, bless his heart, lost all sorts of money investing in various limited partnerships that purchased odd things like cattle and "brain machines." (My father was a brilliant lawyer but not such a great investor.)

The Tax Reform Act of 1986 eliminated passive losses in limited partnerships. If you wanted to deduct a loss, you had to be actively involved in the management of the investment. Limited partnerships didn't count. You had to be the general partner. That changed the scope of many legitimate limited partnerships. They had to make money.

By and large, my mother did pretty well with her real estate limited partnerships. Almost every deal she invested in made some money. But I think she did well for two reasons: (1) she knew the general partner very well, and he had a history of making very successful real estate deals (both in the real estate company he owned and operated and in setting up limited partnerships that invested in real estate), and (2) being in the real estate business herself, she knew what she was buying and had a sense of whether it would go up or down in value.

But let me be clear here: I think limited partnerships in general are tough to analyze. If you don't know the players (including the general partner), don't know the product, and don't know the business, you could be in for a rough ride.

WHAT ARE HEDGE FUNDS?

Years ago, hedge funds used to be places for investors to balance (or hedge) their other investments. Today, they're one of the riskiest investments you can make. Commensurate with that risk is the return: many hedge funds offer returns of 40, 50, or even 100 percent on your money. You need a lot of money to enter the hedge fund game. For many hedge funds, the price for entry is $1 million, and you must have a net worth of at least $2.5 million.

Unlike mutual funds, hedge funds specifically fall outside the scope of the Securities and Exchange Commission (SEC). A hedge fund manager doesn't have to offer you the kinds of financial details that can help you evaluate whether a fund is a good place to park your money. Hedge funds are only for sophisticated (and *very* wealthy) investors.

If you become very wealthy, you'll probably end up hiring a professional money manager long before you enter a hedge fund. But the trend today is to make hedge funds more accessible to the "average investor." That still means operating outside the scope of the SEC, but the entry price may drop to $500,000.

Take a pass on any hedge fund invitations.

SHOULD I BUY GOLD, SILVER, OR OTHER MINERALS?

QUESTION
77

The mental image of Fort Knox has a lot of appeal. I've never been there, but I like to imagine all of the gold owned by Uncle Sam stacked up in neat little bars in sparkling-clean, temperature-controlled rooms, guarded by the kind of infrared futuristic technology we see only in movies (apparently I've been watching too many).

Still, to feel safe and secure, some investors want gold (and, to a lesser extent, other minerals) in their investment portfolio. In many cultures, past and present, gold was worn to show wealth during life, and was part of a burial ritual to pay the person's passage to the world beyond. In times of political or economic crisis, gold could be exchanged for necessities such as bread and milk, or for passage to a safe haven. For a long time, many countries' currencies were backed up by the *gold standard.* Many investors still view gold as a hedge against inflation and other calamities, real or imagined.

But should you invest in gold (other than buying yourself a nice watch as a birthday present)? Over the long term, it doesn't seem to have been a particularly good investment, except for those few speculators who were holding gold when it went to nearly $800 per ounce in 1981. During that distinctly unique period in our economic history (mortgage interest rates, if you recall, were 18 percent), anyone who sold gold made a bundle. Everyone else is still waiting for gold to go back to those lustrous levels.

Unless you've got millions, you've got limited funds to invest. I think you should make the most of them, and gold over the long haul hasn't proven to be a great hedge against anything. If you feel better owning some gold, buy it, or buy a couple of no-load gold funds. *Don't* buy shares of stock in mining companies that claim to have found the richest vein of gold ever. That's pure speculation, and it won't make you feel better about anything.

A better bet is to hedge your portfolio with real estate, Treasury bonds, and other dependable investments. The risks are low and you will actually reap some rewards. If gold does stage a comeback, it will be a surprise to almost everyone.

What about silver? It's true that in the 1980s and 1990s, a few serious investors purchased a sizable investment in silver. The Hunt Brothers even tried to corner the silver market. In the late 1990s, Warren Buffett took a large position in silver. But silver prices have been known to fluctuate even more than gold prices. Silver is not a safe haven. If you have limited resources, there are better places to put your cash.

My advice extends to just about every other metal and precious stone. Don't buy "flawless" diamonds as investments. Their "perfection" is subject to personal interpretation. The only time you should buy diamonds is when they will be worn and enjoyed—by yourself or a special person you give them to.

QUESTION 78

SHOULD I INVEST IN UNDERWATER TREASURE HUNTS, LOTTERY TICKETS, OR TRIPS TO LAS VEGAS?

Compared to some investments, a visit to Las Vegas doesn't look like such a bad bet. On our last trip to Vegas, Sam and I cleared $22 after five days of almost no gambling whatsoever. And our game of choice is Roulette, which has perhaps the worst odds of all.

Enough about where I go on vacation. Let's talk quickly about other investing adventures that may test your forbearance.

You may be tempted by an offer to purchase a interest in a treasure hunt. It might even be structured as a limited partnership. Here's the basic concept. Some grand ship went down in the Atlantic in the 1700s. It has now been located, and you have the amazing opportunity to purchase a share in the expected rewards: probably a sea chest full of gold bullion, plus all the golden, jewel-encrusted tableware, coins, and jewelry that were carried on ships of that caliber in that era.

Sounds glamorous and romantic, doesn't it? You may even be shown color photographs of the treasure that has already been pulled up. The venture is pure speculation; I'd say your odds on hitting the jackpot are somewhat better at a Roulette table. Save the fairy tales for your children. If one of these treasure hunts does hit, you can enjoy the inevitable television special on your local PBS station.

What about investing in films or theater productions? Typically, these deals are structured as limited partnerships. I knew someone who once invested in what she thought was a quality film. She made a few bucks but found out that it was a porn film. She couldn't go see or invite friends to her film, so she gained only some amusing cocktail party chatter. If you support a filmmaker, hoping for cinema gold, don't expect more than an ego boost and perhaps a quick glimpse of your name as the credits roll by.

Theater is also a tough investment, but it can be a lot of fun. You might sink $10,000 into a Broadway show and lose it all because the show closes before it opens. It takes millions of dollars to stage a Broadway production these days. A show could run a full year and still show losses. Your $10,000 or $100,000 will only go so far.

And that brings us to the lottery. Nearly every state has a lottery system in place, and some states join together for unbelievable powerball lotteries where you must have every number and the powerball number to be the winner.

A few winners have had their dreams come true. A Streamwood, Illinois, couple won nearly $200 million in a 1998 powerball lottery. Their choice of cash in a lump sum gave them around $130 million. After taxes, the net amount is about $67 million. (IRS must love lotteries.) The ticket buyer, his wife, and their three sons will pocket about $13.5 million each.

It would definitely be enough for me to live on.

There's nothing wrong with buying lottery tickets, as long as you view the expense as throwaway money. Take it out of your weekly entertainment fund. Stop smoking, and use your cigarette money to buy lottery tickets instead. Your odds of winning an intrastate lottery are 14 million to 1. The odds of winning a powerball lottery are completely unimaginable.

Just don't fool yourself into thinking your lottery tickets are a financial investment.

Planning for Your Retirement

WHAT STEPS DO I NEED TO TAKE TO RETIRE COMFORTABLY?

A baby born in 1999 has a reasonable chance of seeing the year 2100. If he or she decides to retire at what will then be the typical retirement age (sixty-seven, or perhaps even seventy), this relatively young senior may need to fund as many as thirty-three years (or more) of retirement.

That's quite a retirement our grandchildren have waiting for them. We should all be so lucky. You may not live to be 100, but you will probably live longer than your parents did. In 1996, there were 33.9 million people age sixty-five and older in the United States, an 8 percent increase since 1990. The number of Americans in this age group has tripled since 1900. Seniors, especially those 100 years of age or more, make up the fastest-growing segment of the population.

According to the Census Bureau, by the year 2030 (when the last of the baby boomers officially joins the seniors group), there will be around 70 million Americans age sixty-five and over (twice today's number), and they will represent about 20 percent of the population.

So when we talk about retirement here, it's *your* retirement. If you manage to reach age sixty-five, your average life expectancy will be an additional eighteen years (women get a little more estimated time, men a little less). So you're likely to be enjoying life for a long time to come—if you've got enough money to live the way you and your family want to live. If you don't have enough money, your final years will be spent either worrying about how you're going to pay your rent and put food on the table, or working because you have to, not because you want to. Neither option sounds appealing.

A comfortable retirement *is* possible, particularly if you start early. How early? As early as you can. Consider putting away $2,000 into an IRA as soon as you've started earning some money with a paper route or babysitting. (You are eligible to open an IRA once you have earned income no matter how old you are.) If you're age twenty-five and you put $2,000 into an IRA that earns, say, 8 percent annual return, you'll have $608,000 when you're age sixty-five. But if you start when you're age ten, you'll have nearly $2 million. And if you're able to let that chunk sit until you're age seventy-five, it will grow to more than $4 million. (Today's rules say you have to start to withdraw IRA money by the time you're seventy, but the rules may change in another forty years.)

That's the value of compounding. It takes a long time to get going, but then the dollars really start to grow. If you save for forty years, you'll earn more in the last ten years of growth than in the first thirty, thanks to the value of compounding (assuming you have a steady rate of return). And the longer you hold that money, the better off you'll be.

Take a look at the charts on pages 365-366. Individuals may put up to $2,000 into an IRA annually. The Tax Reform Act of 1997 now permits married couples to put $4,000 into an IRA annually even if the spouse doesn't work. Even with just a 6 percent return, the numbers really begin to shine.

The Power of Compounding
$2,000 Annual Contribution, 6 Percent Annual Return

Yearly IRA Contribution	Current Age	Rate of Return	Total Contribution to Age Sixty-Five	IRA Value
$2,000	60	6%	$ 10,000	$ 11,951
2,000	55	6	20,000	27,943
2,000	50	6	30,000	49,345
2,000	45	6	40,000	77,985
2,000	40	6	50,000	116,313
2,000	35	6	60,000	167,603
2,000	30	6	70,000	236,242
2,000	25	6	80,000	328,095

$2,000 Annual Contribution, 9 Percent Annual Return

Yearly IRA Contribution	Current Age	Rate of Return	Total Contribution to Age Sixty-Five	IRA Value
$2,000	60	9%	$ 10,000	$ 13,047
2,000	55	9	20,000	33,121
2,000	50	9	30,000	64,007
2,000	45	9	40,000	111,529
2,000	40	9	50,000	184,648
2,000	35	9	60,000	297,150
2,000	30	9	70,000	470,249
2,000	25	9	80,000	736,584

$4,000 Annual Contribution, 6 Percent Annual Return

Yearly IRA Contribution	Current Age	Rate of Return	Total Contribution to Age Sixty-Five	IRA Value
$4,000	60	6%	$ 20,000	$ 23,091
4,000	55	6	40,000	55,887
4,000	50	6	60,000	98,690
4,000	45	6	80,000	155,971
4,000	40	6	100,000	232,626
4,000	35	6	120,000	335,207
4,000	30	6	140,000	472,483
4,000	25	6	160,000	656,191

$4,000 Annual Contribution, 9 Percent Annual Return

Yearly IRA Contribution	Current Age	Rate of Return	Total Contribution to Age Sixty-Five	IRA Value
$4,000	60	9%	$ 20,000	$ 26,093
4,000	55	9	40,000	66,241
4,000	50	9	60,000	128,014
4,000	45	9	80,000	223,058
4,000	40	9	100,000	369,296
4,000	35	9	120,000	594,301
4,000	30	9	140,000	940,499
4,000	25	9	160,000	1,473,167

Data courtesy of Great Western Financial Securities Corp.

If you and your spouse put away $4,000 every year (8 percent of your gross income if you earn $50,000 per year, and 4 percent of your income if you earn $100,000 per year), for forty years, and earn an average return of 9 percent (the stock market average is around 10 percent over the past seventy years), you'll end up with about $1.5 million. That's a fine start to a financially solid retirement.

Basic Steps You Should Take

But we're putting the cart a little ahead of the horse. Before you plan on how much you'll have, you need to figure out where you are today and what you'll need in the future. Here are seven basic steps you should take in order to retire with the lifestyle you want:

1. *Take inventory of your financial life.* Does the prospect of taking inventory of your life still seem overwhelming? If you've been following this book from the start, you should be almost all the way there. A *life inventory* starts with a current accounting of how much you spend each year, and what you spend it on, right down to the last dollar. Next, figure out your net worth (how much you have minus how much you owe). (For additional help, see Question 4, "How Do I Calculate My Net Worth?" and Question 6, "How Do I Create A Budget That Works For Me?")

2. *Review your insurance coverage.* Assess how well you've protected yourself against life's upheavals. Do you have the proper life, health, home, business, disability, and liability insurance? If you or your spouse or partner dies unexpectedly, are you protected? (See Chapter 5 for more details.)

3. *Write down your financial goals and dreams.* Describe what you hope to accomplish financially, in the long term. Are you hoping to retire early? Do you want your children to have an inheritance? Would you like to earmark money for your grandchildren's education? Have you consulted anyone about protecting your assets from inflation or your estate from taxation? Reread Question 5, "What Are My Financial Goals?" if you need help.

4. *Imagine your perfect retirement.* Think realistically about where you want to live, what lifestyle you hope to have, and what luxuries you hope to be able to afford—and for how many years.

Nearly everyone's goals change when retirement draws near. Get a headstart by picturing clearly the retirement about which you've always dreamed. Estimate how much money you'll need to put your retirement plans into action. Planners suggest that you'll need resources equaling 75 to 80 percent of your current income; if you have champagne dreams, they may be based on having 100 percent or more of your current annual income after you retire. Will the money be there? Every year? (Question 81 can help you figure out most of your expenses.)

5. *Take a long and hard look at your retirement savings.* Do you have what it takes to get you where you want to go? Are you saving as much as you can? Should you be saving more? Pull out a piece of paper and a pen and start writing. Most planners say to count on a 3 percent raise every year, which will basically cover inflation. (Although inflation through the 1980s and 90s *averaged* around 5 percent, the numbers are a bit skewed because inflation went well into the double-digit range during the first half of the 1980s. In the second half of the 1990s, inflation averaged about 1.5 percent.) If your money earns 10 percent, it will double roughly every seven years (see the Rule of 72 chart, on page 372, for a rough estimate of how long it will take you to double your money at various rates of return). If you have $100,000 saved today and work thirty-five more years before you retire, and if you earn 10 percent on your money, you'll end up with approximately $3.2 million in retirement funds. If you have that same $100,000 in savings but retirement is only seven years away, you'll end up with only $200,000 to fund your twenty-five or thirty years of retirement. (Question 82 will take you through the numbers.)

6. *Change your savings or investment strategy to meet your financial goals.* Do your numbers compute? Are you on track for your financial future? If so, congratulations! You're one of few. If not, it's not too late. If there's a discrepancy between what you'll have for retirement and what you need, alter your savings or investment strategy so that you get on track. Save more, or choose slightly riskier investments that offer a higher return. You'll probably have to do both.

7. *Don't just sit there—reevaluate.* Throughout this book, I've encouraged you to take an active role in your financial future. Sit back and relax and you may miss out on one of the best advantages of being young—having many years ahead in which to let

your retirement money compound. Every six months, you should look at where you are and make sure you're on track. Tweak your portfolio as you go through the years. Readjust after you've passed major milestones, such as your children's college graduations—and, perhaps, their weddings.

If you decided to open the book to this Question and dig in, you may be doing your budget and net worth for the first time. If you realize that you're living high on the hog (translation: you're spending more than you take in), it's going to be tough to start saving for retirement when you're paying off credit card bills at 24 percent interest. Go back to Chapter 2, and work through the budgeting worksheet that starts on page 32. Pay off your nondeductible, high-interest-rate debt first, and then start investing for your future. Or, if you can't stand the notion that you're doing nothing for your future, clamp down heavily on your budget, have your employer transfer $100 per month from your paycheck into a 401(k) stock mutual fund, and let the money sit there. That strategy is *in addition to* paying off your debt each month.

Don't Forget about the Real World

Every year or two, Congress passes new laws that can either help or hurt your retirement goals. In the past few years, Congress has been generous. Roth IRAs were created (see Question 80 for more details), and the capital gains tax was lowered from 28 percent to 20 percent for folks in the 28 percent tax bracket or above, and 10 percent for folks in the 15 percent tax bracket. All homeowners, regardless of age, can keep the first $250,000 in profits tax-free (a married couple can keep up to $500,000) when they sell their home, as long as the other requirements are met. The ceiling on how much can be left to heirs tax-free has been raised from $600,000 and will go up to $1 million by the year 2006 (see Question 90 for more details). On the other hand, the age of eligibility for Social Security is on the rise, and Social Security benefits are likely to be taxed at 100 percent by the time today's younger baby boomers and Generation Xers reach age sixty-seven.

Changes like these should alert you to stay abreast of what's happening on Capitol Hill and how it may affect you and your retirement portfolio. Ignore the proposals and decisions before Congress, and you could find yourself preparing for a world that won't exist by the time you're ready to enter it.

The good news is, it's never been easier to stay informed. As we discussed earlier, the Internet, newspapers, magazines, and television (particularly CNBC and CNN) do a terrific job of covering changes that affect your personal finances. All you have to do is tune in.

Mistakes We All Make

No one's perfect. Given the long horizon most of us have until we retire (if we ever do fully retire), and then the years we have in retirement, we'll probably make some classic mistakes along the way. Here are some of the more common slipups and omissions. I'm hoping the list will help you avoid them.

- *Failing to save enough.* Few Americans save adequately for their retirement, but that doesn't preclude turning a little into a lot in a short period of time. Get started, or you'll never get to where you want to be.

- *Believing in too-good-to-be-true investments.* If someone calls you on the phone and offers to double your money via a risk-free investment, you hang up, right? (I hope so!) But many people don't hang up. They put large sums of money into risky investments they don't understand. If a venture sounds too good to be true, it almost certainly is. Why take that risk when so many decent investments are offering a terrific return? If you're bored, take up a hobby, or volunteer. Don't jump into an investment that is going to keep you up at night and may turn you in a direction you want to avoid.

- *Leaving it all up to your "better half."* If you have been assigning all financial decisions to your spouse or partner, get *your* face into the picture. *Both* of you need to know what you have, what you owe, and how much it costs you to live. Don't let the numbers throw you. Personal finance can be easily understood. Once you step in, you'll find that the water's not so cold that you can't stand on your own two feet.

- *Failing to roll over your lump-sum pension distribution.* If you change jobs or retire early, or if your company gets sold, you may receive your pension in a lump-sum distribution. If you roll the money over into a tax-deferred IRA and keep it growing, you've done the right thing. Unfortunately, the U.S. Department of Labor says only 21 percent of folks in this situation do that. The other 79 percent spend the money on themselves or their families, buy into franchises or other business opportunities, or develop home-based businesses. That's all well and good, but unless the business pays off, they may be risking their retirement altogether.

• *Putting your eggs in one basket.* As we discussed earlier, it's far too risky to invest all of your retirement money in one stock, one mutual fund, or even one bond. That's especially true as you get closer to, and enter the early years of, your retirement. Diversification is a good thing. If you hold some of your employer's stock, make sure you're also well diversified not only in different companies in your industry, but in other industries, companies, and countries. And, consider keeping your holdings in your own company to no more than 10 percent of your total retirement fund.

• *Not taking enough risk.* If you don't take enough risk when you invest, you invite the very real possibility that you'll run out of money before you're halfway through your retirement years. Over time, inflation will seriously eat into your buying power. (Remember, in 1953, a first-class stamp cost 3 cents.) Some financial advisers tell their clients to have at least 60 to 70 percent of their assets invested in the stock market (either in individual companies or through mutual funds) at all times. Every investment carries some risk—including the possibility that inflation may eat away the investment until there's nothing left. Learn how to tolerate risk, and incorporate it successfully into your portfolio.

• *Calculating your return incorrectly.* Your return is the percentage gain of your investments *minus the cost of making the investment.* Don't include the dividends that you reinvest when you're calculating your return. If you do dollar-cost averaging, figuring out your real return will be time-consuming. Try keeping track of the approximate price, each month, on the day you make your additional investment. Or, look at your year-end figures and average them out.

• *Making a misguided move.* One thing some folks who have retired and moved to their dream locations find out is that they have not entered the heaven on earth they had pictured. They then re-retire, and move to another location. Picking up your life and moving is expensive (not to mention exhausting), so don't make any sudden changes for a while after you retire. If you sell your

371

house, rent a house or an apartment in the city in which you think you'd like to live, and test it out. If you like it, you can make permanent arrangements. If you don't, you'll have learned a relatively inexpensive lesson.

The Rule of 72

The Rule of 72 is a kind of shorthand. If you divide any number (that represents a rate of return you hope to get) into 72, you find out approximately how many years it will take you to double your money. The chart below covers whole and half-percent interest rates from 1 percent to 10.5 percent.

The Rule of 72 will give you a quick calculation of how quickly your money will grow.

Rule of 72

72 ÷ Interest Rate =	Time Needed to Double Your Money
1.0%	72.0 years
1.5	48.0
2.0	39.0
2.5	28.8
3.0	24.0
3.5	20.6
4.0	18.0
4.5	16.0
5.0	14.4
5.5	13.1
6.0	12.0
6.5	11.1
7.0	10.3
7.5	9.6
8.0	9.0
8.5	8.5
9.0	8.0
9.5	7.6
10.0	7.2
10.5	6.7

It's not hard to live happily ever after. It just takes patience and regular investments in your future.

WHAT ARE MY RETIREMENT ACCOUNT OPTIONS?

Less than half (47 percent) of Americans work for a company that offers a 401(k) retirement program. Of those that are offered a 401(k) plan, only 66 percent participate. A little more than half (51 percent) who participate contribute the maximum amount of money to the plan. But of those who participate, 71 percent have no idea what the maximum amount they may contribute to their accounts is this year. That means just under 16 percent of those Americans eligible to put the maximum into their 401(k) plans actually do. They account for only about 8 percent of all Americans. Is it any wonder why so much ink has been spread worrying about what's going to happen when Social Security goes bankrupt?

Source: Intuit.

According to *The Wall Street Journal*, at the end of December 1997, 26 percent of individuals polled had saved less than $10,000 toward their retirement. Twenty-eight percent had saved between $10,000 and $50,000. Sixteen percent had saved between $50,000 and $100,000. Nineteen percent had saved more than $100,000 for retirement. Eleven percent weren't sure they had saved anything at all.

What about you?

Once you resolve that you want to be (and should be) saving for your retirement, you have to find some place to put your nest egg. Your first preference should be *tax-deductible, tax-deferred options*, followed by other *tax-deferred alternatives.*

Tax-deductible, tax-deferred accounts deliver a double bang for your bucks:

1. You can either exclude your contribution from taxation or deduct the amount you put in from your income, thereby lowering the taxes you pay.

2. You can let your money grow, and defer, until you start withdrawing money from the account, all the taxes you have to pay

on your contributions and earnings. (Most people are in a lower tax bracket by then.)

Let's talk about the basic retirement accounts available to most individuals today.

401(k) Plan

Large companies typically offer this most popular retirement option to their employees. Millions take advantage of it.

A 401(k) plan allows you to put in up to 25 percent of your salary, or up to an annual ceiling of $10,000 (1998 and 1999 amount, but indexed for inflation). All of your contributions, plus your employer's match (if any), cannot exceed $30,000 annually, but that's in addition to your contributions to a company child-care or health-care account. (This arrangement is sometimes referred to as a "cafeteria plan.")

Typically, you'll have a handful of investment options from which to choose: growth stock funds, bond funds, and the employer's stock (don't put too much in that particular basket). If you're really lucky, your employer will match some or all of your contribution; common percentages range between 15 and 50 percent of employees' contribution amount. This is free money, and you should take advantage of every dollar you can. Why? If your employer is matching your contribution with 50 cents on each dollar, it's like earning a 50 percent return every year. If you then add in your annual return (let's say 8 to 12 percent), you're reaping an annual gain of 58 to 62 percent. I don't know where else you can get that kind of return with so little risk. The employer match is truly like receiving free money.

How do I invest? Couldn't be easier. Simply have your employer electronically transfer your contribution (which is deducted from your pay) into a mutual fund that you have designated. Usually, you can transfer all or part of your balance between funds via a telephone call, but this may be possible only at certain times of the year. Check with your plan administrator for details.

What do I need to know? Some 401(k) plans require that you be employed for a certain amount of time before you can participate or before the matching program kicks in. In some matching programs, you have to be employed for a specified number of years before you can be *fully vested* in the plan, which means all the money (your contributions *and* your employer's) are yours. Your own contributions are, of course, vested the moment you join the plan.

You can take your 401(k) contributions with you when you leave your job. You may also be permitted to make an after-tax contribution to the plan. This does not reduce your income for tax purposes, but the money still grows on a tax-deferred basis, which is always a benefit.

You may be permitted to *roll over* or transfer 401(k) proceeds from a prior job into your current 401(k). If not, you're permitted to roll them over into an IRA, or to pay taxes on them and put them into a taxable account [which sometimes works well if you're receiving your 401(k) proceeds in the form of company stock]. If you keep the cash or stock outside of a tax-deferred IRA account, you'll have to pay taxes and penalties because that money is seen as a lump-sum distribution. Some 401(k) programs allow you to borrow funds up to the amount held in your retirement account. (See Question 83 for details on whether this is a good idea.)

Unless you're disabled, if you withdraw funds from your 401(k) before you're age fifty-nine, you'll be subject to an additional 10 percent penalty for premature distribution. (I'll talk more about distributions in Question 85.)

And in the future? Starting in the year 2000, new rules will permit workers in old-fashioned (and going-out-of-style) pension plans to fund larger 401(k) plans, and those who have 401(k) plans will be able to move into pension plans as well.

403(b) and 457 Plans

If you work for a nonprofit organization, or for a school district, police force, or other municipal agency, you may not have a 401(k) offered to you through work. Instead, you may be offered a 403(b) plan or a 457 plan.

These tax-deferred retirement plans are similar to a 401(k). You are allowed to contribute a percentage of your salary up to an annual maximum, though, typically, no matching amount is contributed by your employer.

Unfortunately, 403(b) and 457 plans usually have more limitations and restrictions than 401(k) programs. For example, in a 457 plan, your retirement funds are not set aside in a separate trust; they remain part of the organization's general assets. That could pose an additional risk if something drastic happens to your employer's finances. Quite often, 403(b) plans are set up as annuities. In both, 403(b) and 457 plans, participants usually have fewer investment choices than are offered in 401(k) plans. Why? Sometimes the nonprofit employer requires the investment house managing the plan to take responsibility for the employer's mistakes in crediting accounts. To keep the procedures simple, the investment house offers only a few choices. If you belong to a 403(b) or 457 plan and are unhappy with the investment options being offered to you, you should push for a more open investment climate and more choices.

What do I need to know? The contribution limits for a 403(b) plan are usually the same as for a 401(k) plan. Contribution limits for 457 plans tend to be lower. Check with your plan administrator for details. Also, 403(b) plans do not currently allow employers to match contributions; however, these plans have a *catch-up* provision. If you're making a higher salary now, and didn't fully fund your 403(b) plan over the past three years, you can deposit additional money to make up for the years of underfunding.

Keoghs

If you have self-employment income, you'll want to open this version of a tax-deductible, tax-deferred program. There are several types of Keoghs to choose from:

1. A *profit-sharing Keogh* allows you to contribute up to 15 percent of your self-employed earnings, to a maximum of $30,000 (1998 number indexed for inflation). If you're married and you and your spouse are self-employed, you may put in a maximum of $60,000. If you employ your children to do real work, you can set up a plan for each child. The amount of your contribution can be changed at will.

2. A *money-purchase Keogh* is for entrepreneurs who make a lot of money and know it's going to be there year-in and year-out. Contributions can run as high as 20 percent of self-employed earnings, to the $30,000 maximum. You pick the percentage, and there it stays. Put in less, and you owe a penalty.

3. A *combination Keogh*, also known as a *paired plan*, lets you set a floor for your contributions—say, 8 or 10 percent of your annual income. That's the money-purchase part. Then you set up a profit-sharing plan to contribute the rest of the amount, up to a 20 percent maximum. The $30,000 allowable total is unchanged.

4. In a *defined-benefit Keogh*, you choose the monthly pension you want, and you are allowed to contribute tax-deductible amounts that will get you to that goal. The maximum annual pension amount for a defined-benefit Keogh is over $100,000 per year and is indexed to inflation. There are additional expenses to this kind of Keogh (you'd expect that, given the amount you're allowed to contribute). A fee is charged to set up and administrate the plan. Also, it must be checked by an actuary each year.

What do I need to know? If you are self-employed, but have employees, they must also be covered by the Keogh. If you want to own stocks and bonds, you need a self-directed Keogh trust. Any one of the big fund families—for example, Fidelity, Vanguard, or Schwab—can assist you.

How do I invest? Write yourself a check, or arrange to have the investment house that set up your plan draw cash from your account on a monthly basis.

Simplified Employee Pension (SEP)

This plan, also known as a SEP-IRA, is for self-employed individuals or small business owners. If you qualify, you may contribute up to 15 percent of your annual income, to a maximum of $30,000 (1998 number indexed for inflation). Your contributions are tax-deductible, and earnings are tax-deferred until they're withdrawn.

What do I need to know? There are no annual funding requirements, so you contribute as your business allows. However, you have to put in contributions from everyone in your company. If you set aside 10 percent of your income, you must take 10 percent of your workers' income as well. This plan works well for people who work on their own, with few or no employees.

Savings Incentive Match Plan for Employees (SIMPLE)

In this version of a tax-deferred retirement account, you (the boss) can set aside up to $12,000 per year. If your employees join, you'll have to contribute something to their accounts, up to 3 percent of their annual salary. Workers can contribute up to $6,000 through salary deductions.

What do I need to know? SIMPLE plans can be good for employers, but not as good for employees. If you're an employee, it's in your best interest to join, although your contributions are much more limited than for a 401(k). There's an option for a SIMPLE 401(k), which has easier restrictions than a regular 401(k). You might want to check it out.

Individual Retirement Accounts (IRAs)

A regular IRA (for information on a Roth IRA, see the next section) allows you to contribute $2,000 per year. In addition, your spouse (whether he or she is working full- or part-time, or is a stay-at-home parent) may also contribute up to $2,000 per year. If you and your spouse work and are covered by a retirement plan through work, but your adjusted gross income is below a certain threshold, you're still eligible to contribute. If you're single, your income must be $30,000 (rising to $50,000 in 2005) or less. If you're married, your income must be $50,000 (rising to $80,000 in 2007) or less. If your income is a little over these amounts, you may still be able to deduct part of your contribution.

If you're retired, but still earn an income from investments, pensions, and perhaps even part-time work, you can continue to contribute $2,000 if you're single (up to $4,000 if you're married) to an IRA if your adjusted gross income is $150,000 or less.

What do I need to know? IRAs are an easy investment. You can open one at any number of financial institutions, including a brokerage firm or a bank.

With a conventional IRA, you may not withdraw without penalty (currently, 10 percent) until you're age fifty-nine, and you must begin withdrawals when you're age seventy. You have to stop contributing when you're seventy, though you can continue contributing for your spouse, as long as he or she is under the age limit. When you start to withdraw your retirement funds, you'll owe income tax on the cash, at the percentage for your current tax bracket.

You can open as many IRAs as you want. If you leave a company and have to roll-over your lump-sum pension, you'll want to open a separate IRA for those funds. (See page 379 for details.) However, you are entitled to make only one $2,000 contribution (or $4,000 if you're married and you both qualify) per year.

What kind of IRA do I need if my money gets rolled over from a 401(k) plan? If you get a lump-sum distribution from a former employer and you can't roll it over into your current employer's plan, you can put it into an IRA that you currently hold, or you can open up a new IRA to keep the funds separate. If you keep the funds separate, you may be able to roll them over into a future employer's 401(k) program at a later date. Either way, you only have sixty days to deposit the check, otherwise it's considered a withdrawal and you'll owe taxes and perhaps penalties.

For home buyers and scholars. First-time home buyers of any age may, without penalty, tap their IRAs for up to $10,000 for a down payment or for the closing costs on a home. IRA proceeds can also be used for educational expenses, penalty-free.

Don't forget the IRS. If you die with money left in an IRA, your heirs may pay double tax on that cash. First, income taxes will be due on the money that's left in the IRA. Then, the cash is added to your estate. If your estate is more than the limit (see page 00 for current limits), it may be subject to hefty estate taxes. For estate planning purposes, use up your IRA money first. Also, consider putting money into a Roth IRA, which allows your contributions and earnings to grow tax-free.

Roth IRA

A Roth IRA, a new take on the old IRA for a new generation of future retirees, allows you to contribute up to $2,000 (plus another $2,000 for your spouse) of after-tax money. The initial contribution isn't tax-deductible, but your money grows tax-free, as long as you meet these withdrawal requirements: You must be age fifty-nine or older, and the account must have been open at least five years.

You may withdraw your contributions tax-free and penalty-free at any time. However, if you are under age fifty-nine and you withdraw some of the earnings, you may owe tax on the earnings plus a 10 percent penalty.

First-time home buyers may withdraw up to $10,000 tax-free and penalty-free. The early-withdrawal penalty may also be avoided if you're funding a college education for yourself, your spouse, your children, or your grandchildren, or are paying medical expenses that exceed 7.5 percent of your adjusted gross income.

What else do I need to know? Rothomania, as some people call it, has swept the nation. For many folks, it's a terrific deal. If your adjusted gross income is no more than $95,000 (single person) or $150,000 (married couples filing jointly), you're eligible to contribute. Nonmarried individuals whose adjusted gross income goes up to $110,000, and married couples (filing jointly) whose adjusted gross income goes up to $160,000, may make partial contributions.

Unlike a conventional IRA, you *never* have to withdraw from a Roth IRA account. You can keep contributing as long as you have earned income.

Roth IRAs can be an excellent estate-planning tool. Unlike a conventional IRA, if your Roth IRA has money left over when you die, it passes to your heirs income-tax-free, no matter how much you have in the account. This is another huge benefit.

Nondeductible IRAs

Nondeductible IRAs combine the worst of a Roth IRA and a conventional IRA. You get no deduction up front, and you pay tax when you withdraw the money. There's a mandatory withdrawal at age seventy, and if you withdraw before you're age fifty-nine, you may get hit with penalties as well.

Your nondeductible IRA contributions compound tax-free. But here's something to think about: When you withdraw nondeductible

If you qualify, a Roth IRA is a pretty good deal all around. It allows your funds to grow on a tax-deferred basis forever, even after you die (your heirs could keep it growing). If your tax bracket will stay the same or go up after you retire, a Roth IRA is even better than a conventional IRA, and there is no mandatory withdrawal rule. Also, if you're over age seventy and want to keep saving because you're still working and earning, the Roth IRA is your only option. Keep in mind, of course, that Congress could change the game at any moment and start taxing Roth IRA withdrawals. But right now, that seems unlikely. It's in Congress's best interest to make sure we have income to live on during our retirement, particularly if we retire after Social Security is predicted to be bankrupt. As soon as your kids are working, open a Roth IRA for them. The long-term benefits will be enormous.

IRA contributions, you pay income tax at your current marginal tax rate. If you buy and hold stocks, they also compound tax-free (unless they throw off dividends). When you sell stocks, you pay capital gains tax, as opposed to income tax, and capital gains tax will always be lower than income tax. As with the other forms of IRAs, you can withdraw $10,000 for the purchase of a first home, and pay an un-limited amount of college tuition for yourself, your spouse, or your children or grandchildren. You may also pay medical expenses that exceed 7.5 percent of your adjusted gross income.

What do I need to know? Now that the capital gains tax rate has been lowered, nondeductible IRAs don't offer as much in the way of bene-fits. If you qualify, the Roth IRA is a much better deal.

Pensions vs. Retirement Plans

If you're going to get a pension from your job, congratulations. But don't think you're home free yet. Many pensions yield fixed income: you retire with a certain percentage of your last year's income, or some mathematical-equation amount based on the last few years of income. But rarely will that amount increase with inflation. If you retire at age sixty-five with a $1,500-per-month pension, that's $18,000 per year. Add maybe $10,000 more in Social Security, and you might think you're rolling in dough. But because the $1,500 pension will never increase, its buying power will slowly (or quickly) be eaten away by inflation.

That's why it's important to take advantage today of tax-deductible, tax-deferred retirement accounts in addition to any pen-sion you might receive. You'll want to develop a portfolio of assets that grow over time, to see you through the thirty years of retire-ment you might be lucky enough to enjoy.

Getting Your Money Out

No matter what kind of retirement account you have, if you're under age fifty-nine and one-half and if you start withdrawing money from it for just about any reason, you'll have to pay a 10 percent penalty. Ouch! There are some exceptions:

1. If you're disabled.
2. If you take early retirement and are at least age fifty-five.

3. If you're paying medical expenses that exceed 7.5 percent of your adjusted gross income (for which you can claim a deduction).

4. If you're taking out $10,000 to purchase a first home (only from an IRA or Roth IRA).

5. If you're paying educational expenses for yourself, your spouse, your children, or your grandchildren (IRA and Roth IRA).

6. If you set up a payment schedule to withdraw the money at a certain rate over the rest of your life. This schedule must be in place for five years, or until you reach age fifty-nine, and then you may alter it or stop it without penalty. (Check out IRS Publication 590 "Individual Retirement Arrangements," for more information.)

RESOURCES

There are lots of places you can go for more information on any of these plans and what to do with them. Here are some of the best sources for help:

If you're over age fifty, you can join the American Association of Retired Persons (AARP). Free pamphlets are available on pensions, planning your retirement, and age discrimination in the workplace. Write to the AARP Work Force Programs Department, 601 E Street, NW, Washington, DC 20049, or go online at <www.aarp.org>. The Alliance for Investor Education Web site (www.investoreducation.org) offers investment education, and the Older Investors page has information on retirement planning. The Certified Financial Planner Board of Standards (www.CFP-Board.org) also has general information on financial planning for retirement.

The Consumer Information Catalog (www.pueblo.gsa.gov) lists hundreds of federal publications for consumers. Look in the Money section. Or, write to CIC, Pueblo, Colorado.

Check out the Web sites or offices of the major brokerage firms. Fidelity, Vanguard, and Schwab, for example, offer advice and calculators

Your first source when you want to check out your retirement plan should be your plan administrator. If your employer offers a 401(k), 403(b), or 457 plan, there should be someone who can give you a copy of your plan booklet and answer your questions.

online, plus free brochures and pamphlets to help educate consumers about various retirement options. Sites run by Intuit and Microsoft, and those hosted on AOL may also be consulted.

SHOULD I BORROW AGAINST MY RETIREMENT ACCOUNTS?

You understand the concept: your retirement money is your pot of gold at the end of the work-years rainbow. But you're in your mid-forties, decades away from retirement, and you need cash now. Should you borrow against that pot of gold?

The first question is: Can you borrow against your 401(k) plan, Keogh, or IRA? Some 401(k) plans permit you to borrow against the accumulated value for a short period of time—say, five years. You must reimburse the plan for the principal borrowed, plus a reasonable rate of interest, or pay the dreaded 10 percent penalty plus income taxes (because the loan will then be seen as a distribution). But some 401(k) plans don't permit borrowing, which closes that door.

Under the 1997 Tax Reform Act, you are now permitted to borrow up to $10,000 from your IRA (conventional or Roth) to purchase a first home (either pay points or use as the down payment). You may also pay an unlimited amount of college expenses for yourself, your spouse, your children, or your grandchildren. For people who are self-employed or are full-time parents, opening the IRA spigot was an important piece of good news.

Here are some pointers to keep in mind:

- *Employer-sponsored retirement plans.* If you dip into your retirement savings [a 401(k) or 403(b) plan], you generally must repay the loan within five years. If you use the money to buy a home, there is no legal limit on repayment. *The big issue:* Your employer may or may not permit any borrowing, and the company has the right to set the policy for its retirement plans, even if it's your money. Also, if you leave your job while your loan is outstanding, you'll have to settle up within three months, or the company will treat the loan as a distribution and you'll owe income taxes and penalties on the amount you borrowed.

- *IRAs.* New tax rules permit you to borrow up to $10,000 for the purchase of a first home. You may use the money as a down payment or for closing costs. If you have a Roth IRA, you may borrow from the account for the purchase of a first home, or use it to pay college loans. *The big issue:* Ten thousand dollars isn't that much these days, particularly when the average home costs more than $130,000. You'll be lucky to get a 3 percent down payment plus closing costs, or a 5 percent down payment with a no-cost loan.

- *The cost of borrowing.* The magic of paying yourself back loses a little of its luster if you consider that you're paying back a tax-deductible, tax-deferred account with already-taxed dollars. You'll pay income taxes when you finally withdraw the money, so you're really paying double taxes on the money when you borrow (you pay tax on the money you use to repay your debt, and you pay tax when you withdraw the funds at retirement). That makes the borrowing fairly expensive. But consider this: If you stop contributions to your retirement account while you're repaying the loan, your retirement kitty could be worth at least 20 percent less by the time you retire, according to a study by the General Accounting Office. Look at the alternative. During the five years your retirement account loan would be outstanding, you could double the amount of money you have in the account through prudent investing and your own additional contributions. *The big issue:* Don't borrow from your retirement account unless you can continue to contribute while the loan is outstanding.

The Bottom Line

Look elsewhere for money before you tap a retirement account. If all you have left is your retirement account, look at how big a percentage of the account you want to borrow. If you're borrowing $10,000 but have $200,000 in the account, your loan won't make much of a big difference in your retirement income (particularly if you still have fifteen years or more to let the money grow). But if you're borrowing $10,000 from an account that has only $20,000, or if you are thinking about borrowing half of what you've saved, make sure you have a really good reason. Buying a brand new car isn't a good reason. Buying a home or paying tuition for a college degree or graduate school degree that will increase your earning power might be.

Inevitable Exceptions

A few years ago, *The Wall Street Journal* wrote about Bill and Ann, their two children, and their dog. Bill had many jobs through the year. He finally landed a better-paying job where he could join a 401(k) plan that permitted borrowing. Now, Bill and Ann are on a continuous cycle of borrowing from and repaying Bill's 401(k). They've used the money for a lot of different things, including buying a motorboat.

But what about their retirement? Ann, at age forty-five, had survived a dozen surgeries for cancer and other illnesses. She questioned whether she'd live to see their retirement years. The money they borrow from Bill's 401(k) gives them the freedom and flexibility to enjoy today and to treat themselves and their children to things that make life fun.

Do they worry about tomorrow? Not really. They believe they'll find a way to work things out. Once you've survived cancer, Ann says, the rest seems easy.

If you're going to mortgage your future, you should ask yourself why. If you don't have a good enough reason, think it through again. Remember, every dollar that doesn't accrue on a tax-deductible and tax-deferred basis takes longer to earn the same kinds of returns.

WHAT WILL MY EXPENSES BE WHEN I RETIRE?

QUESTION
82

Overheard on Wall Street:

> *"You hoping to retire early?"*
> *"Yeah. I think I'd like to give it all up when I'm in my forties."*
> *"Really? What's that gonna take?"*
> *"I'm shooting for the tens of millions."*

According to one survey, only about 11 percent of Americans are saving for retirement with a specific dollar amount in mind. Half of those polled said they have no idea how much it will cost them to live after they stop working.

It's tough to save without a goal. But figuring out how much it will cost you to live, in a style that has yet to be determined, is a conundrum. The easy answer? Retirement is going to be pretty expensive. And with inflation, your dollar will be worth a lot less. But that doesn't mean you won't be able to afford your retirement. It simply means you need to plan for what your costs will be.

Predicting the Future

If you're in your twenties or early thirties, with young children, or perhaps some on the way, looking ahead to another forty to sixty years (including your thirty or more years in retirement), is, at best, difficult. Right now you're dazed by diapers and preschool. Thinking about what life will be like when your children have children may be too much to contemplate, particularly after a night when none of you got any sleep. If you're in your forties and fifties, you're probably paying college tuition and wondering how you're going to get through these years financially. Retirement still seems to be an eternity away. The problem is, once you get into your sixties, it's a little late to start thinking about what life might cost and then planning for it appropriately.

In answering this Question, I'm going to lay out some things for you to think about, in an effort to help you define your future retirement.

According to the U.S. Bureau of Labor Statistics, here's how an average sixty-five-year-old-plus urban household spends its money:

Housing	33.8 percent
Food	16.2
Transportation	15.1
Medical care	10.4
Clothing and personal care	6.1
Contributions	5.0
Education, entertainment, and reading	5.3
Other expenses (including travel)	8.1

If this household's annual income is $25,000 per year, they're spending $1,325 per year on education, entertainment, and reading expenses. And that's without taxes.

Figuring Out Your Own Expenses

If you're looking for good news, here it is: No matter what you estimate your expenses in retirement will be, they'll usually be less. Rarely do people spend more than they've estimated. Or, if they do, it's not for long.

One planner actually has clients inflate their retirement numbers. She says: "I assume they're going to live in their current lifestyle. If they tell me they're going to sell their big family home, buy a condo, and put the rest of the money into a cottage in the country, I inflate those numbers. I ask them how much the cottage costs today, and then I push that number up 4 percent a year until their projected retirement date. I project their living expenses will rise 3 to 4 percent per year, and that their money will compound at 10 percent. The numbers will, on average, be fairly accurate. We'll just tweak them every year."

Jeanne and Meyer's Story

When Jeanne and Meyer first married, they moved from their hometown of Chicago to San José to escape the cold. Back then, Jeanne would recall, San José was a small town of perhaps 30,000. (Today, there are more than a million residents in the metro area.)

In 1989, Jeanne and Meyer decided to move back to Chicago, to be near their family during their final years. They brought with them about $200,000 in cash, which, with their pensions and Social Security, they expected would see them through the end of their days. Although they moved into an expensive two-bedroom assisted-living facility, their other expenses were minimal. Together, they lived on perhaps $35,000 per year.

What they didn't count on was living so long. Meyer used to joke that if he had known he was going to live to be nearly ninety-seven, he would've quit spending money years ago. As the years went on, they worried more and more that their money wouldn't last, despite promises from their family that they would be taken care of.

They needn't have worried. Aside from their rent, their expenses dwindled down to nearly nothing. Blessed with relatively excellent health, their greatest pleasure at the end was doing a little shopping and having lunch together at McDonald's. By the time they both passed away in 1998, nine years after "moving home to die," as Meyer used to say, they still had $100,000 in the bank.

Why don't we spend as much as we think we will in retirement? Our wish list may say we're going to play golf every day. But the truth is, no one can play golf 365 days a year. Some days it'll rain. Some days you'll have doctors' appointments. Or perhaps you'll travel. You've got dozens of trips in mind, but few individuals travel 365 days a year. You need days, or maybe months, at home to rest and recover, pay the bills, see your children and grandchildren, or play some golf.

And some things will cost less than you're paying now. As a senior, you're entitled to special travel discounts. You're not working, so you don't need as many new clothes. Your children are grown (provided you aren't taking care of dependent grandchildren), so your food budget goes down. And if you're lucky enough to reach your nineties, it's unlikely you'll pursue the activities you spent money on when you were in your sixties.

Your Retirement Expenses

These will probably be some of your major retirement expenses:

- *Housing.* As we discussed earlier, changes in the tax law now allow you to keep up to $250,000 (for a married couple, up to $500,000) in capital gains tax-free when you sell your home. That leaves you free to sell your home, buy less expensive housing and invest the proceeds. However, even if you buy your retirement home with cash, you'll have some ongoing expenses: a monthly or annual condo or homeowners' association fee, real estate property taxes, homeowner's insurance, maintenance and upkeep, and decorating. Don't assume that your housing costs will fall to nothing.

- *Medical and dental.* On average, Medicare covers about 40 percent of the health costs you'll have in your senior years. You'll likely be on the hook for supplemental health insurance coverage and for extras you may want, such as a single room during hospitalizations. Even if your former employer provides you with coverage in retirement, you'll have some out-of-pocket costs that you should plan for.

- *Other insurance.* Your retirement doesn't mean you can give up homeowner's or renter's insurance (this cost may go up significantly if you purchase a second home), automobile insurance, liability insurance, earthquake or flood insurance, or special riders you may have needed along the way. Some insurance costs may decline, but others will stay the same or will increase.

- *Transportation.* Gertie thought she and her husband, Sam, would be able to get rid of one of their two cars when they retired. After all, they'd both be home, right? So they sold one car. Six months later, Gertie was driving a new car. Having only one car (which spent quite a lot of time with Sam, at various golf course parking lots) severely limited her ability to get around and do what *she* wanted. Bob leases a brand new car every two to three years. He says he doesn't want to be out on the road somewhere with a broken down old car. At age ninety-four, Irving bought a new car. He thought he deserved it, and the other one was getting too old to drive (not to mention that Irving might have been too old to drive). If you can get rid of one of your cars, you will save a bundle on gas, insurance, maintenance, repairs, registration, and fees—and you'll get cash for selling it. But if public transportation in your area isn't what you'd like it to be, or you're unable to take advantage of it, you may prefer to have two cars and budget for the expenses that go with them.

- *Travel.* If it's your life's dream to spend six months in Europe, you should plan for that. If you want to take a major trip every year, plan for that. If your children live across the country and you want to visit them every month, or fly them in, or take them on an elaborate family vacation, plan for that, too.

- *Entertainment and hobbies.* Pat retired and took up metal welding. His hobby costs him about $500 per month in materials and other expenses. Dorothy and her girlfriends take adult education classes that cost $200 each. Another couple goes to dinner every evening (the wife says she cooked for forty years and that was that!) and see a movie twice a week. Whatever you dream about doing in retirement, plan for that cost now. A movie ticket that costs $8 today might cost as much as $20 (or more!) in thirty years.

- *Gifts and contributions.* Many seniors step up their giving, and their volunteer time, as they get older. If you currently give 10 percent of your income away, there's no reason to think you'll stop doing that as you get older. In fact, you may increase your donations to 15 percent or more.

- *Providing for your family.* If it's been your dream to pick up the tab for your grandchildren's college educations, figure that cost will roughly double every twenty years. Or, if your children need a little financial assistance now and then, that's a parent's privilege. If you want to have money to give them while you're alive, plan for it today. (We'll talk about planning for your estate in the next chapter.)

- *Dependent care.* If you have a child who is mentally or physically disabled and will always need help, or if you have a grandchild who may come to live with you, plan to have enough money to take care of the situation in the way you'd want to.

A Worksheet for Your Expenses Today and in the Future

I've worked out a minibudget to help you record how much you spend today and compare the cost of living today with the projected cost of living in the future. Be sure to calculate the cost (in today's dollars) of *everything* you want to do during your retirement.

You can also estimate what you'll be paying in the future by looking at the Useful Charts in Appendix III.

Remember, write down the dollar amounts of living in retirement as if you were going to retire today. If your housing expenses today total $20,000 (including mortgage payments, taxes, and insurance), but your mortgage will be paid off by the time you retire, put down only the cost of taxes and homeowner's insurance. (See page 391.)

If you want to feel good about estimating your expenses in retirement, plan on spending more than you will. That may cause you some pain today (you'll probably have to step up your savings and/or increase your risk in investing), but you'll know that you can satisfy every need, want, and whim when you retire.

Don't get so carried away with retirement planning that you pinch yourself too hard today. If you get a second or third job in order to pay for a lavish retirement, the benefit may come at a high cost. The one thing you can't get back is time spent with your friends and family. If you spend forty years working yourself to the bone so that you can enjoy your retirement, when you get there you may find you have no one with whom you can share it.

WORKSHEET
Your Expenses Today and in Your Retirement

Item	Cost of Living Today	Cost of Living in Retirement
Housing		
Repairs and upkeep		
Medical and dental		
Supplemental medical insurance		
Prescriptions		
Other insurance		
Transportation		
Utilities		
Food		
Clothing		
Travel		
Entertainment		
Education		
Hobbies		
Gifts and contributions		
Dependent care		
Help to family members		
Household furnishings		
Savings and investments		
Miscellaneous		
Subtotal		
Fudge factor*		
Total		

*The fudge factor gives you some cushion, in case you haven't correctly estimated your cost of living. Allow yourself an extra 5 percent of expenses (multiply the subtotal by .05). If that doesn't seem to yield enough, multiply by .10.

QUESTION
83

HOW MUCH MONEY WILL I HAVE WHEN I RETIRE?

Money can't buy me love.
—*The Beatles*

Money may not be able to buy you love. It may not even be able to buy you friendship (though it can certainly buy you sessions with a psychiatrist, who may be nicer to you than your best friend). Only cold hard cash can buy your independence in retirement and give you peace of mind that you won't be beholden to anyone as long as you live.

Now that we've looked at how much retirement is going to cost, we should talk about how much money you'll have coming in to pay for your retirement. If there's a gap between what you think you'll spend and what you know you'll have coming in, you have two choices: (1) go back to Chapter 2 and spend more time figuring out how to rein in your budget and stash away more for your retirement, or (2) trim back your retirement goals and dreams.

Running out of money is a retiree's biggest fear. Knowing they will be financially independent is, for most people, a considerable relief. For some folks, financial independence is everything.

The Effects of Inflation

Before we get to how much cash you'll have in retirement, let's look at how inflation is going to eat away your purchasing power. Say you were given $20,000 in 1976. It would have been worth only $6,900 in 1996, some twenty years later. If you retired on an income of $20,000 in 1976, you'd have needed an income of about $58,000 in 1997 (a 190 percent increase) just to maintain the same purchasing power.

To buy $20,000 worth of goods and services annually during the next twenty years, you'll need to have a total of $286,145 if inflation runs at 4 percent annually; $310,133 if inflation is 5 percent annually; $336,868 if inflation is 6 percent annually; and $366,695 if inflation is 7 percent annually.

In other words, if you have $286,000 in the bank today, your money will last twenty years if inflation is 4 percent but only fifteen years if inflation runs at 7 percent. (These projections assume the money you don't spend continues to grow at an 8 percent annual rate of return.)

The chart below shows that if inflation runs at 7 percent annually, $1,000 today will be worth only about $713 in five years, and about $184 in twenty-five years.

The Impact of Inflation on $1,000, over Time

Years	Rate of Return			
	4%	5%	6%	7%
5	$819	$779	$741	$713
15	549	473	407	362
25	368	287	224	184

Source: T. Rowe Price Associates.

Your Money in Retirement

Now let's look at what kinds of assets you have and how much income you'll receive when you retire. (See pages 394–396.)

The Other Side of the Coin

If you had only assets, your numbers might look pretty good. But most of us have debts that will continue into retirement. Use the worksheet on page 397 to chart debts and to forecast when some of them will be paid off.

> Although you may have more access to your assets in retirement, you should still have a liquid emergency reserve, equal to two months' expenses. In a crisis, you'll have some cash on hand to respond until you can liquidate other assets. Too many retirees live from one benefit check to the next, either not eager or unable to dip into their principal for emergencies. If you don't already have this reserve, make sure you subtract it as a lump sum from one of your assets before you start your calculations.

WORKSHEET
How Much Money Will I Have in Retirement?

1. Retirement Plan Assets (Tax-Deferred). These are assets that typically can't be touched without penalty until you're age 59 ½.

Type of Asset	Total Value	Monthly Income
Employer-paid pension/profit-sharing account	_____	_____
Individual Retirement Account (IRA)	_____	_____
Roth IRA	_____	_____
Employee savings plans: 401(k), 457, 403(b), etc.	_____	_____
Savings Incentive Match Plan for Employees (SIMPLE)	_____	_____
Keogh plans	_____	_____
Simplified Employee Pension (SEP)	_____	_____
Tax-sheltered annuities	_____	_____
Other tax-deferred assets	_____	_____
Total Retirement Plan Assets	_____	_____

2. Short-Term Assets. These are assets that can be liquidated quickly and cheaply. Depending on how long you've held them, they may or may not qualify for capital gains tax treatment (that is, a lower rate than your marginal tax rate).

Type of Asset	Total Value	Monthly Income
Cash	_____	_____
Checking accounts	_____	_____
Savings accounts	_____	_____
Money market accounts, including mutual funds	_____	_____
Certificates of deposit (CDs)	_____	_____
U.S. Treasury bills	_____	_____
Total Short-Term Assets	_____	_____

3. Long-Term Assets. If you have capital gains on any of the following assets, you should subtract 20 percent from that asset's estimated value, to cover the capital gains tax you'll owe if you are in the 28 percent tax bracket (or higher). Subtract 10 percent if you are in the 15 percent tax bracket.

Type of Asset	Total Value	Monthly Income
Stock and bond mutual funds	_____	_____
U.S. Government notes and bonds	_____	_____
Municipal bonds	_____	_____
Corporate bonds	_____	_____
Common stocks	_____	_____
Real estate investment trusts (REITs)	_____	_____
Real estate investments	_____	_____
Partnership interests (limited or general)	_____	_____
Business interests	_____	_____
Annuities (not including those listed under Retirement Plan Assets)	_____	_____
Available trust assets	_____	_____
Other _____	_____	_____
Other _____	_____	_____
Other _____	_____	_____
Total Long-Term Assets	_____	_____

4. Personal Assets. Put down the estimated value for each investment category, but only list the monthly income if you plan to sell the investment to finance your retirement. If you're going to sell your home and buy another one, make sure you record the value of the newly purchased home, plus estimated costs of purchase and sale. It's the *net cash* you're interested in here.

Type of Asset	Total Value	Monthly Income
Personal residence	_____	_____
Vacation home(s)	_____	_____

Timeshare interests _____ _____

Other _____ _____ _____

Other _____ _____ _____

Total Personal Assets _____ _____

5. Other Income. This may include Social Security from this country or another, an inheritance, or a trust that names you as beneficiary.

Type of Asset	Total Value	Monthly Income
Social Security	_____	_____
Inheritance	_____	_____
Trust account	_____	_____
Other _____	_____	_____
Total Other Income	_____	_____

6. Calculation of Total Assets. Transfer to this section the totals in each category, and add them together.

	Total Value	Monthly Income
1. Total Retirement Plan Assets	_____	_____
2. Total Short-Term Assets	+ _____	+ _____
3. Total Long-Term Assets	+ _____	+ _____
4. Total Personal Assets	+ _____	+ _____
5. Total Other Income	+ _____	+ _____
Total Assets	= _____	_____

Type of Debt	Total Debt	Monthly Payment	Estimated Date of Last Payment
Mortgage	_____	_____	_____
Home equity loan(s)	_____	_____	_____
Auto loan(s)	_____	_____	_____
School loan(s) (yours or your children's or grandchildren's)	_____	_____	_____
Loans against pension plan(s)	_____	_____	_____
Loans against insurance policies	_____	_____	_____
Credit card debt	_____	_____	_____
Personal line(s) of credit	_____	_____	_____
Investment or business loan(s) for which you are personally responsible	_____	_____	_____
Margin account loan(s)	_____	_____	_____
Unpaid property taxes	_____	_____	_____
Unpaid IRS taxes	_____	_____	_____
Alimony or spousal/child support	_____	_____	_____
Other _____	_____	_____	_____
Other _____	_____	_____	_____
Total Outstanding Debt	_____	_____	_____

Net Annual Income at Retirement

*Monthly Income from Total Assets _____ $\times 12 =$ _____ per year

Less: Monthly Payment for Total Outstanding Debt – _____ $\times 12 =$ _____ per year

Net Monthly Income = _____ $\times 12 =$ _____ per year

*See previous worksheet, pp. 394–396.

QUESTION 84

HOW DOES SOCIAL SECURITY WORK?

A recent poll indicates that most older baby boomers believe Social Security benefits will be waiting for them (in some form) when they retire. But the youngest of the boomers, and the Generation Xers, aren't so sure. In 2029, when the last members of the baby boom generation (people born in 1946 through 1964) reach age sixty-five, Social Security is expected to go broke. More people will be receiving money than will be paying into it.

Today, over 44 million Americans collect Social Security benefits. Recipients include retired workers and their families, disabled workers and their families, and survivors of workers. In 2029, that number is expected to reach about 58 million. By 2033, forecasters say, Social Security will be able to cover only 75 percent of all benefits due, if payroll taxes stay where they are. At that point, the government can step in with a subsidy, raise payroll taxes, tax benefits, or reduce their amounts. If the federal government can solve the problem sometime soon, with more than a few years' margin, the remedies will be much less painful.

Calculating Social Security

To qualify for Social Security benefits, you must earn income in at least ten years, and earn a minimum amount, set by law, in each of those years. Currently, the annual minimum amount is less than $3,000 per year, but it is tagged to the average wage index and rises each year. If you earned at least the minimum amount for ten years, and retired in 1997 at age sixty-two, you'd now be receiving a monthly benefit of $362, or $4,344 per year. It is difficult to eat and pay rent with that small amount of money, but many elderly Americans do just that.

The largest possible payout in 1997 was $1,609 a month ($19,308 per year) for an eligible person who waited until age seventy to collect benefits. To get that amount monthly, the requirements were: thirty-five years of work while earning the maximum amount taxed for Social Security ($65,400 in 1997). If you work for more than thirty-five years, your highest thirty-five years' worth of wages count. Every year you don't work is counted as a zero.

Important Points to Keep in Mind

1. *Divorced spouses.* If you were married at least ten years, and half of your ex-spouse's benefit is larger than your own benefit, and if you've been divorced for at least two years and are not remarried to someone else, you're entitled to a Social Security check based on your ex-spouse's lifetime earnings. You're eligible to receive checks as soon as you and your ex-spouse reach age sixty-two. Your ex-spouse doesn't even need to know (the payment to you won't reduce his or her own benefit). But if you remarry, you lose the benefit.

2. *Dependent school-age children.* If you receive Social Security and have children under eighteen (nineteen if they're still in high school), you qualify for an extra amount. If you have grandchildren or stepgrandchildren who live with you, and you claim them as dependents, you may also be entitled to a benefit. If you're widowed and are too young to receive Social Security for yourself, but you have young children, you're entitled to receive a benefit until your youngest child is eighteen (nineteen if still in high school).

3. *Changing your name.* If you get married and change your name, get divorced and change your name, change your name because you don't like the one you were born with, or receive income under another name (a pen name or stage name), be sure you notify the Social Security Administration. Otherwise, you might find that your payroll taxes aren't being credited to your account. (It's another good reason to check your benefits periodically.)

How Much Are You Going to Get?

How much do you pay into Social Security? If you're employed by a company, you paid 6.2 percent of your salary, up to about $66,000, in 1998. (This number goes up slightly every year.) Your employer picks up the other 6.2 percent. If you're self-employed, you pay the whole 12.4 percent.

How much will you receive? You can get an estimate of your Social Security benefits by filing an application for a Personal Earnings and

Benefits Statement. Pick up the form at your local Social Security office; or call, toll-free, 800-772-1213; or download the form from the Internet (www.ssa.gov). The form below asks for your name, the age you expect to retire, and how much you think you'll earn, on average, between now and retirement. In about five weeks, you'll receive a statement that shows you how much you've contributed over the years. Check your statement for mistakes. If your contribution is reported as zero for even one year, it can affect your benefits.

If you need 70 to 80 percent of your preretirement income to fund your lifestyle, don't count on Social Security to pay the entire bill. According to the Social Security Administration, your benefits will replace only about 42 percent of your salary as an average wage earner, and less if you earned above-average wages.

Form Approved
OMB No. 0960-0466 [ ] SP

Request for Earnings and Benefit Estimate Statement

[ ] Please check this box if you want to get your statement in Spanish instead of English.

Please print or type your answers. When you have completed the form, fold it and mail it to us.

1. Name shown on your Social Security card:

_____
First Name / Middle Initial

_____
Last Name Only

2. Your Social Security number as shown on your card:

□□□-□□-□□□□

3. Your date of birth _____
Month Day Year

4. Other Social Security numbers you have used:

□□□-□□-□□□□

□□□-□□-□□□□

5. Your sex: [ ] Male [ ] Female

6. Other names you have used
(including a maiden name):

_____

_____

For items 7 and 9 show only earnings covered by Social Security. Do NOT include wages from State, local or Federal Government employment that are NOT covered for Social Security or that are covered ONLY by Medicare.

7. Show your actual earnings (wages and/or net self-employment income) for last year and your estimated earnings for this year.

   A. Last year's actual earnings: *(Dollars Only)*

   $ □□□,□□□.□□

   B. This year's estimated earnings: *(Dollars Only)*

   $ □□□,□□□.□□

8. Show the age at which you plan to stop working.

   □□ *(Show only one age)*

9. Below, show the average yearly amount (not your total future lifetime earnings) that you think you will earn between now and when you plan to stop working. Include cost-of-living, performance or scheduled pay increases or bonuses.

   If you expect to earn significantly more or less in the future due to promotions, job changes, part-time work, or an absence from the work force, enter the amount that most closely reflects your future average yearly earnings.

   If you don't expect any significant changes, show the same amount you are earning now (the amount in 7B).

   Future average yearly earnings: *(Dollars Only)*

   $ □□□,□□□.□□

10. Address where you want us to send the statement.

   _____
   Name

   _____
   Street Address (Include Apt. No., P.O. Box, or Rural Route)

   _____
   City   State   Zip Code

   Notice:
   I am asking for information about my own Social Security record or the record of a person I am authorized to represent. I understand that when requesting information on a deceased person, I must include proof of death and relationship or appointment. I further understand that if I deliberately request information under false pretenses, I may be guilty of a Federal crime and could be fined and/or imprisoned. I authorize you to use a contractor to send the statement of earnings and benefit estimates to the person named in item 10.

   ►

   Please sign your name (Do Not Print)

   _____

   _____
   Date   (Area Code) Daytime Telephone No.

Form SSA-7004-SM(4-95) Destroy prior editions   ♻ Printed on recycled paper

Increasing Your Social Security Benefits

As we discussed, for a wage earner to get a check from Social Security, he or she must earn income in at least ten years, and the amount of income earned must be at least the minimum for that year. Benefits are based on a span of thirty-five years, and every year in which the minimum is not met counts as a "zero" toward ultimate benefits. (Each of the subsequent twenty-five years, after the initial ten, raises the amount of the eventual monthly Social Security check.) To get the largest possible check, you need to work for thirty-five years and earn the maximum amount in each of those years. If you work for more than thirty-five years, the Social Security Administration will substitute lower-paying years for higher-paying years.

The way Social Security is calculated is a real problem for parents who either stay at home to raise their children, or take a few years off and then go back to work. It is particularly a problem for women, who, far more than men, stay at home to raise young children. It's one reason why women tend to receive far smaller Social Security benefits than men, and why more elderly women than men are hovering at or below the poverty line. (The other part of the explanation is that women still earn less than men and live longer than men, and so are living longer on less assets.)

There are a couple of things you can do to raise your benefits. Consider taking a second job to boost your earnings or starting a part-time business at home. You might also consider working part-time while you're at home with your child. In both situations, you'll be contributing something to Social Security, which will increase the amount you'll eventually receive.

When You Can Take Your Social Security Benefits

You're eligible to receive Social Security benefits starting at age sixty-two, but if you take them that early, your benefit will be permanently reduced (that's right, it *never* goes up) by as much as 20 percent. For each month you receive benefits before you turn sixty-five, the Social Security Administration permanently reduces your benefits by $5/9$ of 1 percent. For each year you wait beyond sixty-five (that age will slowly rise to sixty-seven over the next few years), you'll receive an additional 3 percent to 8 percent. When you reach age seventy, all increases stop.

401

If you can get more by waiting, why would you start taking Social Security at sixty-two? Your decision depends on your circumstances. If you're divorced or widowed, and don't have much to live on, Social Security can provide enough to buy you the basics (food, shelter, and clothing) plus perhaps a few extras, like Medi-Gap insurance. If people tend to die early in your family, you might choose to get a few extras now. When you die, your Social Security benefits cease.

Why might you wait? If you don't need the money at age sixty-two (perhaps you're still working), you're wise to wait until you retire to collect. Also, if you'll receive a fixed pension (the amount never changes), you might want a higher Social Security benefit, which will increase to keep pace, approximately, with inflation.

It's comforting to know that Social Security will probably be there to provide some assistance when we retire. But, if that's all you're counting on, you're going to have trouble making ends meet in retirement. Any bright future plans will be out of reach. For a secure and comfortable retirement, you need to fund your tax-deductible and tax-deferred accounts to the maximum, and then grow additional assets from which to draw.

QUESTION 85

WHAT DO I NEED TO KNOW ABOUT WITHDRAWING MY RETIREMENT FUNDS?

After you read this book, I'm betting you'll realize that putting money away for retirement can be a relatively painless experience. I hope that you'll start as early as you can, put away as much as you can, and invest as wisely as possible.

At some point, you will have to start taking some of your money out of your retirement plans and using it for your living expenses. Or, if you take early retirement, or are let go in a restructuring, you might receive a lump-sum distribution from your retirement plan. Either way, there are certain rules you must follow to avoid being penalized.

Lump-Sum Distribution

If you're let go from your job, or you take early retirement, or your company is bought out, you may be eligible to receive a lump-sum distribution from your retirement plan. At that point, you have to decide whether or not to roll over the money into an Individual Retirement Account (IRA).

If you decide on a rollover, you must open the IRA within sixty days of receiving your distribution check. If you handle the money (i.e., receive the check), your company will withhold 20 percent of it for federal taxes. To roll over the entire amount, you'd then have to use additional funds to make up the 20 percent, and apply for a tax refund later.

A better solution is to open the IRA first and then have the money electronically transferred into the account. Or, your company can give you a check payable to the custodian of the new IRA. Your money is then considered to have been distributed "trustee to trustee" (qualified retirement plan to IRA), and you are considered to be out of the transaction. Best of all, no taxes are withheld. It's a clean and easy move.

If you decide not to roll over the money, your employer is required by law to withhold 20 percent for federal income taxes. You will have to pay any additional federal income taxes you owe, and perhaps state and local taxes. In addition, if you're younger than age fifty-nine, you will have to pay the IRS a 10 percent penalty for an early withdrawal of your retirement money, unless you qualify for a specific exemption.

Net Unrealized Appreciation

When is it a good idea *not* to roll over your lump-sum distribution into an IRA? If all, or a large portion, of your 401(k) money is in company stock, you may not want to roll it over into an IRA. A special tax break is available to employees who take their company stock and put it into a regular brokerage account. Instead of paying income taxes on all the money, you pay only on the cost basis of the stock— that is, the cost of the shares when they were bought and placed into your retirement account. This cost is, hopefully, far below what the shares are worth today.

The difference between the cost basis of the shares and their current value is called the *net unrealized appreciation* (NUA). If you put your shares into a brokerage account instead of into an IRA, you'll pay income taxes at your current marginal rate on the cost basis of the shares. Whenever you sell the rest of the stock—a week later or a decade later—you'll only pay capital gains tax (20 percent if you're in the 28 percent tax bracket or above; 10 percent if you're in the 15 percent tax bracket). Either way, you save, if your stock has had significant appreciation.

A warning: This may not be the best choice for everyone. If you're under age fifty-nine, you'll owe a 10 percent penalty in addition to paying income taxes. If you're going to try this, hire an accountant who can help you work through the complex tax rules. Also, check out Internal Revenue Code Section 402(e)(4), which you can find at <www.irs.gov>.

Mandatory Retirement Withdrawals

If you're in the very fortunate position of having enough income or assets to live on without ever tapping your retirement accounts, here's a bit of unhappy news. Whether or not you need it, the government requires you to start withdrawing money from your IRAs, Keoghs, and 401(k) programs the year after you turn age seventy.

There is a minimum amount you may withdraw, and it is based on your life expectancy and the total amount you have available in your retirement accounts. Basically, you divide your retirement account balance by your life expectancy.

Two strategies can help you lower the amount you have to take. First, married couples can use the joint life expectancy. If you're seventy-one, your life expectancy (according to the IRS) is approximately 15.3 years. If you have $500,000 in your retirement accounts, you'll have to withdraw $32,680. But if your spouse is sixty-eight, your *joint* life expectancy (when the second spouse is expected to die) is 21.2 years. So you'd have to withdraw only $23,585. You can link the joint life expectancy to anyone you name as your beneficiary, so it may make sense to name one of your heirs—perhaps a child or a niece or nephew—as your beneficiary (although the rules limit the "age" difference to ten years). Talk to your accountant, tax preparer, enrolled agent, or estate attorney for more details.

You can easily see the lunacy that drives minimum withdrawals. If you live longer than the IRS expects you to, you may run out of money. So you'll withdraw the minimum, pay your income taxes (which is what the IRS really wants) and reinvest the money. What if you don't withdraw? Expect to be hit with a 50 percent penalty for the amount you should've withdrawn but didn't.

The second way to minimize your withdrawals is to recalculate your life expectancy annually. Each year you live, your life expectancy goes down, so you'd have to take out less money. But not every retirement plan allows you to recalculate your life expectancy, and you'll have to make a final decision by April 1 of the year after you turn age seventy.

Roth IRAs

As I explained in Question 80, there are a lot of reasons to like Roth IRAs. If you qualify incomewise, they can be an excellent investment and (as you'll see in the next chapter) estate-tax vehicle.

It's worthwhile noting that, regarding withdrawals of money, Roth IRAs have two other advantages over conventional IRAs. The first is that, with a Roth IRA, you don't have to withdraw any money at all. In fact, you can continue to make contributions (it's after-tax money that's contributed, but the gains grow tax-free) as long as you have earned income—that is, you're still working.

Second, with a conventional IRA, you owe income tax on your contributions and your gains. If you die with money left in your IRA, your heirs pay a double tax: (1) income tax on the remaining money, and (2) if your estate is over the $625,000 (rising to $1 million in 2006) threshold, estate taxes as well.

Odds and Ends

Besides a minimum withdrawal from your retirement account, there is also a maximum amount you can withdraw. (You're smart, so you already see where this is going, right?) If you take out more than the maximum ($160,000 in 1997, indexed to inflation, or a one-time lump-sum withdrawal of $800,000, in 1997), you'd normally be hit with a 15 percent tax penalty. In other words, you'd have to pay yet another tax for saving too much and investing too well. However, the penalties are temporarily suspended for three years, starting in 1997 (and continuing through 1999). This doesn't change the penalties applied to those under age fifty-nine who withdraw money from their retirement accounts.

Although this item won't be available after 1999, I've included it for some readers who may fall into this category and might want to take the larger withdrawal to get it out of their retirement accounts before the three-year permission period ends.

Should You Take It Now or Later?

People often ask whether they should take Social Security as soon as possible or as late as possible. The indecision typically hinges on taking it at age sixty-two or waiting until age seventy. The difference in money can be significant—sometimes twice as much—particularly if you continue working all those years.

But what about pensions? People get laid off or bought out, and employees don't know whether it's in their best interests to cash out early or wait. Should you take a $500 pension at age fifty-five or wait until you're sixty-five and receive more than twice that amount?

A key consideration is how well you'll do if you invest the money on your own. If you think that earning 10 to 12 percent on your money is a piece of cake, you might do better taking the early amount. The other thing to think about is whether you need the money today. If you're earning 10 to 12 percent annually on your investments and do not need the cash, why not let the payments accrue?

A final thought. Is there some danger that your employer might fold? If so, can you get a lump-sum payment instead of the annual pension for life? Talk to your benefits manager about your options.

The Bottom Line

Taking money out of your retirement plans is really dictated by the taxes you're going to pay. Withdraw before age fifty-nine and you'll get hit with a 10 percent penalty on top of the income taxes you owe (unless you qualify for one of the exemptions). Withdraw too much (once we're past the 1999 special withdrawal years) and you'll get hit with a 15 percent penalty. Don't withdraw the minimum, and you'll get hit with a 50 percent penalty on the amount you failed to withdraw. Receive a lump-sum distribution, and the company will withhold 20 percent for federal income tax. Put it into an IRA, and you'll have to make up the 20 percent out of other funds and then apply for a tax refund.

What is the best thing to do with a lump-sum distribution? Electronically transfer your retirement fund money directly into a new IRA, or have your plan administrator make out a check to the custodian for your new IRA account—not to you.

RESOURCES

IRS Publication 590, "Individual Retirement Accounts (IRAs)" offers a lot of details on the rules and requirements. It also contains the life expectancy tables you'll need to calculate your mandatory withdrawals. You can order it by calling, toll-free, 800-829-3676. The American Association for Retired Persons offers a mountain of pamphlets to its members. For membership information, write to AARP, 601 E Street, NW, Washington, DC 20049.

HOW CAN I RETIRE AS A MILLIONAIRE (OR AT LEAST RETIRE EARLY)?

QUESTION
86

Before going to Europe on business, a man drove his Rolls-Royce to a downtown New York City bank and went in to ask for an immediate loan of $5,000. The loan officer, taken aback, requested collateral.

"Well, then, here are the keys to my Rolls-Royce," the man said. The loan officer promptly had the car driven into the bank's underground parking garage for safe keeping, and gave the man $5,000.

Two weeks later, the man walked through the bank's doors and asked to settle up his loan and get his car back. "That will be $5,000 in principal, and $15.40 in interest," the loan officer said. The man wrote out a check, was given his car keys, and started to walk away.

"Wait, sir," the loan officer said. "While you were gone, I found out you are a millionaire. Why in the world would you need to borrow $5,000?"

The man smiled. "Where else could I park my Rolls-Royce in Manhattan for two weeks and pay only $15.40?"

—Joke sent around the Internet; author unknown

In his book, *The Millionaire Next Door*, Thomas Stanley argues that you never know whether your neighbor has $500 or $5 million to his name. That's because people who don't have real wealth often go into debt so they can purchase all of the trappings of wealth. On the other hand, folks with real wealth will often drive ten-year-old cars, take inexpensive vacations, and eat at home.

407

Are your best friends millionaires? You'll never know simply by the car they drive, the clothes they wear, or the house they live in. Many people who drive Range Rovers (at $65,000 each) and wear gold Rolex watches are making monthly payments on $100,000 of credit card debt.

Having a million dollars in the bank is the ultimate economic threshold for many folks. They think having that kind of money means security. It used to. Today, it's certainly a noble sum, but it's nothing special. In ten years, a million bucks may buy half of what it buys today.

Still, if you have $1 million in the bank and invest it at 5 percent, you'll receive $50,000 in interest each year. That's a nice chunk of change to spend each year in retirement.

How do you get there? How do you become a millionaire? Save $91.32 each day for thirty years. If that seems too steep, try putting away $3.00 per day into a tax-deferred account (that's only $1,095 per year). Put that money in a low-cost (no-load, low-expense-ratio) stock mutual fund that will earn about 12 percent annually (the historic return of the stock market is just over 10 percent), and watch it grow for forty years. Want to have $2 million? Leave it in the account for another six years, or put away $2,000 per year.

(To avoid mandatory withdrawals from this account, you'll have to start contributing before age thirty.)

A New Twist

It seems like there are a million schemes to help you earn a million dollars. Maybe some of them work, but most of them don't, and many are outright scams. Occasionally, an idea comes along that sounds like it might work. I don't recommend this path, but I thought I'd include it so you can see the lengths to which some people will go in order to finance their retirement.

DePaul University finance professor Richard Garrigan proposes financing your retirement by using your home equity. It's a little tricky, and again, I'm not recommending that you do this. But it's a clever little numbers game.

In Professor Garrigan's example, the Millers are age thirty-four and have voluntary 401(k) retirement plans at work. They'd like to contribute the maximum and get the 5 percent contribution their employer offers, but they can't because, with two children, they're just making ends meet.

If they take a $100,000 home equity loan at 8.5 percent for ten years, they could draw down on the account to pay themselves back for the money their employer withdraws from their salary to put into their tax-deductible, tax-deferred retirement plan.

If they're earning enough to put in $9,500 each ($19,000 together), at the end of six years, they'll have accumulated $99,728 of debt on the home equity loan ($82,080 in principal plus $24,511 in gross interest minus $6,863 in tax savings). Of course, now they have to pay back the home equity loan, or refinance their home (which, hopefully, has appreciated in value) to pay back the home equity loan at a (hopefully) lower interest rate.

Meanwhile, they've been able to invest $1,583.33 per month in their retirement accounts for six years. At this point, according to Professor Garrigan's plan, they stop putting money into their retirement accounts. By the end of the six years, they have either $141,171 (if the money grew at 7 percent) or $155,342 (if the money grew at 10 percent). In another twenty-five years (a total of thirty-one years), they'd have $808,265 (at 7 percent), or nearly $1.9 million (if the money grew at 10 percent) in their retirement accounts.

This is a complicated example of some pretty creative financing. There are lots of ways it would work better, or not work at all. For example, if one of the Millers' employers contributed 10 percent of their income, instead of 5 percent, there might be significantly more in the kitty. If there were no employer contributions, there would be less. Also, the federal ceiling for contributions rises each year, but you have to be earning a really healthy amount to reach it.

My question is: If this fictitious couple can afford to pay off the home equity loan each year, why can't they curtail their spending enough to make the contributions on their own? It's much simpler to rein in your spending than go through all these financial shindigs (all of which may be perfectly legal) in order to save for retirement. Professor Garrigan says it's because today's young couples don't want to give up anything for the sake of their retirement. They'd rather finance their retirement with debt. Or, they're simply strapped for cash.

> We all face choices in life. Looking toward your retirement, you can either cut back your spending today to pad your future, or you can spend today and hope the future takes care of itself.

409

Retiring Early

The idea of retiring early sounds marvelous. Who wouldn't want to chuck it all and spend the rest of your days relaxing, playing golf or tennis, taking children or grandchildren to lunch, attending classes, shopping, or working out?

What should you do if you want to retire early? As I see it, you have some throwaway options—marry well, inherit a bundle, win the lottery, or rob a bank—but the only strategy that has any dependable record of success is: work hard, and save, save, save. This is how most of us make it in this world. We work hard, sometimes taking on a second or third job, and we save. Spend less than you earn, save the difference, invest it well, and your money will grow enough to fund the retirement (early or late) of your dreams.

Some readers may be disappointed that there are no magic bullets to help them reap an incredible financial windfall when they retire. Sorry, but I don't do magic bullets. For starters, they don't always work. Second, they're typically complicated (like Professor Garrigan's example, discussed earlier). Third, there's a difference between luck and magic. I believe in luck.

I also believe in the old saying that luck is the intersection of opportunity and preparation. You can make lucky things happen by being prepared and walking through doors that are opened for you. And, you can create all sorts of opportunities by opening yourself up to the world. A friend of mine, who is a world-renowned intuitive, says people who open up their souls draw opportunities like a magnet draws nails. You have the power within you to change your life and improve your financial future. You have the power within you to make things happen—even to retire early, if that's your dream.

And everything starts with a dream. Dream about the kind of financial future you want. Then, create a plan of action that will get you there. Stick to your guns, even in the face of temptation ("I have to have that BMW") and retool your plan as the years pass. Before you know it, you'll have achieved all of your financial goals, and set others.

Planning for the
Next Generation

HOW DO I GET MY ESTATE IN ORDER?

At the beginning of this book, I said that most people approach their personal finances the same way they approach a hall closet that hasn't been cleaned out in thirty years. Your estate is the ultimate hall closet. And if you don't clean it up before you go, or if you do a bad job, I promise you, your children or other heirs will never forget you, but not for the reasons you had hoped.

The term *estate* refers to everything you own the moment you pass away. It consists of your real and personal property, including your cash, stocks, retirement accounts, life insurance proceeds, furniture, clothing, artwork, house, car, and other possessions.

Get your estate in order before you die. Leave the necessary papers, like a will or trust agreements, so that your estate can be parceled out in exactly the way you'd do it yourself if you were still alive. Getting your estate in order takes some planning and some knowledge or advice. There's plenty to think about. You need to take into account your minor children; how you want your assets to be distributed; how much you want to "control from the grave," so to speak; the disposition of those assets; and how the current tax laws affect your decisions or wishes.

Here are some of the major issues you should think through before you start working on your estate:

1. *Taxes.* If you are worth more than $625,000, you may want to think about how much you'll pay in estate taxes. Currently, you

may pass along up to $650,000 (rising to $1 million in 2006) tax-free. You'll pay the government anywhere from 37 percent to 55 percent on assets that are over that limit. That possibility should make anyone with real money think about ways to minimize estate taxes.

2. *Minor children.* If you don't leave a will designating who will care for your minor children, your state's law goes into effect, and custody of your children (and any part of your estate that you leave to them) may end up with someone you wouldn't have chosen. If you have children, you need to take action. Today.

3. *Bequests.* If you want your money to go to a certain person, you must put that instruction in your will, or create a trust designating that individual as the beneficiary, or name that person as the beneficiary on your life insurance policies and IRAs. Once again, if you don't set things up in advance, your state law will kick in and your estate will be parceled out according to statute.

4. *Control.* If you want your children to have your money, but not quite yet and not all at once, you should set up an appropriate trust agreement. This will give you some control over what's done with your money, even after you're no longer on the scene.

When I was researching this chapter, the estate planners and estate attorneys I spoke to told me stories about people who tried to extend too much control beyond the grave. You can parcel out your estate any way you want, and do what you can to minimize the taxes the estate will pay. But ultimately, what's right taxwise may be wrong for your heirs. Too many people make the mistake of not discussing these issues with their children ahead of time. If you don't treat all your children equally while you're alive, they will resent you and your differential attitude toward them. If you treat them differently after your death, especially when they have had no inkling of preferential treatment, they will probably resent you and their preferred sibling(s) for the rest of their lives. Explain to them your decisions on bequests, and be sure they understand *and accept* the reasoning behind your actions.

Your Estate Plan of Action

If you're starting from ground zero, you'll need an estate plan to get you going in the right direction. (I talk about many of these concepts in detail later in the chapter. If you want more information, see the questions referenced.) Here are the steps toward setting up your estate.

1. *Calculate your net worth.* List *everything* you own, then deduct *everything* you owe. Your goal is a list of everything you own by yourself or with a spouse or partner: homes, cars, possessions, money, retirement accounts, other investments, and businesses. Don't forget your life insurance proceeds (not the cash surrender value) and any annuities you might own. You may not benefit from life insurance proceeds while you're alive, but your estate will receive them. If your net worth is over $650,000 (in 1999), you may want to consider the estate tax consequences of passing along an estate that large.

2. *Write your will.* A will is a legal document that determines the distribution, after your death, of assets that do not have a named beneficiary, are not controlled by a trust, or are not jointly owned (with rights of survivorship). If your retirement plans, stocks, and life insurance policies have named beneficiaries, these assets will pass directly to the named beneficiaries. (That doesn't take them out of your estate for tax purposes; it just means your will doesn't control what happens to them.) Your will can also name guardians for your minor children or any other children for whom you have custody. Everything that is controlled by your will becomes part of your *probate estate.* Probate is the court-supervised transfer of ownership to your heirs. State law controls probate court, and probate can be extremely expensive.

3. *Decide who should get what.* You need to think about what you have and to whom you want it to go after your death. Do you want to leave everything to your spouse? Do you want your assets divided among your spouse, your children, and your three best friends? Do you want your ailing parents to get a share? You can give your personal or real property to beneficiaries through your will or through a *trust.* Besides being a form of control, a trust can help you minimize your estate taxes. Minor children can't control assets (to buy or sell property, a person must be the legal age in your state, which may be 18 or 21), so if you leave your minor children assets outright, the court

413

will appoint a guardian who will insist your assets be invested in the safest of investments. If you own a business, you'll want to make sure your heirs don't have to sell the business to pay the estate taxes.

4. *Enlist an estate team.* The *executor* will be responsible for gathering your assets after your death, overseeing or handling the probate proceedings, and distributing your assets to your heirs, according to your expressed wishes. You may name your spouse, your child, your attorney, or your best friend as executor. You may even name several people as co-executors. It is important and easier on everyone that at least one executor lives in the state in which you had your legal residence before your death.

The *guardian* will raise your minor children if you and your spouse die. Choose the guardian(s) carefully, and don't have the guardianship come as a surprise. Discuss your decision with any person(s) you are naming as guardian(s), and be sure you have a firm and informed agreement that they will care for and raise your children. Make sure it won't be a financial or emotional hardship for them to raise your children. If you're divorced, the probate judge may or may not follow your wishes. If your children's other parent is still living, the probate judge may award custody to the parent, even though you've explained your reasons for choosing an alternate guardian.

A *trustee* is in charge of one or more of your trusts. You can choose an institution (usually, a bank), but it will charge fees for the service. A family member may or may not charge a fee for his or her services as trustee.

Agents are people you name to make decisions for you in case you can't.

Do you need a separate person for each of these tasks? No. But you may want an additional or separate trustee (other than your children's guardian) to oversee your children's money. Also, depending on the size and complexity of your estate, and whether minor children are involved, the decision load may be too heavy for one person. If your sister is your executor, the trustee of your trust accounts, and the guardian of your children, your death may be tough for her to handle emotionally, in addition to taking in your children and dealing with all of the after-death matters.

A *durable power of attorney* gives someone the right to act on your behalf if you become incapacitated. A durable power of attorney for financial matters allows your agent to buy and sell stock, your home, or other assets. With a durable power of attorney for health care, you designate someone to make health care decisions for you. (This is different from a *living will*, in which you express how you want your health care to be handled at the end of your life. For samples of the Illinois Power of Attorney for Health Care, Power of Attorney for Property, and Living Will, see pages 438–441.)

5. *Create your estate plan.* Talk to one and maybe two different professionals at this point. An *estate planner* (a financial planner with special training in estates) can help you organize your estate and plan how your assets should be distributed. An *estate attorney* can do the same things plus draft the documentation and make sure all arrangements made are legal in your state. In many states, only an estate attorney can actually draft trusts. However, an estate planner, whose hourly fee is less than an attorney's fee, can be hired to get things in order. Try to minimize your estate taxes. An estate planner may recommend: setting up trusts that protect each spouse's unified tax credits; maximizing the unlimited marital deduction; bypassing the surviving spouse and giving bequests directly to children or grandchildren; using life insurance to pay any estate taxes owed; or making charitable gifts. Each of these estate-planning tools is a way to help minimize estate taxes and transfer to your heirs as much of your estate as possible.

6. *Sign all the paperwork.* You can create all the trusts you want, and write a new will each week, but if you don't sign the paperwork, it means nothing. If you create a trust but don't put any assets into it, the trust is meaningless. How do you put assets into a trust? For a home, you must sign and record a new deed that lists the trust as the owner of record. To change stock ownership, you must send the transfer agent, by certified mail, the original certificate for the shares, along with a letter asking that they be reissued in the name of the trust. (If a corporation or its agent is holding shares in your account, you may not have received an actual stock certificate.) To change your bank accounts, you'll have to sign the documents required by each financial institution. To change the beneficiary on your life insurance policy or retirement accounts, you'll have to sign new documentation. Estate attorneys can prepare this paperwork for you, though you'll pay a bit extra for that service. As for your will, until you sign the most

current version (with witnesses present), any older signed version remains in effect. If you don't have a will, state law is in effect.

7. *Prepare a living will.* A *living will* is a vital document. It isn't long—perhaps just a page, double-spaced. In it, you declare that you either want or don't want doctors and emergency medical professionals to do everything in their power to prolong your life in the event of an incurable and irreversible injury, disease, or illness. (For a sample of a living will, see page 438.)

8. *Assign a durable power of attorney.* A durable power of attorney for health care and a durable power of attorney for financial matters are two other extremely useful documents. With a durable power of attorney, you designate someone to act on your behalf, and make decisions for you, if you become incapable of doing so. A durable power of attorney for health care gives someone the authority to make medical decisions for you—hopefully, in accordance with the wishes you've expressed in your living will. An individual who has a durable power of attorney for financial matters can make financial decisions, including selling your home and stocks so that you have enough money to live on. (See Question 96 for more information and a sample of each document.)

If you have assets in several states, their distribution may be covered under different laws. Trusts can be particularly useful in this situation. Ask your estate attorney or financial planner for guidance.

These are complicated topics, and it's important that you have a plan of action. Here is a quick reference list of where to find detailed discussions of these issues:

Topic	Information Source	Page
Holding title to property	Question 88	417
Probate	Question 89	419
Wills	Question 90	421
Taxes	Question 91	424
Trusts	Question 92 to 94	427–430
Charitable giving	Question 95	434
A living will and a durable power of attorney for financial matters	Question 96	436

HOW SHOULD I HOLD TITLE TO MY INVESTMENTS?

As we discussed in Question 40, regarding how to hold title to a home, there are several different forms of ownership, and each has a slightly different effect on how you pass down your assets.

Here's a brief look at the different ways you can hold title to your property:

- *Sole ownership.* You own it, you have the financial responsibility for it, you get the rewards from it, and you can sell it whenever you want. You may also name any beneficiary you want to have it after you die.

- *Joint tenancy with rights of survivorship.* With this arrangement, you both own the property. Should one owner die, the other owner automatically inherits the deceased's interests.

- *Tenancy in common.* You and your co-owner(s) own portions of the property. You may each own equal shares, or the ownership may be in different amounts. And you each have the right to dispose of your share as you wish. Should you die while you own property as tenants in common, your piece of the property goes to your estate, and will be divvied up according to instructions in your will. If you die without a will, the property will be divided up as designated by your state's law.

- *Tenancy of the entirety.* Only a husband and wife can be tenants of the entirety. It means you and your spouse each own the whole property. Tenancy of the entirety can help shield your home from the creditors of one spouse. As long as you both own the home, it's untouchable by creditors of either spouse. When you sell it, or cease using it as your primary residence, creditors may go after the proceeds of the home.

- *Community property.* States that have community property laws are Arizona, California, Idaho, Louisiana, Nevada, New Mexico, Texas, Washington, and Wisconsin. If you have community property, your part of it is divided equally between your spouse and your estate after your death. Community property raises very complex issues, especially if you move to a state that doesn't allow it. Check with your estate attorney or financial planner for advice.

- *Trusts.* Trusts allow you to control and be the beneficiary of your assets, but not to own them. There are two kinds of trusts:

417

(1) revocable trusts, or living trusts, can take the place of a will and keep your estate out of probate court; (2) irrevocable trusts can do that *and* help you minimize your estate taxes.

Why the Way You Hold Title Is Important

From an estate point of view, two issues come up when you own property:

1. *Tax consequences.* As we just discussed, the way you own property controls that property and its disposition after you die. Property owned as joint tenants with rights of survivorship, for example, allows you to automatically pass on ownership by operation of law (in states that have it, and most do). But it may not minimize taxes. A properly drawn irrevocable trust that names you as beneficiary will get that property out of your estate, thereby minimizing your estate taxes.

2. *Probate consequences.* The way you own property determines whether your estate goes through probate. For example, if you have $2 million in a joint brokerage account, you could write wills and create trusts and it wouldn't matter. The account will pass to your co-owner because joint tenancy takes precedence

After you die, the state examines how you've provided for your estate. Do you have a will? If you die intestate (without a will), the state will appoint someone to shepherd your estate through probate, and will parcel out your estate according to state law. If you have a will, your estate will go through probate, after which it will be distributed to your heirs. If you have a revocable trust, your estate will avoid probate and pass directly to your heirs, although you may have excess estate taxes. An irrevocable trust will ensure that your heirs receive as much as they can and, if done properly, will minimize the estate taxes you pay.

It's important to pay attention, while you're alive, to the way you own property. Undoing it after you're gone may be either impossible or extremely expensive. Doing it right the first time, or changing things as your life changes, is how you should handle your financial (and your personal) affairs.

over the wishes you express in your will. Also, probate is expensive, time-consuming, and very public. If you don't want your assets put on public display, spend some time making sure your estate avoids probate.

WHAT IS PROBATE?

QUESTION
89

Probate is a legal process that effectively "cleanses" your assets and distributes them according to instructions left in your will—or, if there is no will, then according to state statute. The cleansing ensures that no claims are attached to your assets before they are distributed to your heirs.

If you die *intestate* (without a will), *probate court* will enforce the state's statutes, name a guardian for your minor children, and appoint an administrator who will handle the court proceedings, contact your heirs, and handle the details. If you have a will, the named *executor* will have the job of collecting your assets, paying any bills or taxes that are owed, and distributing what's left to the rightful heirs.

Almost every estate goes through probate, but you should try to avoid probate court. It is typically expensive and time-consuming. On the expense side, for example, the court-appointed administrator may get a percentage of your estate as a fee. (Your executor may be paid, or may refuse to take a fee.) Either the court-appointed administrator or a family member will have to post a bond (to protect against theft of your money). Filing fees may eat up another chunk of your estate. Timewise, a year or more may pass before the administrator gives proper notice to all known and unknown creditors and can close out the estate.

Finally, probate court is extremely public. A listing of your assets will become part of the public record.

How can you avoid probate court? There's only one way: *Create trust accounts.* If you create the appropriate trusts and actually put assets into them, you should be able to avoid probate. But a revocable trust will not minimize your estate taxes. A properly drawn irrevocable trust should help you minimize the estate taxes your heirs will owe.

If you don't create trust accounts, a valid, written, signed will is your best bet for speeding up the probate process and lowering your probate costs.

Live Rich, Die Cheap

If you want the probating of your estate to happen quickly, easily, and cheaply, consider these issues when getting your estate in order:

- *Get good help.* A session or two with a good estate attorney can help you organize and clean up your estate.
- *Name an heir as your executor.* Banks, lawyers, and court-appointed administrators will take a chunk of your estate as a fee. In some states, attorneys are entitled to legal fees on top of executor fees. Your executor-heir is entitled to a fee, but he or she may refuse it. If you don't want to burden your heirs with executor duties, consider a non-heir sibling, cousin, or friend who may be willing to lend a hand. Also, as we discussed earlier, at least one of your executors should reside in the state (preferably, the city) in which you lived at the time of your death. Why? Because closing your estate will take some time, perhaps a long time, and having at least one of your executors reside in the same state (if not the same city) should be a faster and more economical way of settling your affairs.
- *Leave detailed instructions and lists of assets.* Above and beyond an enforceable will, you should leave a list of all your assets, where they're located, the location's contact-name, address, and phone number, and the location of any keys to safe deposit boxes you may have (in which you've already put your important papers). You should also list your liabilities (mortgages, credit cards debts), your insurance policies (with the policies' contact names and claims phone numbers), and credit cards you hold (with numbers and customer service numbers). Include the name and number of the estate attorney who assisted you. This information should be updated regularly and kept in a very safe place.
- *Make it easy.* As we discussed earlier, there's no need for you to have thirty different brokerage accounts at thirty different firms. Consolidate everything into one or two places. Consolidate your credit cards to just one or two cards with bigger balances. Consolidate your portfolios into one fund family (so you have one statement coming each month, and one place for your heirs to go). Try to buy your insurance from one or two different companies (but if you have long-standing policies, keep them).

- *Keep your beneficiaries current.* How many times have you heard the story about the husband in a second marriage who dies suddenly? His wife, and mother of their three children, finds out too late that his life insurance policy, in force before they knew each other, names his ex-spouse as beneficiary. She gets it all, and the wife and mother ends up with nothing. As your life changes, make sure you change the beneficiaries on your insurance policies, retirement accounts, and other assets. Make sure your trust agreements are updated to include future children and grandchildren.

WHEN SHOULD I DRAW UP A WILL?

A valid, enforceable will could be one of the most important documents you sign. If you don't sign it and have it properly witnessed *and* notarized, your estate will be distributed according to the laws of the state in which you live. Your wishes will be discarded.

In New York, for example, if you die intestate (without a will), your spouse will get one-third of your estate, and your children will get two-thirds. If you don't have children, your parents will inherit. If your parents are dead, your siblings will inherit, and so on. If that works for you, fine. If you want your spouse to get everything, you'll have to write up a will, or follow some of the other suggestions in this chapter.

Some costs will still be associated with executing your will, but they will be far lower than the costs, if you die intestate.

Contesting a Will

One of the problems with allowing the distribution of your estate to be governed entirely by a will is that unhappy heirs, or those who feel they should be heirs but aren't, can contest your will. If you're concerned that someone may contest your will, add to it a *no-contest provision.* This basically says: If you contest the will, you forfeit your entire bequest. (The bequest would have to be worth holding onto.) A no-contest provision won't prevent someone *not named* in the will from contesting it.

Another strategy to avoid probate and protect against having people contest your will is to put your assets in a revocable trust, also known as a living trust. (See Question 92 for details.)

You can't preclude the possibility that someone will contest your will, but by doing it right the first time, and making sure it has been properly signed and notarized, you limit the chances that the will might be altered.

Things Change

Nothing stays the same. After you're gone, your heirs may need to alter the arrangements you made. For example, your will should name the trustees for trusts that you've set up. But if you name a bank as trustee, and the bank doesn't do the job, your heirs may want to remove the bank as trustee and name someone else. Make sure the attorney who drafts your will names a family member or friend as co-trustee with an institution, and provides him or her with the power to remove the institution as trustee of the accounts.

A Good Will Doesn't Have to Be Long

When former Supreme Court Chief Justice Warren Burger died, he left a will that, as wills go, wasn't very long. It all fit on one page. He typed it out on his computer, and it basically said the following:

1. My executors will first pay all claims against my estate.
2. The remainder of my estate will be distributed as follows: one-third to my daughter, Margaret Elizabeth Burger Rose, and two-thirds to my son, Wade A. Burger.
3. I designate and appoint, as executors of this will, Wade A. Burger and J. Michael Luttig.

Justice Burger left an estate estimated to be $1.8 million. Perhaps a little too short and sweet, his will failed to grant the executors the power to sell his real estate (which might require a court order). If his children had been minors, he would've needed to name a guardian for them.

What does this teach us? Wills don't have to be long and complicated. If your estate is in order (i.e., beneficiaries named, trusts established, and so on), you may be able to write your own will.

But be aware: A badly written will is often worse than having no will at all.

Wills in a Box

Where can you get a model of a simple will? Some people turn to the "will in a box."

With all the great technology and software available, and in the interest of saving a few bucks, you might be tempted to write your own will or create your own trust. I strongly advise against trying to write these documents yourself. Wills and trusts are highly complicated these days, and the tax opportunities you'll be trying to maximize are tough to negotiate. Your local stationery store probably sells forms for wills (and perhaps even for trust agreements), and your local computer store will have do-it-yourself-rather-than-hire-a-lawyer software. Leave both products in the stores. Hire a competent professional who can help tailor each document to your needs and who will write you a will that will stand up in case someone contests it.

If you're hell-bent to do this yourself, at least have an attorney review your finished product, to make sure it matches the laws and requirements of the state in which you live.

I can just hear you saying, "But Justice Burger wrote his own will." That's true. But he was a former Supreme Court Chief Justice, a lawyer with many years of practice behind him, and who, undoubtedly, had many lawyer friends who specialize in estates. And, he was represented personally by an attorney.

One more time: Unless you know what you're doing, check with a professional before relying on a will or a trust in a box.

Remember, if you don't sign your will and have your signature witnessed and notarized, the state will consider your latest prior will to be valid. If you don't have any will when you die, the state considers you intestate. Dying intestate can hurt the ones you wanted to help most. Also, remember to leave the original will (signed, witnessed, and notarized) in your safe deposit box. A copy should be in your attorney's files.

423

QUESTION 91

WHAT IS THE UNIFIED TAX CREDIT, HOW MUCH INHERITANCE TAX WILL I PAY, AND HOW MUCH IS THE GIFT TAX?

Federal estate and gift taxes are frequently referred to as *transfer taxes* because they only go into effect when you transfer your assets to someone else. If you do it while you're alive, it's a gift. If you do it after you die, your assets are part of your estate.

The estate and gift tax structures are identical. On anything over the limit, the estate and gift tax rate ranges from 37 percent to 55 percent (on gifts over $3 million). Ouch!

Before you start worrying about how much your kids *aren't* going to get, let's look at the actual "limit." Uncle Sam allows you to pass down $625,000 (in 1998) before estate or gift taxes kick in. This is called the *unified tax credit*. It's referred to as a tax *credit* because you actually get a tax credit equal to the amount of tax you'd owe on $625,000 (or whatever the number is in the year you die) on your estate tax return. (Your executors are required to file two tax returns for you after you've died: your final income tax return, due by April 15 of the year *after* the year you passed away, and an estate return.)

You and your spouse *each* get to pass on $625,000 without incurring gift or estate tax. But to take full advantage of that unified tax credit amount, you have to separate at least some of your assets into two pots. (This may open up another can of worms.) If you plan right, you can give away a combined $1.25 million without triggering any taxes. (See Questions 92 through 94 for information on trusts that can help you minimize estate taxes.)

Go above the limit and it starts to get expensive. The first $625,000 can be given tax-free. The next $100,000 you give away is taxed at 37 percent, so it would cost you $137,000: $37,000 for Uncle Sam and $100,000 to your heirs. Give away $10 million and you'll pay more than half to the government.

Here's what the current gift and estate tax structure looks like:

The first $625,000	Tax-free
$625,000 to $750,000	37 percent
$751,000 to $1 million	39 percent
$1 million to 1.25 million	41 percent

$1.25 million to $1.5 million	43 percent
$1.5 million to $2 million	45 percent
$2 million to $2.5 million	49 percent
$2.5 million to $3 million	53 percent
$3 million and up	55 percent

In addition to the unified tax credit, anyone may give a gift of up to $10,000 (starting in 1999, this amount will be indexed for inflation) to any individual once a year. And you may give this gift year in and year out without it counting against your $625,000 exemption. For example, if you have three children, you may give each child $10,000 once a year. If you're married, you and your spouse may give each child $20,000 per year. If each child is married, you can give that couple (your child and his or her spouse) $40,000. If that family has two children, you may give the family $80,000. When all's said and done, you can give away up to $240,000 per year without having it count toward your $625,000 limit.

But if you give, say, $12,000 to an individual in a single year, that's $2,000 more than is allowed. Instead of paying gift taxes (the giver, by the way, always pays the gift tax) at the time you give the gift, the amount is subtracted from your $625,000 transfer tax exemption. When you die, you'd then be able to leave only $623,000 tax-free (or whatever the limit is by then, minus $2,000). Is there a way to get around that penalty? Give half the gift in one year, and the rest in the next. Or give it from yourself and your spouse.

How does the IRS know what you've given? You are required to report it on IRS Form 709 (you can download the form from <www.irs.gov>). When you've exceeded the $625,000 limit, you'll have to pay gift tax in the year after you make the gift.

Giving Is Cheaper Than Bequeathing

Getting that gift money out of your estate means you ultimately will pay less in estate taxes. Why? Because gift tax is tax-exclusive and estate tax is tax-inclusive. In other words, when you pay gift tax (during your lifetime), the gift and the tax are removed from your estate. If you leave the gift money in your estate until you die, it will be part of

425

the amount on which you'll be taxed. You pay estate tax on *all* of your money, including money used to pay the estate tax due!

This is another example of how we pay tax on tax. A similar situation develops with retirement accounts that you leave to your heirs. Your estate pays estate tax on the entire estate—including your retirement accounts—and then income tax on your retirement account funds.

Another reason to give away gift money while you're alive is that you can play with the value. The estate tax and gift tax are based on the fair market value at the time the gift is made or the time of your death. Some things are easy to value. If you own stock, the fair market value is established at the end of each trading day. If you own a house, the estate will have to hire an appraiser to pin a value on your home. But if you own a closely held business and give away small pieces of it, you may be able to discount the value of the asset for IRS purposes and pass it along while saving a load of gift or estate taxes. (This trick is known as a limited partnership. I know I railed against most limited partnerships as an investment. This is different. As an estate-planning tool, limited partnerships in homes, land, or businesses can be valuable. Ask an estate attorney or financial planner for help in determining whether a limited partnership can be a beneficial estate-planning tool for you.)

Another reason to pass along some or all of your money while you're alive: You get to see your heirs enjoy the money while you're still around.

Other Ways of Giving to Your Heirs Without Giving to the IRS

The government allows you to pay someone else's college tuition or medical bills gift-tax-free. No matter how much they are. The catch? You have to pay the college or medical care source directly.

"But I Don't Have $625,000"

Do you own a home? Do you have life insurance? If you have $200,000 in equity in your home and a life insurance policy for

$500,000, you're already over the limit. If you have only $50,000 in equity in your home, two $140,000 life insurance policies, an IRA you inherited from your mom, worth $65,000, some investments worth $60,000, and a retirement account worth $100,000, that's $490,000 right there. If you're age forty-five, it's likely that your investments will continue to grow and may put you over the limit (whatever it is by then) by the time you're into your sixties.

> If you're young and you already have a stable of assets that's growing nicely, plan as though you're going to be over the limit when you die. If something happens to you suddenly, you'll have everything organized. If it doesn't save you estate or gift taxes, it may spare your heirs a massive headache, just when they're missing you the most.

WHAT IS A LIVING TRUST, AND WHAT IS AN IRREVOCABLE TRUST?

QUESTION
92

There are basically two types of trusts: revocable and irrevocable. A *revocable trust*, also known as a *living trust*, allows you to transfer your stocks, property, and other assets into the trust and become the trust's beneficiary for as long as you live. The trust is revocable: you can change it or cancel it at any time. An *irrevocable trust* can't be changed or altered once it is set up.

The nice thing about a living trust is that it allows you to do everything a will allows you to do, including designating who will be the beneficiary of the trust after you die. It also allows for a speedy transfer of assets, some savings on probate filing fees, and a generally simple way for dealing with assets owned in several states (perhaps you live in Michigan but own a vacation home in Colorado).

Living trusts come in a variety of forms. You'll hear them called "Sweetheart Trusts" or "Living and Loving Trusts." The question you have to ask yourself is: Who retains control? If you retain control over your assets, the trust is revocable and is a simple living trust.

And that's a problem if you were hoping to get your assets out of your estate. Until you give up control, you haven't really given away your money. And if you haven't given away your money, you haven't minimized taxes. That's what an irrevocable trust is for.

With an irrevocable trust, you give up the ultimate control of your money or assets, and control generally rests with those to whom you've given the gift. For example, if you give your nephew $10,000, he can put a down payment on a house or blow the money on buying round after round of drinks for the guys at the local pub. The point is, you no longer have control over the cash or assets, and you can never remove them. But, depending on how you structure the trust, you may still be able to limit what happens to those assets.

When you lose control, the IRS considers that you've given away the money and removed it from your estate. That's when you start to minimize your estate taxes.

How can you maximize the value of your irrevocable trust? There are countless varieties of trusts. Many are legal, some are possibly legal, and the rest you have to wonder about. Here are just two examples. See an estate planner or an estate attorney for other ideas.

1. *Life insurance trust.* You set up a trust and name your four children as the beneficiaries of the trust. Because you and your wife are each allowed to give $10,000 to anyone, you may each make a deposit of $40,000 ($10,000 for each child, from each of you) to the trust. That sets aside $80,000 to pay the premium on a so-called "second-to-die" life insurance policy. With second-to-die insurance, the benefit will be paid out (to the trust, which holds the policy) upon the death of the spouse who dies last. The insurance money is then out of your estate and can be used to pay any estate taxes that are due.

What do I need to know? On gifts like this, the IRS wants to see that you've really given away the money. That's where *Crummey powers* come in. (Mr. Crummey was the first person to do this and successfully fight off the IRS, which said it wasn't legal.) A gift in trust is a gift of the future, not of the present. You make it qualify as a gift of present value by informing the beneficiaries of the trust that they have an opportunity—once a year, for a total of thirty days—to withdraw the money you've placed in the trust to pay for the life insurance premium. If they don't withdraw the money within the specified time frame, the right to do so lapses. (Your beneficiaries would understand that if they did withdraw the money, you'd cease funding the trust.)

2. *Qualified Personal Residence Trust (QPRT).* This type of trust (you may see clones of it listed under several names or acronyms) is a fairly common way of passing along property, over time, at a

discounted rate. Say you start with a property worth $500,000 today. The owner is seventy years old, and he thinks he's going to live another fifteen years. The term of the trust is then set for fifteen years or the day of his death, whichever comes first. Because the property is valued over fifteen years, the present value of the gift, for IRS purposes, is only $76,355. You pay gift taxes on that amount, rather than the $500,000 the property is actually worth.

What do I need to know? If you die during the term of the trust, you haven't saved anything because the property reverts back to your estate, and your heirs inherit it at its fair market value on the day you die. But your losses are limited to what the attorney charged to set up the trust. If you outlive the trust, and the property passes to the beneficiaries, their cost basis is whatever you paid for the property. Let's say the value of the property is $778,000 (assuming 3 percent annual appreciation) after fifteen years. If the combined federal and state death tax bracket is 55 percent, the potential death tax savings is $386,446. When they sell the property, years later, the beneficiaries may still owe capital gains tax. But paying 20 percent of the gain is far cheaper than paying 37 to 55 percent in estate tax. And if they move into the property and it becomes their personal residence, they might be able to claim up to the first $250,000 (or $500,000 if they're married) in tax-free capital gains.

How far can you take a life insurance trust? One woman went to her tax lawyer and said, "I have five married children, and twenty-five grandchildren and great-grandchildren. I want a huge trust that covers them all." She ended up with a trust that had thirty beneficiaries, and she deposited $300,000 per year for three years to pay the insurance premiums.

The cost of drafting a very simple trust ranges from $500 to $2,000. Estate planners might charge $1,000 to $3,000 to organize an entire estate. An estate attorney might charge $2,000 to draft a will and a trust agreement. Shop around, but don't always choose the lowest price. You want your documents to stand up, so hire a professional who really knows what he or she is doing. Ask to check references, and then call a few. (For more tips on hiring an estate planner or an estate attorney, see Question 99.)

WHAT IS A BYPASS TRUST?

A *bypass trust*, also known as a *credit shelter trust* or *exemption trust*, allows married couples to preserve their unified credit exemption. In other words, instead of wasting the $625,000 (or whatever the amount is when you die) that each of us can pass along tax-free, this trust allows you to separate some of your assets and pass them on directly to your children or other heirs, while giving your spouse the lifetime right to the income from the trust.

The need for this trust is rooted in the idea that your spouse can inherit your entire estate tax-free. That's the good news. The bad news is that when your spouse dies, he or she will be able to bequeath only $625,000 tax-free. Because you didn't separate out your $625,000, it's as if your unified credit exemption didn't exist.

How does a bypass trust work? You create a trust with $625,000 worth of your assets, including perhaps your retirement account, life insurance policies, and some stocks and bonds. Your spouse receives the income from the trust for life, plus any principal he or she needs for health, education, or support. When your spouse dies, what's left goes to your children outright.

The important action with a bypass trust (and all trusts) is to actually change the name on all of your assets. For example, instead of owning shares of stock in your name, they'll be owned in the name of your trust. That's called *funding the trust.* If you don't fund the trust, creating it was a waste of time and money because it won't do anything. Even if you direct that everything you own be placed into a trust upon your death, if you and your spouse own your property as joint tenants with rights of survivorship, your spouse will inherit everything outright instead.

WHAT OTHER KINDS OF TRUSTS EXIST?

As I continued researching this chapter, it became clear that every estate attorney (and some folks who aren't estate attorneys) has created various trusts to suit every client's whims and desires. As long as the trusts meet basic IRS definitions and tests, they're probably fine. Trusts can be called by various names, however, so it may be difficult to know exactly what your estate attorney is talking about.

Here are a few more examples of popularly used trusts and estate-planning tools:

- *Grantor Retained Annuity Trust (GRAT).* A GRAT is somewhere between a revocable trust (where you pay no gift taxes but pay hefty estate taxes later on) and an irrevocable trust (minimizes estate taxes). Let's say you have $3 million in tax-exempt municipal bonds (with a 5 percent interest rate). The investment brings in $150,000 per year, but your living expenses are only $50,000 per year. If you die holding the money, Uncle Sam gets about half. By creating a GRAT, you effectively get the money out of your estate. What will you live on? You can set an amount that you'll receive each year from the trust. In addition, you can still manage the trust and buy or sell the stocks or funds now owned by the trust. Like a qualified personal residence trust (QPRT), you choose a term for the trust. Because you're taking money out of the trust and your family doesn't get it outright, the present value of the gift is discounted by the IRS, so less gift tax is due.

- *Grantor Retained Income Trust (GRIT).* This trust is similar to the GRAT, and it works well for nonrelated people. Here's how it works. You transfer your assets into the trust, but retain all of the income for a specified period of time. At the end of the term, what's left goes to your partner or friend. Because your gift is a gift of the future, you're able to take advantage of a significant discount of the value of the money. Why? Because the present value of a gift you're giving in, say, fifteen years, is far less than if you gave it today.

- *Sprinkling trust.* You want your children to have your money, but you're worried about their inheriting a big wad when they're age eighteen or even age twenty-five. So you design an irrevocable trust that parcels out some of your cash over a number of years. One Chicago woman decided her children should get a third of their inheritance when they turned age thirty-five, a third ten years later, and the balance when they reached age fifty-five. Her reasoning? She wanted her children to have a comfortable retirement, and not spend her money on daily living expenses. A doctor had a daughter in a cult that encouraged its members to give all that they owned to the cult's central bank account. Rather than see his money disappear down a deep hole, he instructed the trustee to parcel out the money in little bits to his daughter over her lifetime. Another way to sprinkle an inheritance is to provide a matching amount based on your heirs' earning power. If they earn $15,000, they receive 15 cents on the dollar. Once their income reaches $45,000, they receive a 100 percent matching amount. Sounds good. But suppose you have a daughter who opts to stay at home to raise her children. She may not bring in any income, but is her contribution to her family any less valuable?

• *Limited partnerships.* We've talked about these before, but here's an example of how one really works. Let's say you have a business worth $10 million. If you keep 1 percent of the business (but as general partner, you retain control of all day-to-day operations) and then pass along the rest of the business to your heirs, only the 1 percent that you currently own is included in your estate when you die. Taxwise, you might do fairly well:

1. The present value of the gift is devalued because each limited partner doesn't own enough to control the business.

2. The gift is being given over time (in fact, if you give $10,000 pieces of the business over a long period of time, you may have no taxes to pay at all).

3. Income from a limited partnership is taxed at the heir's current tax bracket, perhaps as low as 15 percent. For an extra layer of control, some estate planners suggest putting the proceeds from each heir's share into a trust.

These are a few examples of the ways estate planners help their clients control their wealth and reduce estate taxes. For more information, you'll want to consult a financial planner, estate planner, or estate attorney.

Mistakes We Make

It's tough to give money away fairly. Even if you divide everything equally, there's no guarantee that someone won't be angry about something. That's the nature of money and property.

But parents often make some classic mistakes when leaving money to their children, relatives, or friends. Here are some things to avoid doing:

1. *Being unfair for no reason.* Just because you think your daughter married well but your son is struggling, this is not a reason for you to give him everything and leave her nothing but a token payment. If you distinguish between your children without even a glimmer of explanation, you're setting up the family to crack into pieces. If you're going to leave money and property unequally, have a solid reason for doing so, and communicate that reason to your family.

2. *Failing to communicate.* This is the second biggest mistake people make with their estates. An unequal distribution of assets might at least be understood if you leave a lengthy letter explaining yourself. Even better, sit down with your kids and have a heart-to-heart talk about what you have, where you've decided it should go, and why. Money-grubbing or spendthrift children may never change, but you'll die knowing you've tried to explain the whys of your estate, and given them the opportunity to ask you questions. After you're gone, it's too late.

3. *Failing to plan your estate.* If you don't leave your estate in good order, someone's going to have to come in and clean it up. Estate attorneys say that heirs are often bitter when more of an estate goes to the government than is necessary. Maybe you've failed to pay your real estate taxes for the past four years, and your home has been sold, and now the back taxes have to be paid and the property bought back. Adding this kind of mess on top of the emotional weight of a close friend's or family member's death is often enough to send your heirs over the edge.

4. *Doing something because someone else says to do it.* Your estate needs to make sense to only one person—you. If you're married, it should make sense for you and your spouse. Don't allow guilt to make you do things you know aren't right. Likewise, don't hire someone you can't trust, and don't use financial instruments you don't fully understand (like complicated trusts).

Planning your estate should give you a sense of comfort. If it doesn't, there's probably something wrong. Look into the source of your discomfort, and take the steps necessary to correct it. Remember: As your life changes, so should your estate plan.

433

HOW SHOULD I GIVE A GIFT TO A NONPROFIT ORGANIZATION?

Big gifts always get publicity. Two hundred million dollars here, $30 million there. Add it all up and pretty soon you're talking about real money.

You don't have to give a lot for your gift to make a difference to your personal finances. Giving offers an opportunity to put your money where your mouth is. If you don't like drunk drivers careening through neighborhoods, you can give a gift that will support Mothers Against Drunk Drivers (MADD). If you're religious, you can give to your church, temple, or synagogue. If you want to help abused women, you can give to a shelter.

The opportunities for giving are endless. Once you decide where you want your money to go, you need to figure out the best way of making your donation.

If you give your gift outright, while you're alive, you'll be allowed to take a tax deduction. If the gift is large enough, it may offset all of your income for the year. But you'll lose control of the money. If you give your gift through a *charitable trust*—that is, a trust whose beneficiary is a nonprofit organization or charity—it can continue to generate income for you, while taking assets out of your estate and producing a nice tax deduction in the year you make your gift.

For example, if you owned $5 million of IBM stock and sold it today, you'd pay $1 million in capital gains taxes and have $4 million left over. When you die, your estate will pay slightly more than $2 million in estate taxes. So, out of the $5 million, you'll be left with only $2 million, or 40 percent of your original investment.

However, if you put $1 million of IBM stock into a charitable remainder income trust, you and your spouse will receive dividends for life, you'll eliminate the capital gains tax you would have owed, your estate will have less money in it, and you'll have a nice tax deduction. I've used a large figure, but it works nearly as well if you have a smaller pool of assets.

Here is a sampling of some of the different kinds of trusts available for charitable gifts:

- *Charitable Remainder Income Trust (CRIT)*. You give a major asset (like stock or artwork) to a qualified charity. The asset is sold, and the proceeds are put into a trust account you've set up in advance. The trust is managed by the charity or an investment manager. You (and your spouse) receive income from the trust as long as you live. When you die, the charity gets everything.

- *Charitable Lead Trust (CLT).* A CRIT in reverse. You give your assets to the charity, which places them in a trust. The charity receives income as long as you live. When you die, the assets are turned over to your heirs.

- *Life estate agreement.* You give your home to a nonprofit organization, and are allowed to live in the home for the rest of your lives. When you sign over the home, you receive a tax deduction. When you die, the property goes to the charity.

- *Life insurance trust.* You purchase life insurance and name the charity the beneficiary. You give much more than you'd otherwise be able to, and your estate gets a far bigger deduction after you die.

- *Charitable trust with insurance.* You decide to give a certain amount of assets to a charity. You put these in a charitable trust and then purchase life insurance equal to the assets you're giving away. You then put the life insurance in the trust. When you die, the trust hands your assets over to the charity, but the life insurance proceeds are distributed to your heirs.

- *Gift annuity.* Many nonprofit organizations, universities, or charities offer gift annuities. You buy into the gift annuity, and it pays you a fixed income for life. When you die, the charity gets the asset. Your tax benefit is based on when you start taking payments from the charity.

- *Pooled income fund.* This is basically a mutual fund for charities. You put money in (i.e., donate it to the fund) and, as it grows, you give more money than you might otherwise have been able to give.

Many planners today are using aggressive valuation techniques when calculating the present value of a gift for IRS purposes. Make sure you're comfortable with these tactics. If you're not, you'll spend your final years wondering whether the IRS is going to catch you.

If you're making a gift to a large, well-established charitable organization, you shouldn't pay any fees at all for setting up the trust. Many of these organizations will do it for you. They've become very sophisticated about doing the paperwork. In that way, they know it's getting done.

The Bottom Line

There are some great tax incentives for giving money. And yet, few wealthy people who can truly afford to do so actually give as much as they might. Partly, this is a control issue. Many people just can't let go of their money. What they don't realize is that, by giving their wealth away, so much more will come back to them. Giving isn't something to be done only for tax purposes. If you can afford it, giving is the right thing to do. And in a world where right and wrong often seem topsy-turvy, helping out those who are less fortunate is always a solid and satisfying move.

WHAT IS A LIVING WILL, AND WHAT IS A DURABLE POWER OF ATTORNEY?

QUESTION 96

The last piece of your estate plan should be the writing of your living will, durable power of attorney for health care, and durable power of attorney for financial matters.

A living will is a statement that tells the world how you want to die. If you're injured in a horrible accident, or develop an incurable

If you want your living will to be effective, you need to make its existence known to the people who care about your health most: your spouse, your family, your best friends, and your doctor. You should give a signed copy of your living will to your doctor and have him or her attach it to your permanent records. There have been cases where a living will has been on file and life-prolonging methods were used anyway. You have a better chance of your wishes being followed if you make them known.

disease, and you're very near the end of your life, you can use a living will (signed earlier) to declare that you don't want your life prolonged unnecessarily.

On page 438 is a living will declaration, valid only in the State of Illinois. Your state may offer one with similar wording.

Signing a living will can be tough. Basically, you're signing a declaration that recognizes you won't live forever. But having a living will can help to smooth out what is often a horribly rough period. You personally may or may not know or recognize the effects, but your living will may save your family from an emotional dispute over what your last wishes really were.

Durable Powers of Attorney

As we discussed earlier, a durable power of attorney gives the person you designate—your *agent*—broad powers to act on your behalf. There are two principal types of powers of attorney: (1) a power of attorney for property (also known as a power of attorney for financial matters) and (2) a power of attorney for health care.

A power of attorney for property gives your agent the power to pledge, sell, or otherwise dispose of your real estate or other personal property without giving you advance notice or seeking your approval. Your agent must act on your behalf, but he or she has pretty broad powers. Unless you limit the term, you typically assign a power of attorney indefinitely. You can end a term by revoking the grant.

A power of attorney for health care gives your agent the right to make health care decisions for you, if you become incapable of making them yourself. Besides deciding what medical treatment you should receive, your agent has the power to admit you to, or have you discharged from, a hospital, nursing home, or other institution. Your agent also has the power to refuse or withdraw medical treatment. A durable power of attorney for health care can be more important than a living will. Too often, a living will never comes to anyone's attention because no one knows where it is. If you give a durable power of attorney for health care to a family member or friend, and provide that person with a copy of your living will, your wishes stand a far greater chance of being followed.

Living Will Declaration

This declaration is made this ____ day of _____ 1998. I, _____,
 being of sound mind, willfully and voluntarily make known my desires that my
moment of death shall not be artificially postponed.

If at any time I should have an incurable and irreversible injury, disease, or illness
judged to be a terminal condition by my attending physician who has personally
examined me and has determined that my death is imminent except for death delaying
procedures and has verified that determination in writing, I direct that such
procedures which would only prolong the dying process be withheld or withdrawn and
that I be permitted to die naturally with only the administration of medication,
sustenance, or the performance of any medical procedure deemed necessary by my
attending physician to provide me with comfort care.

In the absence of my ability to give directions regarding the use of such death
delaying procedures, it is my intention that this declaration shall be honored by my
family and physician as the final expression of my legal right to refuse medical or
surgical treatment and accept the consequences from such refusal.

_____
Name

City of _____

County of _____

State of _____

The declarant is personally known to me and I believe _____ to be
of sound mind. I saw the declarant sign the declaration in my presence and I signed the
declaration as a witness in the presence of the declarant. I did not sign the declarant's
signature above for, or at the direction of, the declarant. At the date of this instrument,
I am not entitled to any portion of the estate of the declarant according to the laws of
interstate succession or, to the best of my knowledge and belief, under any will of
declarant or other instrument taking effect at declarant's death, or directly financially
responsible for declarant's medical care.

_____   Residing at   _____
                                            _____

_____   Residing at   _____
                                            _____

_____   Residing at   _____
                                            _____

Source: State of Illinois Statute.

ILLINOIS STATUTORY SHORT FORM POWER OF ATTORNEY FOR HEALTH CARE

(NOTICE: THE PURPOSE OF THIS POWER OF ATTORNEY IS TO GIVE THE PERSON YOU DESIGNATE (YOUR "AGENT") BROAD POWERS TO MAKE HEALTH CARE DECISIONS FOR YOU, INCLUDING POWER TO REQUIRE, CONSENT TO OR WITHDRAW ANY TYPE OF PERSONAL CARE OR MEDICAL TREATMENT FOR ANY PHYSICAL OR MENTAL CONDITION AND TO ADMIT YOU TO OR DISCHARGE YOU FROM ANY HOSPITAL, HOME OR OTHER INSTITUTION. THIS FORM DOES NOT IMPOSE A DUTY ON YOUR AGENT TO EXERCISE GRANTED POWERS; BUT WHEN POWERS ARE EXERCISED, YOUR AGENT WILL HAVE TO USE DUE CARE TO ACT FOR YOUR BENEFIT AND IN ACCORDANCE WITH THIS FORM AND KEEP A RECORD OF RECEIPTS, DISBURSEMENTS AND SIGNIFICANT ACTIONS TAKEN AS AGENT. A COURT CAN TAKE AWAY THE POWERS OF YOUR AGENT IF IT FINDS THE AGENT IS NOT ACTING PROPERLY. YOU MAY NAME SUCCESSOR AGENTS UNDER THIS FORM BUT NOT CO-AGENTS, AND NO HEALTH CARE PROVIDER MAY BE NAMED. UNLESS YOU EXPRESSLY LIMIT THE DURATION OF THIS POWER IN THE MANNER PROVIDED BELOW, UNTIL YOU REVOKE THIS POWER OR A COURT ACTING ON YOUR BEHALF TERMINATES IT, YOUR AGENT MAY EXERCISE THE POWERS GIVEN HERE THROUGHOUT YOUR LIFETIME, EVEN AFTER YOU BECOME DISABLED. THE POWERS YOU GIVE YOUR AGENT, YOUR RIGHT TO REVOKE THOSE POWERS AND THE PENALTIES FOR VIOLATING THE LAW ARE EXPLAINED MORE FULLY IN SECTIONS 4-5, 4-6, 4-9 AND 4-10(b) OF THE ILLINOIS "POWERS OF ATTORNEY FOR HEALTH CARE LAW" OF WHICH THIS FORM IS A PART (SEE THE BACK OF THIS FORM). THAT LAW EXPRESSLY PERMITS THE USE OF ANY DIFFERENT FORM OF POWER OF ATTORNEY YOU MAY DESIRE. IF THERE IS ANYTHING ABOUT THIS FORM THAT YOU DO NOT UNDERSTAND, YOU SHOULD ASK A LAWYER TO EXPLAIN IT TO YOU.)

Power of Attorney made this _____ day of _____, 19_____.
(month)   (year)

1. I, _____
(insert name and address of principal)

hereby appoint: _____
(insert name and address of agent)

as my attorney-in-fact (my "agent") to act for me and in my name (in any way I could act in person) to make any and all decisions for me concerning my personal care, medical treatment, hospitalization and health care and to require, withhold or withdraw any type of medical treatment or procedure, even though my death may ensue. My agent shall have the same access to my medical records that I have, including the right to disclose the contents to others. My agent shall also have full power to make a disposition of any part or all of my body for medical purposes, authorize an autopsy and direct the disposition of my remains.

(THE ABOVE GRANT OF POWER IS INTENDED TO BE AS BROAD AS POSSIBLE SO THAT YOUR AGENT WILL HAVE AUTHORITY TO MAKE ANY DECISION YOU COULD MAKE TO OBTAIN OR TERMINATE ANY TYPE OF HEALTH CARE, INCLUDING WITHDRAWAL OF FOOD AND WATER AND OTHER LIFE-SUSTAINING MEASURES, IF YOUR AGENT BELIEVES SUCH ACTION WOULD BE CONSISTENT WITH YOUR INTENT AND DESIRES. IF YOU WISH TO LIMIT THE SCOPE OF YOUR AGENT'S POWERS OR PRESCRIBE SPECIAL RULES OR LIMIT THE POWER TO MAKE AN ANATOMICAL GIFT, AUTHORIZE AUTOPSY OR DISPOSE OF REMAINS, YOU MAY DO SO IN THE FOLLOWING PARAGRAPHS.)

2. The powers granted above shall not include the following powers or shall be subject to the following rules or limitations (here you may include any specific limitations you deem appropriate, such as: your own definition of when life-sustaining measures should be withheld; a direction to continue food and fluids or life-sustaining treatment in all events; or instructions to refuse any specific types of treatment that are inconsistent with your religious beliefs or unacceptable to you for any other reason, such as blood transfusion, electro-convulsive therapy, amputation, psychosurgery, voluntary admission to a mental institution, etc.):

_____
_____
_____
_____
_____
_____

(THE SUBJECT OF LIFE-SUSTAINING TREATMENT IS OF PARTICULAR IMPORTANCE. FOR YOUR CONVENIENCE IN DEALING WITH THAT SUBJECT, SOME GENERAL STATEMENTS CONCERNING THE WITHHOLDING OR REMOVAL OF LIFE-SUSTAINING TREATMENT ARE SET FORTH BELOW. IF YOU AGREE WITH ONE OF THESE STATEMENTS, YOU MAY INITIAL THAT STATEMENT; BUT DO NOT INITIAL MORE THAN ONE):

_____   I do not want my life to be prolonged nor do I want life-sustaining treatment to be provided or continued if my agent believes
(Initialed) the burdens of the treatment outweigh the expected benefits. I want my agent to consider the relief of suffering, the expense
             involved and the quality as well as the possible extension of my life in making decisions concerning life-sustaining treatment.

_____   I want my life to be prolonged and I want life-sustaining treatment to be provided or continued unless I am in a coma which
(Initialed) my attending physician believes to be irreversible, in accordance with reasonable medical standards at the time of reference.
             If and when I have suffered irreversible coma, I want life-sustaining treatment to be withheld or discontinued.

_____   I want my life to be prolonged to the greatest extent possible without regard to my condition, the chances I have for recovery
(Initialed) or the cost of the procedures.

(THIS POWER OF ATTORNEY MAY BE AMENDED OR REVOKED BY YOU IN THE MANNER PROVIDED IN SECTION 4-6 OF THE ILLINOIS "POWERS OF ATTORNEY FOR HEALTH CARE LAW" (SEE THE BACK OF THIS FORM). ABSENT AMENDMENT OR REVOCATION, THE AUTHORITY GRANTED IN THIS POWER OF ATTORNEY WILL BECOME EFFECTIVE AT THE TIME THIS POWER IS SIGNED AND WILL CONTINUE UNTIL YOUR DEATH, AND BEYOND IF ANATOMICAL GIFT, AUTOPSY OR DISPOSITION OF REMAINS IS AUTHORIZED, UNLESS A LIMITATION ON THE BEGINNING DATE OR DURATION IS MADE BY INITIALING AND COMPLETING EITHER OR BOTH OF THE FOLLOWING:)

3. (   ) This power of attorney shall become effective on_____
(insert a future date or event during your lifetime, such as court determination of your disability, when you want this power to first take effect)

4. (   ) This power of attorney shall terminate on_____
(insert a future date or event, such as court determination of your disability, when you want this power to terminate prior to your death)

(IF YOU WISH TO NAME SUCCESSOR AGENTS, INSERT THE NAMES AND ADDRESSES OF SUCH SUCCESSORS IN THE FOLLOWING PARAGRAPH.)

5. If any agent named by me shall die, become incompetent, resign, refuse to accept the office of agent or be unavailable, I name the following (each to act alone and successively, in the order named) as successors to such agent:

_____
_____

For purposes of this paragraph 5, a person shall be considered to be incompetent if and while the person is a minor or an adjudicated incompetent or disabled person or the person is unable to give prompt and intelligent consideration to health care matters, as certified by a licensed physician.

(IF YOU WISH TO NAME YOUR AGENT AS GUARDIAN OF YOUR PERSON, IN THE EVENT A COURT DECIDES THAT ONE SHOULD BE APPOINTED, YOU MAY, BUT ARE NOT REQUIRED TO, DO SO BY RETAINING THE FOLLOWING PARAGRAPH. THE COURT WILL APPOINT YOUR AGENT IF THE COURT FINDS THAT SUCH APPOINTMENT WILL SERVE YOUR BEST INTERESTS AND WELFARE. STRIKE OUT PARAGRAPH 6 IF YOU DO NOT WANT YOUR AGENT TO ACT AS GUARDIAN.)

6. If a guardian of my person is to be appointed, I nominate the agent acting under this power of attorney as such guardian, to serve without bond or security.

7. I am fully informed as to all the contents of this form and understand the full import of this grant of powers to my agent.

Signed_____
(principal)

The principal has had an opportunity to read the above form and has signed the form or acknowledged his or her signature or mark on the form in my presence.

_____   Residing at:_____
(witness)

(YOU MAY, BUT ARE NOT REQUIRED TO, REQUEST YOUR AGENT AND SUCCESSOR AGENTS TO PROVIDE SPECIMEN SIGNATURES BELOW. IF YOU INCLUDE SPECIMEN SIGNATURES IN THIS POWER OF ATTORNEY, YOU MUST COMPLETE THE CERTIFICATION OPPOSITE THE SIGNATURES OF THE AGENTS.)

Specimen signatures of agent (and successors).   I certify that the signatures of my agent (and successors) are correct.

_____   _____
(agent)   (principal)

_____   _____
(successor agent)   (principal)

_____   _____
(successor agent)   (principal)

AMERICAN LEGAL FORMS © 1990 Form No. 800
CHICAGO, IL   (312) 372-1922

Page 1

Illinois Power of Attorney Act Official Statutory Form
755 ILCS 45/3-3, Effective January, 1993

ILLINOIS STATUTORY SHORT FORM POWER OF ATTORNEY FOR PROPERTY

(NOTICE: THE PURPOSE OF THIS POWER OF ATTORNEY IS TO GIVE THE PERSON YOU DESIGNATE (YOUR "AGENT") BROAD POWERS TO HANDLE YOUR PROPERTY, WHICH MAY INCLUDE POWERS TO PLEDGE, SELL OR OTHERWISE DISPOSE OF ANY REAL OR PERSONAL PROPERTY WITHOUT ADVANCE NOTICE TO YOU OR APPROVAL BY YOU. THIS FORM DOES NOT IMPOSE A DUTY ON YOUR AGENT TO EXERCISE GRANTED POWERS; BUT WHEN POWERS ARE EXERCISED, YOUR AGENT WILL HAVE TO USE DUE CARE TO ACT FOR YOUR BENEFIT AND IN ACCORDANCE WITH THIS FORM AND KEEP A RECORD OF RECEIPTS, DISBURSEMENTS AND SIGNIFICANT ACTIONS TAKEN AS AGENT. A COURT CAN TAKE AWAY THE POWERS OF YOUR AGENT IF IT FINDS THE AGENT IS NOT ACTING PROPERLY. YOU MAY NAME SUCCESSOR AGENTS UNDER THIS FORM BUT NOT CO-AGENTS. UNLESS YOU EXPRESSLY LIMIT THE DURATION OF THIS POWER IN THE MANNER PROVIDED BELOW, UNTIL YOU REVOKE THIS POWER OR A COURT ACTING ON YOUR BEHALF TERMINATES IT, YOUR AGENT MAY EXERCISE THE POWERS GIVEN HERE THROUGHOUT YOUR LIFETIME, EVEN AFTER YOU BECOME DISABLED. THE POWERS YOU GIVE YOUR AGENT ARE EXPLAINED MORE FULLY IN SECTION 3-4 OF THE ILLINOIS "STATUTORY SHORT FORM POWER OF ATTORNEY FOR PROPERTY LAW" OF WHICH THIS FORM IS A PART (SEE THE BACK OF THIS FORM). THAT LAW EXPRESSLY PERMITS THE USE OF ANY DIFFERENT FORM OF POWER OF ATTORNEY YOU MAY DESIRE. IF THERE IS ANYTHING ABOUT THIS FORM THAT YOU DO NOT UNDERSTAND, YOU SHOULD ASK A LAWYER TO EXPLAIN IT TO YOU.)

Power of Attorney made this _____ day of _____, _____
                                                         (month)   (year)

1. I, _____
                              (insert name and address of principal)

hereby appoint: _____
                              (insert name and address of agent)

as my attorney-in-fact (my "agent") to act for me and in my name (in any way I could act in person) with respect to the following powers, as defined in Section 3-4 of the "Statutory Short Form Power of Attorney for Property Law" (including all amendments), but subject to any limitations on or additions to the specified powers inserted in paragraph 2 or 3 below:

(YOU MUST STRIKE OUT ANY ONE OR MORE OF THE FOLLOWING CATEGORIES OF POWERS YOU DO NOT WANT YOUR AGENT TO HAVE. FAILURE TO STRIKE THE TITLE OF ANY CATEGORY WILL CAUSE THE POWERS DESCRIBED IN THAT CATEGORY TO BE GRANTED TO THE AGENT. TO STRIKE OUT A CATEGORY YOU MUST DRAW A LINE THROUGH THE TITLE OF THAT CATEGORY.)

(a) Real estate transactions.
(b) Financial institution transactions.
(c) Stock and bond transactions.
(d) Tangible personal property transactions.
(e) Safe deposit box transactions.
(f) Insurance and annuity transactions.

(g) Retirement plan transactions.
(h) Social Security, employment and military service benefits.
(i) Tax matters.
(j) Claims and litigation.
(k) Commodity and option transactions.

(l) Business operations.
(m) Borrowing transactions.
(n) Estate transactions.
(o) All other property powers and transactions.

(LIMITATIONS ON AND ADDITIONS TO THE AGENT'S POWERS MAY BE INCLUDED IN THIS POWER OF ATTORNEY IF THEY ARE SPECIFICALLY DESCRIBED BELOW.)

2. The powers granted above shall not include the following powers or shall be modified or limited in the following particulars (here you may include any specific limitations you deem appropriate, such as a prohibition or conditions on the sale of particular stock or real estate or special rules on borrowing by the agent):

_____

_____

_____

_____

_____

3. In addition to the powers granted above, I grant my agent the following powers (here you may add any other delegable powers including, without limitation, power to make gifts, exercise powers of appointment, name or change beneficiaries or joint tenants or revoke or amend any trust specifically referred to below):

_____

_____

_____

_____

_____

(YOUR AGENT WILL HAVE AUTHORITY TO EMPLOY OTHER PERSONS AS NECESSARY TO ENABLE THE AGENT TO PROPERLY EXERCISE THE POWERS GRANTED IN THIS FORM, BUT YOUR AGENT WILL HAVE TO MAKE ALL DISCRETIONARY DECISIONS. IF YOU WANT TO GIVE YOUR AGENT THE RIGHT TO DELEGATE DISCRETIONARY DECISION-MAKING POWERS TO OTHERS, YOU SHOULD KEEP THE NEXT SENTENCE, OTHERWISE IT SHOULD BE STRUCK OUT.)

4. My agent shall have the right by written instrument to delegate any or all of the foregoing powers involving discretionary decision-making to any person or persons whom my agent may select, but such delegation may be amended or revoked by any agent (including any successor) named by me who is acting under this power of attorney at the time of reference.

(YOUR AGENT WILL BE ENTITLED TO REIMBURSEMENT FOR ALL REASONABLE EXPENSES INCURRED IN ACTING UNDER THIS POWER OF ATTORNEY. STRIKE OUT THE NEXT SENTENCE IF YOU DO NOT WANT YOUR AGENT TO ALSO BE ENTITLED TO REASONABLE COMPENSATION FOR SERVICES AS AGENT.)

5. My agent shall be entitled to reasonable compensation for services rendered as agent under this power of attorney.

(THIS POWER OF ATTORNEY MAY BE AMENDED OR REVOKED BY YOU AT ANY TIME AND IN ANY MANNER. ABSENT AMENDMENT OR REVOCATION, THE AUTHORITY GRANTED IN THIS POWER OF ATTORNEY WILL BECOME EFFECTIVE AT THE TIME THIS POWER IS SIGNED AND WILL CONTINUE UNTIL YOUR DEATH UNLESS A LIMITATION ON THE BEGINNING DATE OR DURATION IS MADE BY INITIALING AND COMPLETING EITHER (OR BOTH) OF THE FOLLOWING:)

6. (   ) This power of attorney shall become effective on_____

_____
(insert a future date or event during your lifetime, such as court determination of your disability, when you want this power to first take effect)

7. (   ) This power of attorney shall terminate on _____
(insert a future date or event, such as court determination of your disability, when you want this power to terminate prior to your death)

(IF YOU WISH TO NAME SUCCESSOR AGENTS, INSERT THE NAME(S) AND ADDRESS(ES) OF SUCH SUCCESSOR(S) IN THE FOLLOWING PARAGRAPH.)

8. If any agent named by me shall die, become incompetent, resign or refuse to accept the office of agent, I name the following (each to act alone and successively,

in the order named) as successor(s) to such agent: _____

_____

For purposes of this paragraph 8, a person shall be considered to be incompetent if and while the person is a minor or an adjudicated incompetent or disabled person or the person is unable to give prompt and intelligent consideration to business matters, as certified by a licensed physician.

(IF YOU WISH TO NAME YOUR AGENT AS GUARDIAN OF YOUR ESTATE, IN THE EVENT A COURT DECIDES THAT ONE SHOULD BE APPOINTED, YOU MAY, BUT ARE NOT REQUIRED TO, DO SO BY RETAINING THE FOLLOWING PARAGRAPH. THE COURT WILL APPOINT YOUR AGENT IF THE COURT FINDS THAT SUCH APPOINTMENT WILL SERVE YOUR BEST INTERESTS AND WELFARE. STRIKE OUT PARAGRAPH 9 IF YOU DO NOT WANT YOUR AGENT TO ACT AS GUARDIAN.)

9. If a guardian of my estate (my property) is to be appointed, I nominate the agent acting under this power of attorney as such guardian, to serve without bond or security.

10. I am fully informed as to all the contents of this form and understand the full import of this grant of powers to my agent.

Signed_____
(principal)

(YOU MAY, BUT ARE NOT REQUIRED TO, REQUEST YOUR AGENT AND SUCCESSOR AGENTS TO PROVIDE SPECIMEN SIGNATURES BELOW. IF YOU INCLUDE SPECIMEN SIGNATURES IN THIS POWER OF ATTORNEY, YOU MUST COMPLETE THE CERTIFICATION OPPOSITE THE SIGNATURES OF THE AGENTS.)

Specimen signatures of agent (and successors)   I certify that the signatures of my agent (and successors) are correct.

_____   _____
(agent)   (principal)

_____   _____
(successor agent)   (principal)

_____   _____
(successor agent)   (principal)

(THIS POWER OF ATTORNEY WILL NOT BE EFFECTIVE UNLESS IT IS NOTARIZED, USING THE FORM BELOW.)

State of _____   )
) SS.
County of_____   )

The undersigned, a notary public in and for the above county and state, certifies that_____,
known to me to be the same person whose name is subscribed as principal to the foregoing power of attorney, appeared before me in person and acknowledged signing and delivering the instrument as the free and voluntary act of the principal, for the uses and purposes therein set forth (, and certified to the correctness of the signature(s) of the agent(s)).

Dated:_____

(SEAL)   _____
                                              Notary Public
                                              My commission expires_____

(THE NAME AND ADDRESS OF THE PERSON PREPARING THIS FORM SHOULD BE INSERTED IF THE AGENT WILL HAVE POWER TO CONVEY ANY INTEREST IN REAL ESTATE.)

This document was prepared by:

_____

Durable powers of attorney are also important if you have a slow-moving but incurable disease. The time will come when you'll be incapable of making decisions that have to be made. If you don't designate an agent, a committee may decide whether you receive a certain treatment, and feelings will be hurt on all sides. Taking care of these important duties is one of the not-so-nice features of growing old, but it will help you and your family.

Each state has a form in its statutes that confers a power of attorney. Power of attorney forms are reprinted on pages 438–441 from an Illinois statute.* They are only valid in Illinois, but they won't be too dissimilar from powers of attorney in your state. A local stationery shop (one that carries legal forms) should have the power of attorney forms you need for your state. To be sure you've signed the correct form, check with your estate attorney.

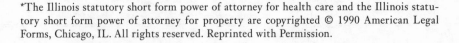

Knowing When You
Need Help

HOW DO I FIND THE RIGHT KIND OF HELP?

Some people always seem to pick good people to help them get where they want to go. Others just make bad folks sound great, perhaps because they're embarrassed by how badly their selection turned out.

There's only one reliable way to select good people to work for you: *Do your homework*. Guessing doesn't cut it. Referrals from relatives often produce only mediocre results. And don't even ask whether you should dig into the Yellow Pages and choose the biggest ad you see. ("They pay so much for the ad, they must be worth it" is a common conclusion.) If you make a poor choice, keeping the nonperforming person around only worsens the situation.

What kind of help is available? This chapter offers a quick list of suggestions and indicates some of the important questions you should ask. The most important question is: Are you—and whoever else is going to use this adviser, counselor, broker, attorney, or agent—comfortable with your choice?

Investment Broker or Investment Adviser

Do you need a stockbroker? Not really, if you know the stock you want to buy. If you want recommendations and analyses of various companies before you make your decision, then perhaps you do. A better choice may be an investment firm, especially if you intend to purchase shares of a mutual fund, or shares of stocks that are not available through dividend reinvestment plans (DRIPs). If you have significant assets, you may want to hire a registered investment adviser.

Stockbrokers currently come in three flavors: (1) full service, (2) discount, and (3) super discount. Full-service brokers are supposed to provide you with advice and counsel about your investments. They may even tell you what stock to buy. For these tidbits, you pay them a hefty fee. A discount broker takes less commission to complete a trade for you, but typically doesn't offer advice. A super discount broker offers only electronic trading (via the Internet or telephone), at a price that's hard to beat. You can trade online for as little as $5 per trade.

Should I hire a broker? That depends on how you want to trade your portfolio. If you're comfortable doing it yourself online or via the telephone, you'll probably want to find a brokerage firm, that offers a wide range of investments, plus access to Fidelity, Vanguard, or other high quality mutual funds, and set up your accounts there. It's nice to have your broker's office relatively close by (if you're selling and don't have your stocks in "street name," you can get the shares to your broker and close your sale within three business days), but a nearby location is not mandatory. In fact, with all the information out there in Internet Land, you may find you need a broker only if you decide to start trading bonds, shorting stock, or buying and selling puts and calls. Or, at times, you may simply need advice, assistance, and guidance.

What questions should I ask? You should know about your adviser's educational and professional background. You'll also want to write down the broker's Central Registration Depository (CRD) number. If you have the number, you can check whether any complaints have been filed against the broker. If he or she doesn't give you a CRD, ask for his or her Social Security number. If that's a problem too, you're correct to wonder whether the broker is hiding some bad bit of past notoriety. Call the National Association of Securities Dealers public disclosure phone center (800-289-9999) and your state securities regulator.

Make sure your stockbroker passed the "Series 6" and "Series 7" exams. A Registered Investment Advisor (RIA) certificate is proof that your adviser has passed an exam and can now sell the products he or she represents. A broker or adviser may also be a Certified Financial Planner (CFP), a Certified Fund Specialist (CFS), a Chartered Mutual Fund Consultant (CMFC), or a Chartered Financial Analyst

(CFA). Of them all, the CFA is the best designation; it requires the most training.

As with all people you hire, know how much you're going to have to pay up front. Ask about clients and caseloads. Do you have to give the broker a minimum, or can you trade ad hoc? Whatever you do, don't hand over a check at the first meeting.

Financial Planner

A financial planner should be able to help you organize your personal finances, get yourself on a budget, plan for future expenses, and help secure your retirement. In addition, a financial planner may sell investments or insurance, and make trades of stocks, bonds, and mutual funds for your account.

Financial planners are paid in one of three ways: (1) they receive a commission based on the products they sell to you; (2) you compensate them on an hourly basis, just as you would an attorney (they are then operating as fee-only financial planners), or (3) they take a percentage of the total dollars they manage for you. Which is the best method of compensation? If you pay your adviser on a fee-only basis, you eliminate the conflict of interest that is present if your financial planner is also taking a commission on the investments he or she is recommending. A small percentage of your money might be okay, but commissions can amount to a hefty sum. If you're not making many trades and your money is just sitting in your account, you may be paying a lot of money for virtually no work. Get specific details about compensation, and ask the planner to disclose any and all fees that he or she may collect if you purchase any kinds of products.

Should I hire a planner? A good planner is going to motivate you to pare down your expenses, reform your budget, and save for the big financial goals you've laid out. This very personal process can be quite emotional. Some planners act as financial psychiatrists for clients, helping them work out their emotional problems, and their money blocks so that they can get on with the rest of their lives.

What questions should I ask? Financial planners usually register in the state in which they work, but they don't need any formal training or education to guide you. That's a scary thought. If you're just starting out, look for someone who has real skills and the right kind of background, and who has been in business for a long time.

Ask what credentials the financial planner has. Certified Financial Planner (CFP) or Chartered Financial Analyst (CFA) will be a typical status. Certified public accountants (CPAs) are sometimes designated Personal Financial Specialists (PFS). An Enrolled Agent (EA) can act on your behalf in dealing with the IRS.

Do all these labels mean anything? Having at least a couple of them (say, a CFA and a CFP) could mean someone has put considerable time and effort into learning about the financial world.

If estate planning is in your future, be sure to ask whether your financial planner is qualified to help you plan your estate. Some financial planners specialize in estate planning.

Where do I find one? Check out some of these places for names and number, and then start whittling down your list: Institute of Certified Financial Planners (800-282-7526); International Association for Financial Planning (800-945-IAFP); National Association of Personal Financial Advisors (888-FEE-ONLY); American Institute of Certified Public Accountants (request PFS designations) (800-862-4272); and Investment Counsel Association of America (202-293-4222).

Insurance Agents

The first agent I bought insurance from was the father of a friend of mine. I was renting, had just been robbed, and lost a few pieces of jewelry my great aunt had left me. The next agent was a friend of my first cousin. The third was the son of my father-in-law's insurance agent. He was nice enough, but didn't seem particularly interested in helping us with our growing insurance needs. That's when we started buying some of our insurance directly from various companies.

In retrospect, I should have taken my own advice: done homework rather than simply hire someone to whom I was referred. Instead of taking tips or using someone recommended to you, consider interviewing several agents before you hire someone. It might even be easy and relatively inexpensive for you to purchase insurance on your own.

Should I hire one? Sometimes, you just can't find a good insurance agent. They're out there, but you've got to hunt them down. Do you absolutely need one? No, but it may make your life simpler, and a good agent who has your best interests at heart can be a great help in understanding different products and buying the right insurance for you and your family. If you want to try buying insurance directly from different companies, refer to Chapter 5 and call some of the numbers listed there. Even if you sign up with an agent, call a few companies directly to make sure the quote your agent is giving you is really the best deal you can get.

What questions should I ask? Your insurance agent must be licensed by the state in which you live. Find out which companies he or she represents, or whether the agent is an independent.

Be sure to find out how the agent charges for his or her services. Typically, agents work on a commission basis, which can influence their recommendations.

Where do I find a good one? Ask your friends, relatives, doctor, and business associates. Many Internet sites offer referrals, but make sure you check them out with your state's insurance commissioner's office.

Real Estate Agents

If you're going to buy a home, you'll most likely want to have a real estate agent—preferably, a buyer broker—to assist you. If you're selling, and you think you can do it better, faster, and cheaper than an agent, by all means, step into those FSBO (for sale by owner) shoes and see how they fit. If you haven't unloaded your home after two months, consider hiring an agent. Are you prepared for the enormous amount of work that goes into selling your own home? A good broker can be a great help.

Whom does the agent really represent? Make sure you know whom the real estate agent you select really represents. Real estate agents come in a variety of forms. Buyer broker agents represent the fiduciary interests of buyers, except when they represent sellers in the same transaction. If a single broker represents both sides in the same transaction, he or she is a dual agent. If you're buying, hiring a dual agent is like hiring the seller's attorney to represent you, too. Conventional agents represent the seller, even if they're shepherding the buyer from showing to showing. Exclusive buyer agents never represent sellers (no conflict of interest there). Transactional brokers are dual agents who claim they have no legal liability because they represent neither party (which makes one wonder why anyone would pay them a full, let alone double, commission).

Confused? The home you buy will likely be your single biggest purchase, and probably your largest single investment. Having the right agent on your side can help you navigate these often-muddied waters.

What questions should I ask? Make sure the agent (or broker) regularly works in the neighborhood in which you're interested, and deals with homes in your price range. You should aim to hire one of the top brokers in an office. You can find out their names by talking to the managing broker. The busiest broker may or may not work in your area or your price range. Keep working your way down the list until you find a top broker who does both.

Ask what the office's sales volume is, and what the average sales price has been during the past year. Talk to at least three brokers or agents from three different firms, and test whether personal rapport can develop with them. Working with an agent through a purchase or sale is a lot like a short-term marriage. You want it to be a happy one.

Real estate agents have taken a minimum number of hours of specialized training and have passed a state licensing examination. Brokers have taken additional classes and have logged at least one year of experience. Are brokers better? Not necessarily. The practice of real estate is unique. A broker's license is a goal only for people who want to open up their own office or be the managing broker of an office.

Ask how the agent expects to be compensated. Traditionally, the seller pays the commission, even if the buyer uses a buyer broker. If the buyer uses an exclusive buyer broker, however, the commission arrangement may alter. If you are the seller, the commission is fully negotiable. See my book, *100 Questions Every Home Seller Should Ask*, for details on how to negotiate the listing agreement, including the commission that you'll ultimately pay.

How do I find a real estate agent? Visit local open houses. Go online and check out the sites of local offices. Go to the national Web sites of the major real estate firms, like Century 21 (www.century21.com) or Coldwell Banker (www.coldwellbanker.com). You might also ask your friends, relatives, and neighbors about the agency they used and whether they were happy with their choice. Upon request, your state board of Realtors can send you a list of members. (Remember, Realtors® are members of the National Association of Realtors. It doesn't include everyone who holds a real estate license.) Finally, look in the local paper. Who is running the ads you like? If you're selling your home, that's the kind of exposure you'll want.

Accountants, Tax Preparers, and Enrolled Agents

Yes, you can do your own taxes. There are excellent software programs that will lead you through the process. The question is: Do you want to? If you don't, accountants, tax preparers, and Enrolled Agents can assist you.

Should I hire one? To be perfectly honest, the tax preparation software now available is so good that anyone with a computer, some time, and the desire to do so should be able to file his or her own tax return, especially if the data are relatively simple. If your return is more complicated and requires filing several schedules, you may want a professional to lend a hand and advise you about tax strategies.

A tax preparer might be someone at H&R Block, who actually assists you in filling out your income tax forms. A Certified Public Accountant (CPA) has had the necessary education (and passed tough exams) and should know his or her way around a tax form. An Enrolled Agent (EA) is a former IRS employee who has passed an exam and may now represent clients before the IRS. Whatever you do, don't rely on the IRS staff for tax help. Studies have shown that you're as likely to get the wrong answer as the right one.

What questions should I ask? Find out the qualifications of the person you're hiring. You don't want to mess around with the IRS. You need someone who will sign your return as the preparer and, if necessary, will defend the numbers on your tax return.

Ask about fees and how much you are expected to pay for each service. Tax preparers may charge per return or per hour, or may ask a flat fee. Enrolled Agents and CPAs typically charge by the hour.

It should go without saying (but I'm saying it anyway) that you shouldn't hire someone who has had previous "difficulties." If the adviser, agent, or broker you've selected has had complaints filed against him or her, why should you be the test case to see whether he or she has reformed? Research any active or past complaints registered against the individual you're considering. Try to find out what the problems were and how the situations were resolved, or simply look for someone else. You're entitled to a professional who has integrity, not someone who slipped through a crack in the systems.

Where do I find them? The Accreditation Council for Accountancy and Taxation (703-549-ACAT) will give you names of accredited tax preparers in your neighborhood. The National Association of Enrolled Agents (800-424-4339) will do the same for EAs who work near you. Your state will have its own local and/or regional CPA organization(s). You may also contact the local office of a large accounting firm in your area for a referral.

HOW WILL I KNOW IF I NEED HELP?

Knowing you need help is the easy part. You simply feel overwhelmed, like you're drowning. You can't cope, and you know you can't cope.

Asking for help is the tricky part. Sometimes we get immobilized by our needs and our fears. This is what classically happens with Money Block. You get so agitated by what's supposed to get done that you end up shutting down and not doing anything.

Financial advisers, brokers, planners, attorneys, and CPAs can only help you so far. As we discussed earlier, you can have all kinds of trusts, but if you don't deposit your assets into those trusts, they're meaningless. The same is true for financial help. If you don't follow professionals' recommendations, you may wind up throwing away a lot of good money.

How much should you pay for good financial advice? You get what you pay for, so going cheap isn't always the best thing to do. If you want the advice but don't want to spend a lot of money, you're setting yourself up for a conflict you may not be able to resolve. If you want to save money, try doing on your own some of the things I talk about in this book. It's as easy to trade on the Internet yourself as it is to pick up a phone and call your broker (and the Internet doesn't take lunch breaks!). Finally, there's nothing wrong with paying for a little handholding, especially at the beginning, but I want you to feel strong enough to take on your own personal finances and run with them. You can do it. All you have to do is trust yourself a little and then take the first step.

Before Money Block sets in, you might want to step back, take a short walk around the block, and try to identify what you're afraid of doing. By identifying what you really don't want to do, you'll be able to break through your Money Block and get going.

Hot Tips and Cold Calls

As I was writing this final chapter, the phone rang in my office. After confirming that I was Ms. Glink, the caller wanted to know whether he could give me a quote for replacing the windows in my house. "No," I said. "Well, we do patio restoration and enclosures," he said. "We don't have a patio," I said. "We can build one for you," he said. I could picture the gleam in his eye.

I'll admit to a momentary pause, since we're in the middle of planning a renovation of our home. Then I said, "No, thanks," and hung up the phone.

I get at least five solicitations each weekday, plus a few on the weekends. The offers are for everything from replacing my roof and landscaping my yard to refinancing my mortgage and getting a new long-distance service. On top of that, two to three credit card solicitations arrive weekly in the mail.

And then there are the young men (it's always men who seem to call me, although certainly plenty of women do cold calling) with smooth voices, who ask for my husband, Sam. Some of these men act casual on the phone, as if they know my husband. Some are serious, as if they have important information for him. When I identify myself as his wife, and ask whether I can assist them, they always say they'll call back.

What's going on here? These are stockbrokers who are *cold calling* my husband to try to persuade him to give them money to manage. Or, perhaps they're just cold calling him to see whether he's interested in the amazing stock tip they have for him today.

Ho-hum. If it were such a great stock tip, I can guarantee you these callers would be mortgaging themselves to the hilt, plunking their money in the market, taking their payoff, and retiring to an island in the Pacific. (I have a similar response to investment newsletters. If they know so much, why are they sharing it with me, a complete stranger?)

The truth is, nothing good ever comes of a cold call. If someone calls you on the phone with a "great" deal, thank them politely and hang up. It's a tough policy, but it has stood me in good stead through the years. I may miss a once-in-a-lifetime opportunity, but I'll also miss millions of other scams, bad investments, and loser deals just waiting for a patsy.

I'm not going to sit around waiting for someone to pin a tail on this donkey.

Telephone, e-mail, and postal solicitations have become big business. But it's your house, your telephone, your computer. You have the right to say, "No, take me off your list permanently," and hang up. I always ask to be removed from whatever list they're using, and I threaten to report them if they don't do it. Am I actually removed from these endless lists? Who knows? By law, I'm supposed to be. But standing up for myself makes me feel that I'm doing something that's in my own best interests. I encourage you to do the same.

QUESTION 99
WHAT SHOULD I DO IF MY FINANCIAL ADVISERS HAVEN'T TREATED ME WELL?

If someone you hired, to whom you paid good money, isn't giving you the service or treatment you want or deserve, by all means *open your mouth!* The old cliché still works: The squeaky wheel gets the oil.

Here are the steps you should take if you're not being treated correctly:

1. *Complain, loudly and often.* Start with the person you hired. Initiate a good, honest, face-to-face talk about what you thought you were getting and what you feel you've received instead. If the message isn't getting through, delivery your complaint through the ranks and eventually to the top person at the company. But be sure you're able to document the problems.

2. *File a complaint.* If you're having trouble with a particular company, go to the state agency that licenses that company. For example, if your insurance agent has been promising you one thing and delivering another, contact the insurance commissioner in your state. If you have a problem with a real estate agent, go to the state agency that licenses real estate agents and brokers. You

can also file a complaint with your local Better Business Bureau. (Call the Council for Better Business Bureaus at 703-525-8277 for a local complaint number.)

3. *Don't recommend the service.* When Lisa was buying a house, she asked her sister Karen to recommend an attorney. Karen gave her an attorney's name, and Lisa hired him. She had a bad experience. When she told Karen about it, Karen mentioned that, with that same lawyer, things hadn't gone particularly well for her, either. If you have a bad experience with various individuals, *don't recommend them.* Perhaps if enough people steer customers away, they'll go out of business!

4. *When all else fails, sue.* Lawyers like to say that lawsuits are expensive, time-consuming, and heart-breaking, and that's if you win. But if you haven't been treated well, if you've been bilked out of money, if a broker has made unauthorized trades on your account, you may have legal remedies you can pursue. If you're interested in finding out what your legal options are, consult with an attorney who specializes in the field in which you've had the problem. For example, if you're having problems with your stockbroker, don't call your real estate attorney—unless you're only asking for a recommendation to an attorney who specializes in investment cases.

When things go wrong in a financial relationship, usually everyone can shoulder a little bit of blame. Before you start throwing lawsuits around, think about why you're so upset. Are your calls not being returned fast enough? Did the financial strategy your planner suggested lose money? Were you forced into accepting investments that were just plain wrong for you? Was there unauthorized trading on your account? Were you demanding and unreasonable? If you think you were part of the problem, consider sitting down with the adviser (perhaps with his or her manager present as a mediator) and working things out. If that doesn't satisfy you, move on. There are plenty of qualified planners, brokers, accountants, Enrolled Agents, and real estate agents who would love to work for you and help you achieve your financial dreams.

QUESTION 100

NOW WHAT?

If you've read my answers to 100 questions, congratulations. You've taken an enormous step toward achieving your financial goals. But it's only your first step. Now you have to go out and make things happen.

The thought of going out and making something happen affects each of us in different ways. Some of us are paralyzed. It's the old Money Block surfacing again, keeping us from doing something we know is absolutely in the best interests of ourselves and the people we love.

Some of us are frightened by what we might discover when we open that hall closet door. Go on, crack it open. Let some air and sunshine in. You might find it's in better shape than you remembered. If you organized things well enough at some point, long ago, your financial closet may only be slightly overgrown. It may need pruning rather than a gut job. On the other hand, your finances may be in serious disarray. That can be scary, but you now have the tools you need to start in and get things organized. You've learned how to:

- Organize your paperwork.
- Create a budget that will carry you through paying off your debt until retirement.
- Fix your credit.
- Figure out whether it's better to buy or lease your next car or truck.
- Get the insurance you need to protect your loved ones.
- Put real estate to good personal financial use.
- Make smart decisions when it comes to marriage and children.
- Take advantage of your tax opportunities.
- Understand your investments.
- Plan for your retirement.
- Organize your estate.
- Hire the right kind of financial help.

That's a lot of know-how.

The bottom line is: These tools should give you the confidence you need to take hold of your personal finances today:

- You now know enough to begin to secure a wonderful and comfortable financial future for yourself and those you love.

- You've laid the groundwork for a lifetime of knowledge about your current investments and for the future decisions you'll make along the way.

- You no longer have to feel powerless against personal finance professionals who try to sell you things "for your own good." You now know where to go to find out what you need to know to make intelligent choices for yourself and your family.

As you go about charting your course, you'll begin to experience the enormous satisfaction that comes with the adept handling of your personal finances. You'll watch your money grow, and take pride in knowing *you* made those decisions. And over the years, your fears about money will dissipate. Your Money Block will disappear. You'll realize that no matter how much you actually earn, you can create the retirement of your dreams, leave an orderly estate, and pass along to your children and grandchildren all of the knowledge and information you've gleaned.

Making your own financial decisions won't always be easy. You may well encounter some obstacles along the way. And you might make some mistakes—although I hope you'll miss the majority of them. We've all walked miles in the shoes you're about to put on. The truth is, making smart financial decisions isn't brain surgery. You now have the tools you need to turn your finance dreams into reality. And you have the power to protect the ones you love.

And in the end, that's all you need.

Appendix I

Top 10 Mistakes We Make with Our Personal Finances

There's nothing wrong with making a mistake. It happens all the time. Even the "experts" make mistakes. But you'll really have problems if you don't learn from your mistakes, keep making the same ones over and over again.

Consider this list, then, as a road map. The road to a solid financial future depends on your ability to find a path through the thicket of information and nonsense thrown your way. Surely there will be other mistakes besides these that you might make. (For a list of common investing mistakes, for example, see pages 327–331.) But I hope this list will tell you where the biggest potholes lie—where most people stumble or lose their way.

And if you know what to look out for, well, that's half the battle won.

1. Putting off 'til tomorrow. Do you clean your closets first or are you too busy doing just about anything else? If you're a procrastinator by nature, you'll find it easier and easier to pass on the active management of your personal finances. The problem with "I'll get to it later" is that by the time you *do* get around to making a move, the opportunity may have passed. Procrastination is also the first step to a major Money Block. If you keep putting off your personal finance chores, the pile will grow ever larger. To keep the procrastination monster at bay, try breaking your personal finances into bite-size pieces that are more easily finished.

2. Spending more than you earn. Unfortunately, millions of Americans live above their means and will likely be struggling financially for the rest of their lives. Getting your budget under control isn't just about creating a solid base from which you can launch your financial future. Psychologically, when you finally pay off your debts, a huge weight will lift from your shoulders. Casting away the albatross will free you to dream big and create a new reality for yourself and your family.

3. Not saving enough. Building wealth isn't about how much money you earn each year; it's about how much money you don't spend. And in some cases, fortunes are found in the pennies, not the dollars, saved. As long as you don't spend everything you earn, you will start to accumulate assets. If you haven't saved enough in the past, you should start saving more today. If you save $3.29 per day, every day for the next 30 years, you'll have saved $36,000. If you invest that money and achieve a 10 percent return, you'll end up with more than $197,392. Remember, it's the pennies you save every day that will make you rich.

4. Failing to pay off your high-interest, non-deductible debt. It's hard to save when you're in debt up to your ears. And if your debt is costing you some 24 percent a year, you'll be hard-pressed to dig yourself out. Start by paying off your highest-interest, nondeductible debt. If you have the cash on hand, pay off everything that isn't tax deductible. The 2 percent you're probably earning on that $5,000 you have stashed away would be put to far better use if you paid off your credit cards.

5. Looking for the big kill. The problem with looking for the "big kill," or the one perfect investment, is that you'll look forever and not find it. That's because it really doesn't exist. You'll more likely be struck by lightning than you'll win the lottery. Focusing so much attention looking for the investment that's going to solve all your financial problems wastes a lot of time and energy, and there is the very real risk you'll take a hot tip from a cold call and end up doing something you'll regret later.

6. Letting your emotions interfere with your investment strategy. Your investments are not your children, your parents, your best friends, or your pets; nor should they be your sole reason for living. But when it comes to our investments, we tend to get emotional just when we should step back and take a fresh look at the situation. Setting up an investment structure should help keep your emotions out of the equation. Set your goals clearly in writing—when you've achieved them, you can create others. Finally, don't regret a loss, or hang onto a losing investment longer than you know you should. If you need to take a loss, do it, learn from it, and be smarter the next time.

7. Trying to time the market. No one can time the market. Believing you have a system that will allow you to always buy at the low and sell at the high is a sure way of getting yourself into trouble. The best way to invest in the market is to be steady and consistent. Dollar cost averaging, a system by which you invest the same amount each month no matter what is happening in the market, is the safest and best way for most people to invest.

8. Failing to diversify your investments. The stock market will rise and fall many times throughout your years as an investor. The only way to keep yourself insulated against the worst is to hang on for the long run and diversify into various investments. That means keeping your portfolio balanced with stocks, bonds, cash, and other investments so that you can sleep at night, no matter which direction the market is going.

9. Chasing the investment flavor of the month, week, day, or minute. As a corollary, if you try to invest in the hottest mutual fund, you're bound to lose money. That's because fund managers tend to jump around, particularly after they've had a good year. The fund managers you want to follow are those who get a solid return, year in and year out, and have weathered many market ups and downs. Also, beware of falling into the trap of believing that short-term trends will continue forever. Remember, past performance is no guarantee of future results, and the market can change on a dime.

10. Not taking enough risk. Probably the biggest mistake we make with our personal finances is not taking enough risk. That's because we've been warned from the time we're very little not to do risky things. So we don't take enough risk with our investments because we're afraid of losing it all. But "losing it all" is a phrase that really refers to gambling. If you're smart about your personal finances, and you thoroughly investigate companies before you buy their stock, then you're investing, not rolling the dice. And in that case, as long as time is on your side, the odds that you'll lose it all are very, very small.

Appendix II

5 Simple Things You Can Do to Improve Your Personal Finances

After researching and writing this book, I've come to the conclusion that anyone can improve their personal finances by taking a few simple steps. If you follow these suggestions, you're sure to see a dramatic improvement in the size and shape of your investments and the way in which you feel about them.

1. Take responsibility for your investments. Did someone hold a gun to your head when you made your last investment? The answer, I'm sure, is no. So why are you blaming everyone else because the investment didn't do as well as you had hoped? The truth is, it's a lot easier to get a hot tip from a cold call than it is to go out and do your own research. That involves work! Taking responsibility for your investments means you have to act like a grownup. You can't blame anyone else for your procrastination or your mistakes.

2. Invest only in things you understand. So much money is lost by folks who think they understand an investment—and don't. The most successful investors are the ones who keep it simple: Don't invest in anything you can't explain to a child.

3. Develop an investment strategy and stick with it. Do you have an itchy trigger finger? If you do, you might find yourself selling an investment on a dime because you heard from a colleague that someone on television reported something negative and your favorite stock dropped a point. (A television report probably isn't the best reason to buy or sell an investment, although it could be a reason for you to do some further investigation.) To combat itchy trigger finger syndrome, develop an investment strategy and then stick with it. If you simply react to everything, you'll end up losing nearly every time. Remember, just because you can trade online for $5 a trade doesn't mean you must.

4. Accept that you'll never buy low and sell high every time. No one can time the market, including the experts. As long as you consistently sell for more money than you bought, you can still make a lot of money in the stock market.

5. Don't obsess about your investments. If you find yourself unable to think about anything else except your finances, you've got real problems. The pot of gold might be at the end of the rainbow, but if you're so focused on finding it, you might miss the beauty of the rainbow itself. Instead of obsessing on whether the value of your portfolio went up or down today, focus on other things. Get a hobby. Volunteer your time in a homeless soup kitchen. Read a book to your child or grandchild. Perspective is a good thing. If you have too much time to think about your money, you might end up making a really bad decision for all the wrong reasons.

Appendix III

A Few Useful Charts

The following nifty little chart will help you figure exactly what kind of taxable return you'll have to generate just to stay ahead of inflation. The game, of course, is to beat inflation. That's when your money really starts to grow.

Useful Chart 1
The Investment Returns Required to Maintain the Purchasing Power of Money

	Inflation Rate (%)												
	4	*6*	*7*	*8*	*9*	*10*	*11*	*12*	*13*	*14*	*16*	*18*	*20*
Tax Bracket													
0	4.0	6.0	7.0	8.0	9.0	10.0	11.0	12.0	13.0	14.0	16.0	18.0	20.0
10	4.5	6.7	7.8	8.9	10.0	11.1	12.2	13.3	14.4	15.6	17.8	20.0	22.2
15	4.7	7.1	8.2	9.4	10.5	11.8	12.9	14.1	15.3	16.4	18.8	21.0	23.6
20	5.0	7.5	8.7	10.0	11.2	12.5	13.7	15.0	16.2	17.4	20.0	22.4	25.0
25	5.3	8.0	9.3	10.7	12.0	13.3	14.7	16.0	17.3	18.6	21.3	24.0	26.6
30	5.7	8.6	10.1	11.4	12.9	14.3	15.7	17.1	18.6	20.2	22.8	25.8	28.6
35	6.2	9.2	10.8	12.3	13.8	15.4	16.9	18.5	20.0	21.6	24.6	27.6	30.8
40	6.6	10.0	11.7	13.3	15.0	16.1	18.3	20.2	21.7	23.4	26.6	30.0	33.4
45	7.2	10.9	12.7	14.5	16.4	18.2	20.0	21.8	23.6	25.4	29.0	32.8	36.4
50	8.0	12.0	14.0	16.0	18.0	20.0	22.0	24.0	26.0	28.0	32.0	36.0	40.0

Source: Money Managers Advisory. Used with permission.

At my current _____% tax bracket and at my _____% projected rate of inflation, I will have to earn _____% on a taxable investment just to break even.

Useful Chart 2

How a single investment of $100 grows over 30 years with interest compounded annually.
For a $1,000 investment, simply add a zero.

Days	Years	5.00%	6.00%	7.00%	8.00%	9.00%	10.00%
365	1	$105.00	$106.00	$107.00	$ 108.00	$ 109.00	$ 110.00
730	2	110.25	112.36	114.49	116.64	118.81	121.00
1,095	3	115.76	119.10	122.50	125.97	129.50	133.10
1,460	4	121.55	126.25	131.08	136.05	141.16	146.41
1,825	5	127.63	133.82	140.26	146.93	153.86	161.05
3,650	10	162.89	179.08	196.72	215.89	236.74	259.37
5,475	15	207.89	239.66	275.90	317.22	364.25	417.72
7,300	20	265.33	320.71	386.97	466.10	560.44	672.75
9,125	25	338.64	429.19	542.74	684.85	862.31	1,083.47
10,950	30	432.19	574.35	761.23	1,006.27	1,326.77	1,744.94

Days	Years	11.00%	12.00%	13.00%	14.00%	15.00%	16.00%
365	1	$ 111.00	$ 112.00	$ 113.00	$ 114.00	$ 115.00	$ 116.00
730	2	123.21	125.44	127.69	129.96	132.25	134.56
1,095	3	136.76	140.49	144.29	148.15	152.09	156.09
1,460	4	151.81	157.35	163.05	168.90	174.90	181.06
1,825	5	168.51	176.23	184.24	192.54	201.14	210.03
3,650	10	283.94	310.58	339.46	370.72	404.56	441.14
5,475	15	478.46	547.36	625.43	713.79	813.71	926.55
7,300	20	806.23	964.63	1,152.31	1,374.35	1,636.65	1,946.08
9,125	25	1,358.55	1,700.01	2,123.05	2,646.19	3,291.90	4,087.42
10,950	30	2,289.23	2,995.99	3,911.59	5,095.02	6,621.18	8,584.99

Useful Chart 3

How a $100 investment grows over 30 years compounded monthly.
For a $1,000 investment, simply add a zero.

Months	Years	5.00%	6.00%	7.00%	8.00%	9.00%	10.00%
12	1	$105.12	$106.17	$107.23	$ 108.30	$ 109.38	$ 110.47
24	2	110.49	112.72	114.98	117.29	119.64	122.04
36	3	116.15	119.67	123.29	127.02	130.86	134.82
48	4	122.09	127.05	132.21	137.57	143.14	148.94
60	5	128.34	134.89	141.76	148.98	156.57	164.53
120	10	164.70	181.94	200.97	221.96	245.14	270.70
180	15	211.37	245.41	284.89	330.69	383.80	445.39
240	20	271.26	331.02	403.87	492.68	600.92	732.81
300	25	348.13	446.50	572.54	734.02	940.84	1,205.69
360	30	446.77	602.26	811.65	1,093.57	1,473.06	1,983.74

Months	Years	11.00%	12.00%	13.00%	14.00%	15.00%	16.00%
12	1	$ 111.57	$ 112.68	$ 113.80	$ 114.93	$ 116.08	$ 117.23
24	2	124.48	126.97	129.51	132.10	134.74	137.42
36	3	138.89	143.08	147.39	151.83	156.39	161.10
48	4	154.96	161.22	167.73	174.50	181.54	188.85
60	5	172.89	181.67	190.89	200.56	210.72	221.38
120	10	298.91	330.04	364.37	402.25	444.02	490.09
180	15	516.80	599.58	695.54	806.75	935.63	1,084.97
240	20	893.50	1,089.26	1,327.68	1,618.03	1,971.55	2,401.92
300	25	1,544.79	1,978.85	2,534.35	3,245.13	4,154.41	5,317.39
360	30	2,670.81	3,594.96	4,837.71	6,508.47	8,754.10	11,771.68

Useful Chart 4

*How a $100 investment grows over 30 years with interest compounded quarterly
(every three months). For a $1,000 investment, simply add a zero.*

Quarters	Years	5.00%	6.00%	7.00%	8.00%	9.00%	10.00%
4	1	$105.09	$106.14	$107.19	$ 108.24	$ 109.31	$ 110.38
8	2	110.45	112.65	114.89	117.17	119.48	121.84
12	3	116.08	119.56	123.14	126.82	130.60	134.49
16	4	121.99	126.90	131.99	137.28	142.76	148.45
20	5	128.20	134.69	141.48	148.59	156.05	163.86
40	10	164.36	181.40	200.16	220.80	243.52	268.51
60	15	210.72	244.32	283.18	328.10	380.01	439.98
80	20	270.15	329.07	400.64	487.54	593.01	720.96
100	25	346.34	443.20	566.82	724.46	925.40	1,181.37
120	30	444.02	596.93	801.92	1,076.52	1,444.10	1,935.81

Quarters	Years	11.00%	12.00%	13.00%	14.00%	15.00%	16.00%
4	1	$ 111.46	$ 112.55	$ 113.65	$ 114.75	$ 115.87	$ 116.99
8	2	124.24	126.68	129.16	131.68	134.25	136.86
12	3	138.48	142.58	146.78	151.11	155.55	160.10
16	4	154.35	160.47	166.82	173.40	180.22	187.30
20	5	172.04	180.61	189.58	198.98	208.82	219.11
40	10	295.99	326.20	359.42	395.93	436.04	480.10
60	15	509.23	589.16	681.40	787.81	910.51	1,051.96
80	20	876.09	1,064.09	1,291.83	1,567.57	1,901.29	2,304.98
100	25	1,507.24	1,921.86	2,449.10	3,119.14	3,970.18	5,050.49
120	30	2,593.10	3,471.10	4,643.09	6,206.43	8,290.35	11,066.26

Useful Chart 5

How a $100 investment grows over 30 years with interest compounded daily.
For $1,000 investment, add a zero.

Days	Years	5.00%	6.00%	7.00%	8.00%	9.00%	10.00%
365	1	$105.13	$106.18	$107.25	$ 108.33	$ 109.42	$ 110.52
730	2	110.52	112.75	115.03	117.35	119.72	122.14
1,095	3	116.18	119.72	123.37	127.12	130.99	134.98
1,460	4	122.14	127.12	132.31	137.71	143.33	149.17
1,825	5	128.40	134.98	141.90	149.18	156.82	164.86
3,650	10	164.87	182.20	201.36	222.53	245.93	271.79
5,475	15	211.69	245.94	285.74	331.97	385.68	448.08
7,300	20	271.81	331.98	405.47	495.22	604.83	738.70
9,125	25	349.00	448.11	575.36	738.74	948.51	1,217.83
10,950	30	448.12	604.88	816.45	1,102.03	1,487.48	2,007.73

Days	Years	11.00%	12.00%	13.00%	14.00%	15.00%	16.00%
365	1	$ 111.63	$ 112.75	$ 113.88	$ 115.02	$ 116.18	$ 117.35
730	2	124.60	127.12	129.69	132.31	134.98	137.70
1,095	3	139.09	143.32	147.69	152.18	156.82	161.59
1,460	4	155.26	161.59	168.19	175.05	182.19	189.62
1,825	5	173.31	182.19	191.53	201.35	211.67	222.52
3,650	10	300.37	331.95	366.84	405.41	448.03	495.13
5,475	15	520.57	604.79	702.62	816.29	948.34	1,101.74
7,300	20	902.20	1,101.88	1,345.75	1,643.58	2,007.32	2,451.53
9,125	25	1,563.62	2,007.56	2,577.54	3,309.32	4,248.83	5,455.03
10,950	30	2,709.92	3,657.66	4,936.82	6,663.27	8,993.40	12,138.27

Have you ever wondered how much money you'd have if you invested $100 per month (or $1,200 per year) for the rest of your life? These two charts will give you an idea of how your money will grow over time, at various rates of return.

Useful Chart 6

If you invest $100 per month, or $1,200 per year, how much money will you have?

Years	6.00%	7.00%	8.00%	9.00%	10.00%	11.00%	12.00%
1	$ 1,200.00	$ 1,200.00	$ 1,200.00	$ 1,200.00	$ 1,200.00	$ 1,200.00	$ 1,200.00
5	6,764.51	6,900.89	7,039.92	7,181.62	7,326.12	7,473.36	7,623.42
10	15,816.95	16,579.74	17,383.87	18,231.52	19,124.91	20,066.41	21,058.48
15	27,931.16	30,154.83	32,582.54	35,233.10	38,126.98	41,286.43	44,735.66
20	44,142.71	49,194.59	54,914.36	61,392.14	68,730.00	77,043.40	86,462.93
25	65,837.41	75,898.85	87,727.13	101,641.08	118,016.47	137,295.97	160,000.64
30	94,869.82	113,352.94	135,939.85	163,569.05	197,392.83	238,825.05	289,599.22
35	133,721.74	165,884.25	206,780.16	258,852.91	325,229.24	409,907.47	517,996.20
40	185,714.36	239,562.13	310,867.82	405,458.93	531,111.07	698,191.28	920,509.70
45	255,292.22	342,899.17	463,806.74	631,030.48	862,685.80	1,183,966.27	1,629,876.04
50	348,403.09	487,834.72	688,524.19	978,100.27	1,396,690.23	2,002,525.38	2,880,021.90

Useful Chart 7

If you invest $250 per month, or $3,000 per year, how much money will you have?

Years	6.00%	7.00%	8.00%	9.00%	10.00%	11.00%	12.00%
1	$ 3,000.00	$ 3,000.00	$ 3,000.00	$ 3,000.00	$ 3,000.00	$ 3,000.00	$ 3,000.00
5	16,911.28	17,252.22	17,599.80	17,954.13	18,315.30	18,683.40	19,058.54
10	39,542.38	41,449.34	43,459.69	45,578.79	47,812.27	50,166.03	52,646.21
15	69,827.91	75,387.31	81,456.34	88,082.75	95,317.45	103,216.08	111,839.14
20	110,356.77	122,986.48	137,285.89	153,480.36	171,825.00	192,608.50	216,157.33
25	164,593.54	189,747.11	219,317.82	254,102.69	295,041.18	343,239.92	400,001.61
30	237,174.56	283,382.36	339,849.63	408,922.62	493,482.07	597,062.63	723,998.05
35	334,304.34	414,710.64	516,950.41	647,132.26	813,073.11	1,024,768.66	1,294,990.49
40	464,285.90	598,905.34	777,169.56	1,013,647.34	1,327,777.67	1,745,478.20	2,301,274.26
45	638,230.54	857,247.93	1,159,516.85	1,577,576.20	2,156,714.51	2,959,915.68	4,074,690.10
50	871,007.71	1,219,586.79	1,721,310.47	2,445,250.67	3,491,725.59	5,006,313.46	7,220,054.75

Glossary

Abstract (of Title)   A summary of the public records affecting the title to a particular piece of land. An attorney or title insurance company officer creates the abstract of title by examining all recorded instruments (documents) relating to a specific piece of property, such as easements, liens, mortgages, etc.

Accelerated Benefit   A rider that allows a terminally ill person to cash in a policy before he or she dies and collect up to 95 percent of the policy's face value.

Acceleration Clause   A provision in a loan agreement that allows the lender to require the balance of the loan to become due immediately if mortgage payments are not made or there is a breach in your obligation under your mortgage or note.

Accumulation Fund   The savings component of a universal life insurance policy. The money in this fund earns interest and goes to pay the higher cost of the mortality charge as you age. As long as you pay enough to fund the mortality charge, you can skip payments if your funds dry up. And, if you contribute enough to the accumulation fund early, on the interest earned on your initial payments may be enough to pay the premium later on.

Acquisition or Bank Fee   The average fee you'll pay to the car dealer at the start of the lease. Typically $300–400, not negotiable.

Addendum   Any addition to, or modification of, a contract. Also called an amendment or rider.

Adjustable-Rate Mortgage (ARM) A type of loan whose prevailing interest rate is tied to an economic index (like one-year Treasury Bills), which fluctuates with the market. There are several types of ARMs, including one-year ARMs, which adjust every year; three-year ARMs, which adjust every three years; and five-year ARMs, which adjust every five years. When the loan adjusts, the lender tacks a margin (its profit) onto the economic index rate to come up with your loan's new rate. ARMs are considered far riskier than fixed-rate mortgages, but their starting interest rates are extremely low, and in the past five to ten years, people have done very well with them.

Adjusted Gross Income Your income reduced by contributions to retirement accounts, alimony payments, and certain other exclusions.

Agency A term used to describe the relationship between a seller and a broker, or a buyer and a broker.

Agency Closing The lender's use of a title company or other party to act on the lender's behalf for the purposes of closing on the purchase of a home or refinancing of a loan.

Agent An individual who represents a buyer or a seller in the purchase or sale of a home. Licensed by the state, an agent must work for a broker or a brokerage firm.

Agreement of Sale This document is also known as the contract of purchase, purchase agreement, or sales agreement. It is the agreement by which the seller agrees to sell you his or her property if you pay a certain price. It contains all the provisions and conditions for the purchase, must be written, and is signed by both parties.

Amortization A payment plan which enables the borrower to reduce his debt gradually through monthly payments of principal and interest. Amortization tables allow you to see exactly how much you would pay each month in interest and how much you repay in principal, depending on the amount of money borrowed at a specific interest rate.

Annual Mileage Allowance The number of miles included as part of an automobile lease.

Annual Percentage Rate (APR) The total cost of your loan, expressed as a percentage rate of interest, which includes not only the loan's interest rate, but factors in all the costs associated with making that loan, including closing costs and fees. The costs are then amortized over the life of the

469

loan. Banks are required by the federal Truth-in-Lending statutes to disclose the APR of a loan, which allows borrowers a common ground for comparing various loans from different lenders.

Any-Occupation Policy A type of private disability insurance that pays if—from the insurer's perspective—you can't work at any job for which your education and training qualify you.

Application A series of documents you must fill out when you apply for a loan.

Application Fee A one-time fee charged by the mortgage company for processing your application for a loan. Sometimes the application fee is applied toward certain costs, including the appraisal and credit report.

Appraisal The opinion of an appraiser, who estimates the value of a home at a specific point in time.

Articles-of-Agreement Mortgage A type of seller financing which allows the buyer to purchase the home in installments over a specified period of time. The seller keeps legal title to the home until the loan is paid off. The buyer receives an interest in the property—called equitable title—but does not own it. However, because the buyer is paying the real estate taxes and paying interest to the seller, it is the buyer who receives the tax benefits of home ownership.

Asset Allocation A term used to express your choice among different types of asset classes and styles. You might have growth or value funds, which are mutual funds typically focused on companies that are growing quickly or companies that are perhaps out of favor temporarily, and are typically priced cheaply relative to their assets, profits and potential. Your fund may be international (holding shares of international companies or indices) or domestic (holding shares of U.S. companies only). It might contain large cap (focused on huge corporations), mid-cap (medium companies), or small-cap (small companies) stocks.

Assumption of Mortgage If you assume a mortgage when you purchase a home, you undertake to fulfill the obligations of the existing loan agreement the seller made with the lender. The obligations are similar to those that you would incur if you took out a new mortgage. When assuming a mortgage, you become personally liable for the payment of principal and interest. The seller, or original mortgagor, is released from the liability, and should get that release in writing. Otherwise, he or she could be liable if you don't make the monthly payments.

Balloon Mortgage   A type of mortgage which is generally short in length, but is amortized over 25 or 30 years so that the borrower pays a combination of interest and principal each month. At the end of the loan term, the entire balance of the loan must be repaid at once.

Blue Chips   Large, well-established companies that offer investors some growth with a solid dividend. Companies listed on the S&P 500 are frequently referred to as blue chip stocks, capable of weathering even the worst market fluctuations.

Bond   A loan to a government (federal or municipal) or a corporation. You earn interest on your money as well as a promise to get your principal back.

Bond Fund   A bond fund is a short-hand way of talking about a mutual fund made up of bond issues.

Broker   An individual who acts as the agent of the seller or buyer.

Building Line or Setback   The distance from the front, back, or side of a lot beyond which construction or improvements may not extend without permission from the proper governmental authority. The building line may be established by a filed plat of subdivision, by restrictive covenants in deeds, by building codes, or by zoning ordinances.

Buy Down   An incentive offered by a developer or seller that allows the buyer to lower his or her initial interest rate by putting up a certain amount of money. A buy down also refers to the process of paying extra points up front at the closing of your loan in order to have a lower interest rate over the life of the loan.

Buyer Broker   A buyer broker is a real estate broker who specializes in representing home buyers. Unlike a seller broker or conventional broker, the buyer broker has a fiduciary duty to the buyer, because the buyer accepts the legal obligation of paying the broker. The buyer broker is obligated to find the best property for a client, and then negotiate the best possible purchase price and terms. Buyer brokerage has gained a significant amount of respect in recent years, since the National Association of Realtors has changed its code of ethics to accept this designation.

Buyer's Market   Market conditions that favor the buyer. A buyer's market is usually expressed when there are too many homes for sale, and a home can be bought for less money.

Calls   When a company or bond issuer orders preferred stock or bond holders to turn in their stock or bonds for money.

Capital Gain   A profit made on the sale of stocks, bonds, real estate, or other assets.

Capitalized Cost (or **Gross Capitalized Cost**)   This is the price of the car that the dealer uses to construct the lease. It also includes all the items and services that come with the car in the lease. A crucial number, it is negotiable.

Capitalized Cost Reduction   Your down payment. It is negotiable. If you're trading in a car, the value of the trade-in should be applied to either the capitalized cost reduction or your monthly payments.

Capital Loss   The loss taken on the sale of stocks, bonds, real estate, or other assets.

Certificate of Title   A document or instrument issued by a local government agency to a homeowner, naming the homeowner as the owner of a specific piece of property. At the sale of the property, the certificate of title is transferred to the buyer. The agency then issues a new certificate of title to the buyer.

Cash Surrender Value (Cash Value)   The amount available in cash upon voluntary termination of a policy by its owner before it becomes payable by death or maturity. This amount is typically paid in cash or paid-up insurance.

Cash Value Policy   A category of life insurance including whole life, universal life and variable universal life that combines the death benefit with a savings component. The insurance policy is broken down into two parts: the mortality charge (the part that pays for the death benefit) and a reserve (the savings component that earns interest). As you get older, the cost of the death benefit rises. In addition to interest, the reserve might receive an annual dividend, depending on how many policies have been paid out and how well the insurer has invested the premiums it has received.

Catastrophic Care   Most health insurance policies cover catastrophic care, including such procedures as transplants, complex neonatal care, severe burns care, or trauma care.

472

Chain of Title   The lineage of ownership of a particular property.

Churning   Also known as twisting, churning is an attempt by an unscrupulous agent from an insurance company to cancel your existing policy and replace it with a new one, drawing down your cash value (called "juice" in industry jargon) to pay for it. This activity generates additional commission for the agent and may result in your having to pay more down the line.

Classified Shares   Mutual fund shares grouped alphabetically. "A" shares are traditional load fund where you pay the broker right off the top of your investment. "B" shares still pay a commission, but the mutual fund puts up the money and then gradually withdraws it from your account. "C" and "D" shares are sometimes called level-load funds. The broker gets no commission up front, but instead gets an annual fee (called a trail commission) from the investor's account.

Closed-Ended   A mutual fund that has closed its doors to new investors and their cash in order to maintain its size and position in the market.

Code-and-Contention Coverage (Building Code Coverage)   A homeowner's insurance rider that covers the cost of meeting new building codes that may have gone into effect after your home was built and to which any new homes built are subject. Also known as an Ordinance-and-Law Rider.

Common Stock   A share of ownership in a company.

Conditionally Renewable Policy   A type of private disability insurance policy that may be renewed at the insurer's discretion.

Consumer Federation of America (CFA)   A nonprofit association of consumer interest groups that works to further the consumer interest through educational programs and advocacy. The CFA pays particular attention to those in need, including children, elderly persons living on fixed incomes, and the poor.

Consumer Price Index (CPI)   A measure of the changes in price of all the goods and services that urban households purchase for consumption. The CPI is used as an economic indicator, a policy guide, a means to adjust income payments for inflation, and a means to determine the cost of school lunches, to mention a few of its uses.

Contrarian Fund   A contrarian fund is one that is positioned against conventional wisdom. So when Asia was headed into a recession during the late 1990s, contrarian international funds went in and began swooping up the stocks of companies, betting that they'd come back.

Cost-of-Living Adjustments (COLAs)   A rider that can be added to a long-term care policy under which the policy owner's benefits increase to keep pace with the consumer price index (CPI).

Convertible Bond   A bond is one that can be converted into shares of stock.

Corporate Bond   A bond issued by a corporation.

Coupon   The actual interest payment made on each bond. If you have a $5,000 bond paying 7 percent interest, you will receive $350 each year, most likely in two $175 payments. The $350 is the coupon. The interest rate of the bond is also referred to as the coupon rate. The name originates from how you used to collect your interest (and still do with some bonds). You'd actually clip a coupon and bring it in to receive your interest. Today, this is often done electronically, with the interest simply deposited in your bank account.

Current Yield   The coupon interest payment divided by the bond's price. This will fluctuate based on where interest rates are and what you could currently sell your bond for in the marketplace.

Debt Service   The total amount of debt (credit cards, mortgage, car loan) that an individual is carrying at any one time.

Deferred Compensation Plan   Employees may put a limited portion of their pre-tax earnings into a deferred compensation plan, like a 401K or Keogh. The earnings are excluded from tax calculations, and grow tax-free until the funds are withdrawn at retirement.

Dependent   An individual for whom the taxpayer provides over half of the support for the calendar year. This could be a child, spouse, relative, or nonrelative living as a member of the taxpayer's household.

Discount   Newly issued bonds are typically sold at some sort of discount. So a bond that has a face value of $1,000 and sells for $925 has a $75 discount. When interest rates rise, bonds are discounted more because you need a less expensive bond to achieve the same interest rate.

Diversified Funds   According to the Diversified Mutual Fund Investment Act of 1940, a mutual fund calling itself diversified must spread its assets around. Seventy-five percent of its assets must be divvied up so no more than 5 percent of the fund's assets are invested in a single stock.

Funds that do not call themselves diversified may invest a larger percent of their holdings in a single stock.

Dividends   Your share of a company's profits, typically paid out in quarterly installments. To find out how much you'll receive, multiply the dividend (published in your local paper) by the number of shares you own.

Endorsement   The amendment of a policy usually by means of a rider.

Equity   Your share of ownership in a company. Stockholders are often referred to as equity investors, because they invest in the equity of a company.

Estimated Tax Payments   If you are self-employed, or have significant dividend income or investment income in addition to your regular salary, you must make tax payments based on the estimated tax you'll owe at the end of the year. Your estimated tax payments must equal either 100 percent of the tax you paid in the previous year or 90 percent of your total tax for the current year.

Exemption   You may take an exemption, from your adjusted gross income for yourself, your spouse, and any dependents. The exemption basically excludes money from taxation.

Fee Simple   The most basic type of ownership, under which the owner has the right to use and dispose of the property at will.

Fiduciary Duty   A relationship of trust between a broker and a seller or a buyer broker and a buyer, or an attorney and a client.

Filing Status   A declaration as to your personal status (i.e., married, single, separated, dependents or not). Your filing status will determine your standard deduction, the tax rate table you'll use to compute your tax liability, and the deductions and credits to which you're entitled.

First Mortgage   A mortgage that takes priority over all other voluntary liens.

Fixture   Personal property, such as a built-in bookcase, furnace, hot water heater, and recessed lights, that becomes "affixed" because it has been permanently attached to the home.

Foreclosure   The legal action taken to extinguish a home owner's right and interest in a property, so that the property can be sold in a foreclosure sale to satisfy a debt.

401(k) Plan   A defined contribution plan for employees. Some companies do not offer this benefit, but if they do, you may contribute up to a maximum set by the government and indexed to inflation. For 1998 and 1999, the 401K limit was $10,000 (although you have to earn enough to put that much away). As an additional benefit, some employers match contributions up to a certain dollar limit or percentage.

403(b) Plan   A retirement plan offered by certain religious, charitable, or public organizations. It operates much like a 401(k) plan.

Fund of Funds   A mutual fund that is made up of other mutual funds. The idea here is that you're not diversified enough by choosing a diversified mutual fund. So you buy one fund that diversifies by purchasing several different funds.

Fund Supermarket   An investment firm (often called a family) that offers not only its own mutual funds, but the ability to invest in the mutual funds or other investment firms. The nice thing about this is that all of your investments in these funds would be displayed on one statement from your primary family. On the down side, sometimes supermarkets will tack on additional charges for investing in funds outside the family if that fund doesn't separately pay a commission.

GAP Insurance   This stands for guaranteed auto protection and you need it if you're leasing. This insurance will pay the balance on the lease and the early termination penalties if the car is stolen or totaled. Negotiate to have it included with your lease payment.

Gift Letter   A letter to the lender indicating that a gift of cash has been made to the buyer and that it is not expected to be repaid. The letter must detail the amount of the gift, and the name of the giver.

Good Faith Estimate (GFE)   Under RESPA, lenders are required to give potential borrowers a written Good Faith Estimate of closing costs within three days of an application submission.

Grace Period   The period of time after a loan payment due date in which a mortgage payment may be made and not be considered delinquent.

Graduated Payment Mortgage A mortgage in which the payments increase over the life of the mortgage, allowing the borrower to make very low payments at the beginning of the loan.

Growth Stock A company that is focusing on growing above all else. All profits are typically reinvested into the company to keep it growing quickly, so little if any dividends are paid.

Guaranteed Cost Replacement A type of homeowner's insurance that guarantees to rebuild your home no matter what the cost and has a rider built in to take care of inflation. On some policies, insurers might only pay to rebuild your home up to 120 to 125 percent of your policy amount. It's up to you to stay on top of how much it will cost to rebuild your home.

Guaranteed Renewable Policy An insurance policy that must be renewed as long as the insured pays the premium on time. Typically, an insurer cannot make any changes to a guaranteed renewable policy other than to increase the premium rate for an entire class of policy holders.

Hard Asset Funds A mutual fund that holds a portion of its assets in gold or silver, or other commodities like these, or in indices that are based on hard assets. Hard asset funds may also be invested in real estate.

Hazard Insurance Insurance that covers the property from damages that might materially affect its value. Also known as homeowner's insurance, it may also include personal liability and theft coverage.

Health Insurance Portability and Accountability Act Effective July 1, 1997 this act specifies that if a person has been covered by insurance during the past 12 months, a new insurer cannot refuse to cover that person nor can it force him or her to accept a waiting period when joining a new group plan.

HMO (Health Maintenance Organization) An organization that provides a wide range of comprehensive health care services for a specified group at a fixed periodic payment. An HMO can be sponsored by the government, medical schools, hospitals, employers, labor unions, consumer groups, insurance companies, and hospital-medical plans.

Holdback An amount of money held back at closing by the lender or the escrow agent until a particular condition has been met. If the problem is a repair, the money is kept until the repair is made. If the repair is not made, the lender or escrow agent uses the money to make the repair. Buyers and

477

sellers may also have holdbacks between them, to ensure that specific conditions of the sale are met.

Homeowner's Association   A group of homeowners in a particular subdivision or area who band together to take care of common property and common interests.

Homeowner's Insurance   See hazard insurance.

Home Warranty   A service contract that covers appliances (with exclusions) in working condition in the home for a certain period of time, usually one year. Homeowners are responsible for a per-call service fee. There is a homeowner's warranty for new construction. Some developers will purchase a warranty from a company specializing in new construction for the homes they sell. A homeowner's warranty will warrant the good working order of the appliances and workmanship of a new home for between one and ten years; for example, appliances might be covered for one year while the roof may be covered for several years.

Hostile Takeover   When a company purchases another against the will of the purchased company's management.

Housing and Urban Development, Department of (HUD)   This is the federal department responsible for the nation's housing programs. It also regulates RESPA, the Real Estate Settlement Procedures Act, which governs how lenders must deal with their customers.

Inception Fees   These are the upfront fees that the car dealer will require you to pay, including your first monthly payment, refundable security deposit, DMV fees, and possibly an acquisition fee. You'll have to come up with this cash upfront, even if you're getting a "no money down" lease. If you're paying a down payment, you'll have to add that in as well.

Income Replacement Policy   A category of private disability insurance that covers the difference between what you earned prior to the disability and what you now earn doing a different job.

Income Stock   A company that tends to pay out more of its profits to shareholders (in the form of dividends) and put less resources toward growth.

Indemnity Plans   A type of health care insurance set up as a fee-for-service plan. You get something done, you pay for it. Typically there are no restrictions on care, and the plan coverage kicks in when you reach a certain deductible. Unlike an HMO, you (or the doctor's office) will also have to bill the insurance company. The nice thing about indemnity plans is that you can see the doctor you choose and seek second opinions or specialists anywhere in the country. On the other hand, it's the most expensive way to go, and not every employer offers this plan.

Index Funds   These are mutual funds designed to mimic the movements of a particular index. For example, a fund trying to mimic the movement of the S&P 500, will either purchase every stock on the S&P 500 in the same ratio that those stocks appear on the index, or will purchase a representative sample of companies that closely approximate the index. Since index funds rarely change their holdings, they are typically cheap to hold and may do better for investors over the long haul.

Individual Retirement Account (IRA)   An account to which any individual who earns income may contribute up to $2,000 per year. The contributions are tax-deductible, and the earnings grow tax-free although they may be taxed upon withdrawal.

Initial Public Offering (IPO)   A young company hoping to finance future growth will often go public to raise additional funds. Many IPOs rise dramatically the first day of the offering, then settle back down to a more reasonable share price. Some investors try to get in on the ground floor of an IPO and then sell their shares within the first day or week.

Inspection   The service an inspector performs when he or she is hired to scrutinize the home for any possible structural defects. May also be done in order to check for the presence of toxic substances, such as leaded paint or water, asbestos, radon, or pests, including termites.

Installment Contract   The purchase of property in installments. Title to the property is given to the purchaser when all installments are made.

Institutional Investors or Lenders   Private or public companies, corporations, or funds (such as pension funds) that purchase loans on the secondary market from commercial lenders such as banks and savings and loans. Or, they are sources of funds for mortgages through mortgage brokers.

Interest   Money charged for the use of borrowed funds. Usually expressed as an interest rate, it is the percentage of the total loan charged annually for the use of the funds.

Interest-Only Mortgage   A loan in which only the interest is paid on a regular basis (usually monthly), and the principal is owed in full at the end of the loan term.

Interest Rate Cap The total number of percentage points that an adjustable-rate mortgage (ARM) might rise over the life of the loan.

Joint Tenancy An equal, undivided ownership in a property taken by two or more owners. Under joint tenancy there are rights of survivorship, which means that if one of the owners dies, the surviving owner rather than the heirs of the estate inherits the other's total interest in the property.

Keogh A retirement plan for employees of unincorporated businesses or self-employed individuals. You may contribute up to 25 percent of your earned income, to a maximum of $30,000.

Landscape The trees, flowers, planting, lawn, and shrubbery that surround the exterior of a dwelling.

Late Charge A penalty applied to a mortgage payment that arrives after the grace period (usually the 10th or 15th of a month).

Lease Charge or Money Factor This is the complicated way dealers calculate lease payments. Similar to an interest rate, and you should multiply the money factor by 2400 to approximate the annual percentage rate of your lease. It is not negotiable, but differs from lease-to-lease, car-to-car, and company-to-company. Usually it is not disclosed—that's because car companies are not required to under Regulation M.

Lease with an Option to Buy When the renter or lessee of a piece of property has the right to purchase the property for a specific period of time at a specific price. Usually, a lease with an option to buy allows a first-time buyer to accumulate a down payment by applying a portion of the monthly rent toward the down payment.

Lender A person, company, corporation, or entity that lends money for the purchase of real estate.

Lessee You, or the person leasing the vehicle. In apartment leases, the lessee is the renter.

Lessor The leasing company, bank or finance company that buys the car from the dealer and leases it back to you. The name of the lessor should be listed on the back of the contract. In an apartment rental agreement, the lessor is the landlord.

Letter of Intent   A formal statement, usually in letter form, from the buyer to the seller stating that the buyer intends to purchase a specific piece of property for a specific price on a specific date.

Leverage   Using a small amount of cash, say a 10 or 20 percent down payment, to purchase a piece of property.

Lien   An encumbrance against the property, which may be voluntary or involuntary. There are many different kinds of liens, including a tax lien (for unpaid federal, state, or real estate taxes), a judgment lien (for monetary judgments by a court of law), a mortgage lien (when you take out a mortgage), and a mechanic's lien (for work done by a contractor on the property that has not been paid for). For a lien to be attached to the property's title, it must be filed or recorded with local county government.

Life Cycle Funds   These are mutual funds specifically designed to mirror what many experts feel are optimum ratios of stocks and bonds throughout the different stages in your life. You may be able to choose from 3 or 4 funds, one designed for 20 to 30-year-olds, one for 40 to 50-year-olds, and so on.

Listing   A property that a broker agrees to list for sale in return for a commission.

Loan   An amount of money that is lent to a borrower, who agrees to repay it plus interest.

Load   A sales charge that can range from 1 to 7 percent. It might be a front-load (payable when you buy into the fund) or a back-load (payable when you cash out). You typically pay this because you want the service of a financial professional selecting and building your portfolio. Your load may decrease the longer you hold the fund. If you cashed out in the first year, you'd pay 6 percent. Cash out three years later and the load may only be 3 percent.

Loan Commitment   A written document that states that a mortgage company has agreed to lend a buyer a certain amount of money at a certain rate of interest for a specific period of time, which may contain sets of conditions and a date by which the loan must close.

Loan Origination Fee   A one-time fee charged by the mortgage company to arrange the financing for the loan.

Loan-to-Value Ratio   The ratio of the amount of money you wish to borrow compared to the value of the property you wish to purchase. Institutional investors (who buy loans on the secondary market from your mortgage company) set up certain ratios that guide lending practices. For example, the mortgage company might only lend you 80 percent of a property's value.

Location   Where property is geographically situated. "Location, location, location" is a broker's maxim that states that where the property is located is its most important feature, because you can change everything about a house, except its location.

Lock-In   The mechanism by which a borrower locks in the interest rate that will be charged on a particular loan. Usually, the lock lasts for a certain time period, such as 30, 45, or 60 days. On a new construction, the lock may be much longer.

Long-Term Care Insurance   Insurance that covers the cost of long-term care in a nursing home, other custodial care settings, or at home.

Maintenance Fee   The monthly or annual fee charged to condo, co-op, or townhouse owners, and paid to the homeowner's association, for the maintenance of common property. Also called an assessment.

Management Buyout   When the individuals running a company get together, borrow money, and buy most or all of its common shares.

Market Price   On any given day, your bond will be worth more or less than the face value. That's because the bond market is continually active, with traders bidding up and down the value of bonds based on the current interest rate of the day. When interest rates rise, bonds are worth less (because it takes a smaller amount of capital to earn the same amount of interest). When interest rates fall, bonds are worth more (because it takes a greater amount of money to earn the same amount of interest.)

Market Sector   The categorizing of companies based on the industry in which they operate. Some sectors include technology and transportation.

Matured Bond   A bond that has been paid back in full.

Medicaid   State public assistance programs to persons who are unable to pay for health care. Title XIX of the federal Social Security Act provides matching federal funds for financing state Medicaid programs.

Medicare   A program of Hospital Insurance (Part A) and Supplementary Medical Insurance (Part B) protection provided under the Social Security Act.

Medicare Supplemental Insurance (Medigap or MedSup)   A term used in reference to private insurance products that supplement Medicare insurance benefits.

Merger   When two companies voluntarily join together. Sometimes mergers are really takeovers, where one company ends up becoming the dominant presence.

Mortgage   A document granting a lien on a home in exchange for financing granted by a lender. The mortgage is the means by which the lender secures the loan and has the ability to foreclose on the home.

Mortgage Banker   A company or a corporation, like a bank, that lends its own funds to borrowers in addition to bringing together lenders and borrowers. A mortgage banker may also service the loan (i.e., collect the monthly payments).

Mortgage Broker   A company or individual that brings together lenders and borrowers and processes mortgage applications.

Mortgagee   A legal term for the lender.

Mortgagor   A legal term for the borrower.

Multiple Listing Service (MLS)   A computerized listing of all properties offered for sale by member brokers. Buyers may only gain access to the MLS by working with a member broker.

Municipal Bond   A bond offered by a local municipality. Munis, as they are commonly known, are not taxed by the federal government.

Negative Amortization   A condition created when the monthly mortgage payment is less than the amount necessary to pay off the loan over the period of time set forth in the note. Because you're paying less than the amount necessary, the actual loan amount increases over time. That's how you end up with negative equity. To pay off the loan, a lump-sum payment must be made.

Net Asset Value (NAV)   The value per share of a mutual fund. This is similar to a stock price.

483

No-Fault Insurance   A legal policy adopted by some states that abolishes liability for a death or injury caused by a motor vehicle regardless of the accident's cause. An injured party cannot sue another driver unless a particular crime or hazard is proven. Drivers in states with no-fault insurance laws can buy *personal injury protection*, which means you pay for your injuries and the other driver pays for his or her injuries.

No-Load   These are mutual funds that charge no fees to buy in or cash out. There are other charges, however. Check the funds *expense ratio* to find out how much you're being charged.

Non-Cancelable Policy   A policy specifying that, as long as you pay your premiums on time, the insurer can't raise your premium and can't cancel your policy.

Opened-Ended   This is a mutual fund that continues to welcome new investors and their cash.

Open-End Lease   When you bring the car back, the dealer compares the actual value of the car with the residual value stated in your lease contract. If the actual value is less than the stated residual value, you make up the difference. If, by chance, the car has retained more of its value, the dealer pays you.

Operating Expense Ratio (OER)   Also known as the expense ratio, the OER is the cost of administering and managing a mutual fund, including salaries and bonuses paid. This can run .05 to 2 percent per year.

Option   When a buyer pays for the right or option to purchase property for a given length of time, without having the obligation to actually purchase the property.

Optionally Renewable Policy   A contract of health insurance in which the insurer reserves the right to terminate the coverage at any anniversary or, in some cases, at any premium due date, but does not have the right to terminate coverage between such dates.

Ordinance-and-Law Rider   See **Code-and-Contention Coverage**

Origination Fee   A fee charged by the lender for allowing you to borrow money to purchase property. The fee—which is also referred to as points—is usually expressed as a percentage of the total loan amount.

Ownership   The absolute right to use, enjoy, and dispose of property. You own it!

Own-Occupation Policy A type of private disability insurance that pays if you can't work at your specific job.

Package Mortgage A mortgage that uses both real and personal property to secure a loan.

Paper Slang usage that refers to the mortgage, trust deed, installment, and land contract.

Par The bond's face value. A $1,000 bond will have a par value of $1,000. The term par may be a bit confusing because even if your bond is worth $10,000, par also refers to 100, as in 100 percent of a bond's value. So you may hear that your bond cost 95, which means 95 percent of par. That means you'll get a 5 percent discount, and pay $950 for every bond with a $1,000 face value. If the bond cost 116, that means it's 116 percent of par, or cost you $1,160 for a bond with a face value of $1,000.

Partial Disability Coverage A benefit sometimes found in disability income policies providing for the payment of reduced monthly income in the event the insured cannot work full time and/or is prevented from performing one or more important daily duties pertaining to his or her occupation.

Penalty A fine levied by the IRS. You may pay a flat dollar fee or a fee based on an interest charge for unpaid taxes, failure to pay taxes, failure to make estimated tax payments, failure to make federal tax deposits, or filing late.

Personal Articles Rider Coverage designed to insure property of a moveable nature. The coverage typically protects against all physical loss, subject to special exclusions and conditions.

Personal Injury Protection First-party no-fault coverage in which an insurer pays, within the specified limits, the wage loss, medical, hospital and funeral expenses of the insured.

Personal Property Moveable property, such as appliances, furniture, clothing, and artwork.

PITI An acronym for Principal-Interest-Taxes-and-Insurance. These are usually the four parts of your monthly mortgage payment.

Pledged Account Borrowers who do not want to have a real estate tax or insurance escrow administered by the mortgage servicer can, in some circumstances, pledge a savings account into which enough money to cover real estate taxes and the insurance premium must be deposited. You must then make the payments for your real estate taxes and insurance premiums from a separate account. If you fail to pay your taxes or premiums, the lender is allowed to use the funds in the pledged account to make those payments.

Point   A point is one percent of the loan amount.

POS (Point of Service) Plans   A health insurance plan that permits an individual to choose providers outside the plan yet encourages the use of network providers. This type of plan is also known as an open-ended HMO or PPO.

Possession   Being in control of a piece of property, and having the right to use it to the exclusion of all others.

Power of Attorney   The legal authorization given to an individual to act on behalf of another individual.

PPO (Preferred Provider Organization)   An arrangement whereby a third-party payer contracts with a group of medical care providers who furnish services at lower than usual fees in return for prompt payment and a certain volume of patients.

Pre-Existing Condition   A physical condition that existed before the effective date of coverage.

Preferred stock   A special class of stock that may have certain voting privileges. Companies typically pay a fixed, high dividend whose return is similar to what you'd get on a bond. While the price of preferred stock can rise, common stock prices typically rise faster than preferred stock.

Prepaid Interest   Interest paid at closing for the number of days left in the month after closing. For example, if you close on the 15th, you would prepay the interest for the 16th through the end of the month.

Prepayment Penalty   A fine imposed when a loan is paid off before it comes due. Many states now have laws against prepayment penalties, although banks with federal charters are exempt from state laws. If possible, do not use a mortgage that has a prepayment penalty, or you will be charged a fine if you sell your property or refinance your loan before the penalty period has expired.

Prequalifying for a Loan   When a mortgage company tells a buyer in advance of the formal application approximately how much money the buyer can afford to borrow.

Presumptive Disability   A type of private disability insurance that presumes its holder to be fully disabled and entitled to full benefits if he or she loses his or her sight, speech, hearing, or some other specified faculty.

Price to Earnings Ratio (P/E)   This is the price of the stock divided by a company's earnings per share. Typically, newspapers will publish a company's P/E ratio in the stock market tables. When a company's stock has a high P/E ratio, its earnings have risen rapidly and investors have bid up the price of the stock even higher, guessing that continued high growth is in the company's future.

Principal   If you're getting a home loan, the principal is the amount of money you borrow. If you're buying a bond, the principal is the amount you're lending. Typically, you'll buy bonds with a face value of $1,000. If you buy a $1,000 bond, your principal is $1,000.

Private Mortgage Insurance (PMI)   Special insurance that specifically protects the top 20 percent of a loan, allowing the lender to lend more than 80 percent of the value of the property. PMI is paid in monthly installments by the borrower.

Property Tax   A tax levied by a county or local authority on the value of real estate.

Proration   The proportional division of certain costs of home ownership. Usually used at closing to figure out how much the buyer and seller each owe for certain expenditures, including real estate taxes, assessments, and water bills.

Purchase Agreement   An agreement between the buyer and seller for the purchase of property.

Purchase Fee   This is a fee you'll pay in addition to the purchase option price if you do decide to purchase your leased car at the end of the lease term. Typically, it's about $250–300 and it is negotiable.

Purchase Money Mortgage   An instrument used in seller financing, a purchase money mortgage is signed by a buyer and given to the seller in exchange for a portion of the purchase price.

Purchase-Option Price The price you'll pay to buy the car at the end of the lease. Typically, it's not negotiable, but it may be tied into the number of miles you're allotted each year. A car that's driven 15,000 miles a year will be less valuable than a car driven only 10,000 miles a year.

Quit-Claim Deed A deed that operates to release any interest in a property that a person may have, *without a representation that he or she actually has a right in that property*. For example, Sally may use a quit-claim deed to grant Bill her interest in the White House, in Washington, DC, although she may not actually own, or have any rights to, that particular house.

Real Rate of Return Your rate of return with a bond consists of two pieces: The interest you've earned on the bond and the actual market value of the bond (it could be above or below face value when you sell it). If the market value of the bond has appreciated, you may have to pay capital gains on the rise in value. The interest you earn is taxed like income.

Real Estate Land and anything permanently attached to it, such as buildings and improvements.

Real Estate Agent An individual licensed by the state, who acts on behalf of the seller or buyer. For his or her services, the agent receives a commission, which is usually expressed as a percentage of the sales price of a home and is split with his or her real estate firm. A real estate agent must also be a real estate broker or work for one.

Real Estate Attorney An attorney who specializes in the purchase and sale of real estate.

Real Estate Broker An individual who is licensed by the state to act as an agent on behalf of the seller or buyer. For his or her services, the broker receives a commission, which is usually expressed as a percentage of the sales price of a home.

Real Estate Settlement Procedures Act (RESPA) This federal statute was originally passed in 1974, and contains provisions that govern the way companies involved with a real estate closing must treat each other and the consumer. For example, one section of RESPA requires lenders to give consumers a written Good Faith Estimate within three days of making an application for a loan. Another section of RESPA prohibits title companies from giving referral fees to brokers for steering business to them.

Realtist A designation given to an agent or broker who is a member of the National Association of Real Estate Brokers.

Realtor A designation given to a real estate agent or broker who is a member of the National Association of Realtors.

Recording The process of filing documents at a specific government office. Upon such recording, the document becomes part of the public record.

Redemption Fee Typically a charge that's imposed on people who redeem their shares within a short period of time. It might be 90 days or 3 years. Some funds impose a .25 percent redemption fee no matter when you cash out. Why? This is another way for funds to be profitable. But there may be some additional costs if too many people take their money out at exactly the same moment. Funds have to keep some money in cash reserves in case people want to redeem their shares. If too many people want to redeem their shares all at once, the fund would have to sell some stock, perhaps at not the most fortuitous time.

Redlining The slang term used to describe an illegal practice of discrimination against a particular racial group within a certain geographical area by real estate agents and lenders and insurance agents. Redlining typically occurs when lenders decide certain areas of a community are too high risk and refuse to lend to buyers who want to purchase property in those areas, regardless of their qualifications or creditworthiness.

Regulation M The revised federal rules that went into effect at the end of 1997. Regulation M standardized and simplified leasing forms and language. While it requires dealers to disclose all sorts of information, it does not require them to disclose the money factor (also known as the lease rate).

Regulation Z Also known as the Truth in Lending Act. Congress determined that lenders must provide a written Good Faith Estimate of closing costs to all borrowers and provide them with other written information about the loan.

Replacement Insurance Guarantees that the insurer will pay for the cost of replacing the home in its current condition. This is a less expensive form of homeowner's insurance than *Guaranteed Cost Replacement Insurance* and it typically won't pay to bring your home up to current standards.

Reserve The amount of money set aside by a condo, co-op, or homeowners' association for future capital improvements.

Residual Value   How much the dealer says the car will be worth at the end of the lease term. Typically, this is not negotiable.

Roth IRA   The Tax Relief Act of 1997 created a Roth IRA, which allows non-deductible, after-tax contributions of up to $2,000 per year. As long as you hold the IRA for at least 5 years, and meet other requirements the gains are tax free. In addition, you are not required to make a minimum contribution each year, and there is no age limit for additional contributions.

Sale-Leaseback   A transaction in which the seller sells property to a buyer, who then leases the property back to the seller. This is accomplished within the same transaction.

Sales Contract   The document by which a buyer contracts to purchase property. Also known as the purchase contract or a contract to purchase.

Sales Tax   In most areas, a lease is considered the same as a purchase. So you'll pay sales tax on your purchase. That's one reason to think carefully about where you purchase or lease your vehicle. You might only pay 7.5 percent sales tax instead of 8.75 percent depending on where you buy or lease your car. And when you're talking about a $20,000 car, saving 1.25 percent means saving $250.

Savings Bonds   A bond backed by the U.S. government, savings bonds (which come in different series, like EE and HH) can be purchased in small amounts, either directly from a bank, the Treasury Department, or through a broker. They're non-transferable, and are not traded as are other government offerings. In September 1998, the Government began selling an inflation-indexed savings bonds. The I-bond guarantees that your return will out-pace inflation, and is actually based on the rate of inflation plus a fixed rate of return, perhaps 3 to 3.5 percent.

Savings Incentive Match Plan for Employees (SIMPLE-401(k) or IRA)   A pension plan for employers with 100 or fewer employees (who earn at least $5,000 per year). The employer must match the employee contribution, which is limited to a dollar amount that is indexed for inflation. (The 1998 contribution limit for employees was $6,000.)

Second Mortgage   A mortgage that is obtained after the primary mortgage, and whose rights for repayment are secondary to the first mortgage.

490

Seller Broker   A broker who has a fiduciary responsibility to the seller. Most brokers are seller brokers, although an increasing number are buyer brokers, who have a fiduciary responsibility to the buyer.

Settlement Statement   A statement that details the monies paid out and received by the buyer and seller at closing.

Shared Appreciation Mortgage   A relatively new mortgage used to help first-time buyers who might not qualify for conventional financing. In a shared appreciation mortgage, the lender offers a below-market interest rate in return for a portion of the profits made by the home owner when the property is sold. Before entering into a shared appreciation mortgage, be sure to have your real estate attorney review the documentation.

Simplified Employee Pension (SEP-IRA)   This is a type of pension plan used by small businesses. The employer's contributions are excluded from the employee's taxable salary, and may not exceed 15 percent of the employee's salary or the current dollar amount set by the government ($30,000 in 1998), whichever is less.

Social Security   Under the Social Security Act of 1935, the government established the Social Security Administration to provide retirement benefits, disability income, and Medicare for working individuals and their spouses.

Special Assessment   An additional charge levied by a condo or co-op board in order to pay for capital improvements, or other unforeseen expenses.

Specialty Funds   A mutual fund that specializes in one particular market sector or industry, or even a specific piece of an industry.

Spin-Off   A company may divide itself into several pieces, giving new shares in the company to current shareholders. Your 100 shares of stock in one company may turn into 300 shares if the company divides itself into three, and rewards stockholders with one share in each new company for each share currently held.

Standard Deduction   If you decide not to itemize your deductions, or if you can't, you may opt for the standard deduction, an amount set by the government and indexed for inflation.

Stock Rights   Your right as a shareholder to purchase new shares, often at a discount. Sometimes you'll see this if you have an account at a Savings

& Loan that announces it intends to go public. Account holders are offered the right to purchase shares of stock in the company before the initial public offering.

Subagent   A broker who brings the buyer to the property. Although subagents would appear to be working for the buyer (a subagent usually ferries around the buyer, showing him or her properties), they are paid by the seller and have a fiduciary responsibility to the seller. Subagency is often confusing to first-time buyers, who think that because the subagent shows them property, the subagent is "their" agent, rather than the seller's.

Subdivision   The division of a large piece of property into several smaller pieces. Usually a developer or a group of developers will build single family or duplex homes of a similar design and cost within one subdivision.

Subvented Lease   A lease that's subsidized (typically by the auto manufacturer) in order to get rid of a certain kind of car. Subvented leases can be exceptional deals, and they are often the only way that leasing may be cheaper than owning (unless you pay cash, in which case a well-negotiated car purchase will almost certainly be cheaper than any lease you could get).

Surrender Value   *See* **Cash Surrender Value**

Takeover   When one company purchases another. Takeovers are considered to be friendly but there is often a lot of ill will as the company that was taken over adjusts to the new corporate culture.

Tax Audit   A formal examination of your tax return by IRS auditors.

Tax Bracket   A range of income which must pay a certain level of taxes. The higher your income, the higher your tax bracket, and the more tax you pay.

Tax Credit   A dollar-for-dollar amount subtracted directly from the taxes you owe.

Tax Lien   A lien that is attached to property if the owner does not pay his or her real estate taxes or federal income taxes. If overdue property taxes are not paid, the owner's property might be sold at auction for the amount owed in back taxes.

Tax Shelter   Investments entered into for the sole purpose of lowering your tax burden.

492

Taxable Income   Your gross earnings minus deductions and exclusions.

Tenancy by the Entirety   A type of ownership whereby both the husband and wife each own the complete property. Each spouse has an ownership interest in the property as their marital residence and, as a result, creditors cannot force the sale of the home to pay back the debts of one spouse without the other spouse's consent. There are rights of survivorship whereby upon the death of one spouse, the other spouse would immediately inherit the entire property.

Tenants in Common   A type of ownership in which two or more parties have an undivided interest in the property. The owners may or may not have equal shares of ownership, and there are no rights of survivorship. However, each owner retains the right to sell his or her share in the property as he or she sees fit.

Tender Offer   When a company wants to takeover another company, it will offer a price per share that is typically above the market price. You will be asked to tender, or surrender, your shares for the higher price. In reality, after the tender offer is made, the market price for your stock will go up and match the offer (if it doesn't match the offer, there is some concern in the market that the deal may not go through).

Term (Bonds)   Short-term bonds run up to 3 years in length. Intermediate bonds are from 3 to 10 years in length. Long-term bonds run up to 30 years in length. Generally, the bonds that pay the best are the long-term bonds. However, you'll only earn an extra percentage point or so on your money for which you'll have to tie it up for a long period of time. Financial planners say a better bet is to purchase intermediate-term bonds, which are more flexible.

Term (Car Lease)   How long the car lease lasts. Generally, you won't want to get a lease for longer than 3 years. Too many things can start to go wrong with a leased car in it's 4th or 5th year, and the likelihood that you'll get some nicks and dings increases.

Term (HomeLoan)   The length of your mortgage.

Title   Refers to the ownership of a particular piece of property.

Title Company   The corporation or company that insures the status of title (title insurance) through the closing, and may handle other aspects of the closing.

493

Title Insurance   Insurance that protects the lender and the property owner against losses arising from defects or problems with the title to property.

Torrens Title   A system of recording the chain of ownership for property, which takes its name from the man who created it in Australia in 1858, Sir Robert Torrens. While that system was popular in the nineteenth century, most cities have converted to other, less cumbersome, systems of recording.

Total Return   Your total return are your dividends plus the gain or loss in the price of the company's stock. If the stock rises 5 percent and your dividends are 2 percent, your total return is 7 percent.

Transaction Fees   The costs mutual funds incur when they buy and sell shares of stock on the open market.

Treasuries   The federal government offers three types of products to raise money. They are Treasury Bills (also known as a T-Bills), Treasury notes, and Treasury bonds. Uncle Sam uses the money raised from the sale of these three products to pay for social and spending programs. Collectively, this debt is our national debt. It is considered fail-proof, since it is backed by the U.S. government.

Treasury Bills (T Bills)   These are government-backed securities, with a minimum purchase price of $1,000. They are offered in 3-month, 6-month, and 12-month lengths. You buy the T-bill at a discount which, when divided by the effective cost, equals your rate of interest. (So if you purchase a $10,000 T-bill for $9,300, your interest rate is $700 ($9,300 = .08 or 8 percent.) The discount is deposited immediately into your account, and the rest of the face value arrives on the day the bond matures. You have the option of rolling over your T-bill for another period. Since T-bills, like all offerings from the Treasury Department are backed by the full faith and credit of the U.S. government, they're considered just about the safest investments around.

Trust Account   An account used by brokers and escrow agents, in which funds for another individual are held separately, and not commingled with other funds.

12(b)-1 Fees   These are a mutual fund's marketing expenses. They include everything from printing brochures to picking up the cost of entertaining or compensating brokers who put their clients into the fund.

Umbrella Liability Policy   Insures losses in excess of amounts covered by other liability insurance policies; also protects the insured in many situations not covered by the usual liability polices.

Underwriter   One who underwrites a loan for another. Your lender will have an investor underwrite your loan.

Universal Life Insurance   A flexible premium life insurance policy under which the policyholder may change the death benefit from time to time (with satisfactory evidence of insurability for increases), vary the amount or timing of premium payments, and choose the investment vehicle for his or her premiums. Premiums (less expense charges and commissions) are credited to a policy account from which mortality charges are deducted and to which interest is credited at a rate that may change from time to time.

Variable Interest Rate   An interest rate that rises and falls according to a particular economic indicator, such as Treasury Bills.

Viatical Settlement   Payment of a portion of the proceeds from life insurance to an insured who is terminally ill.

Void   A contract or document that is not enforceable.

Voluntary Lien   A lien, such as a mortgage, that a homeowner elects to grant to a lender.

Waiver   The surrender or relinquishment of a particular right, claim, or privilege.

Warrants   Sometimes when you buy preferred stock or bonds of speculative companies, you get a warrant, or the right to buy additional shares of stock at a pre-determined price. This sounds great, but the company usually has the right to call in the warrants, forcing you to exercise them (i.e., buy stock at the current price) or receive a few cents for each warrant you hold.

Warranty   A legally binding promise given to the buyer at closing by the seller, generally regarding the condition of the home, property, or other matter.

Wash Sale   If you sell stocks and repurchase them within 30 days prior to or after the sale.

Withholding   An ongoing deduction from your paycheck that is sent, by your employer on your behalf, to the IRS.

Withholding Allowance   One withholding allowance is available for each personal and dependent exemption that you're entitled to take. You may also take additional exemptions to compensate for deductions and credits you plan to use. You may change your withholding allowances during the year if your income will be higher or lower than you planned.

Wrap Accounts   Your broker might offer to wrap your mutual funds in with other investments you own, and keep an eye out on all of it, for a 1 to 3 percent wrap account fee. Another wrap account is a mutual fund that has no up front load, but charges a fixed percentage of assets each year to cover the cost of the commission, management and expenses.

Yield to Call   If interest rates go down, your bond issuer will want to re-finance his debt. That means he'll call in your bond as soon as he can. If your bond has 5 years until the call date, you'll want to calculate the yield to call, since the bond issuer may not let the bond mature.

Yield to Maturity   If you hold your bond until it matures and reinvest every interest payment at the interest rate on your bond, you would end up with your yield to maturity. If you spend your interest payments, or rein-vest them at a lower rate (like in a passbook savings account), your yield to maturity will be less. If you invest them at a higher rate, your yield to maturity will be higher.

Zero Coupon Bonds   Zero coupon bonds pay no interest throughout the bond term. However, you buy the bond at a steep discount that includes the implied interest rate. For example, a $1,000 bond paying 8 percent, might be purchased for $456. At the date of maturity, you'd collect $544 in interest. The Treasury department offers zeros (as they're commonly called), as do municipalities and some corporations.

Zoning   The right of the local municipal government to decide how different areas of the municipality will be used. Zoning ordinances are the laws that govern the use of the land.

Acknowledgments

Each time I sit down to begin writing a new book, I wonder how I'm going to fill its pages. As the writing begins, new sources, interns, assistants, readers, and editors turn up to lend a hand. And I am, as always, profoundly grateful for their excellent help and guidance. Without it, this book would never have been written.

Although there are literally hundreds of professionals, experts, economists, professors, students, parents, children, self-employed entrepreneurs, and company CEOs who contributed in one way or another to this book, the following individuals went far beyond the call of duty to provide me with all sorts of information, anecdotes, and assistance. I would specifically like to thank accountant Mark Luscombe, CCH, Inc.; Catherine Williams, CCCS of Greater Chicago; Michael Miller, attorney, FTC Chicago office; Richard Coorsh, Health Insurance Association of America; Loretta Waters, Insurance Information Institute; Kathy Kristof, syndicated personal finance columnist and author; Chuck Jaffe, syndicated mutual funds columnist and author; Don Reiser, Ameritas Insurance; mortgage broker Dick Lepre, HomeOwners Finance Center in San Francisco; Elaine Waxman, David Hall, and Rick Druker, Coldwell Banker in Chicago; David Doyle and Cameron King, Countrywide Home Loans; David Lereah, chief economist, Mortgage Bankers Association of America; James Annable, chief economist, First Chicago NBD; Manhattan-based attorney Stephen Long; and Susan Dziubinski, editor, *Morningstar Fund Investor*, whose patient explanations crystallized many important mutual fund issues for me.

497

I also wish to thank my readers, who took chunks of the manuscript and offered invaluable suggestions. I am grateful for their time and many talents: Phil Ravid, of Ravid & Bernstein, whose ability to clearly explain the most difficult issues is unparalleled; Ronald Kalish, who helped shape this book when it was just an outline and whose sharp eyes noted a few important missing pieces; Bill Valentine, of Valentine Ventures, who squeezed time to read this book by pushing into his workout schedule; Bob Gianni, whose memory of his father trading the family car for his newborn brother's hospital bill seems to me the essence of the personal choices we all make in our lives; Nancy Coutu, of Money Managers Advisory, whose advice is sound and true; Susan D. Snyder, of Sachnoff & Weaver, Ltd., who makes trusts easy to understand; and Richard Garrigan, professor of finance with DePaul University, who continues to think up unusual ways people can retire comfortably. Any mistakes you find in this book are mine, and mine alone.

I cannot be in five places at once, but for awhile there, it seemed as though I could. For that magic, I must thank the marvelous assistance of my researchers and interns, each of whom contributed immeasurably to what this book has become: Colleen DeBaise, who spent six months collecting articles, doing interviews, and pretending to be interested in buying Volkswagon cars—all in the name of getting priceless information from car dealers; Amy Frangipane, whose relentless cheeriness brightened many a writing afternoon and who, along with Lise Halpern, did such a terrific job of booking and producing my radio program, *Real Estate USA*, that I didn't have to worry about it one bit; Nada Milakovic, whose organization and writing skills are to be envied; Liz Stanton, who finished assignments faster than I could prepare new ones and was always up for a challenge; Dina Gavrilos, who helped keep everything in perspective; and Janice Matsumoto, whose calm manner and clarity of purpose started everything off so long ago.

As an author, I've had the most unique and wonderful publishing experiences. I am surrounded by talented, smart, and hard-working professionals who just happen to be the kind of people with whom you'd choose to spend your free time. I am deeply grateful to my attorney Ralph Martire, of the Chicago law firm; Much Shelist Freed Denenberg, of Ament & Rubenstein, P.C., for his continuing friendship, counsel, and guidance about intellectual property matters and fine wine selections; and to my agent and great friend, Alice Martell, who takes on each new project as if it were the only one on her plate.

The Times Books staff is just incredible. Nancy Land, of Publications Development Company of Texas, once again produced a marvelous interior; Mary Beth Roche and Diane Henry (now in MBA-land) have overseen four years of terrific, coordinated publicity for all of my books; Kate Larkin stepped into Diane's shoes as if she had been there forever; Peter Bernstein also has stepped so ably to the plate; Kristin McGowan ensures things run as smoothly as they can in a busy publishing house; and, of course, my deepest thanks go to my editor and great friend, Times Books Associate Publisher Carie Freimuth, for believing in me and in this book and infecting the entire Times Books team with her unbridled enthusiasm.

Other close friends were enormously supportive, including Leonora Shaw and Gene Galperin, Gerhard and Emanuele Plaschka, Geoff and Michelle Kalish, Ellyn Rosen, Karen Egolf, Ellen Shubart, Pamela Sherrod, Janet Franz, Ann Hagedorn, and Beth and Mark Kurensky; all contributed anecdotes, good cheer, and invitations for dinner. (They knew I'd eventually surface.) My old friend Rick Mawrence appeared out of nowhere, pitched in, and made me smile on days I didn't think I could. Only an e-mail away, Wendy Miller saw the light at the end of the tunnel, each time propping me up enough to write the next chapter. Visionary Sonia Choquette told me I'd finish this book on time. She was right, though I never really believed it. Pat Clinton is the kind of friend and editor you always hope to have by your side. And, Thea Flaum has been a mentor and close friend for nearly twenty years, and I am grateful when she shares her thoughts and wisdom.

There's a lot of my family, both past and present, in this book, and it would have been truly difficult to finish without their love, encouragement, and memories of the way things used to be. I'd like to thank my in-laws, Stan (who called the 1998 stock market drop about four months ahead of time and remained bearish as we went to press) and Margo, Mitch and Alice, Brad and Maru, Linda and Simon, Kiki and Mike, Marya and Tim, Judy and Alvin, for the occasional babysitting, dinners eaten, guest rooms occupied, and for remembering that this book wasn't only about real estate; my mother-in-law, Marilyn, the family's newest e-mail junkie, for allowing me to spend most of my "vacation" writing on my laptop while staring out onto the Merrimac River from her porch; Grandma Betty (who always knew how to balance a budget even when ends didn't meet), and my late step-grandfather, Irving, for sending ruggelah and grapefruit; Karen and Dennis Bookshester, Jacki Bookshester, and Alli and Al Rogoway, who are

499

so important to all of us; Uncle Rich, for sharing stories about his personal finances and those of my grandfather's; my sisters, Phyllis and Shona, for being the best aunts and friends, and always understanding when I couldn't make a family get-together; my brother-in-law, Jonathan, for being a wonderful uncle and offering me a few tidbits from his experiences in the financial industry; and, my mother, Susanne Glink, Grandma Extraordinaire, who managed in the last sixteen years to create an incredible career as one of the top real estate agents in Chicago, and through hard work, smart savings, and savvy investing, has achieved nearly all her financial dreams.

Finally, I would have never finished this book without the unstinting help of my husband and best friend, Samuel J. Tamkin, the world's best real estate attorney, radio show producer, and editor, who continues to believe all my wildest dreams will come true.

Index

About the Author

ILYCE R. GLINK is an award-winning, nationally syndicated journalist who specializes in personal finance and real estate. Her articles have been published in the *Chicago Tribune, Chicago Sun-Times, Washington Post, Los Angeles Times, San Francisco Chronicle, San Diego Union-Tribune, Worth* magazine, *Working Woman, Chicago* magazine, and many other publications. Her weekly newspaper column, "Real Estate Matters," is read by millions of people coast to coast. She is the host of *USA*, a live, nationally syndicated weekly radio show and a nationally syndicated daily feature *The Real Estate Minute*. She also has appeared on hundreds of other radio and television programs, including the *Today* show, *Oprah*, CNN and CNBC. She is the author of three previous books: the best-selling *100 Questions Every First-Time Home Buyer Should Ask*), *100 Questions Every Home Seller Should Ask*, and *10 Steps to Home Ownership*. She is currently writing another book about personal finance and updating her website <www.ThinkGlink.com>.